Gerrit J. Dimmendaal
Nurturing Language

Anthropological Linguistics

Edited by
Svenja Völkel and Nico Nassenstein

Advisory board

Kate Burridge
N. J. Enfield
Birgit Hellwig
Paul Kockelman
Simon Overall
Jack Sidnell
James Slotta

Volume 2

Gerrit J. Dimmendaal
Nurturing Language

Anthropological Linguistics in an African Context

DE GRUYTER
MOUTON

ISBN 978-3-11-152272-2
e-ISBN (PDF) 978-3-11-072663-3
e-ISBN (EPUB) 978-3-11-072714-2
ISSN 2701-987X

Library of Congress Control Number: 2022942577

Bibliographic information published by the Deutsche Nationalbibliothek
The Deutsche Nationalbibliothek lists this publication in the Deutsche Nationalbibliografie; detailed bibliographic data are available on the internet at http://dnb.dnb.de.

© 2024 Walter de Gruyter GmbH, Berlin/Boston
This volume is text- and page-identical with the hardback published in 2022.
Cover image: _jure/iStock/Getty Images Plus
Typesetting: Integra Software Services Pvt. Ltd.
Printing and binding: CPI books GmbH, Leck

www.degruyter.com

In memory of Kenneth L. Hale (1934–2001)
linguist, anthropologist, and humanist

Preface

This book grew out of a practical need to produce a textbook on anthropological linguistics for teaching purposes. The fact that it was completed when the present author no longer had any teaching obligations, due to reaching retirement age, hopefully makes its publication not entirely superfluous for others.

There is no monograph on anthropological linguistics with a special focus on Africa. A central goal of the present study, therefore, is to make at least part of the extensive literature available to a wider public, including on the African continent, in order to show what the data from Africa tell us about the various issues currently (and formerly) debated in the anthropological-linguistic literature, in order to arrive at a kind of synthesis from which further investigations may be initiated. While African scholars have played an important role in developing the field of anthropological linguistics so far, it is hoped that the present monograph will encourage more academics from that part of the world to take part in the debate on the role played by culture in structuring languages. The actual motivation for writing this monograph, consequently, is similar to the reasons for publishing the monograph *Historical Linguistics and the Comparative Study of African Languages* (Dimmendaal 2011), where the role (ideally) played by African languages in our understanding of language change is a central theme.

As with this previous monograph, the present author may again be subject to *ad hominem* attacks in animose reviews, being accused of "rambling prose" and the use of a "meandering style" (as one reviewer of the monograph on historical linguistics put it). Still, it is hoped that the present contribution contains sufficiently rich datasets (or at least references to additional datasets of a whole range of authors whose contributions might otherwise slide into oblivion) to satisfy the critics. These datasets are presented with a wink to the "empiricists" amongst us, as the author's own presentations of data are based on interviews with a range of speakers, rather than on interviews with just one (semi-)speaker of a language far away from the actual speech community. If readers feel tempted to write an alternative textbook focusing on what they think is more important or empirically well-founded, one can only encourage them to go ahead.

The intellectual stance propagated in Dimmendaal (2011) with respect to language change is the same as the position defended in the present study, namely that language is "Lamarckian", i.e., highly flexible and always adapting to the needs of its users, who feed or nurture this precious product of human evolution in a rather intriguing variety of ways. As already suggested by the title, this monograph emphasizes the interplay between culture and cognition as reflected in language, supporting the case for a nurturing device in the nature/nurture debate.

Ferdinand de Saussure, the pioneer of the synchronic study of language, distinguished between *langue* and *parole*, with *langage* being the cover term for these two components, whereby *parole* corresponds to language use and *langue* represents the abstract system of rules. This distinction is still relevant in modern linguistics, including from a theoretical point of view. Constraint-based approaches, and, associated with these, the stipulation of principles of Universal Grammar, are particularly prominent within the generative paradigm and the work of its most prominent protagonist, Noam Chomsky. On the other hand, those focusing on the role played by language use, and the corresponding differential structuring of languages emerging from this constellation, tend to emphasize the co-evolution of language and culture (e.g., Evans and Levinson 2009 in their influential contribution).

No doubt somewhat paradoxically to some readers, the present author does not see any principled contradiction between the investigation of language use on the one hand and formal, constraint-based approaches to the study of language as a rule system on the other. To use the words of the great Roman Jakobson in one of his publications (Jakobson 1960: 377): *Linguista sum; linguistici nihil a me alienum puto*, 'I am a linguist; nothing linguistic is alien to me', thereby paraphrasing the Latin saying *Homo sum; homini nihil a me alienum puto*, 'I am human; nothing human is alien to me.' Mind-reading and intersubjectivity in language use (including inter-brain synchronization) of course play a key role in social interaction. But there is also evidence for language acquisition in a non-interactive way, for example by autistic individuals. Kissine (2020) argues that the entire autistic spectrum is characterized by life-long deficits in intersubjective communication and persistent difficulties in understanding other people's perspectives. In that sense, autism constitutes a unique profile within which linguistic competence is dissociated from communication skills. Nevertheless, individuals with such impairments acquire structural language in a non-interactive way, using it from an egocentric perspective. Language structures consequently can also be investigated without a "theory of mind", as illustrated in Dimmendaal, Schneider-Blum, and Veit (to appear), in a study on argument properties in Tima, a language which also plays a role in the present monograph. Such alternative approaches are therefore best treated as clusters of interconnected theories, where our present understanding of language does not allow us to make strong claims on what is nature and what is nurture; see also the discussion and reactions to Kissene's (2020) article in *Language* 97(3). It is the crossroad of these two polar domains which makes this discipline so fascinating, a view also shared, it seems, by the person in whose memory this book was written, somebody the author had the honour of meeting a couple of times, about whom another leading linguist wrote: "Surely no one could equal Ken Hale in linguistic acumen and insight" (Dixon 2010: 107).

This book could not have been written without the support of a number of people. I would like to thank the rector of the University of Cologne, Prof. Axel Freimuth, for bestowing the Leo-Spitzer Prize upon me in 2013, which allowed me to focus more on research than on teaching and administration for three years. I probably also owe this opportunity to my colleague Nikolaus Himmelmann, to whom I express my deep gratitude here as well. It was this unique chance to focus more on research for a few years which kept me motivated to continue my academic research, as it also allowed me to start working on the present monograph and other studies at a rather critical point in my life, when I was about to abandon academia.

A range of other people who all contributed, in one way or another, to making the publication of this book possible, need to be mentioned here. The valuable input of Gertrud (Trudel) Schneider-Blum cannot be emphasized enough. Her academic commitment, in particular to the documentation of the Tima language and culture in Sudan through her extensive and thorough fieldwork in the Tima speech community, also provided a significant impetus for the present monograph.

Special thanks are due to several people, including the wonderful Lennart Attenberger, Jan Knipping, Milo Reinmöller, and Emmanuel Tekpertey, who helped in so many ways to make the publication of this book possible, from the retrieval of literature and help with formatting issues to comments on the contents. The editors of the series, Nico Nassenstein and Svenja Völkel, are to be thanked for having taken the initiative to make this publication possible, as well as for their extensive comments on an earlier draft of the present contribution. I would also like to express my deeply felt gratitude to Mary Chambers for polishing up my English, for raising important editorial questions, and for her contributions in formatting the manuscript. Monika Feinen's professional contribution concerning maps and graphics is also gratefully acknowledged here.

I would also like to thank my colleagues at the Institut für Afrikanistik und Ägyptologie, as well as various colleagues elsewhere in the Philosophische Fakultät, University of Cologne, for being so supportive and for creating an agreeable intellectual atmosphere. Several colleagues particularly need to be mentioned in this respect: Taluah Reginald Asangba, Agnes Brühwiler, Richard Bussmann, Birgit Hellwig, Muhsin Ibrahim, Meike Meerpohl, Angelika Mietzner, Alice Mitchell, Helma Pasch, Anne Storch, Nataliya Veit, and Thomas Widlok.

In addition, a range of colleagues elsewhere played a significant role in my anthropological-linguistic endeavours: Alexandra (Sasha) Aikhenvald, Suzan Alamin, Felix Ameka, Azeb Amha, David Barasa, Abeer Bashir, the late Tucker Childs, Didier Demolin, Alex de Voogt, R. M. W. (Bob) Dixon, German Dziebel, Abdelrahim Mugaddam, Serge Tornay, Rainer Vossen, and Hirut Woldemariam.

Students have always been important to me, as they legitimized my position as an academic. I express a warm and deeply felt "thank you" to students from various departments at the University of Cologne who have attended my courses in anthropological linguistics over the past two decades. Last but not least, my wonderful colleagues from the Universidade de São Paulo, Brazil, Alexander Cobbinah, Esmeralda Vaillati Negrão, Margareda Petter, Luciana Raccanello Storto, and Evani Viotti, as well as their students, are also thanked here for raising various questions and for commenting on different claims made by myself and others interested in the field of anthropological linguistics during a course in March 2020.

Hengelo, December 2021

Acknowledgements

Special thanks

to Angelika Mietzner for permission to reproduce the music notes for example (163);

to the Max-Planck-Institute for Psycholinguistics, Nijmegen (the Netherlands) for allowing the use of pictures from the Space Kit.

to Oxford University Press for the reproduction of Figure 11.

Contents

Preface —— VII

Acknowledgements —— XI

List of figures —— XVII

List of pictures —— XIX

List of maps —— XXI

List of tables —— XXIII

List of abbreviations —— XXV

1 Introduction —— 1

2 Lexical semantics and the contribution of cognitive anthropology —— 8
    2.1 Kinship terminology —— 8
    2.2 Numeral systems —— 16
    2.3 Bionomenclature —— 24

3 Lexical semantics and the contribution of cognitive linguistics —— 37
    3.1 Colour —— 37
    3.2 Body-part nomenclature —— 56
    3.3 Olfactory cognition —— 61

4 **Spatial orientation —— 69**
    4.1 Physical space —— 71
    4.2 Social space —— 91
    4.3 Social deixis and the co-evolution of language and culture —— 98

5 **Language and habitual thought —— 104**
    5.1 The roots of linguistic relativism —— 105
    5.2 The name strategy —— 108
    5.3 Grammar and cognition —— 110
    5.4 On WEIRD people and cognitive tests —— 119

6 Onomastics —— 124
- 6.1 Anthroponymy —— 125
- 6.2 Toponymy —— 138
- 6.3 Names and avoidance or endearment strategies —— 140

7 The ethnography of communication —— 152
- 7.1 Hymes' etic framework —— 152
- 7.2 Greeting strategies —— 162
- 7.3 Parting strategies —— 169
- 7.4 Elaborating upon the SPEAKING model —— 173

8 The contribution of interactional sociolinguistics —— 186
- 8.1 Language socialization across cultures —— 187
- 8.2 Dyadic and triadic modes of communication —— 192
- 8.3 Language ideologies —— 194
- 8.4 Performance —— 204

9 Emotions and the sounds of silence in a cross-cultural perspective —— 211
- 9.1 The expression of emotions —— 212
- 9.2 The meaning of silence —— 224

10 Cultural conceptions of face —— 232
- 10.1 Politeness strategies —— 232
- 10.2 Impoliteness strategies —— 245
- 10.3 "First wave" and more recent approaches —— 252

11 Conversation analysis —— 269
- 11.1 Conversation analysis as a model —— 269
- 11.2 Asking the right questions —— 280
- 11.3 Overlap in conversations —— 284
- 11.4 Pre-expansions and pre-closing strategies —— 289

12 Non-verbal communication —— 298
- 12.1 Facial expressions —— 301
- 12.2 Gestures —— 306
- 12.3 Sign language —— 319

Appendices

Appendix I: Kinship terminology in Tima (Schneider-Blum and Veit 2022) —— 325

Appendix II: Colour chart as used in Tornay (1978) —— 327

Appendix III: Politeness strategies (Brown and Levinson 1987) —— 329

Appendix IV: Transcriptional symbols in conversation analysis —— 331

References —— 333

Subject index —— 373

Language index —— 379

List of figures

Figure 1 Basic colour terms (Berlin and Kay 1969) —— **42**
Figure 2 Colour-encoding sequence (Kay and McDaniel 1978) —— **44**
Figure 3 Generic space for the Tima concept -hɛh 'light, bright' —— **46**
Figure 4 Tima colour terms and their prototypical representatives (Schneider-Blum 2013a) —— **48**
Figure 5 Body-part nomenclature (Andersen 1978) —— **57**
Figure 6 Moving straight ahead in southwestern Ethiopia —— **69**
Figure 7 Spatial orientation in Dutch and Guugu Yimithirr (Foley 1997) —— **76**
Figure 8 Spatial orientation in Tenejapa Tzeltal (Foley 1997) —— **79**
Figure 9 Spatial description for objects in Tenejapa Tzeltal (Foley 1997) —— **80**
Figure 10 Single-file and face-to-face model (inspired by Heine 1997) —— **81**
Figure 11 Testing cognitive attention paid to number and shape (Lucy 1992b) —— **112**
Figure 12 Triad sets contrasting shape and material as a basis for classification (Lucy 1992b) —— **113**
Figure 13 The Müller-Lyer illusion —— **120**
Figure 14 The interjection *ahe* framed within Natural Semantic Metalanguage (Amberber 2001) —— **184**
Figure 15 Possible strategies for doing FTAs (Brown and Levinson 1987) —— **235**
Figure 16 Pénc conversation threads in a Wolof village —— **286**
Figure 17 Tonal melody of a whistled Cherang'any utterance (Mietzner 2016) —— **299**
Figure 18 Gesturing in Guugu Yimithirr —— **318**

List of pictures

Picture 1	Mancala players in Madagascar on the left and in Rwanda on the right	19
Picture 2	Impression of a European forest	22
Picture 3	The concept of *cì-bí* and *k-áyí* in Tima	27
Picture 4	Are pythons snakes or not?	33
Picture 5	The beaver as a kind of fish during the late Middle Ages	34
Picture 6	Turkana names for skin patterns of cows (Ohta 1987)	52
Picture 7	Body-part nomenclature in Tima (Schneider-Blum 2013a)	59
Picture 8	Screenshots from a video showing !Xóõ speakers taking part in the odour test	63
Picture 9	Front page of Lucassen (1994)	70
Picture 10	Mound of magnetic termites in northern Australia	77
Picture 11	Man and Tree game (Mietzner 2016: 265)	82
Picture 12	Going up/down the street and turning left/right at the traffic lights	85
Picture 13	The front or back of an envelope	86
Picture 14	*Saola* as shown on stamps in Vietnam	136
Picture 15	Leave taking among Turkana after a meeting (*Lorang's Way*)	172
Picture 16	Lokatukan performing an ox song (*Lorang's Way*)	177
Picture 17	Central area of the Tima	219
Picture 18	Snapshot from a National Geographic documentary	229
Picture 19	Cover of the monograph by Ovid Demaris (2019) on Lucky Luciano	230
Picture 20	Lorang scolding at Abei	239
Picture 21	Lorang chuckling on hearing Abei's reply	239
Picture 22	Lorang scolding a young boy	246
Picture 23	Lorang criticizing his son	246
Picture 24	Great Britain's former Prime Minister Theresa May	248
Picture 25	Screenshot of ELAN	277
Picture 26	Haiǁom Bush camp in ǀGomais (Mangetti-West, Namibia)	282
Picture 27	Wolof village square meeting	286
Picture 28	Lorang emphasizing the name of a rich Dodoth (Karimojong) person	288
Picture 29	Sign in a café in Gulu	296
Picture 30	Screenshot from YouTube on "teeth kissing" in Bamako (Mali)	303
Picture 31	Former president of the USA, Donald Trump, lashing out at journalists	305
Picture 32	President Xi Jiping, President of the People's Republic of China	305
Picture 33	Holding the wrist instead of shaking hands	310
Picture 34	Socializing within the family (*Lorang's Way*)	311
Picture 35	Naingiro talking about Lorang's life	312
Picture 36	Lorang explaining about life	312
Picture 37	Lorang explaining about knowledge	313
Picture 38	Lorang pointing at the homestead of one of his wives	315
Picture 39	Lorang scolding a young boy	315
Picture 40	Lorang explaining about directions	316
Picture 41	Expressing the height of humans as against animals in Acholi	316
Picture 42	ELAN screenshot of a picture accompanying an utterance	319

List of maps

Map 1 Southwestern Ethiopia and the approximate home area of the Suri people —— 71
Map 2 The Marakwet area west of the Kerio River, viewed from the north —— 92
Map 3 The southward migration of eastern Bantu languages —— 145

List of tables

Table 1	Numerals in Logo (Goyvaerts 1980) —— 17	
Table 2	Numerals in Ngiti (Kutsch Lojenga 1994) —— 18	
Table 3	Botanical life-forms and implicational relationships (Brown 1984) —— 25	
Table 4	Zoological life-forms and implicational relationships (Brown 1984) —— 30	
Table 5	Basic colour terms in some African languages (Berlin and Kay 1969) —— 42	
Table 6	Tima colour terms —— 48	
Table 7	Mursi colour terms (Turton 1980) —— 53	
Table 8	Tima body-part nomenclature —— 58	
Table 9	Kuteb odour terminology (Koops 2009) —— 62	
Table 10	!Xóõ odour terms (Demolin et al. 2016) —— 63	
Table 11	Aligning classifications of frames of reference (Levinson 2003a) —— 74	
Table 12	Metaphorical extensions of 'right' and 'left' in Marakwet (Moore 1986) —— 91	
Table 13	Amharic pronouns (Hoben 1976) —— 96	
Table 14	Bari names (Spagnolo 1933) —— 127	
Table 15	Akan days and male and female birthday names names (Agyekum 2006) —— 129	
Table 16	Female names in Tima —— 129	
Table 17	Gborbo Khrahn names and corresponding pronominal reference (Bing 1993) —— 134	
Table 18	Greeting in Tuareg (Ag Youssouf, Grimshaw, and Bird 1976) —— 162	
Table 19	Greeting in Wolof (Irvine 1979) —— 165	
Table 20	Sources of Yabacrâne lexicon (Nassenstein 2016a) —— 209	
Table 21	Conversational maxims (Grice 1975) —— 234	
Table 22	(Im)politeness models and terminological variation —— 255	
Table 23	Pronouns in Korean (Byon 2006) —— 258	
Table 24	Methodologies contributing to an understanding of communicative competence —— 264	
Table 25	Turn-taking rules (Sacks, Schegloff, and Jefferson 1974) —— 270	
Table 26	Action types in the conversational analysis of Hoymann (2010) —— 282	
Table 27	Frame-and-scenario model of a complaint (Kießling, Neumann, and Schröter 2011) —— 292	
Table 28	Verbal gestures in Wolof (Grenoble, Martinović, and Baglini 2015) —— 306	
Table 29	Arm positions in Ts'ixa pointing gestures (Fehn 2011) —— 320	

List of abbreviations

A	final -a on nouns
ABS	absolutive
AFF	affirmative
AS	aspect marker
ASC	associative
ATT	attitude marker
CFM	contrastive focus marker
COM	comitative
COMPL	complement
COP	copula
CP	centripetal
DEF	definite
DEM	demonstrative
DIR	directive, directional
EE	epenthetic vowel
EGO	egocentric marker
ENCL	enclitic
EXCL	exclamative
F	feminine
FOC	focus
FUT	future
GEN	genitive
HAB	habitual
IDEO	ideophone
IMP	imperative
IND	indicative
INF	infinitive
INFER	inference
INS	instrumental
INTJ	interjection
IPFV	imperfective
IS	inflectional suffix
LOC	locative
M	masculine
MP	modal particle; model person
N	neutral
NC	noun class
NEG	negation
NMZ	nominalizer
NOM	nominative
NUM	numeral
OB	object
OIR	other-initiated repair
PART	partitive

PASS	passive
PFV	perfective
PL	plural
POSS	possessive
PST	past
PRED	predicative
PREP	preposition
PROG	progressive
PRS	present
PSN	personal name
Q	question
QPLR.INFER	polar question proposition inferred
QT	quotative
REFL	reflexive
REL	relative
RT	reactive token
S, SU	subject
SEQ	sequential
SG	singular
SM	subject masculine
SN	singular neuter
SUB	subjunctive
TOPIC	topic
UR	unit reference
VEN	ventive
VOC	vocative
1	first person
2	second person
3	third person

1 Introduction

The scientific discipline which has come to be known as "anthropological linguistics" grew out of the anthropological concern for language as an integral part of culture. Duranti (1997a: 1–2) points out that this label and "linguistic anthropology" have been used interchangeably by pioneers in the field such as Hymes (1964: 23). In his textbook *Linguistic Anthropology*, Duranti (1997a: 2) defines this field "*as the study of language as a cultural resource and speaking as a cultural practice*" (emphasis in the original text). He further argues that the interest lies "in language as both a resource for and a product of social interaction, in speech communities as simultaneously real and imaginary entities whose boundaries are constantly being reshaped and negotiated through myriad acts of speaking" (Duranti 1997a: 6).

Ahearn (2012) is a further informative monograph on linguistic anthropology, with a strong focus on sociological issues such as ethnicity, gender, power, race, and sexuality, as in the early monographs on linguistic anthropology by Parrot Hickerson (1980) and Saville-Troike (1982).

In his monograph *Anthropological Linguistics*, Foley (1997: 3) describes the discipline as "that sub-field of linguistics which is concerned with the place of language in its wider social and cultural context, its role in forging and sustaining cultural practice and social structures". And so it views language "through the prism of the core anthropological concept, culture, and as such, seeks to uncover the meaning behind the use, misuse or non-use of language, its different forms, registers and styles" (Foley 1997: 3).

The present study also focuses primarily on language rather than cultural practices (the latter being a set of symbolic resources that constitute the social fabric), while using insights from both linguistics and anthropology. It thus focuses less on ethnographical implications or theories of culture, and more on linguistic implications and theories of language, by drawing examples mainly though not exclusively from African speech communities, because these have been underrepresented in textbooks on anthropological linguistics so far. In his rich contribution, William (Bill) Foley also treats topics such as language evolution, the philosophical background of the discipline, language standardization, and literacy. These issues are not addressed in the present study. In contrast to Foley (1997), however, the present contribution discusses themes which these days are widely held to be part of the "anthropological linguistics programme", such as conversation analysis or non-verbal communication.

The interest in language as a window to culture has a long tradition. The founding father of linguistic anthropology, Franz Boas (1858–1942), was a key figure historically in this endeavour, and so he may be called the "Galileo of linguistic anthropology", in parallel with Claude Lévi-Strauss (1958: 162) in his characterization of the anthropologist W. H. K Rivers (1864–1922) as the "Galileo of anthropology". Boas was the first professor of anthropology at a university in the United States, initially at Clark University (Maine), and later on at Columbia University in New York. His famous introduction in *The Handbook of American Indian Languages* (1911), written at the instigation of one of his mentors, John Wesley Powell (director of the Bureau of Ethnology), is one of the first documents on linguistic anthropology.

Like Boas, another pioneer of anthropology, Bronisław Malinowski (1884–1942), who did most of his research among Melanesian communities, stressed the importance of "native terminology" as documents of local thinking (Malinowski 1923). His contributions and those of other influential 20th century pioneers like (in alphabetical order) Richard Bauman, Joseph H. Greenberg, John Gumperz, Dell Hymes, Joel Sherzer, Edward Sapir, and Benjamin Lee Whorf are discussed in the following chapters, as are more recent authors in this rapidly developing field.

The roots of linguistic anthropology or anthropological linguistics (depending on one's focus) actually date back to the first part of the 19th century. Inspired by the extensive collections of grammars and other materials of Lorenzo Hervás y Panduro on Amerindian languages, the German politician and scientist Wilhelm von Humboldt produced *Le prodige de l'origine des langues: Essai sur les langues du Nouveau Continent* (*The Wonder of the Origin of Languages: Essay on the Languages of the New Continent*) in 1812, followed by another pioneering study, *Über das Entstehen der grammatischen Formen und ihren Einfluss auf die Ideeentwicklung* (*On the Origin of Grammatical Forms and their Influence on the Development of Ideas*) in 1822. Based on his experience of a range of languages across the world, von Humboldt aimed to link linguistic data with the ideas or ways of thinking of its speakers.[1]

Among the pioneers in the field from the United States shortlisted above, there is one name, that of Joseph H. Greenberg, which deserves special attention. His important contributions on inductive methods in anthropological linguistics, as well as on language typology and historical linguistics, were essential to the development of these disciplines as empirically-oriented sciences. His observations on being a linguistic anthropologist and becoming a linguist, as well as on the controversies between different schools of linguistics are discussed in Green-

---

[1] Readers who want to know more about the intellectual predecessors of Wilhelm von Humboldt who were also interested in investigating language as the embodiment of a world view, such as Kant, Hegel, or Herder, are referred to the relevant sections in Foley (1997).

berg (1986), and are still worthwhile reading for those of us interested in the sociology of science.

In Europe, it was mainly linguists from France with an interest in culture who helped to enhance the field of anthropological linguistics in the 20th century. André-Georges Haudricourt (1911–1996), a pioneer in the investigation of little-studied Asian languages within their cultural and natural environment (in particular involving botany) at the *Centre National de la Recherche Scientifique* in Paris, also inspired another leading French scholar in the field of anthropological linguistics, Jacqueline M. C. Thomas; see Bouquiaux (2004) and Bouquiaux and Thomas (2013), as well as the collection of studies in Motte-Florac and Guarisma (2004), for a discussion of "ethnolinguistics" (*ethnolinguistique*), which is still the preferred term for this field in some parts of Europe, as against the Anglo-American label "anthropological linguistics".

Another "hotspot" for research on the interaction between language and culture is found in Japan, as should also become clear from the various scholars from this country quoted in Dimmendaal (2022c). Whereas French scholars concentrated mainly on central Africa, Japanese scholars have been and still are mainly active in research projects with a focus on southern and eastern Africa.

A major issue cutting across different research traditions, both historically and regionally, is the question of the extent to which nurture or the social environment in which we grow up plays a central role, or alternatively, whether much of who we are and what we do is governed by nature. As already suggested by the title of this monograph, the present author supports a nurturing device in the presentation of the various issues currently occupying anthropological linguists, a position also defended in an earlier study on the interaction between language, culture, and cognition (Dimmendaal 2015a). However, as should be clear from the preface and from the discussions in the following chapters, this "battle of theories" is not a matter of either/or, but rather a matter of degree in the present author's view.

Chapters 2 and 3 approach the nurture/nature debate from the vantage point of lexical-semantic fields (sometimes referred to by the term "ethnosemantics"), more specifically concerning kinship, bionomenclature, numeral systems, colour, body-part nomenclature, and olfactory cognition. As argued below, there are clear-cut cognitive constraints on the kind of variation found cross-linguistically so far. Moreover, both the more universal tendencies and the cultural elaborations found within these semantic fields can be accounted for by "prototype theory", a concept which also plays a role in subsequent chapters.

The cross-linguistic and cross-cultural investigation of spatial orientation in different communities across the world has also started to play a central role in the nature/nurture debate, as discussed in Chapter 4, where a distinction is drawn between physical space and the more abstract (metaphorical) social space. In this chapter a theoretical notion is introduced which plays a role at different stages in this monograph, that of "conceptual blending". The discussion of two phenomena involved in social deixis, namely inclusivity and the egocentric perspective, serves as an illustration of the co-evolution of language and culture.

"Universalists" and "relativists" have been involved in, at times, heated debates regarding the question of whether tacit knowledge of speakers about language structures interacts with habitual thinking, or more generally, with their cognitive system. Chapter 5 provides a brief historical survey of linguistic relativity, a claim about the links between language and cognitive experiences primarily associated with two influential proponents, Edward Sapir and Benjamin Lee Whorf. This chapter discusses the cognitive and cultural meaning of structural differences between languages at the lexical, grammatical, and pragmatic level, the third domain revolving around the culture-specific production and interpretation of speech acts. The same chapter starts with an anecdote from the author's personal experience, as do several subsequent chapters. The motivation for this "intersubjective intrusion" is twofold. First, it serves as an illustration of a claim made in Section 5.4, namely that – like the proverbial man in the street – scientists are not necessarily exempt from the influence of their own cultural background in their analytical endeavours; second, these anecdotes should help to illustrate the important distinction in anthropological linguistics between etic and emic perspectives, or (phrased differently) between the "outsider's" view of scientists as against the "insider's" perspective from members of a community under study, a binary distinction which plays a significant hermeneutic role in the present book.

Chapter 6 on naming strategies serves as a bridge between the discussion of lexical and grammatical domains on the one hand and language use (pragmatics) on the other, the latter being central in subsequent chapters. The chapter includes a survey of naming strategies for individuals' names and the transition between phenotypes and genotypes. Name avoidance and names as terms of endearment are also discussed here, in order to illustrate how culture may affect semantic structures.

The remaining chapters are about language sociality, or more specifically about social interaction and the role played by culture, as well as the communication channels employed (including non-verbal communication). Conventionalized speech, as manifested in greeting and parting strategies, is central to Chapter 7, which also introduces a descriptive and analytical model commonly referred to as the ethnography of communication. More specifically, this chapter illustrates etic and emic approaches towards an analysis of the various functions of speech as first argued for in a foundational article by Hymes (1962) on the "ethnography of speaking". Based on the latter model, also known as "the ethnography of communication", Chapter 7 presents the so-called "frame-and-scenario" model of language use, based on elaborations upon Hymes' model, as well as on insights from cognitive grammar.

When quoting from or summarizing different sources on speech community x in language y in the present monograph, the original parlance is usually retained, thereby leading to the realization that we are sometimes talking about stereotypes, as such labeling suggests the presence of monolithic units, whether concerning ethnic groups or specific languages. In actual fact, of course, the situation tends to be more complex. Moreover, the identification of a certain phenomenon in speech community x or language y may also be misinterpreted as a statement on their unique character, whereas in actual fact such features may be widespread in the area, across the continent, or globally. Chapter 7 therefore also discusses older and more recent views on concepts such as "speech community", "community of practice", and "language variety".

Chapter 8 introduces concepts from interactional sociolinguistics which also play a role in anthropological linguistics these days. It starts with a discussion of differences in language socialization across cultures. In addition, various conventionalized speech styles involving the interactional dimension of language are illustrated, such as dyadic and triadic communication. More generally, this chapter addresses language ideologies as found in different communities of practice, as well as the role played by performances in this respect. Concepts like "languoid", "stylect", and related concepts such as "metrolingualism" and "(trans)languaging" are discussed within this context.

To follow this up, in Chapter (9), the descriptive and analytical tools introduced in Chapters 7 and 8 are used for an investigation of emotions as reflected in grammar and language use. Remaining silent is one widespread strategy for containing emotions. The same chapter therefore also discusses the cultural meaning of silence, since the absence of speech has a range of alternative meanings across cultures as well.

One of the notions introduced in Hymes' model for the description and analysis of fashions of speaking is that of speech norms. This latter concept plays a central role in a highly influential study by Brown and Levinson (1987) on politeness strategies and the concept of "Face" from a cross-linguistic point of view, which is introduced in Chapter 10. In more recent times, a range of contributions have appeared on so-called "impoliteness" strategies, as illustrated in the same chapter. Chapter 10 also presents a dynamic conceptualization of the frame-and-scenario model of language use in social interaction, as introduced in Chapter 7, by incorporating critique on these (im)politeness models as "rational" or "objectified" models of (im)politeness.

Chapter 11 introduces a further, more recent domain of anthropological linguistics, that of conversation analysis. While initial publications based on this model appeared in the 1960s, its application to the analysis of verbal interactions in speech communities outside the United States (where this model was developed for English originally) is of more recent origin. The same chapter also discusses some of the modern technical tools helping scholars to document the multimodal facets of language in a cultural context.

Last, but certainly not least, non-verbal communication is discussed (in Chapter 12). More specifically, the role played by facial expressions, gestures, and signs – the latter sometimes assumed to constitute the evolutionary basis of language as used by modern humans – are discussed here.

Throughout this monograph, it is claimed again and again that there is an interaction between "language", "culture", and "cognition". Of course, all three labels refer to rather abstract notions, whereby authors also disagree as to what is or is not part of these concepts. As pointed out above, Chapter 8 goes into more detail concerning the notion of "language" in its manifold manifestations. Cognition also involves a range of dimensions, going from perception as a sensorial activity, to learning and remembering, and to argumentation and planning. However, in the present monograph the main focus is on perception. Culture also comprises everything that is man-made, both tangible and intangible. Central in the present study is the concept of habitus, as developed, in particular, by Pierre Bourdieu (1930–2002), for example in Bourdieu (1994), and defined by Thompson (1991: 12) in his introduction to the scholarly work of this sociologist as "a set of dispositions which incline agents to act and react in certain ways. The dispositions generate practices, perceptions and attitudes which are regular without being consciously coordinate or governed by any 'rule'". Habitus was also used as a concept by the sociologist Marcel Mauss several decades earlier (e.g., Mauss 1968), and ultimately goes back to the philosophical concept of *hexis* in Ancient Greek (associated primarily with Aristotle), which may be translated as 'disposition acquired by habituation'.

The semiotic triangle formed by language, culture, and cognition is also central to a more recent multidisciplinary approach called "cultural linguistics". Inspired by Palmer (1996) and his monograph of the same title, there have been several contributions by different scholars combining Boasian traditions in anthropological linguistics with ethnosemantics as developed by cognitive anthropologists, and the ethnography of speaking with insights from cognitive linguistics under the label "cultural linguistics", in particular by Farzad Sharifian (1964–2020), founding editor of the *International Journal of Language and Culture*. Sharifian (2017a, 2017b) presents an overview of this inspiring interdisciplinary approach centring around the study of language and cultural cognition. However, many of the topics treated under this heading are also part of anthropological linguistics, as becomes clear from the studies in *The Handbook of Language and Culture*, edited by Farzad Sharifian (2015). For this reason, the present author prefers to treat the burgeoning body of literature produced under this heading as part of the tradition which has come to be known as anthropological linguistics.

2 Lexical semantics and the contribution of cognitive anthropology

The early interest of anthropologists in language as a window into culture led to interesting discoveries on the structure of lexical-semantic fields in languages, the latter representing collections of words covering different conceptual fields within the language of a speech community. Words may refer to objects, but they may also reflect concepts categorizing the latter. For example, words like *blue*, *green*, and *yellow* refer to a semantic field or category in English called "colour".

The investigation of semantic fields was first practised by scholars with respect to kinship terminology in the 19th century, and extended into various other lexical domains such as bionomenclature and colour terminology in the 20th century, in particular in cognitive anthropology, a branch of anthropology in which the investigation of language is seen as an important source for the investigation of cultural schemas (or schemata) as conceptual structures of individuals. The form and function of these latter abstractions, which also play a key role in the present monograph, are discussed in Chapter 7.

For cognitive anthropologists, research in these lexical-semantic domains often involves longitudinal research among a specific social group, learning to speak their language (moderately or fluently), and practising participant observation as part of the methodology. The brief historical survey of research on kinship terminology below should serve as a starting point for the question of the extent to which these research endeavours are successful or whether they require an additional perspective on the investigation of lexical-semantic fields. More specifically, the following two sections introduce the analytical concept of prototypicality; moreover, a methodological problem is introduced, which the pioneer of linguistic anthropology, Franz Boas, was already struggling with in his fieldwork among First Nation communities along the Pacific coast, namely how to get at the actual meaning of words in other languages.

2.1 Kinship terminology

Research on social groupings based upon kinship ties, and taking the nuclear family with ascending and descending generations linked to the latter as a basis, was initiated in the 19th century by Morgan (1871), with two central notions: consanguinity, i.e., relationships by blood, and affinal relationships, i.e., relationships by marriage. Correspondingly, one finds residential kin groups, and in addition there are consanguinal kin groups ("blood relatives"), the latter based on a rule of common descent rather than common residence.

Starting out from the nuclear family, typically a married man and woman with their offspring, there is "*polygyny* or the marriage of one man to two or more wives at a time, *polyandry* or the coexistent union of one woman with two or more men, and *group marriage* or a marital union embracing at once several men and several women", as stated by Murdock (1949: 24). The Cross-Cultural Survey, a project initiated in 1937 and organized by the Institute of Human Relations at Yale University (New Haven, USA), aimed at a catalogue of "any known" aspects of a society's culture. Its originator, the author referred to above, George P. Murdock, arrived in his monograph *Social Structure* (1949) at a classificatory system of family structures through a comparison of kinship terminologies in a wide range of languages, thereby summing up the state of the art at the time. Based on the usage of kinship terms in one specific group as a "prototype", or in the area where it was most prevalent, Morgan (1871) established six types: Crow, Eskimo, Hawaiian, Iroquois, Omaha, and Sudanese. Murdock (1949) arrived at a total of eight types of kinship terminology (cousin terminology). In addition to the six kinship systems already established by Morgan (1871), he identified the Australian and the Dravidian types of system.

In a follow-up study, Murdock (1968) arrived at seven basic types based on the classification of siblings. Appendix I lists these and discusses one subtype, the Melanesian or Relative Sex type, which is illustrated for Tima, a language of the Nuba Mountains in Sudan in Appendix I.[2] In what is probably the most thorough recent contribution on the subject, Dziebel (2007) arrives at still another typology. These and other important anthropological contributions should not concern us here, as the focus in the present chapter is on the non-biological use of kinship terminology.

After the pioneering work of Murdock and his colleagues, a range of anthropologists elaborated upon these contributions by fine-tuning the model. Goodenough (1956) and Lounsbury (1956, 1964) moved kinship studies in a new direction inspired by structural linguistics in the second half of the 20th century, where observations on systematic oppositions in the sound structure (phonology) of

---

[2] The Tima and their language figure rather prominently in the present monograph, as the in-depth investigation of their language and culture over a period of fifteen years by a team consisting of the present author, as well as (in alphabetical order) Suzan Alamin, Abeer Bashir, Meike Meerpohl, Abdelrahim Mugaddam, Gertrud Schneider-Blum, and Nataliya Veit, has resulted in a wealth of anthropological and linguistic information. The frequent reference to (the) Turkana in Kenya is related to the fact that the present author also did extensive fieldwork on this language, primarily for his doctoral dissertation, published as Dimmendaal (1983).

languages are common, for example between sounds with the same point of articulation in the vocal tract but differing in terms of phonation, i.e., produced with the vocal cords in the larynx vibrating (voiced) or not (i.e., voiceless), as with *b* versus *p*, *d* versus *t*, or *g* versus *k* in English. All of these consonants are produced through a closure somewhere in the vocal tract (the upper and lower lip, the tongue and the tooth ridge, or the palate and the back of the tongue blade, respectively), which is why they are called stops. Similarly, with grammatical structure there are paradigmatic oppositions between singular and plural pronouns in English: *I* versus *we* or *(s)he* versus *they*. Inspired by this type of structural analysis with entities sharing features and being distinguished by other features, Lounsbury (1956) presents a kinship analysis of the Republican Pawnee, who once spoke a language in the Great Plains of the United States before they were deported to a reservation in Oklahoma in the 19th century. Their kinship system belongs to the so-called Crow type (in the terminology of Morgan 1871). Lounsbury (1956: 167) also points towards translation problems for the Pawnee kinship terms, if English is used as the metalanguage. Thus, the term *tiwátsiriks* may be translated as 'uncle'; but as pointed out by him, it may also refer to "great-grandfather, two great-great-uncles, and certain cousins, once, twice or thrice removed".

Stating the defining features of the class is hence a major analytical challenge, as is true for sound systems in languages. Thus, in English, *b* and *p* are defined by the common features "bilabial" (produced with the lips), "stop" (complete closure of the upper and lower lip), and by the distinctive feature "voiced" versus "voiceless" (with the vocal cords vibrating or not vibrating). Consonants like *z* or *s* also show the contrastive feature "voiced" versus "voiceless", as with *b* and *p*, but they are distinct from the latter in that they are "alveolar", i.e., produced by using the teeth ridge and the tongue blade as points of articulation, with partial (rather than complete) occlusion of the airstream during pronunciation, i.e., they are "fricatives". According to Lounsbury (1956), kinship systems (for example, of the Crow type, as found among the Pawnee) are characterized by focal and non-focal kin members of increasing distance from Ego sharing different numbers of features, similarly to the structure of sound systems or grammatical systems. Such componential analyses (or decomposition by means of features that are either shared or not) ideally reflect the cognitive organization of kinship systems and languages.

The classification into six major types of kinship system, elegant at first glance, which goes back to Morgan (1871), suggests that there are universal human experiences in the process of socialization, which have been applied numerous times, including with respect to groups whose kinship systems have been described in more recent times, thereby showing their continued validity as empirical generalizations about social structures. See, for example, the detailed account of kinship terminology, or kincepts, by Onyango-Ouma and

Aagaard-Hansen (2020) in Luo, a language spoken in western Kenya and in neighbouring regions of Tanzania and Uganda, as one example. However, this is not the entire story.

What looked like a successful empirical endeavour and a major step forward in attempts to come to grips with variations between different communities in the organization of kin relations and corresponding kinship terminologies has been criticized as reflecting the investigator's understanding of the system, and not necessarily the native speaker's conceptualization. Authors like Burling (1964: 426) even asked the question as to whether this type of research was "God's truth or hocus-pocus?" Research on the way speakers use kinship terms in different languages has made clear that pragmatic considerations also need to be taken into account in order to understand the symbolic meaning of lexical concepts within this semantic domain. Kinship terms are usually genealogically-based, but not all kin members necessarily meet these criteria. Moreover, these terms are not necessarily biologically defined, as the following two examples should illustrate.

Santandrea (1944) is an early source on the extended, non-biological use of kinship terms in an African speech community. The author, who worked as a missionary in Eastern Africa, discusses terms of address versus terms of reference as used among the Luwo in (what is now) South Sudan. For example, amongst better acquainted people, *cwor nyar-a* (lit. 'husband of my daughter') may be used by women when addressing youths or physically fit men, as terms of endearment. Non-kin persons may also be addressed as *kwo-a* (lit. 'my grandfather') or *xo-na* (lit. 'my grandmother') if they are old, thereby expressing a deeply rooted affectionate family relationship in this speech community.

In his investigation of the pragmatics of kin terms in Kituba (Democratic Republic of the Congo), Mufwene (1988: 443) points out that in this language "there is nothing marked with the plural forms *ba-tatá* 'fathers' and *ba-mamá* 'mothers' when reference is being made collectively either to Ego's genitor/pater and his 'brothers and sisters' or to his/her genitrix/ mater and her 'brothers and sisters'". The marker *ba-* in these words marks plurality. Moreover, parents may also address their children with *tatá* or *mamá* in order to "connote, or implicate, a special affection and/or good disposition" (Mufwene 1988: 447). As Mufwene argues, these examples make it clear that kinship terms often have a prototypical meaning but with semantic extensions. One reason why such semantic modifications may occur has to do with endearment. But there are additional cultural reasons for such semantic elaborations through metaphorical or metonymic extension, such as politeness or deference, as further discussed in Chapter 6.

Mufwene (1988: 443) also points out: "Aside from the genitor/pater and the genitrix/mater, for whom no qualification is ordinarily provided, the other members of the kin classes *tatá* and *mamá* are often modified with the words *nkénto* and *bakála*, respectively, when the sex of the referent is different from that of the prototype. Thus *tatáa nkénto* 'female father' and *mamáa bakála* 'male mother' are not bizarre in Kituba". The latter two concepts in Kituba are not discussed any further by the author.[3] But as the following example, that of the "female husband", illustrates, such inversions of gender roles and corresponding non-biological use of kinship terms are common cross-linguistically.

The practice whereby a woman is legally accepted as a man has been described for communities in western Kenya, for example by Oboler Smith (1980) for the Nandi, where traditionally only men can hold and manage land and livestock. In their society, a female husband should always be a woman of advanced age who is barren or has failed to bear a son, and who marries a woman (by paying bride-wealth). The purpose of the union is to provide a male heir, as only a man can hold and transmit property (livestock and land) to heirs. The demographic reality is that not every woman gives birth to a son, and so woman-woman marriage is one solution to this problem. The intention is that the wife of a female husband should bear sons who themselves will become their female father's house's male heirs in the property system. Unmarried girls with a child, or girls pregnant by a man who refuses to marry them, quite often apparently become (or rather, became) the wives of female husbands. After marriage, "the wife and her children ideally occupy a separate dwelling from that of the female husband to facilitate the wife's relationship with her consort" (Oboler Smith 1980: 77). "Nevertheless, the wives of female husbands and other observers confirm that they are not promiscuous, but that they have a long-standing relationship with a male friend (*sandet*)" (Oboler Smith 1980: 79).

A woman who has taken a wife is said to become a man (*muren*, which may also be translated as 'warrior'), or, as Nandi speakers would say: *kagotogosta komostab murenik* 'she has been promoted to male status' (Oboler Smith 1980: 74). Female husbands tend to be addressed as *kogo* 'grandmother' by their wives and children in Nandi, according to Oboler Smith (1980: 77), who also points out that apart from this convention there is little unanimity among speakers concerning proper ways of addressing female husbands by others, in spite of the existing ideology of being a man in the area of kinship terminology (Oboler Smith 1980: 85). What these examples illustrate is that cultural behaviour may result in the modification or change in the meaning of kinship terms through bridging contexts, i.e., new meanings may emerge by applying terms to new social contexts, or new terms may be generated to express new concepts, as further discussed in Section 6.3.

---

3 As pointed out by Svenja Völkel (personal communication, 2021), the gender marking seems only "bizarre" because the English translation is inappropriate. A more appropriate translation for *tatá* may be 'father and his sublings' or 'patrilateral kin of one generation above ego'.

Similar systems are known to occur, or used to occur, in neighbouring communities speaking related (Nilotic) languages (Mietzner 2016: 191), or genetically unrelated (Bantu) languages, for example among the Gusii, from whom the custom probably originated (Oboler Smith 1980). Huber (1969) describes this custom for a speech community known as Simbiti (Simbĕtĕ, who consider themselves to be part of an ethnic grouping called Suba) in northern Tanzania, where the so-called "woman marriage", in the local perspective of the community members, is seen as a "mother-in-law" and "daughter-in-law" relationship in terms of kinship reference, whereby the former has no male offspring and the latter is treated as the wife of a ficticious or deceased son.[4] Unfortunately, the author does not give any information on terms of address used by the community. The custom was already disappearing when Hugo Huber published his article, but traditionally there were preferential rules for the male person actually begetting the "daughter-in-law"s' male descendants, thereby securing legal progeny.

The following case study by Marshall (1976) of the kinship system of the !Kung (who live in parts of Botswana, northern Namibia, and southern Angola) serves as a final example that generational terms play a role in their culture, but that this is not the entire story. In her discussion, Lorna Marshall observes that trying to fit the kin terms of this speech community into a genealogical framework does not match the conceptualization of the kin terms by the speakers. The whole system of terms of reference and address can change, for example, regardless of genealogical relationship, merely by changing one's name: "Names may be changed, and, when they are, the person is reclassified and the kin terms applied to him or her are changed accordingly" (Marshall 1976: 236). In the "generational method", people are classified by their consanguineous (kin) or affinal relationships (those acquired through marriage) to each other, and terms are applied on that basis. In the so-called "homonymous method" (based on shared personal names), people are classified with those that have the same names. Here, the name is the factor that gives them their terminological position. The confusing aspect for outsiders is the fact that if X is named after Y (or, as Lorna Marshall formulates it, "if X is named for Y"), he partakes of Y's identity and, to some extent, he shares Y's position, that is, he has kin terms applied to him in certain instances as though he were Y. Moreover, he applies terms to others as though they were the persons they were named "for" (Marshall 1976: 228). Thus, if a relative is named for somebody's sibling (i.e., brother or sister), this person applies sibling terms to the relative. However, as observed by Marshall (1976: 207), the homonymous method is never applied to the nuclear family, nor to primary affines.

---

[4] Third gender as a phenomenon is well known from the cultural history of mankind in different parts of the world, as shown in the volume edited by Herdt (1994).

Various other examples are known from the anthropological literature. Based on such descriptions of the non-biological use of kinship terms, theoretical anthropologists like Needham (1971: 5) went as far as to claim that "there is no such thing as kinship, and it follows that there can be no such thing as kinship theory". As claimed by the same author, fatherhood and motherhood depend not on procreation and parturition but on social convention. The lexeme naming a focal type, for example *father* in English, is 'a parent who has sired a child' as the centre around which other meanings orient themselves, such as 'priest' (in which case it is usually written with a capital in English, *Father*). Semantic extensions of prototypes reflect graduated sets of similarities following from culture-specific elaborations, as with the use by the Catholic Church and some other Christian churches of the terms for 'father' and 'mother'. In actual fact, genitor is not the only designation of the term *father* or *mother* in many languages.

Schneider (1984) is another author claiming that kinship terms are structured in social terms, and hence encode cultural knowledge, rather than being based on genealogical reproduction. The author argues that the Yapese, who live on the island of Yap in the Pacific Ocean, do not have a term that can be reasonably translated as 'father', in a genealogical sense: "the relationship between *citamangen* and *fak* may not properly be translated as 'father' and 'child,' and is indeed not even a kinship relationship according to certain [genealogical] definitions of that term" (Schneider 1984: 78). The author does not reject the possibility of there being culturally identified relationships between one person and another, but rather the presumption that these "kinship relationships" are biological, with its attendant universal genealogical grid. The presumed reproductive basis has been introduced, he suggests, because kinship has been defined by European social scientists, and European social scientists use their own folk culture as the source of many of their ways of formulating and understanding the world around them.

As these case studies show, the field of kinship studies in anthropology has been in turmoil over the last few decades, either being pronounced "dead", or then again being declared central to human affairs by different authors. In this respect, the scientific debate was and still is characteristic of the debate which also permeates anthropological linguistics or linguistic anthropology today: To what extent do shared cognitive structures between humans play a role in the conceptualization of language structures, and where does culture come in? The controversy on the meaning of kinship terminologies lingers on, as is the case for other semantic fields, as we shall see hereafter.

The question is, what to replace it with? The position taken in the present study is that these and other empirical generalizations (for example on bionomenclature, colour, and other semantic fields discussed below) can be saved as empirical generalizations, if we assume a prototype approach with culture-specific elaborations. In his monograph *The Genius of Kinship*, Dziebel (2007) presents a thorough empirical study based on a database of some 2,500 kinship vocabularies from languages across the globe, including roughly 600 African languages, 140 Australian languages, 500 Austronesian languages, 200 Papuan languages, 350 languages of Eurasia (excluding Indo-European languages), 440 North and Middle American Indian languages, and 200 South American languages. As Dziebel (2007: 190) points out, critics like Needham (1971) failed to replace genealogy with anything logically comparable. One intriguing outcome of the diachronic investigation reported on by Dziebel (2007: 313–339) is the fact that the evolution of kin terminologies shows an amazing stability across language families. This correlation suggests that speakers of expanding languages (and consequently of expanding language families) tend to keep inherited kinship systems, except when strong language contact occurs. These claims have been confirmed more recently by Manfredi (to appear), who shows that Niger-Congo languages tend to have classificatory and generation-oriented kin terminologies, whereas Nilo-Saharan languages tend to have descriptive kin terminologies.

Dziebel (2007: 131) also states that "[a] more economical way would have been to have added, from the very start, two more variables, 'death' and 'divorce' to the minimalist definition of kinship as a social reality that has to do with birth and marriage". Dziebel's intellectual stance is taken as a basis for the analysis of cultural elaborations of lexical-semantic fields such as kinship terminology and other domains in the present study. This semiotic approach to signs involves the postulation of a prototypical representative with semantic extensions or elaborations upon the word or other units of morphological analysis functioning as the paragon or prototype. The term "morpheme" is the primary lexical unit of a word carrying meaning and cannot be reduced to smaller constituents carrying semantic content, as with the word *prototype*, which consists of the morphemes *proto-* and *type* (as also occurs in other words).

In order to find out what such semantic maps with a focal-peripheral ordering look like in a particular language, one could ask speakers whether term A is a good example or representative of a specific concept, for example 'biological father' or 'biological mother' for the two kinship terms in Kituba mentioned above: *ba-tatá* 'fathers' and *ba-mamá* 'mothers'. If the answer is negative, one could ask speakers why. Both of these words consist of two morphemes, and share the presence of a morpheme *ba-*, belonging to a closed (finite) set of function morphemes marking plural (or singular, depending on the form) of nouns, and labeled "prefix", as it precedes a lexical root, the latter belonging to an open set; instead of *-tatá* or *-mamá* a few thousand other nominal roots could follow this prefix, and new forms may be added, for example by borrowing from other languages.

The next section gives further examples of lexical domains containing elements carrying prototypical meanings, but it also illustrates a methodological pitfall, when trying to arrive at a proper understanding of terms, and thereby of prototypical meanings, in a foreign language.

2.2 Numeral systems

Various linguists probably associate the name of the late Joseph H. Greenberg primarily with language typology and the genetic classification of the languages of Africa and other parts of the world. But the same scholar also made essential observations within the field of anthropological linguistics. Greenberg wrote his doctoral dissertation in anthropology at Yale University on the pre-Islamic religion of the Hausa, northern Nigeria (published as Greenberg 1946). Apparently, it was the Cross-Cultural Survey initiated in 1937 by the Institute of Human Relations at the same university (mentioned above in Section 2.1) which provided the real impetus for Greenberg's own work on linguistic universals and language typology, namely by extending this broad comparative approach to include as many languages as possible, thereby revealing universal principles of human language on the basis of inductive methods, particularly in order to support such claims with a strong empirical base.[5]

Greenberg initiated a research tradition that also had its impact on anthropological linguistics. As the principal instigator of new methods of dynamic comparison in linguistics (comparing languages from a genetic as well as from a typological point of view), Greenberg himself extended the study of implicational scales in lexical-semantic domains such as kinship terminology (Greenberg 1980).

As an experienced scientist, Joseph Greenberg was fully aware of the potential complexity of explanatory mechanisms behind the observed diversity for kinship terminology (and, by extension, for other lexical-semantic fields), as shown by the following statement:

> [t]hey [the kinship studies] provide the possibility, through the analysis of highly specific and formally manageable phenomena, of disentangling the contribution various causal factors (social, historical, psychological, linguistic and, I should add, evolutionary) make to an important cultural phenomenon. (Greenberg 1980: 31)

---

[5] Readers are also referred to the interview with Joseph H. Greenberg by Paul Newman (1991), where the former presents his views on the historical links between research in anthropology and linguistics.

In an earlier typological contribution, Greenberg (1978) had arrived at around fifty generalizations regarding numeral systems in languages, for example that in every numerical system certain numbers receive simple lexical representation. Another example is that the existence of multiplication implies the existence of addition. Several prototypical numeral systems figure prominently as fundamental bases in the numeral systems of languages: base-5, 10, 20, 4, and 12. The reader is also referred to Beller and Bergen (2008) for an interesting account of numerical cognition between evolution and culture.

Only a few of Greenberg's generalizations and implicational universals, formulated more than four decades ago, have required modification over the years, for example the claim that zero is never expressed as part of a numeral system. Maya hieroglyphs from the Precolumbian Americas show that they used zero as part of their mathematical system. Moreover, the zero was used as a concept in India before it was transferred to mathematical systems in Europe in the 11th century. Some of Greenberg's other claims are illustrated below.

The examples in Table 1 from Logo, a language spoken in the northeastern corner of the Democratic Republic of the Congo, illustrate the use of addition as well as multiplication in a language with a base-5 system. The information is based on Goyvaerts (1980), although the data and analysis are derived from a bachelor's thesis by a student from the Institut Supérieur Pédagogique de Bukavu in the Democratic Republic of the Congo; unfortunately, this source is not identified. The etymology for 'six' in Logo is not clear from a synchronic point of view. Addition and multiplication are illustrated in the expression for 'seven hundred': (20 x 5) x 5 + (20 x 5) x 2.

Table 1: Numerals in Logo (based on Goyvaerts 1980).

alo	'one'	kazaya	'six'
iri	'two'	nzi drya iri	'seven'
na	'three'	nzi drya na	'eight'
su	'four'	nzi drya su	'nine'
nzi	'five'	mudri	'ten'
mudri drya alo	'eleven'	nya-ɓa alo	'twenty (lit. eat person one'
nya-ɓa drya mudri	'thirty (lit. twenty plus ten)'	nya-ɓa iri	'forty'
nya-ɓa nzi	'one hundred	nya-ɓa nzi drya nyaɓa nzi iri	'seven hundred'

Using the word for 'person, human being' (through metonymic extension, as most human beings have twenty digits) to indicate 'twenty' is widespread across Central and Eastern Africa. Majangir, in southwestern Ethiopia, for example, uses the metaphorical expression *rumer dīt* 'the whole person' (Joswig 2019: 302). The word for 'ten' in Majang, *á:rn*, "apparently goes back to *áríŋ*, the plural of *àrí* 'hand'" (Joswig 2019: 302). Using the word for 'hand, arm' to indicate 'five' is also common in the area, as in Nyangatom, a language spoken south of the Majang area, *-kàn(ɪ̀)*.

The vigesimal system (i.e., the people/digits equation) is combined either with a quinary (base-5) system, as in Logo above, or a decimal (base-10) system. The latter type is widespread not only across Africa, but also in other parts of the world. But interesting additional systems are found, involving binary (base-2), ternary (base-3), and quaternary (base-4) systems. Hammarström (2010) presents a discussion of rare features in numeral systems that are either universal (for example base-3 systems), or areal in nature, i.e., restricted to certain parts of the world (for example base-12 systems); Greenberg (1978: 289) points towards such an area, namely the duodecimal systems of Plateau Benue-Congo languages in central Nigeria, which are being replaced by a decimal system through the influence of the Chadic language Hausa (and presumably by the British educational system inherited from colonial times).

In Ngiti, a language spoken in the Democratic Republic of the Congo, a decimal system is now replacing the more archaic base-4 system (Kutsch Lojenga 1994: 355–358); only a few old people apparently still remembered the traditional four-based numeral system in the 1990s. It survived longest in its use for important elements in social life: a) for the dowry, b) in court cases, c) in wartime, for counting arrows in a quiver (32 arrows per quiver), and d) for the famous "bao" game, which has four rows of eight, i.e., 32 holes, and four grains for each of eight holes, i.e., 32 grains for each player. All other numerals are derived from these by means of a suffixed form *-vi*, expressing 'minus one, lacking one'. It can be attached to each of the above, to yield the forms listed in Table 2.

Table 2: Numerals in Ngiti (Kutsch Lojenga 1994).

atdí ~ otdí	'one'	otsi-vi (12 – 1)	'eleven'
ɔyɔ ~ ayɔ ~ ɔlyɔ	'two'	otsi	'twelve'
ìbhʉ	'three'	otsi dɔ̃ atdí (12 + 1)	'thirteen'
ìfɔ	'four'	otsi dɔ̃ ɔyɔ (12 + 2)	'fourteen'
mbo	'five'	ɔpɨ-vi (16 – 1)	'fifteen'
aza	'six'	ɔpɨ	'sixteen'
àrʉbhʉ	'seven'	ɔpɨ dɔ̃ atdí (16 + 1)	'seventeen'
àrʉ	'eight'	ɔpɨ dɔ̃ ɔyɔ (16 + 2)	'eighteen'
àrʉgyètdí ~ àrɨgyètdí	'nine'	àbà-vi (20 – 1)	'nineteen'
idrɛ	'ten'	àbà	'twenty'

Numbers from 'eleven' onwards in Ngiti are formed by means of subtraction and addition in combination with the morphologically simplex forms. 'Eleven' is formed by means of a compound (or suffix) -*vi* expressing 'minus/ lacking one, *otsi-vi* (lit. 'twelve minus/lacking one'); 'thirteen' is *otsi dɔ̄ atdí* (lit. 'twelve plus one'). In this more archaic system, the word 'twenty' is not based on 'body', but instead is expressed by an underived form, *àbà*, as are higher numbers, such as *àròtsí* 'twenty four', *àdzōro* 'twenty eight', or *wǎdhì* 'thirty two'.

The base-5 system was probably more widespread in the Central African region, as we find traces in many Bantu languages (which are spread in a region from Cameroon to Kenya and further south); consider, for example, *nane* from *na-ne*, 'and-four', the word for 'eight' in Swahili, the language of wider communication in eastern and central Africa. As pointed out by Zaslavsky (1999: 39), there are widespread, formally similar terms across the Niger-Congo family in West Africa (which also includes the Bantu languages of central and southern Africa) for the lower numerals: *li/di* 'two', *ta* or *sa* 'three', and a nasal consonant with a vowel for 'four', something like *ne*.

Bao is the regional Swahili name for what is known as the Mancala game in scientific literature (de Voogt 1997); Picture 1 shows players in Madagascar and Rwanda (courtesy of Alex de Voogt, with permission from the persons shown).

Picture 1: Mancala players in Madagascar on the left and in Rwanda on the right.

In languages with a quinary system, the word for 'five' tends to be derived from the word for 'hand', as in Turkana (Kenya), *-kàn(ɪ)*. As pointed out by Zaslavsky (1999: 46) in her continent-wide survey of numeral systems, 'ten' in African languages may be expressed by 'two hands', 'nine' as 'hand and hand less one', and 'twelve' as 'six times two'. In Malinke, a language spoken in Guinea, Liberia, and Sierra Leone, *kononto* 'to the one of the belly' is used as a metaphorical expression reflecting the nine months of pregnancy (Zaslavsky 1999: 429).

Ndimele and Chan (2016) present a survey of numeral systems in around thirty languages of Nigeria. The latter author also built up an extensive database of numeral systems in languages of the world, which is available online.[6] Blažek (1999) also discusses numeral systems in a range of languages in Africa as well as in other parts of the world, with a special focus on possible etymologies for numerals.

Counting with the fingers is an additional ingenious invention found across the continent and of course elsewhere in the world (Zaslavsky 1999: 30–31, 37, 47–51). In this way, social interactants can cross language borders without necessarily speaking the other person's language. Moreover, counting with the fingers allows interactants to negotiate about prices without hearing the results of the bargaining. Gulliver (1958), on counting with the fingers in Arusha (in Tanzania) and Turkana (in Kenya), and Leyew (2004) on counting with the fingers in various languages of eastern and central Africa, are among several sources for this phenomenon.

Extended gesture counting relying exclusively on the human body appears to be restricted to Papua New Guinea. For example, in Kaluli, names for body parts also serve as numbers. Starting with the lower left hand and moving up towards the head, the word for the little finger, *agel*, is used metaphorically for the number 'one', while 'elbow' *agato* is used for 'nine', the word for 'eye', *si*, may also refer to 'sixteen', etc.[7] This rather ingenious invention again allowed speakers of different languages to negotiate about prices in multilingual settings without necessarily speaking the other person's language.

Some languages in Papua New Guinea use the human body as a source domain for counting in an even more extensive way, for example Kobon, as described by Comrie (2011). In this community, counting starts with the little finger of the left hand and progresses through other fingers, the wrist and other parts of the arm up to the shoulder, across the collarbone and the breastbone, and goes down the right arm to finally end with the little finger. From there, the counting may continue in the opposite direction until the little finger of the left hand is reached with the number '46'.

Zaslavsky (1999: 52) discusses additional phenomena related to counting, such as the taboo on counting of human beings, domestic animals, and valuable possessions, as this may "lead to their destruction".

---

6 See [https://mpi-lingweb.shh.mpg.de/numeral/] (accessed 20 January 2021).
7 A number of such systems are illustrated on YouTube, for example for a language called Foe: [https://www.youtube.com/watch?v=H13Se4nBPDA] (accessed 10 February 2021).

Various strategies have been reported in the literature for record-keeping with respect to higher numbers. Zaslavsky (1999: 93–97) mentions the use of sticks, ropes, pebbles, or grains, for example. Among the Nuer, "one corn grain represents ten items (. . .). They count ten objects and put one corn grain separately to remember the amount counted. Two grains mean twenty, three grains mean thirty, and so on". A similar system is found among the Gumuz (Leyew 2004: 253). Other communities in the area, like the Opo and Komo, use small sticks in their counting, whereby one stick or a bent finger means 'twenty'. Among the Komo, a knot in a rope is used as a tallying method for 'twenty' (corresponding to their vigesimal counting system). The Anywa, in the border area between Ethiopia and South Sudan, who have a decimal counting system, use small sticks as a record of ten counted objects each (Leyew 2004: 253; Leyew also points towards the strong influence of the lingua francas Amharic, Arabic, and Oromo on numeral systems in the area). In his discussion of vanishing counting systems across the world, Harrison (2007: 161–200) mentions a similar system of counting with piles of pebbles among the Kpelle in Liberia. Huylebrouck (2019) also presents a fascinating historical interpretation of mathematics on the African continent.

Zaslavsky (1999: 19) discusses a picture of a bone, assumed to be over 20,000 years old, found on the shore of Lake Edward in the Democratic Republic of the Congo, and showing a calendrical or numeration system of the fishing and hunting folk who lived there, suggesting knowledge of multiplication.

But extensive numeral systems are not necessarily part and parcel of all speech communities in human history. Güldemann (2018) discusses the status of cardinal numbers in the common ancestor of one Southern Khoisan group (referred to as the Tuu family by the author), whose modern representatives have small quantifier sets ('one', 'two', 'three', 'many'). When comparing these between the extant members of the group (several of which became extinct before they were properly described), the conclusion is that "[s]tructural diversity across the family (. . .) does not support the assumption of an older paradigmatic coherence of quantifiers" (Güldemann 2018: 143). In other words, their part-of-speech status, morphosyntactic behaviour, and etymological relationships differ considerably across the family. The author furthermore makes reference to an early source, Planert (1905: 159), where it is pointed out that there were other means of communication reflecting the notion of cardinality, namely gestures.

In an early source on the Damara in Namibia, Galton (1853) observed that "[i]n practice, whatever they may possess in their language, they certainly use no numeral greater than three (. . .) yet they seldom lose oxen: the way in which they discover the loss of one, is not by the number of the herd being diminished, but by the absence of a face they know."⁸ In his typological investigation of numeral systems, Greenberg (1978: 291) remarks that "[t]here may be actual regression where a people changes its mode of life through external circumstances. For example, the BUSHMAN [San] languages of South Africa usually have no numeral higher than 3, yet at least 4 seems reconstructable for the larger stock.

Picture 2: Impression of a European forest.

Regressions in lexical domains are of course to be expected if language is an adaptive system. Ask an average child in a European or American metropole to recall what (s)he just saw after having looked at a picture of a local forest (Picture 2). Most likely, the answer from an English-speaking child, for example, will be "trees . . .", rather than "a beech, an oak, a birch . . .". The satirical observation made by McWhorter (2014: 16), whose monograph is discussed in Chapter 5, namely that

---

8 Hale (1975: 295) observes for the Australian aboriginal language Wa(r)lbiri: "I believe that it would be correct to say that there is no single linguistic convention which is employed in situations in which the activity of counting, or exact enumeration, is a practical necessity".

"the idea of marveling that people without numbers don't take to math", or that "tribes without cars don't drive" is well taken from this perspective, especially if we extend it to "people who live in western urban jungles don't take to nature". Those familiar with nature, on the other hand, have a handy way of internalizing these perceptions and categorizing the stimuli along a convenient pattern provided by the lexicon of the language(s) they speak best.

Globalization and the growing role of regional and national languages of wider communication clearly have an impact on the structure of lexical-semantic fields in smaller languages. Smolders (2016) describes such influence from the numeral system of Amharic, a language of wider communication in Ethiopia, on T'apo (also known as Opuuo), a language of western Ethiopia. Here the older system involved a base-5/base-20 system built on the concepts of 'hand' and 'body', respectively, as is common in the area. In the new system, which appears to involve calquing (copying of the system without borrowing of the actual words) from Amharic, the body concept is reinterpreted in a base-10 system. While speakers still use *k'ōj* 'hand' for 5 and 'double hand' for 10, they use 'the body of two men' for 20, 'the body of three men' for 30, and so forth.

(1)
	new system	original system	
	k'ōj-ā-sōk'-ɛ́n	k'ōj-ā-sōk'-ɛ́n	'ten'
	hand-LOC-two-3N.POSS	hand-LOC-two-3N.POSS	
	ēs-í-bì-sōk'á	ēs-í-ù-ɖjān	'twenty'
	body-ASC-PL-two	body-ASC-SG.M-one	

Heine (1997: 18–34) also discusses synchronic and diachronic aspects of numeral systems in different parts of the world, including a discussion of the reanalysis of a decimal-vigesimal system as a duodecimal system (based on the numeral 12) in Munda, a language spoken in eastern India, based on Stampe (1976).

Evans (2009) gives further interesting examples of cultural contexts as selectors for lexical structure, i.e., the co-evolution of language and culture in numerical systems. Evans (2010: 167–200) provides a discussion of endangered numeral systems on a global basis. What the T'apo calquing system suggests is that cultural selection may indeed result from the domination of a regional or national language. Alternatively, the system of an earlier language spoken language may be transferred into the new dominant language, as in French *quatre-vingt* 'eighty' (lit. 4x20), a loan translation (calque) from a vigesimal system, as used by speakers of Celtic languages in the area before the Romance language French became dominant.

2.3 Bionomenclature

During the latter part of the 18th century and the beginning of the 19th century scientific methods were developed for organizing plants and animals into families and orders, for example by the biologist Jean-Baptiste Lamarck. These in turn formed the basis for systematics in biology, for example Charles Darwin's evolutionary concepts of phyla and "the tree of life".

Interest in classifications of our natural environment received an important impetus from Europe's global commercial expansion, which brought knowledge about alternative ways in which people classify nature in different parts of the world. It was these latter taxonomies that were of primary interest to scientists. Harshberger (1896) introduced the term "ethnobotany" for the study of the use of plants by indigenous people. The label "ethno-" has since been used to describe other types of ethnoscientific studies, or ethno-methodologies, aiming at local understandings of the natural and social worlds, such as "ethnoastronomy", "ethnomathematics", "ethnomedicine", "ethnomusicology", or "ethno-poetics".[9] The scientific investigation of these domains is sometimes referred to as "ethnographic semantics" or "ethnosemantics". The more general cover term for such "non-scientific" approaches, "folk taxonomy", is defined by Mathiot (1962: 343) as "the grouping of entities according to the category labels given to them by the culture". Readers interested in the potential link between such lexical taxonomies and cognition are referred to the informative contribution by Hill (1988).

Ethnobiological classifications have interested a range of scholars over the past century. Conklin (1955), for example, published a fascinating study on colour categories in relation to plant taxonomies in Hanunóo, a language of the Philippines. Conklin (1972) presents an extensive bibliography of older references on folk classification. But, inspired by the Greenbergian inductive approach towards lexical-semantic fields, research moved in another direction from the 1980s onwards.

Brown (1984) claims that, cross-linguistically, hierarchies can be identified in the domain of bionomenclature along lines similar to Greenberg's generalizations with respect to numeral systems and kinship terminology. Based on data from 188 languages, Brown (1984: 25) arrives at the following hierarchy:

---

[9] Anthropological linguistics has also been referred to as ethnolinguistics, as pointed out in Chapter 1, but this label tends to be avoided by most scholars these days, as it is associated with the term "ethnos" or "ethnic group", which is widely held to be a problematic concept in the social sciences.

Table 3: Botanical life-forms and implicational relationships (Brown 1984).

No life-forms (2)
Tree (7)
Tree + grerb (21)
Tree + grass (14)
Tree + vine (1)
Tree + grerb + vine (51)
Tree + grerb + grass (13)
Tree + grerb + bush (6)
Tree + grass + vine (6)
Tree + grass + bush (2)
Tree + grerb + grass + vine (31)
Tree + grerb + vine + bush (8)
Tree + grass + vine + bush (7)
Tree + grerb + grass + vine + bush (14)

The implicational scales above signify that one may come across languages without a separate word for 'tree' as a life-form taxon (Brown 1984: 133–134). As shown in Table 3, there are two languages in his scale with no life-forms (i.e., no basic term), namely Southern Paiute (in the United States), and Iwaidja (Australia). The term "grerb" in this list is a cover term for 'grass' plus 'herb', occurring at stage 2, whereas at stage 3 we find terms for 'tree' and 'grerb'. Stage 4 languages distinguish between 'tree', 'grerb', and 'vine', according to this typology, and stage 5 languages have words for 'tree', 'grerb', 'grass', and 'vine', as in Daga, a Trans-New Guinea language of Papua New Guinea, which has the following system, according to Brown (1984: 183):

(2)   oma   'tree, wood'
       rarema   'grerb (herb)'
       ut   'grass (grass + weed)'
       damik   'vine'

The words for 'tree' in Brown's sample have an average length of 4.56 segments, whereas 'bush' has 6.22, according to Brown (1984). There is probably a correlation between the segmental length (as well as the morphological complexity) of a word and its basicness. High frequency of usage results in shortening of words, and is most likely to be the main reason for this formal characteristic (Dimmendaal 2011: 54–55, 101–103, 228–230, 258).

According to Brown (1984), synchronic differences between languages further represent a unidirectional development or specialization, related to the level of technology and general means of subsistence of the speech communities involved, i.e., a strongly evolutionary perspective is assumed by the author.

However, precaution is in order for a number of reasons. The amount of data amassed by Brown (1984) is impressive, but the method used has its empirical problems in terms of observational and descriptive adequacy (Dimmendaal 2015b), because all languages are forced into a specific template, a phenomenon sometimes also observed with respect to other lexical domains, as further illustrated below. What does the research method used by Brown (1984) look like in concrete terms? For quite a few languages in the database, the word for 'tree' also refers to what would be called 'wood' in English. So how does the author know that the primary meaning is 'tree', rather than 'wood', in a specific language? In the Uto-Aztecan language Shoshoni, for example, the primary meaning is 'wood' (Brown 1984: 146). Nevertheless, 'wood' does not appear in the list with "growth stages".

Brown (1984: 183) lists Carapana (a language spoken in Colombia) as a "stage 5" language with words for 'tree', 'grerb', 'grass', and 'vine'. On closer inspection, the term in this language translated as 'grerb (grass + herb)' refers to three types: *moitĩẽ* 'useless stuff', *capuniriĩẽ* 'hurtful stuff', and *carorije* 'bad stuff'. These three terms thus stand in meaningful paradigmatic contrast to each other, a feature which is not reflected in the translation 'grerb (grass + herb)'.

But there is another fundamental problem, central to any attempt to use folk taxonomies in order to arrive at cross-linguistically and cross-culturally interesting generalizations on cognitive systems. It has to do with proper translation, or more specifically with finding a one-to-one translation for words in an unknown language which may have no correspondence with our own or with the metalanguage used in a scientific publication, as the following examples should help to make clear.

One of the approximately forty languages spoken in the Nuba Mountains in Sudan, an area roughly the size of Scotland, is Tima, which is spoken by some 7,000 people in the western part of the Nuba Mountains. As their language is endangered as a result of the encroaching role of Sudanese Arabic in day-to-day interactions, the Tima wanted a writing system for their language, with primers for primary schools in order to be able to teach their vanishing language to children. In addition, they wanted a book with all the plants and trees in their area in order to teach children about traditional medicine and the use of flora for other purposes. This resulted in a book produced for schools in the Tima area, containing the names of Tima plants and trees and their corresponding Latin names, which was produced by Gertrud Schneider-Blum in 2007.[10] Interestingly, when seeing this botanical guide, Tima speakers immediately noticed that the picture of the baobab tree in the book was not taken in their home area, but somewhere else in the Nuba Mountains. This shows that larger trees also function as landmarks for geographical orientation. (Picture 3 kindly provided by Gertrud Schneider-Blum.)

Picture 3: The concepts of *cì-bí* and *k-ʌ́yí* in Tima.

---

10 This information can also be accessed through the online version of the Tima-English dictionary (Schneider-Blum 2013): [http://tima-dictionary.mine.nu/] (accessed 20 February 2021).

When pointing at a tree (in the English sense), as in the picture on the top left, Tima speakers tend to give the Tima name for the tree first, for example *k-ʌ́cùk* (singular), *y-ʌ́cùk* (plural) for 'baobab', a tree whose fruits and leaves are eaten, whose bark is used for rope-making and whose wood is used for bed-making. When asked whether there is a common name corresponding to *tree* in English or *shajara* in Arabic, the answer usually is *cì-bí* (singular), *ì-bí* (plural). And so one may think one has collected the proper translation in Tima for the English or Arabic terms. However, this is incorrect. When trying to apply these Tima words to botanical phenomena, it turns out that they are used for what are called 'trees' and 'shrubs' as well as 'perennials' in English. Tima speakers make a basic division between *cì-bí* (singular) / *ì-bí* (plural) and flora lasting one year (i.e., one wet and one dry season), *k-ʌ́yí* (singular) / *y-ʌ́yí* (plural). The latter includes what is called 'grass' in English, but also the plant shown on the lower right (*Ipomea cordofana*), whereas the plant on the lower left (*Ricinus communis*) is classified as a kind of *cì-bí*.

There is no overarching term for 'tree' in Tima, whose speakers thus agree with the great botanist Linnaeus (Carl von Liné, 1707–1778) that a concept like *tree* in English is scientifically problematic (Dimmendaal 2015a: 128–130). Cases such as the one sketched above also tell us that one has to be rather careful with empirical generalizations about taxonomic terminology in folk biology, because of potential errors in translation, a problem which extends into other lexical domains as well. This does not imply that it is impossible to arrive at implicational scales; on the contrary, it most likely is (as shown for numeral systems, for example).

The confusion about the meaning of *cì-bí* in Tima may remind some readers of the story of the word *kangaroo* in English. When Captain James Cook and his crew met with aboriginal people on the coast of what is now known as Queensland in northern Australian in 1770, they learned the word *gangurru*. This comes from the traditional language of the Guugu Yimithirr people of Far North Queensland, and means 'large black kangaroo', referring to one species, the *eastern grey kangaroo*. In English, this term came to be used to refer generically to the species *kangaroo*.

The mathematician and philosopher Willard Van Orman Quine (1908–2000) refers to this indeterminacy of translation as the problem of "radical translation" in his monograph *Word and Object* (Quine 1960: 26–90). Alien concepts can be carried into English (as the metalanguage) in different ways, each acceptable on its own, so there is no way to choose between various renditions, for example when a language helper for the unknown language Arunta exclaims *gavagai!* upon seeing a rabbit. What does this utterance mean? 'Lo, a rabbit!', or 'Lo, food!', or 'Let's go hunting'? Since other translations may also be compatible with the conjectural evidence available to the investigator at that point in time, an indeterminacy of translation pops up. No unique interpretation, or "radical translation", is possible without further research, because a "radical interpreter" has no way of telling which of many possible meanings the speaker has in mind. The first translation may be ruled out by asking whether this was the same *gavagai* as the earlier one. But such an investigative question can only be asked once the linguist has mastered the Arunta language to some extent.

The "indeterminacy of translation", especially of abstract words not directly attached to observation, in a language which one is trying to understand, is not always easy, as anybody who has done linguistic or anthropological fieldwork knows. The anthropologist Franz Boas was already aware of this problem of the inscrutability of reference which sometimes occurs in this respect. Translation is an interpretive task, whereby one tries to present the categories of one conceptual system in terms of another, functioning as the metalanguage, in order to make shared understandings possible. Glosses are necessary, but they should be considered neither as definitions nor as exact equivalents, as pointed out by Lounsbury (1956: 163); this view was also expressed by Boas, who argued against translating the Kwakiutl principle of kin groups into any English word, for example. Instead of trying to fit the Kwakiutl system into some larger model, he tried to understand their beliefs and practices in their own terms. For example, whereas he had earlier translated the Kwakiutl word *numaym* as 'clan', he later on argued that the word is best understood as referring to a bundle of privileges, for which there is no English word.

What these examples show is that approaches to lexical semantics sometimes rely on denotational overlap with English words (or any other metalanguage into which terms are translated) to establish the meanings of words. Any cross-linguistic typology of semantic categorizations in the lexicon, as represented through folk taxonomies, should take the actual meanings and semantic oppositions in languages as a basis, rather than bracketing these out. The polysemous nature of the word translated as 'tree' in Daga, where it could also mean 'wood', is common cross-linguistically, as suggested by the examples in Brown (1984). In many African languages, the word for 'tree' may also be translated as 'medicine' (or vice versa), as with *yaàt* in Acholi (spoken in Uganda). Whether one meaning is more basic than the other, and if so, which one, cannot be determined on *a priori* grounds.

The following phenomenon, related to nomenclature about fauna from a cross-linguistic and cross-cultural perspective, serves as a further illustration of this epistemological problem. In a range of languages belonging to the Niger-Congo family (in particular those spoken in the forest zone of West Africa), the word for 'animal' is the same as the word for 'meat', the lexical root usually being something like *nam* or *nyam*. As observed by Greenberg (1983: 15–18), this feature extends into neighbouring Afroasiatic and Nilo-Saharan languages (which together with Niger-Congo constitute the three largest language families on the continent).

The author surmises that the primary meaning is indeed 'meat' for a number of reasons. First, in Niger-Congo languages with two distinct words the original root is usually retained with the meaning 'meat', whereas there is an innovated root or word meaning 'animal'. Second, there are languages like Tonga (spoken in Zambia and Zimbabwe) where the morphologically simple form is *nyama* 'meat', whereas the form derived by means of a noun-class prefix *mu-*, *munyama*, means 'animal'.

Similar implicational hierarchies and corresponding "growth stages" to those described with respect to flora are argued for on the basis of data from 144 languages by Brown (1984: 26) with respect to zoological terms (Table 4), ranging from no life-form taxon, to 'fish' (stage 1), and finally to 'mammal'. Again, because of methodological problems in the proper interpretation of lexical meanings, these probably reflect cross-linguistic tendencies, rather than implicational scales.

Table 4: Zoological life-forms and implicational relationships (Brown 1984).

No life-forms (1)
*Fish (2)
*Snake (1)
*Bird + snake (9)
*Fish + snake (6)
*Bird + fish (1)
*Bird + fish + snake (46)
Fish + wug + mammal (1)
Bird + wug + mammal (1)
Bird + snake + mammal (1)
*Bird + fish + snake + wug (23)
*Bird + fish + snake + combined wug-mammal (3)
Bird + snake + wug + mammal (3)
Bird + fish + snake + wug + mammal (22)
Bird + fish + snake + wug + combined wug-mammal (2)
Bird + fish + snake + wug + mammal + combined wug-mammal (1)

As shown by the numbers between parentheses (representing the number of languages in Brown's study with the specific system), some patterns are far more common than others: 'bird + snake' (stage 2), 'bird + fish + snake' (stage 3), 'bird + fish + snake + wug (worm + bug)' (stage 4), 'bird + fish + snake + wug + mammal'.

Berlin (1992) proposes an ethnobiological taxonomic structure with six ranks, representing categories by hierarchical inclusion, comparable to the Linnaean taxonomy, and representing evolutionary history:

Unique beginner (Kingdom) → life-form → intermediate → generic → specific → varietal

As pointed out by Berlin (1992: 15), "[t]he rank dubbed 'intermediate' was proposed cautiously and tentatively, its validity to be determined only by future research". The present author interprets this category as an attempt to allocate non-typical or less salient representatives of a taxon (which are discussed below as part of prototypicality theory).

An example of the five remaining strata in the proposed hierarchy can be found in Conklin's (1962) description of peppers in Hanunóo (Philippines). For example, the unique beginner 'herbacious plant (*qilamnun*) includes 'peppers' (*laadaq*) as a life form; the latter contains 'houseyard peppers (*laada.balainun*) as a generic subclass (as against 'wild peppers', *laada.tirin. dukun-tin-bayaq*); 'houseyard peppers' are divided into 'houseyard chili pepper' (*laada.balaynun. mahaarat*) and 'houseyard green pepper' (*laada.balynun.tagnaanam*) as specific domestic peppers. Each of these categories contains names for different varieties.

In his discussion of folk-biological ranking, Berlin (1992) refers to English concepts such as 'plant' or 'animal' as life forms or kingdom ranks. These in turn can be divided into 'life-form' ranks such as 'tree', 'grass', 'fish', or 'bird'. Each of these contains generic ranks such as 'oak', 'clover', 'dog', and 'shark'. According to Berlin (1992), these form the core of ethnobiological classifications. These generic species contain "folk-specific" ranks like 'white oak' or 'poodle', which in turn may be subdivided into "folk varietal" ranks (like 'toy poodle' or 'swamp white oak'). Taxonomies like these are hence based on relationships of contrasts and inclusion ("kind of" relations). Specific terms like 'oak' contrast with 'birch', for example, but are included within higher-level terms like 'tree' as the next hierarchical level in languages like English, where the latter term contrasts with terms like 'herb' or 'grass'.

Legère (2020: 734–735) notes that the taxon PLANT is widespread in Bantu languages. At the same time it should be noted (as the author does) that this taxon "is not accepted as the unique beginner, but only as a life form (sometimes even restricted to cultigens) like a few others, but not higher in the hierarchy" by speakers of different Bantu languages. In this way, it has the same status in Bantu languages like Swahili as *mti* 'tree', which is in paradigmatic contrast with *mmea* 'small, non-woody (annual) plant, non-tree'. In another Bantu language, Mpiin

(Democratic Republic of the Congo), there is a four-way contrast for life-forms (Koni Muluwa 2010, quoted in Legère 2020: 736).

(3) bítir   'herbs'
    miʃí   'climbers, vines'
    miti   'trees'
    nswâs   'shrubs'

At the level of specific taxa, the largest numbers of terms tend to be found, but these rarely exceed 500 items (Foley 1997: 116). Specifics or subgeneric taxa are a further more common feature of such taxonomies. The scientific taxonomy and corresponding Latin names of trees and plants in Tima, as found in the primer produced by Schneider-Blum (2013a), were provided by the Sudanese botanist Burai Mukhtar Hamed (Kordofan University).

(4) kìṛìr kùtún   'Acacia laeta'
    kìṛìr kwálwàl   'Acacia senegal'
    kìṛìr kìtʌ́k   'Acacia mellifera'
    kùrùh   'Acacia albida'
    kʌ́ʌ́hɨ̀l   'Acacia nubica'
    kàrkíɲáŋ   'Acacia nilotica'

With their pioneering contributions, Brown (1984) and Berlin (1992) triggered a debate about the nature of ethnobiological folk taxonomies and the question of the extent to which such taxonomies are again culturally mediated, parallel to the discussion among anthropologists about the meaning and use of kinship terminology. Berlin (1992: 285–288) points out that utilitarian criteria as well as cognitive factors determine the structure of folk classification. Consequently, not all plants or animals are necessarily part of ethnobiological classifications; biological distinctiveness or phenotypic salience in the local habitat of a community plays a role as well (Berlin 1992: 21).

Hunn (1982) argues that there are two competing models of folk biological classification: 1. the Taxonomic Hierarchy Model, and 2. the Natural Core Model. With the latter conceptualization (of which Eugene Hunn himself is a protagonist), one allows for gradable membership or categorial contiguity, and thereby for transitions in folk biological taxonomies; moreover, this model accounts for the fact that phenomena in the natural environment are not necessarily categorized (or lexicalized) and may be left unclassified instead. Hunn (2006: 259) concludes that "science is not just a product of Renaissance genius and modernist dedication, but rather an impulse common to all humanity" (Hunn 2006: 259).

Life-form taxa may therefore be biologically highly diverse, covering a wide range of generic taxa, as in Karam, a Trans-New Guinea language, where the term *as* refers to 'frog, small marsupial, rodent' (Bulmer and Tyler 1968). Atran, Medin, and Ross (2004) point out that for the Itza Maya villagers, typicality is based not on similarity but on knowledge of cultural ideals. Hence, the wild turkey is a typical bird because of its rich cultural significance, even though it is in no way similar to most other birds. For speakers of the Mayan language Tzeltal in Mexico, adult lepidoptera (butterflies and moths) are of little interest. Their larvae, on the other hand, are carefully sorted into 16 terminal folk taxa, as some are edible, others attack crops, and still others acquire painful defensive ornamentation (Hunn 1982: 831). In other words, classifications may be essence-based and reflect utilitarian factors, for example edible versus inedible, or poisonous versus non-poisonous. For speakers of the Central Khoisan language Khwe (Khoe), the python (a snake which is not poisonous but instead strangles its victims) is not a snake because it is eaten by humans (Picture 4).

Picture 4: Are pythons snakes or not? (picture kindly provided by Willem van Zyl).

For Western minds, which find such classifications somewhat abstruse, a brief look at medieval history in Europe may help to show that such utilitarian perspectives were also found in that part of the world. During the late Middle Ages, fish, living in water as an element of special sanctity, could be eaten during fasting times. But the beaver as a mammal was also classified by religious leaders as a kind of fish (Picture 5), since it lived in and along the water and its tail looked "fishy", and consequently one was also allowed to eat this animal (which was still quite common across Europe in those days). In this way, religious dietary restrictions regulating what kinds of food one should abstain from, such as meat or animal products like eggs or cheeses, were adapted to the needs of the common people. Apparently, typicality is not necessarily based on biological aspects, but may also reflect social similarity; moreover, this type of typicality reflects the salience or function of or human interest in a species in a specific community, something which is clearly better accounted for within the Natural Core Model of folk taxonomies.

Picture 5: The beaver as a kind of fish during the late Middle Ages.

In parallel with kinship terminology and numeral systems, concepts in bionomenclatural classifications may consequently also be treated in terms of prototypes. The latter are categorized, not on the basis of a checklist, but as the most typical and less typical members of a set, which implies that there are degrees of membership, sometimes with vague boundaries. The concept "degree of membership" derives from fuzzy set theory in logic, whereas the concept of "most typical members" derives from prototype theory, as propagated in particular by Rosch (1978). Both concepts are applied in the discussion in this chapter, as well as in Chapter 3. For a detailed discussion of these two theories, including some differences between the two, the interested reader is referred to López Rúa (2003: 60–136). Central to such approaches should always be the specific terms used in a language and the semantic range covered by these terms.

As a consequence of such degrees of typicality, there are also "fuzzy sets", which allow speakers to be creative or to be deliberately ambiguous in their linguistic usage. This conceptualization of cognitive structures allows one to explain both the biological and the culture-specific manipulation of meanings, not only with respect to kinship terminology and bionomenclature, but also for other domains, such as colour terminology, as discussed in Chapter 3.

Rather than having mutually exclusive taxa that jointly exhaust the domain, the Natural Core Model also envisages that members are assigned a place in the category according to their degree of membership or to the features they share with the most typical or central members, i.e., through family resemblance rather than through discreteness. The category of 'birds' in English, for example, is somewhat heterogeneous in that members such as *ostrich, penguin, starling* or *blackbird* do not all fulfil features on a checklist like being able to fly. From this it follows that some features may be less salient than others for speakers of a particular language. Such a model consequently also allows for the allocation of intermediate taxa, such as 'bats', which can fly but do not lay eggs.

From the discussion above one might get the (wrong) impression that American cognitive anthropologists are the only scientists to have contributed to our knowledge of "ethnoscience" (also known as ethnoepistemology or ethnosemantics). In fact, in France, pioneers like André-Georges Haudricourt combined an interest in linguistics with anthropology and botany. He was also co-founder in 1976 of a research centre whose goal it still is to investigate little-documented languages within their cultural environment, called LACITO (*Langues et Civilisations à Tradition Orale*).

Haudricourt also inspired scholars like Jacqueline Thomas, Serge Bahuchet, and others. The encyclopaedic dictionary of Thomas et al. (2013) on the Aka is but one example of his intellectual influence. The linguistic fieldguide by Bouquiaux and Thomas (1971), *Enquête et description des langues à tradition orale*, and its English translation from 1992, *Studying and Describing Unwritten Languages*, also contains various drawings of plants and animals, or utensils and other culturally relevant objects. Several of the French titles of monographs and articles referred to in the present study are studies emerging from the tradition initiated by Haudricourt.

Most speech communities (today as in the past) do not live "in vitro", but rather interact with speakers of other languages, albeit to differing degrees. Multilingual situations characterized by a high degree of lexical and grammatical borrowing also tend to manifest the transfer or replication of lexical categorization strategies. Hayward (1991) lists over forty examples from Ethiopia, which has been argued to constitute such a convergence area.[11]

The examples illustrate metaphorical extensions shared between Cushitic, Omotic, and Semitic languages, such as 'draw water', which also means 'copy, imitate'. But this convergence also involves the categorization of nature, e.g., the division between 'small birds' and 'large birds' in Amharic (Semitic) and Oromo (Cushitic) (Hayward 1991: 147).

---

11 For further discussion, including of criticism of this postulation of language union in Ethiopia, the interested reader is referred to Dimmendaal (2011: 203–209).

	all small birds	all large birds	
(5)	wäf	amora	Amharic (Semitic)
	šimbira	allaattii	Oromo (Cushitic)

Leyew (2011) describes botanical terminologies in three Ethiopian languages, Awngi and the distantly related language Shinasha, as well as the genetically unrelated language Gumuz, all spoken in densely forested regions. Awngi distinguishes between 'tree', 'shrub/herb', 'climber', and 'grass' as taxonomic concepts, whereas in Gumuz and Shinasha the concept of 'shrub/herb' is a diminutive from the word for 'tree' (i.e., 'small tree'). There is no word which may be translated as 'plant' in these Ethiopian languages. Legère (2020) confirms this pattern, the absence of a unique beginner term PLANT, for Bantu languages, which are spoken in an area ranging from Cameroon to Kenya and south of this region.

D'Andrade (1995: 93–94) also observes that "in a number of cultures there is no rank zero term for the plant domain. For example, there is no single term for "plant" in Tzeltal or Aguaruna. However – and this is a crucial point – this does not necessarily mean that there is no concept for "plant". The evidence that such a concept can exist without a term is quite strong for both the Tzeltal and Aguaruna. First, in the systems investigated to date which lack a zero-level term, there are numerous terms for parts of plants and stages of plant growth that are applied *only* to plants. But interestingly, in collecting more than 20,000 specimens, informants never selected organisms other than plants (from the perspective of a speaker of English); mushrooms and other fungi were not considered to fall within the domain. Such experiments show that cognition has to be studied independently of language too.

Roulon-Doko (1999) makes similar observations with respect to the Gbaya 'Bodue (Central African Republic), concerning bionomenclatural terminology and the con-ceptualization of nature as reflected in the way speakers talk about this domain. The author, who is fluent in the language of these people traditionally living as hunter-gatherers, also provides evidence against the Taxonomic Hierarchy Model.

3 Lexical semantics and the contribution of cognitive linguistics

The research interests of cognitive anthropologists in the 1990s moved away from lexical research, instead focusing on "cultural model" research, as shown by Blount (2011: 19) in his historical survey of the field. "Cultural models" are defined as "presupposed, taken-for-granted models of the world that are widely shared (although not necessarily to the exclusion of other, alternative models) by the members of a society and that play an enormous role in their understanding of the world and their behavior in it" (Quinn and Holland 1987: 4). The goal of cultural model research is "a description of the organization of knowledge and its link to what is known about how humans think" (Blount 2011: 19). From the 1990s onwards, it was cognitive linguists, in particular, who pushed research on lexical semantics (as well as discourse) forwards. Cognitive linguistics as a branch of linguistics uses knowledge from cognitive psychology and neurobiology to understand the structure of language, as illustrated for the notion of "colour" below.

The actual roots of this research agenda among cognitive linguists are to be found in the 1960s. One such highly influential early publication by a cognitive anthropologist and a cognitive linguist is that of Berlin and Kay (1969), *Basic Color Terms*. Their model of the colour space as reflected in human language has since been used as a key example of the predominance of nature over nurture in cognitive experiences as reflected in the lexicon (and beyond). This is also the reason why relatively many pages are dedicated to colour as a cognitive phenomenon here. "Universalists" hold that there are innate constraints, while "relativists" hold that nature (or our cognitive system) may set its constraints, but that nurture is crucial when it comes to explaining differences between languages and thus between speech communities.

Berlin and Kay (1969) chose colour as an appropriate domain in which to scrutinize the doctrine of linguistic relativity. There had been at least fifteen years of interdisciplinary concord that colour constitutes the paradigmatic example of semantic and cognitive arbitrariness, as pointed out by MacLaury (2009: 248), and so it was time for Berlin and Kay (1969) to challenge this assumption.

3.1 Colour

The investigation of colour terminology across languages has a longer tradition than the investigation of kinship terminology or other lexical domains discussed in the present chapter and in Chapter 2. The British politician and four-time Prime

Minister of Great Britain, William Ewart Gladstone (1809–1898), was a scholar in his free time and had a special interest in Homer's epics the *Iliad* and the *Odyssey*.[12] His three-volume *Studies on Homer and the Homeric Age* (1858) included a chapter on Homer's perception and use of colour. For Gladstone, the use of words like *oinops* 'wine-faced' (οἶνοψ), in order to describe the colour of the sea as well as that of oxen, was most confusing. He concluded that the ancient Greeks' sense of colour differed from that of modern humans (in the 19th century), a difference which was adduced to an inability of the former to differentiate between specific colours, i.e., an undeveloped state of colour perception compared to people living more than two thousand years later. As a matter of fact, Gladstone's translation problem is at the heart of the matter, lingering on today, as we shall see below, and resulting from an underestimation of the power of culture, as Deutscher (2010: 40) puts it.

Interest in colour was also manifest in the scholarly work of the German philologist Lazarus Geiger, who gave a plenary lecture in 1867 at the Assembly of German Naturalists and Physicians in Frankfurt, "On the Color Sense in Primitive Times and its Evolution", which was published in 1878. Geiger also believed that the "defects" in the colour vocabulary of speakers of ancient Greek, Vedic, and Avestian must be anatomical in nature. Deutscher (2010: 45) gives a detailed historical contextualization of these views and points out that at the time Darwin had just published his evolutionary model *On the Origin of Species*. Geiger (1878) also related cross-linguistic differences in colour terminology to evolutionary progression, and more specifically to an emerging sensitivity to the prismatic colours, starting with a sensitivity to red. In his first "cross-cultural" evolutionary theory of colour names, Geiger assumed an additive progression of at least six stages. First, "black" and "red" (as meta-categories) were named, suggesting a vague conception of something coloured; second, "black" and "red" stood in contrast to one another; third, "yellow" was registered; fourth, "white", previously included in "red", was distinguished; fifth, "green" developed from "yellow"; sixth and last, "blue" developed. Geiger argued that so-called "primitive" people had fewer colour names because they were physiologically underdeveloped.

But another constellation in Germany around the same time made it clear that differences in colour terminology had nothing to do with physiological limitations. During the times of Emperor Wilhelm II (1859–1941), the animal dealer and entrepreneur Carl Hagenbeck, who founded a zoo in Hamburg (to which

---

12 The modern view on these impressive arts of work from the ancient Greeks is that these epic poems are the result of a patchwork of a great number of popular ballads cobbled together from different poets over different periods.

he also gave his name), also organized a large-scale "ethnic-event" Menagerie in 1874, where people from different parts of the world were displayed together with their housing and equipment on the extension of a park. In this way such different groups as Lapps (i.e., Sami), Nubians from Sudan and Egypt and other African communities (including "Hottentots", i.e., San from the German colony of Southwest Africa, now called Namibia), Eskimo (i.e., Inuit) from Canada and Greenland, and Fuegians from the Terra del Fuega at the southern tip of South America were exhibited as human figures in order to give visitors a picture of their daily life. As a matter of fact, between 1810 and the beginning of the Second World War some 35,000 people from outside Europe appeared in exhibitions in cities such as London, Paris, and Berlin, in line with the colonial hegemony. Shocking pictures of these exhibitions can be found on the internet.

Virchow, one of the founding fathers of modern medicine, was also chairman of the German Society for Anthropology, Ethnology and Prehistorical Studies, and tried to give an academic "coating" to these performances. In line with the science of his time, he examined participants in the people shows by surveying their head shapes and bodies, in order to come to a better understanding of the development which humans had undergone.

Virchow also investigated the sense of colours with "Nubians" (of whom it is not clear which language they spoke, as there are several Nubian languages). They were exhibited in the Berlin Zoo in 1878 and were shown skeins of wool by Virchow, who concluded that those interviewed displayed "anomalies of colour vocabulary" (presumably because Nubian languages do not make a lexical distinction between the colours that are referred to in German as *blau* ('blue' in English) and *grün* ('green' in English). Nevertheless, they were quite able to discriminate colours in all parts of the spectrum, as demonstrated by the way those interviewed sorted and matched coloured papers and wools. Virchow concluded that the way in which colour terms are or are not used says absolutely nothing about the general cognitive ability of people to generate linguistic expressions for colours. (See Andree 1878 and Kirchhoff 1879 for a discussion.)

The linguistic-anthropological investigation of colour also had origins in cognitive anthropology, and can be traced back again to Boas, and more specifically to his 1881 dissertation on sea-water colours in Eskimo (Inuit).

Research on the interaction between language and cognition by using experimental methods is generally assumed to have started in the 1950s, when Brown and Lenneberg (1954) reported on their experiments investigating the link between the codeability of 320 Munsell colour chips and their memorability. This chart contains 320 colour chips as stimuli showing different hues ("colouredness") and different degrees of brightness (light reflectance of a colour) and saturation (i.e., strength of hue within a colour; pastel colours, for example, are desaturated). Alongside these chromatic colours, there are nine achromatic colours (those without hue, i.e., white, black, and intermediate shades of grey) in the system.[13]

In a follow-up study, using the same colour chips, Lenneberg and Roberts (1956) published the results of their experimental studies of colour terminology among speakers of the First Nation language Zuni, who were asked to encircle the ranges of pre-elicited terms on acetate laid over a 320-chip Munsell array. In addition, participants in the experiment were asked for a focus of each term, in order to compare the results with those for American English speakers. These authors used the Munsell colour chart under the assumption that in this way it was possible to objectively characterize and compare language categories in terms of their denotational referents, since colour was assumed to be a universal phenomenon, having boundaries which could be plotted on known dimensions, and with contiguous shared boundaries between colours. They defined the category of colour as being composed of the three psychophysical dimensions or perceptual attributes already mentioned above: hue (intensity, colouredness), value (lightness, luminosity, dominant wavelength), and chroma (saturation, purity).

"Colour" itself was not an issue for Roger Brown and Eric Lenneberg; it was presupposed. Only variations in the manner of dealing with what one conceives of as "colour" were at issue, using categories of English as the metalanguage for describing so-called objective reality. This type of research would set the trend for investigations in the domain of colour terminology for the next decades.

In their seminal contribution *Basic Color Terms* (1969), the anthropological linguist Brent Berlin and the cognitive linguist Paul Kay initiated a second era of colour research by using an inductive framework, taking into account as many languages as possible.[14] Berlin and Kay questioned the fundamental assumption of most previous colour research, namely that colours form an even perceptual continuum, pointing towards the arbitrary nature of this semantic domain from a cognitive point of view. Instead, Berlin and Kay claimed that the human visual system sets constraints on the range of variation in semantic structure, i.e., on universal colour space.

"Basic" (as reflected in the title of their book) for these authors implies that a colour term is monolexemic, i.e., its meaning is not predictable from the meaning of its parts. Thus, *blu-ish* (consisting of two morphemes *blue-* and *-ish*) is not basic,

---

[13] The Munsell colour chart can be found on the internet under the following link: [https://figshare.com/articles/figure/_The_Munsell_color_chart_as_used_by_the_World_Color_Survey_/943517] (accessed 17 January 2021).
[14] Google Scholar mentions more than 9,000 citations of this highly influential monograph (accessed 17 February 2022).

because its meaning is included in (a subset of) the term *blue*; moreover, it is not morphologically simple (as it consists of two morphemes). A basic colour term should also not be derived from some other form, for example *orange* in English, which is coterminous with the name of a fruit in this language, and also constitutes a borrowing from French. Furthermore, as a term, it should refer to a wide range of objects. A term like *blonde* is therefore not a basic colour term in English, as it is used only to refer to *pale yellow* or *gold* hair (as non-basic colour terms). Furthermore, the term should also be psychologically highly salient (dominant), easily elicited, and appearing at the beginning of elicitation lists, i.e., it should be mentioned by most speakers.

The measuring device or stimulus array in *Basic Color Terms* again consisted of the Munsell colour chart system. For their typological study, Berlin and Kay (1969) consulted language helpers (foreign students at the University of California at Berkeley) speaking twenty different languages, and forty speakers of Tzeltal in Mexico, with data on another seventy-eight languages being based on the investigation of sources. On the basis of these investigations, they arrive at a list of maximally 11 "basic colour terms". Moreover, they concluded that some of these terms are more basic than others, i.e., that there are implicational universals between them reflected in seven stages. These terms are written in capitals (WHITE etc.) by the authors in order to express a metalanguage, rather than the English use or meaning of these terms. At Stage I, only two terms are found, whose best representatives are to be found in what would be called *WHITE* and *BLACK* in English. At Stage II, RED is added, and at Stage III either GREEN or YELLOW is encoded, while at Stage IV, whichever of these categories was not encoded at Stage III will receive its own term. At Stage V, six term languages are found, also encoding BLUE. Stage VI languages have a separate term for BROWN, while at Stage VII, with eight terms, PURPLE, PINK, ORANGE or GREY may be lexicalized as a basic colour term.

Berlin and Kay (1969) conclude that the division of the colour spectrum in languages is not arbitrary, but rather governed by cognitive constraints. Moreover, the implicational relations holding between the different terms imply, for example, that if a language has a basic term for BROWN (in a corresponding English translation), it also has a basic term for BLUE, but not vice versa. Berlin and Key (1969: 45) furthermore point out that GREY appears to occur as a "wild card", showing up at various points in the evolutionary sequence (compare Figure 1). Encoding other perceptual categories into "basic colour terms" thus follows a fixed, partial order in the history of any language. Berlin and Kay (1969) assume seven evolutionary stages, in which "focal" colours are encoded by the following basic terms:

```
                        VIII PURPLE
I BLACK        IV GREEN                    IX PINK
       III RED       VI BLUE   VII BROWN         X ORANGE
II WHITE       V YELLOW              XI GREY
```

Figure 1: Basic colour terms (Berlin and Kay 1969).

The languages presented in Table 5 constitute a small selection from Africa in Berlin and Kay (1969), with different numbers of "basic colour terms". It should be noted that Ngombe, which is spoken in the Democratic Republic of the Congo and Congo-Brazzaville, is classified as a Chadic (Afroasiatic) language by Berlin and Kay (1969: 48), although it is actually a Bantu (Niger-Congo) language.

Berlin and Kay (1969) were already aware of a number of conceptual problems with their model. In their database there are languages showing "underdifferentiation", like Cantonese, which does not have a term for BROWN, although it does have terms for PINK and GREY (Berlin and Kay 1969: 35). Russian, which has two basic terms for BLUE, *goluboj* and *sinij*, displays "overdifferentiation" (Berlin and Kay 1969: 35).

Table 5: Basic colour terms in some African languages (Berlin and Kay 1969).

Stage I (two terms)	Ngombe DRC/BRA	*bopu* white [WHITE] *bohindu* black [BLACK]
Stage II (three terms)	Shona (Zimbabwe)	*cicena* white, green, yellow [WHITE] *citema* black, blue *cipswuka* red, purple, orange [RED]
Stage IIIa (four terms)	Ibibio (Nigeria)	*àfíá* [WHITE] *èbúbít* [BLACK] *ǹdàídàt* [RED] *àwàwà* [GREEN]
Stage IIIb (four terms)	I(g)bo (Nigeria)	*nzu* white, grey [WHITE] *ojī* black [BLACK] *uhie* red, dull red [RED] *odo* mustard, yellow, tan, green-yellow [YELLOW]
Stage IV (five terms)	!Kung (Botswana, Namibia, Angola)	*!gow* white, grey [WHITE] *žho* black [BLACK] *!gā* red, rust [RED] *|ouŋ* violet, blue, green [GREEN] *gow* orange, yellow, tan [YELLOW]

Table 5 (continued)

Stage V (six terms)	Hausa (Nigeria)	fări white [WHITE] băķi black [very dark blue, very dark green [BLACK] ja red [RED] algashi green grass-green, emerald green) [GREEN] nawaya yellow [YELLOW] shuḍi blue [BLUE]
Stage VI	Bari (South Sudan)	lo'kwe white, pure, holy [white] lurnö [black] lo'tor red, reddish [RED] ló-ngem green [green] lo'forong yellow [YELLOW] murye blue [blue] lo'jere brown [brown]
Stage VII	Dinka (South Sudan)	yer, mabior white car, macar black lual, thith-lual red toc green mayen yellow maŋok, mayɛn brown thith-lual purple thith-lual pink malɔu grey

But the actual empirical problems of the proposed model are more fundamental in nature. Apart from "underdifferentiation" and "overdifferentiation", there is a third issue, the notion of "basic", as discussed below. Fourth, the question is raised below as to what extent the use of the Munsell colour chart as a primary source for the listing of terms is problematic from a methodological point of view, if one tries to understand the meaning of terms for "colour" in another language. Before these four problematic domains are discussed, the modified models by Kay and McDaniel (1975, 1978) and Kay, Berlin, and Merrifield (1991) are discussed first.

Kay and McDaniel (1978) present a slightly revised encoding sequence, with GRUE capturing 'green plus blue' and with GREY operating as a "wild card", potentially popping up at any stage, as shown in Figure 2.

Kay and McDaniel (1978) also aim to provide a neurophysiological basis for colour perception, thereby basing their work on research by de Valois, Abramov, and Jacobs (1966) and de Valois and Jacobs (1968) on the neural representation of colour in the pathways between the eye and the brain at some remove from the retina (which is the innermost, light-sensitive layer of tissue of the eye). Based on neurophysiological research with macaque monkeys, whose visual system

$$\begin{pmatrix}\text{WHITE}\\ \\ \text{BLACK}\end{pmatrix} \rightarrow \begin{matrix}\text{[GRUE]} \rightarrow \text{[yellow]}\\ \text{[RED]}\\ \text{[brown]} \quad \text{[yellow]} \rightarrow \text{[GRUE]}\end{matrix} \rightarrow \begin{pmatrix}\text{green}\\ \text{and}\\ \text{blue}\end{pmatrix} \rightarrow \rightarrow \begin{pmatrix}\text{purple}\\ \text{pink}\\ \text{orange}\end{pmatrix}$$

I   II   III*   IV   V   VI   VII

←———————— grey ————————→

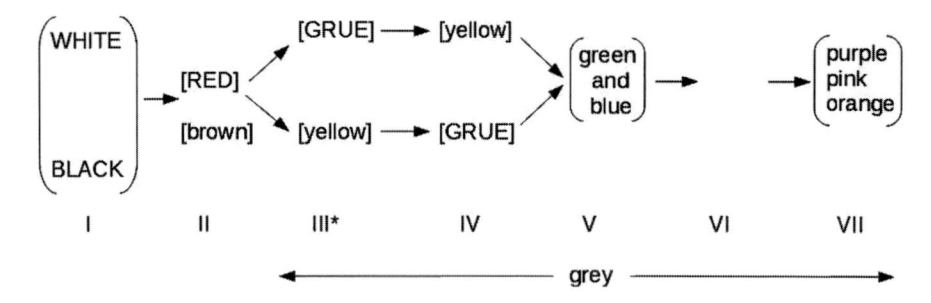

Figure 2: Colour-encoding sequence (Kay and McDaniel 1978).

is similar to that of humans, these neurobiologists discovered that there are six types of colour-sensitive (post-retinal) cells, four of which are responsible for the reception of hue (focal primary colours "blue", "yellow", "red", and "green"), and two for brightness ("black" and "white"). These cells are arranged in pairs (blue-yellow cells, red-green cells, and light-darkness cells). Berlin and McDaniel (1975) argue on the basis of such receptors for basic focal non-primary colours that the latter result from "fuzzy union"; "pink", for example, results from the "fuzzy union" of "red" and "white", and "orange" is found in the region where "red" and "yellow" overlap. Such "composite" colour terms thus refer to colour categories comprising more than one of the focal primary colours established by de Valois, Abramov, and Jacobs (1966) and de Valois and Jacobs (1968).

The four types of cells responsible for the reception of hue, and thereby for four fundamentally distinct neural response processes, help to establish composite categories or "macro-colours" consisting of various combinations of the basic hues ("red", "yellow", "green", and "blue"); macro-colours can have variable foci, both intra-societally and cross-societally. Russell de Valois' neurobiology research team also found evidence for the presence of a separate channel, "consisting of brightness-sensitive and darkness-sensitive cells that inform us regarding the whiteness or blackness of a stimulus" (Kay and McDaniel 1978: 627). These then would be responsible for the presence of terms for the achromatic colours "black" and "white" (if English is used as a metalanguage).

In order to further back up the empirical basis of the model, Kay, Berlin, and Merrifield (1991) present the results of their assessment of colour naming systems in 111 languages from their World Color Survey. According to the same authors, only nine out of 63 logically possible types of composite colour categories are attested cross-linguistically, including "yellow/green/ blue" and "white/yellow".

Inspired by developments in semantic theory, Kay, Berlin, and Merrifield (1991) also incorporate prototype theory and categorization in terms of "fuzzy sets" (rather than foci or discretely contrasting semantic features) in their representation of colour terms. The latter are assumed to be formed by "fuzzy logical operations" of "fuzzy union" and "fuzzy intersection", resulting in the so-called "composite" categories already mentioned above. Composite categories are unions of two or three fuzzy sets, i.e., "named color categories that comprise more than one of the colors that have been established by neurobiologists, independently of language, to correspond to fundamentally distinct neural response processes" (Kay, Berlin, and Merrifield 1991: 14).

What is described by Berlin and McDaniel (1978) as "fuzzy union" would seem to correspond to a much more widespread and well attested cognitive phenomenon called "conceptual blending" by Fauconnier (1985) and Fauconnier and Turner (2002), as one characteristic cognitive principle the human mind operates with. In their system, the blending frequently involves two inputs (as the simplest type), but there does not seem to be any principled reason why more complex types of blending should be excluded. Fauconier (1985: 171) gives an example based on the English sentence *You're driving me into my grave*, which presents a blend of three input spaces resulting in a new meaning: "[A] space of graves and burial, a space of life with aging and growing weakness, and a space of motion along a path. The integrated scene in the bend of someone being slowly pushed into a grave inherits structure selectively from all three" (Fauconnier 1985: 171).

From the 1970s onwards a range of authors set out to test the claims made by the authors above. Jernudd and White (1983) present the results of an experiment carried out with 27 speakers of Fur (For) and Sudanese Arabic in Sudan, who were asked to describe the colours of the Munsell colour chart. Variation occurred between speakers because terms were used which would not fulfil the criteria of "basicness"; speakers also differed as to the number of terms they used. Nevertheless, 93% percent of the Fur (For) speakers consulted used the five "basic terms" for BLACK, WHITE, RED, GREEN, YELLOW in their language; when six terms were used, BLUE and BROWN were the primary choice; whenever seven terms were used, PURPLE was also part of this set. Roughly similar figures were found in the naming task with Sudanese Arabic speakers. Such experiments do indeed confirm the notion of "basicness" in this semantic domain for these languages. Nevertheless, interpretations of speakers' behaviour are not always this straightforward.

Can the modified conceptualiziation of "colour", as proposed by Kay, Berlin, and Merrifield (1991), solve (some of) the conceptual problems of Berlin and Kay listed above, for example that of "underdifferentiation"? In the following cognitive account of the concept -*hɛh* 'bright' in Tima (illustrated in Figure 3), the blending process would involve, first, a "generic space" containing the schematic conceptual structure common to the input spaces at any moment in the development of an integration network (Fauconnier and Turner 2002: 8). In the case of colour terms, this common generic space centres around fundamental neural responses as input (with a neurological basis), from which three are selected: YELLOW, GREEN, and BLUE. These are projected onto another space, the blend. The emerging concept represents a conceptual integration or fuzzy union of these inputs (YELLOW, GREEN, and BLUE) and results in a third space, in this case that of the Tima concept -hɛh, which may be translated as 'light, bright', or 'yeen'.

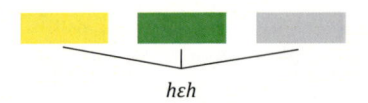

Figure 3: Generic space for the Tima concept -hɛh, 'light, bright'.

Interestingly, in early studies of Northwest Coast languages in Canada, Boas (1891) already observed that the latter have a common pattern in which 'light blue', 'light green', and 'yellow' are interlaced in diverse ways (corresponding to what is called 'yeen' here). The term *qancar* in Burunge (Tanzania) also refers to 'green, yellow, blue' (Segerer and Vanhove 2019: 291; personal communication with Roland Kießling).

If fundamental neural responses lie at the basis of colour vision, examples from languages like Tima (or other languages, such as Burunge (Tanzania) or Kwakiutl (Canada)) can only be explained if we assume that so-called composite colours (of which "yeen" may be one, just like "pink") are the result of a phenomenon called "fuzzy union" by Berlin and McDaniel (1978), and "blending" by Fauconnier (1985). The emerging notion in that case would result from the perception of these colours by cells responsible for the fundamental neural responses for (what are called in English) "blue", "green", and "yellow". This notion would cover lightness or brightness, rather than hue, in a language of this type, like Tima.

Over the years, different authors have also pointed towards other languages manifesting "overdifferentiation" with respect to colour terminology. Hardman (1981), for example, discusses data from Jaqaru (Peru), a language with eight basic colours, four of which cover what is called *red* in English. It has also been pointed out by Hickerson (1971) that by stringent application of Berlin and Kay's criteria, one could reduce a language from Stage VII to Stage II. Wescott (1970) also demonstrates the multitude of problems which can arise in applying Berlin and Kay's criteria for basicness in his analysis of Bini (a language spoken in Nigeria, also known as Edo). Depending on one's criteria, one could reduce languages seemingly rich in colour vocabulary, such as Tongan (Svenja Völkel, personal communication), to a language without basic colour terms. In Jörai (which is spoken in Vietnam), there are 23 basic colour terms but no single word that translates as 'colour', according to Dournes (1978).

In a more recent critical account, Roulon-Doko (2019) discusses data from Gbaya, a language spoken in the Central African Republic which does not lexically distinguish colour from the visual aspects resulting from a variety of parameters, such as material or physical state. As is true for many languages, there is no generic term for 'colour' in Gbaya. Instead, speakers may use *dàp*, which can be translated as 'pattern'; alternatively, they use a compound with the word for 'body', *tè*, for visual descriptions in general, as in the following example (no translation given for -*kènà*):

(6) tè-kènà 'bright green'

The three Gbaya terms translating as 'black', 'red', and 'white', respectively, are (dynamic) process verbs, for example *fɛŋ* "1. bleach, become white, fade (intransitive); 2. depreciate, humiliate, soil, whiten (transitive)". The corresponding derived adjective *fɛŋa* means 'faded, humiliated', with other meanings depending on the noun with which it combines (Roulon-Doko 2019: 140). When a stative meaning is to be expressed, corresponding adjectives are used, for example *bú* 'white'. In addition, Gbaya has 82 so-called "adjective-adverbs" for the colour domain, for example different shades of "white": *kpúŋ-kpúŋ* 'white', *kábá-kábá* 'very white', *kpɔ́ɔ́-kpɔ́ɔ́* 'very white' (whereby the reduplication suggests that they are ideophonic in nature, expressing degrees of intensity).

"Black" or "dark", and "white" or "light" are presumably related to human experience with the rising and setting of the sun, i.e., with dynamic processes (expressed by verbs in many languages). But "red" also tends to be treated as a dynamic verb (rather than an adjective expressing a state). Again, there is probably a deeply rooted evolutionary reason for this. Being able to recognize the colour of fruits that have ripened in nature has tremendous evolutionary advantages, as it is essential for the survival of different species. Hominids and birds have receptors for the colour "red", as shown through experiments. When captive chimpanzees are shown a green (unripe) tomato and a red (ripe) tomato, for example, they immediately go for the red one. Being able to recognize what is called *red* in English as a colour plays an important role in nature.

The modified model as propagated by Kay, Berlin, and Merrifield (1991) does not solve fundamental problems caused by systems manifesting "underdifferentiation" or "overdifferentiation". These "biological facts" cannot account for the fact that languages like Tima use one and the same term to describe a domain in the colour spectrum covered by three terms in English: *green*, *blue*, and *yellow*. Foley (1997: 156) points out that such systems are attested in Asia, Australia and Oceania, North America and South America. But similar systems are common in Africa, in particular in languages in the Sahel region and neighbouring areas. One of these languages, Tima (spoken in the Nuba Mountains in Sudan), has a system as shown in Figure 4 (Dimmendaal 2015a: 131, based on Schneider-Blum 2013a).

-tún	-tɨ́k	-rdí	-hɛ́h	-kùlùmó
black	white	red	yellow green blue	brown

Figure 4: Tima colour terms and their prototypical representatives (Schneider-Blum 2013a).

Several of these terms may be modified in Tima in the same way in which *scarlet* may modify *red* in English, whereby the prefix *a-* expresses a predication in the singular ('it is . . .').

Table 6: Tima colour terms.

a-tun hərhər	'dark (with the connotation of being dirty)'
a-tun kulumkulum	'beautifully dark'
a-tɨk	'white'
a-tɨk cɛhcɛh	'pearly-white'
a-rdi wɛlwɛl	'light red''
a-rdi t̪ɪbɪt̪ɪbɪk	'brightly red'
a-hɛh kʌyi	'green (like grass)'
a-hɛh t̪art̪ar	'light green'
a-hɛh t̪urt̪ur	'bright green'
a-hɛh kɨrɨndi	'yellow (like millet)'
a-hɛh wɛlwɛl	'light blue'
a-hɛh wʌlwʌl	'bright blue'

The Tima examples also manifest another phenomenon, called the Frequency Code, after Ohala (1984: 9). On the basis of a cross-linguistic study, Ohala (1984) concludes that words denoting or connoting smallness tend to exhibit a disproportionate incidence of vowels and/or consonants characterized by high acoustic frequency. High front vowels (like *i*) have a high so-called F2 (fundamental frequency), whereas low back vowels (like *ɒ*) have the lowest F2 value.[15] The Tima examples show that specific vowels correspond with visual experiences involving the perception of colour terms, as in the contrasting examples *-hɛh ṭarṭar* versus *-hɛh ṭurṭur*, or *-hɛh wɛlwɛl* versus *-hɛh wʌlwʌl*. Whether such associations with colour are more widespread cross-linguistically is not known.

Some readers may argue that the Tima do indeed distinguish between "yellow", "green", and "blue", as shown by the modifying adverbs (whose reduplicative structure suggests that these are ideophonic words). But note that these "non-basic" terms (in the sense of Berlin and Kay 1969) have the same complex morphological structure as shades of WHITE like *off-white* in English. Moreover, as Table 6 illustrates, Tima distinguishes between two types of "red", *-rdi wɛlwɛl* and *-rdi ṭɪbɪṭɪbɪk*. These forms consequently have the same status paradigmatically as, for example, *-hɛh kʌyi*, translated as 'green' in English, versus *-hɛh kirindi*, translated as 'yellow' in English. Note also that, whereas 'green/ blue/ yellow' persists as "undissolved", Tima does have a separate lexeme for 'brown', which is lower on the implicational scale proposed by Berlin and Kay (1969). As pointed out by Foley (1997: 156), "[t]his grouping of YELLOW/GRUE poses formidable problems for Kay and McDaniel's grounding of generalities of basic colour terms in innate perceptual properties of the human colour vision system, specifically, the subsystems based on opposing colours. Yellow and blue (member of the composite category GRUE) are opposing poles of the same subsystem". Indeed, if these subsystems based on oppositions form the universal grounding for human colour categorizations, it is hard to understand how yellow and blue could be conflated in a single named category. The problem of "yellow" is that it may be associated in a composite category with "red" or "white" or both, or with "green" and, through "green", with "blue", and so on. The proposed neurophysiological wiring is embedded in the opposition of "warm" and "cool" colours: "yellow" and "red" are "warm", "green" and "blue" are "cool" colours.

Kay, Berlin, and Merrifield (1991: 18) in fact admit that no explanation is available for these problematic cases. Evidently, language-specific or culture-specific differences do not override "neurophysiological constraints". Moreover, of

---

15 The phonetic symbols here and elsewhere in this study are those used by the International Phonetic Association (IPA) in order to describe sounds in a uniform way.

the over sixty logically possible systems a range of systems are not attested. But it is not clear how such systems – which are not that uncommon – should be explained. McLaury's (1992) suggestion of assigning a pivotal role to the brightness (luminosity) dimension, rather than hue, in order to explain such systems, is the most plausible explanation for the grouping of yellow/green/blue. Indeed, the best translation for the corresponding term in Tima, -hɛh, is 'light, bright' (Schneider-Blum 2013a: 129). The Tima term -hɛh also makes it clear that it is not possible to determine which meaning is more "basic" than the other, "yellow", "green", or "blue". Consequently, Berlin and Kay's convention of capitalizing the term expressing "the most basic meaning" in the corresponding metalanguage (in their monograph English) is not followed hereafter, as this presupposes that it is always possible or useful to identify a macro-colour with one prototype as the "best representative".

Apart from issues involving "underdifferentiation" and "overdifferentiation", there is the question of what "basic" means: "basic" to whom? One prominent opponent of the Berlin-and-Kay paradigm needs to be mentioned here, the anthropologist Serge Tornay. Tornay (1973) describes colour terminology for Nyangatom, a language spoken by semi-nomadic and agricultural people in southwestern Ethiopia. Tornay (1978a: IX–LI) also criticizes the "evolutionistic" perspective of Berlin and Kay (1969), instead favouring "culturalism" in the perception of colour, as it is not possible to predict the level of technology of a particular speech community on the basis of the number of "basic" colour terms. With eight terms (Stage VII), the Nyangatom in southwestern Ethiopia would represent "une société à technologie avancée, sinon une société industrielle! [a society with an advanced technology, if not an industrial society!]" (Tornay 1973: 87).

Nyangatom has eight terms for colour, which play a role primarily when referring to cattle:

(7) -aukwan 'white'
    -kiryon 'black'
    -araŋan 'red'
    -pus 'green-blue'
    -ñaŋ 'yellow'
    -mug 'brown'
    -kopurat 'pink'
    -oŋwar 'grey'

These may also be combined in order to describe less saturated colours or complex colour patterns of cattle. The same terms may also be combined with words describing patterns, in particular with respect to cattle, but also with respect to human beings. Thus, the Nyangatom name for the anthropologist Serge Tornay himself was *Lo-kori-ɲaŋ* 'the spotted yellow one' (Serge Tornay, personal communication). The term *-kori* is derived from the lexical root for 'giraffe', whereas historically (though not synchronically), *-ɲaŋ* is probably related to the word for 'crocodile', *a-kɪɲaŋ*. Serge Tornay received this nickname because of his tanned skin and freckles. Such combinations suggest that from a conceptual point of view colour terms and terms expressing patterns belong to one and the same cognitive domain for speakers of this language.

From a linguistic point of view, Nyangatom and Turkana are dialects of one and the same language, and so most of the terms listed for Turkana patterns in Picture 6 below (from Ohta 1987) also occur in Nyangatom. As one speaker of Turkana (whose pastoral culture is also similar to that of the Nyangatom) once explained to the present author, it is important to be able to provide a precise description of individual animals, not only of cows, but also of sheep and goats, because this is the only way to get an animal back if it runs off and joins another herd. This is what makes these various terms, including those for colour shades, "basic" to people with such a cultural background.

One way of testing whether the colour terms and the pattern terms are equally basic to pastoralists speaking these languages would be to do the kinds of tests that are common in psycholinguistics. One could test how many milliseconds speakers of Nyangatom, Dinka, or other languages in the area spoken by pastoralists need in order to identify either the colour or the pattern of cows shown on a computer screen. If there is no significant difference in reaction time, the two cognitive domains apparently have the same (level of) significance, as reaction time is known to be a good indicator of frequency of usage and corresponding "basicness".

Cattle traditionally constitute the primary aesthetic locus of Dinka society and that of other pastoral groups in the area, which is also reflected in an extensive terminology for the different types of trained horns (Coote 1992). Pastoral communities in Eastern Africa usually have a rich vocabulary with numerous terms describing colour patterns in cattle. With respect to the Dinka in South Sudan (who speak a related language), Lienhardt (1961: 13) observes that their "very perception of colour, light, and shade in the world around them is (. . .) inextricably connected with their recognition of colour configurations in their cattle. If their cattle-colour vocabulary were taken away, they would have scarcely any way of describing visual experience in terms of colour, light and darkness".

A1. —meri
    —kori

A2. —ngorok
    —komoli

B1. —bubuo

B2. —kapeli

B3. —kedikedi

B4. —koli

B5. —linga

B6. —lukwa

B7. —ngole

B8. —ngora

B9. —aze

B10. —thili

B11. —tulya

B12. —wazi

Picture 6: Turkana names for skin patterns of cows (Ohta 1987).

Turton (1980) extends the observations made for Dinka by Lienhardt (1961) to Mursi, another language spoken mainly by pastoralists in southwestern Ethiopia, which has nine colour terms characterized as basic (following the criteria of Berlin and Kay 1969). As Table 7 illustrates, Mursi has basic colour terms corresponding to "pink" and "grey" as its corresponding focal colours in English, although colour distinctions "higher on the hierarchy", such as "green" and "blue", are not distinguished in this language.

As pointed out in Turton (1980), there is not a single colour term in the Mursi language that does not also refer to shades of colour for cattle. In other words, cattle serve as a model to represent differences between categories of colour and patterns which are universally recognized. David Turton arrives at the structure for Mursi colour terms presented in Table 7.

Table 7: Mursi colour terms (Turton 1980).

Mursi term	colour chips	cattle
koroi	black (including some blues)	
holi	white	
golonyi	red	brown with preponderance of red; reddish-brown, when applied to cattle)
biley	yellow	brown with preponderance of yellow; yellowish-brown; tan, when applied to cattle
chagi	green-blue	slate grey; bluish-grey; ash coloured, when applied to cattle
rege	pink	flesh-coloured
lulumi	brown	dirty white; grey, when applied to cattle
gidangi	grey	dirty white; grey, when applied to cattle
sirwai	blue-violet	a combination of reddish-brown and black, the two colours shading into one another to give a satiny lustrous appearance, when applied to cattle

Thus, in Mursi, a term like *chagi* refers to the colour of grass or the sky. But when applied to cattle, a speaker of English would describe such cows as *gidangi* 'grey'; see also Dimmendaal (1995, reprinted in Dimmendaal 2015a: 101–126) for a discussion of such intercultural "confusion".

Apparently, one has to distinguish between the use of colours in the bovine and non-bovine universe, i.e., depending on the material or texture involved, not only in Mursi, but in many other languages. And this brings us to a fourth reason why the Berlin-and-Kay model (with subsequent elaborations) has its problems. A major issue in terms of our understanding of lexical items in another language concerns the semantic range covered by words (whether referring to colour or to other lexical-semantic domains), as the translation for the term *-hɛh* in Tima already indicates. Ideally, the elicitation of words belonging to such lexical-semantic fields is conducted in the target language in order to gain access to the contextual schemas through which speakers apprehend context and corresponding meanings, a strategy followed for example by Serge Tornay and David Turton during their many years of fieldwork among the Nyangatom and Mursi, respectively.

One of the languages playing a role in Berlin and Kay's (1969) analysis of colour terminology is Hanunóo, a language from the Philippines which is characterized as a Stage III language by Berlin and Kay (1969: 64). Hanunóo has basic colours with foci in 'white', 'black', 'red', and 'green'. The term *(ma)raraʔ* covers shades of 'red', 'maroon', 'orange', and 'yellow', whereas *(ma)latuy* covers shades of 'green', 'yellow', and 'light brown'. However, Berlin and Kay (1969: 64) choose RED and GREEN, respectively, as the macro colours representing the basic (prototypical) meaning of these terms. The authors base their interpretation on the classic contribution on colour terminology in Hanunóo by Conklin (1964), who points out that "what appears to be colour 'confusion' at first may result from an inadequate knowledge of the internal structure of a colour (sic) system and from a failure to distinguish sharply between sensory reception on the one hand and perceptual categorization on the other" (Conklin 1964: 191). According to him, *(ma)raraq* (also represented as *ma)raraʔ*) and *(ma)latuy* reflect an opposition between dryness or desiccation and wetness or freshness (succulence) in visible components of the natural environment, respectively. Hence, it should not come as a surprise – since these are not colour terms – that both terms may cover shades of "yellow" in the metalanguage, English, as in the translations above. For somebody living in the northern hemisphere, fresh vegetation may indeed be associated with "green" (hence the choice for GREEN), but anybody who has been to tropical areas knows that "fresh" leaves may indeed have other colours as well, including yellow, while dead and therefore dessicated plants and trees may also take on a yellow colour.

What these Hanunóo show is that detaching the labeling from the material is artificial and potentially leads to arbitrary choices on the part of the researcher. Conceptual problems of this type abound in the literature. In an early account of travels across Central Africa, Nachtigal (1879; translation 1972) already described the use of colour terms in Arabic as spoken in the region within respect to skin colours (pp. 170–171). The term *asfar* 'yellow' was also used by speakers consulted by Gustav Nachtigal to describe the skin colour of speakers of Arabic, Karanga, and Maba in the area, while *azraq* 'grey' described the skin colour of some Arabic-

and Maba-speaking individuals but also the skin colour of many Daju and Mimi speakers in the area.

Bender (1983) observes that the terms for 'green' and 'blue' may also be applied to the perception of human skin colours in northern Sudanese Arabic. The author bases his study on the work of a B.A. student in linguistics from the University of Khartoum, Ahmed el Bedawi Mustafa Omer el Tinay, himself a speaker of Sudanese Arabic. In the latter language, somebody's (skin) colour, *loonu*, may be *azrak* 'blue' or *axḍar* 'green' (for somebody with a very dark complexion, itself a genetic adaptation to the intensive radiation from the sun in savannah areas).

Such semantic extensions usually only strike us as "weird" if one comes across them in a foreign language. But semantic extensions like these of course also occur in languages like English, where *red* may be used as a descriptive term for specific natural hair colours (and so not necessarily the dyed hair of punks). Former President of the United States Barack Obama and current Vice-President Kamala Harris describe themselves (or are described by others) as "black", when referring to their skin colour. By taking the Munsell colour chart as a basis, the lexical meaning of colour terms in languages is simply reduced to denotational meanings in the metalanguage.

A speech community may have a concept of "colour" without having a word for it. But the mere fact that not all languages have a word for 'colour' should at least provide us as investigators with a hint that not all people necessarily treat the connection between the lexical item and the object or referent as a socially or materially decontextualized "natural categorization of nature". Instead, they may ask "What kind of skin, fur or pattern is that?", and get an answer translated in English as 'green' when referring to human beings in Sudanese Arabic, or 'blue-violet' when talking about cattle in Mursi.

Some readers may interpret the discussion here as an instance of what has come to be known as the "bongo-bongo-ist" stance of ethnographers (Douglas 1996: xxxv). This stance involves a tendency to come up with a counterexample from some language when a theoretician makes a general claim about cultures or languages. But this is certainly not what the present author is aiming for. Visual physiology no doubt also plays a role in the perception and categorization of colour, setting constraints on the cultural construction of colour categories. However, our current understanding of the human cognitive system cannot help us in any way in explaining the tremendous variation between languages in terms of the semantic domains potentially covered by "colour terms", as different dimensions are involved, for example material (skin colour of human beings and animals) or physical state (succulent or dessicated, ripe or unripe, dirty or clean). How speakers acquire knowledge about "green people" (Sudanese Arabic) or "pink cows" (Mursi) is largely unknown. The question of how cognition constrains culture will thus remain unanswered until further progress has been made in the field of neurophysiology, in particular concerning the regions in the brain that are responsible for identifying similar patterns.

The question of where colour terms come from, whether "basic" or not, has been addressed by various authors. Within an African context, Payne (2020) investigates the areal distribution of colour terminology in sub-Saharan Africa, both in relation to major language families such as Afroasiatic, Niger-Congo, and Nilo-Saharan, but also to smaller language families. Grimm (2012) is a case study on the borrowing of colour terms in Gyeli, a language spoken by tropical forest foragers ("pygmees") in Cameroon, from a neighbouring agricultural community speaking Bulu, whose speakers have borrowed terms from French. Segerer and Vanhove (2019) present an interesting investigation of lexical sources for colour terms and their corresponding morphosyntactic behaviour from 350 African languages. According to them, the terms go back mostly to terms for vegetables (258), followed by lexemes referring to the mineral kingdom (72), animals (54), food- and body-related on a par (26 and 27), and atmospheric elements (16). Colexification of colour terms with either 'ripe' or 'unripe, raw, uncooked' are particularly common. Of course, the authors are fully aware of the methodological problems involved in this type of data gathering, which to a large extent depends on dictionaries and wordlists, and consequently determining which meaning is more basic with polysemous words is problematic. In terms of borrowing, the French word *bleu* and English *blue* are commonly found in African languages (Segerer and Vanhove 2019: 333). This is not unexpected, as these languages are official languages in a range of former colonies on the continent.[16]

3.2 Body-part nomenclature

Among the topics treated in the four volumes emerging primarily from a typological project directed by Charles A. Ferguson and Joseph H. Greenberg at Stanford University on Language Universals between 1967 and 1976, and published as Greenberg, Ferguson, and Moravcsik (1978b), there is a contribution on body-part terminology by Andersen (1978), which appeared in the same volume as the

---

16 It would also be interesting to know to what extent speakers transfer lexical-semantic meanings from their first language into "new Englishes" (or other former colonial languages). Völkel (2016) shows that in Tongan English (spoken in the Pacific), for example, kinship terms are used with another scope of meaning than in standardized English. A proper anthropological understanding of the Tongan kinship system helps to understand the modified meaning and usage in Tongan English.

article by Greenberg (1978) on numeral systems discussed above. The study by Elaine Andersen is introduced here because it constitutes another illustration of the impact of this type of scientific research in anthropological linguistics, which is also relevant for a proper understanding of spatial orientation below.[17]

The inductive methods and implicational hierarchies emerging from the type of research discussed above with respect to bionomenclature, colour, and numeral systems, are based on methods ultimately going back to the research on kinship initiated in the 1940s. After having familiarized himself with this method as a PhD candidate in anthropology working on the pre-Islamic religion of the Hausa (in Nigeria and neighbouring countries), Joseph H. Greenberg introduced these methods into typological linguistics – and anthropological linguistics as well. The Dobbs Ferry Conference on Language Universals in New York in 1961 played an essential part in inaugurating this period of strong interest in generalizations about languages in general, as pointed out by the editors Greenberg, Ferguson, and Moravcsik (1978b: v) in their preface to Volume 1 of *Universals of Human Language*, the first of four volumes emerging from large scale typological comparisons of languages concerning phonetics and phonology, word structure, and syntax.

Andersen (1978) shows that languages tend to have more terms for the upper parts of the body than for the lower parts, and more for the front than the back. What is more, languages usually do not distinguish more than five levels, as shown for English in Figure 5. When going down this hierarchy, one tends to find more morphologically complex forms, as with *fingernail* in English. In line with this type of research, Elaine Andersen also arrives at specific implicational scales (if one finds "b", there should also be "a", though the reverse is not necessarily true). For example, if a language has a separate word for 'toe', it also has a word for 'finger' (as in English), but not vice versa.

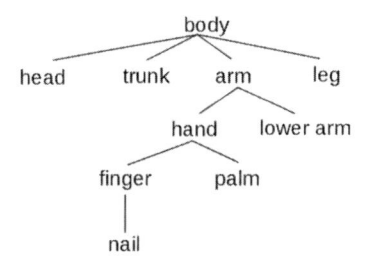

```
                    body
         ┌──────┬────┴───┬──────┐
       head   trunk    arm     leg
                      ┌──┴──────┐
                    hand    lower arm
                   ┌──┴──┐
                finger  palm
                  │
                 nail
```

Figure 5: Body-part nomenclature (Andersen 1978).

---

17 The investigation of body part nomenclature as such has a long history with respect to the study of African languages; Homburger (1929) is one of the earliest sources.

Languages may use the same term for both finger and toe, as in Romanian, where the digit of the hand is referred to as *deget*, and the word for 'toe' is referred to as *deget de la picior*, i.e., as the 'digit of the leg/foot'. Also, unlike English, some languages do not distinguish between 'foot' and 'leg'; in Swahili, 'finger' is referred to as *kidole* or *kidole cha mkono* 'the digit of the arm', and 'toe' is called *kidole cha mguu* 'digit of the leg'.

When testing these claims for a language such as Tima in Sudan, a language which was not part of the database used by Andersen (1978), the following terms for body parts can be identified (as further illustrated in Table 8).

Table 8: Tima body-part nomenclature.

Tima term	English translation	Tima term	English translation
káàh	'head'	kùdú kàɽɕ́m	'elbow'
kìdɛ́k	'neck' (also 'self')	kìrɛ̀mʊ̀ŋ	'wrist', 'ankle'
kə̀rábʊ̀	'shoulder'	kɨ̀mʌ́n kɨ̀dɨ̀ɨ̀	'toe'
pɨ̀rʌmpɨ̀rʌ̀ŋ	'chest'	kɨ̀mʌ́n kɨ̀dɨ̀ɨ̀ kʊ̀kwɔ̀lɔ́ŋ	'big toe (lit. small leg/foot big)'
yáh íyíí	'ribs (lit. heads of eyes)'	kùrúŋò	'knee'
k(w)àlók	'upper arm'	kìdíí	'leg+foot'
kɨ̀dʌwún	'arm+hand' (also twenty-four hours, full day)	kɨhɨɨr	'calf (back part of the lower leg)'
kɨ̀mʌ̀nʌ́ kɨ̀dʌwún	'finger'	kùdú kɔ̀dɔ̄r	'heel'
kɨ̀mʌ́n kɨ̀dʌwún kʊ̀kwɔ̀lɔ́ŋ	'thumb (lit. small hand/arm big'		'thumb'

The following examples from Tima (based on Schneider-Blum 2012) illustrate another widespread phenomenon in languages, namely semantic widening through conceptual blending processes. The following examples illustrate these three types of polysemy.

(8) kɔ́nɔ̀   1. ear; 2. cooking spoon, ladle' (metaphorical extension)
    kááyìm 1. mussel; 2. spoon (metonymy)
    kwáá   1. *Tamarindus indica*; 2. cross-battens of roof frame; 3. rod (synecdoche)

Whereas cross-linguistically such semantic extensions are often culture-specific, deriving from the daily experiences of the variable physical and social world people live in, body-part terminology manifests some significant universalistic tendencies. Visual properties or characteristics related to form or shape

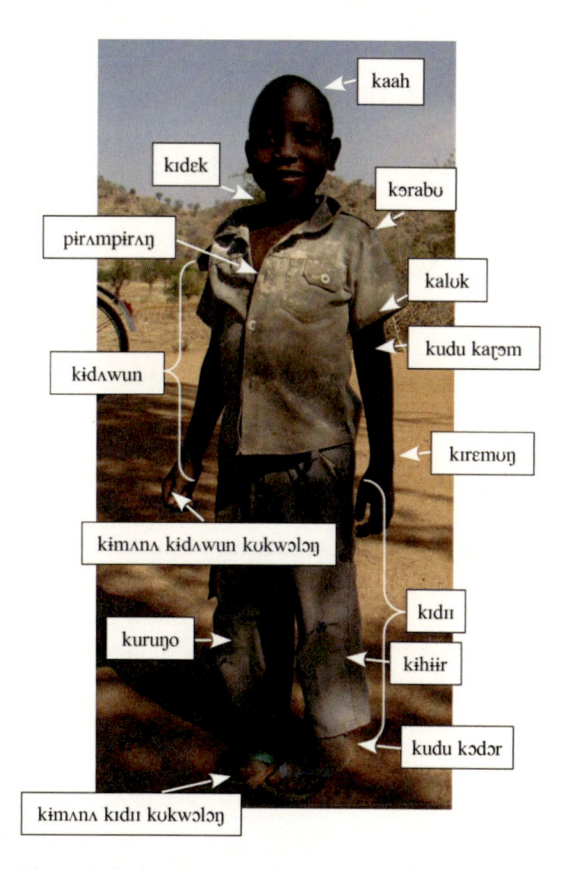

Picture 7: Body-part nomenclature in Tima (Schneider-Blum 2013a).

and spatial proximity usually play an important role, for example 'eye' > 'face' through metonymic extension (Andersen 1978: 358). Other preferred metaphors appear to have a more regional distribution, as for 'stone, kernel, pit, seed' and 'eye' in eastern Africa, as in Baale (Ethiopia) *kɛɛré* 'eyes, seeds' (author's data). Here, cognitive significance in terms of shape presumably is crucial.

There is also a widespread tendency towards an anthropomorphic projection onto specific parts of the body, for example with the digits. 'Thumb' is referred to as 'chief of hand' in Igbo, or 'chief of finger' in Amharic, whereas Mende refers to 'thumb' as 'male of hand' (Brown and Witkowski 1981: 602).[18] Similar metaphorical extensions are found in languages of the Americas or in Asia. The Amerindian

---

[18] The translation as 'hand' rather than 'arm' or 'arm+hand' in these African languages is based on the original sources.

language Dakota has 'mother of hand' and Quechua 'mother finger' for 'thumb'. Mandarin Chinese has 'mother finger' and Japanese 'parent finger' for 'thumb' (Brown and Witkowski 1981). The generic space involved here with respect to the two input spaces is created by adults and their children and digits consisting of two thumbs and the fingers as smaller digits. The cognitively more prominent entities, referring to animates (human beings), serve as the basis for this instance of conceptual blending of kinship terminology and body-part terminology.

Additional examples of metaphorical extensions for body-part terminology are found in Heine (1997: 131–154). Kraska-Szlenk (2014) also discusses common semantic extensions for body-part terms in various African and Amerindian languages, along with language-specific semantic extensions and corresponding cultural models. Examples of this cross-linguistic convergence in conceptualization and metaphorical or metonymic lexical transfer (or "embodied emerging universals"), according to the author, are: heart, liver, stomach as the locus of emotions, and hand as instrument of possession with extensions into notions like power and control.

The reader is also referred to a special issue of *Language Sciences* edited by Enfield, Majid, and van Staden (2006), where different authors show that the human body constitutes a common source domain in the conceptualization of objects and abstract notions in various target domains.

This anthropomorphic centring plus projection onto physical objects, which is widespread on the African continent, is also attested in Marakwet (Kenya), as shown in Moore (1986). Marakwet as a name covers three closely related varieties belonging to the Kalenjin cluster, and consisting of Cherang'any (or Western Marakwet) Endo (or Northeastern Marakwet), and Talai (or Southeastern Marakwet). Its speakers traditionally build their villages on the slopes of the Cherangany escarpment, Kenya. Their daily movement from their residential areas to the fields on the valley floor is a constant process of moving down and up. Marakwet speakers use the antonyms 'uphill' (*doka*) and 'downhill' (*nwun*) in describing these relative positions. Agricultural land on the valley floor furthest away from the village in the hills is referred to in Marakwet as *bar kel* 'land of foot', the land nearest to the villages as *bar mat* 'land of head', and the fields in between as *bar quem* 'land of middle/waist' (Moore 1986: 56).

Apart from conceptual blending between body-part terminology and spatial orientation, blending between body-part terminology and physical objects within the homestead appears to be common. In Päri, South Sudan, houses may also be seen as bodies, hence expressions such as *ko otto* 'wall (lit. chest of house)', or *waŋ otto* 'window (lit. eye of house)' occur as examples of interfield metaphors, i.e., between two semantic fields. Intrafield metaphorical and metonymic extensions (i.e., within the same field, in this case that of body-part nomenclature) also occur, as in *waŋ um* 'nostril (lit. eye-nose)', as shown in Simeoni (1978: 23).

Bonvillain (1993: 82) aptly states that the widespread use of corporeal metaphors probably results from the central importance human beings attribute to their own bodies. "We extend the imagery of body to inanimate objects and to descriptions of activities. It is a process of observing and experiencing the world through human eyes and by analogy with human form". At the same time, it is important to keep in mind that languages do not necessarily use the anthropocentric frame of reference, as further discussed in Chapter 4. Turning this claim into a "universal" could consequently be "a major ethnocentric error", as Levinson (2003a: 24) formulates it.

3.3 Olfactory cognition

The chemical and neuropsychological dimensions of olfactory cognition are fairly well understood today, as shown by Zucco et al. (2012) in their edited volume *Olfactory Cognition – From Perception and Memory to Environmental Odours and Neuroscience*.[19] At the same time, however, the actual variant inventory of odour terms across languages has gone largely unnoticed in the scientific literature. As with other lexical domains discussed above, the general assumption appears to have been that a "biological" account suffices to understand this cognitive domain. Nevertheless, the importance of the cultural dimension involved in this semantic field can no longer be ignored.

Smells appear to have become the subject of taboo in urbanized western societies over the past few centuries, and languages spoken by these communities tend to be lexically poor in this respect. Not necessarily so in other parts of the world. Majid and Burenhult (2014) point out that cross-cultural research suggests that there may be cultures where odour terms play a larger role. The Jahai of the Malay Peninsula are one such group. The authors tested whether Jahai speakers could name smells as easily as colours in comparison to a matched English group. They found that Jahai speakers have at least twelve words to describe smells and find it as easy to name odours as colours, whereas English speakers struggle with odour naming. In Maniq, spoken in southern Thailand, there are fifteen different words for smells (Wnuk and Majid 2014). Traditionally, the Jahai and Maniq are hunter-gatherer communities. But of course such systems are not restricted to communities with this type of subsistence economy.

In Kuteb, a language spoken south of Tarok in Nigeria and Cameroon, there is also a rich set of terms, as Table 9, adapted from Koops (2009), illustrates.

---

[19] More recently, scientists have also discovered that there are receptors for smells on the tongue.

Table 9: Kuteb odour terminology (Koops 2009).

Kuteb term	English circumscription
ashwáe	'smell of fermented cassava, guinea corn sprouts'
aság	'smell of fresh fish, raw dog meat'
ará/arwá	'smell of rotten eggs'
kushi	'smell of soap or a dirty cloth'
kusinn	'smell of a cobra or musk shrew'
a.ham/ku.ham	'smell of sour beer'
kuya/kupí	'smell of smoked meat, perfume'
rika	'smell of frying palm kernels'
aruwub	'smell of rotting mushrooms'
icwu/kucwu	'smell of day-old porridge or of a dead body'
rikpankwer	'smell that causes discomfort'
kubyinkun	'smell of concentrated palm wine'
nyinyi	'a sharp, acidic smell'
rika	'smell of frying palm kernels'

Storch and Vossen (2007) illustrate the rich vocabulary for smells and tastes in Jur-Lwoo, a language spoken in South Sudan by people with an agricultural economy (who are also specialists in iron working; Storch 2014: 11). Storch and Vossen (2007: 227) point out that there are probably hundreds of words denoting smells and tastes, and that these exhibit semantic precision and lexical specialization that is otherwise observed among ideophones in Jur-Lwoo. The authors give the following examples:

(9) cạ̀ù   'fish before being cooked'
    kúr   'smell of flowery perfume'
    tiụ̀   'smell of pus'
    cér   'smell of urine'
    lệm   'flowers, pollen collected by bees'
    wàj   'fermented flour'
    bàd   'smell under armpits'
    pèèd 'rotten meat'
    kééj 'smoke which brings tears to one's eyes'
    ŋìr   'unripe beans'
    kọ̀t   'light air of flowers'
    tị́g   'non-castrated he-goat'

Demolin et al. (2016) give an detailed description of odour terms in !Xóõ, a language spoken by small dispersed groups of semi-nomadic people in southwestern Botswana. Five female and five male speakers took part in an experiment, in which they had to identify and describe the odours produced by fluids or materials in 37 flasks; these involved some natural smells (e.g., smoked fish) but mainly smells that were synthetic, although these do occur in nature (such as ammonia or isoborneol). Picture 8 shows screenshots from a video recording of !Xóõ speakers taking part in the odour test (courtesy of Didier Demolin). These speakers were also asked to group the flasks according to the similarity of odours, and divide them into pleasant and unpleasant smells. As shown in Table 10, terms for the latter dominate, a tendency attested in various other languages, as shown by Boisson (1997), who compares data from 60 languages in nine language families. Boisson (1997) also found that negative stimuli are less subject to variation between speakers. Moreover, his tests showed that the temporal factor (old versus fresh or recent odours) is relevant, as well as the intensity of the smell, variables which are also reflected in the !Xóõ vocabulary.

Picture 8: Screenshots from a video showing !Xóõ speakers taking part in the odour test.

Table 10: !Xóõ odour terms (Demolin et al. 2016).

|nuʔã	'odour of sex organs (unpleasant)'	gǀkxʔáa	'stench of faeces or very rotten meat (unpleasant)'
!gáʔba	'odour of sex organs (unpleasant)'	dtxóʔlu	'stench of rotten meat'
!Gūā	'odour of semen, sex organs'	gǂkxʔõa	'rotten meat (unpleasant)'
gūhʔu	'unwashed vagina smell, rotten'	dtxʔái	'rotten meat (unpleasant)'
ǂgálita, ǂxái	'insect whose odour is similar to that of sex organs'	ǂqúi	'rotten'
ǁgúʔa	'odour of urine (unpleasant)'	ǁqólu	'odour of burnt gelatine (animal hoofs or human nails) (unpleasant)'
góhʔlo	'old urine, stench of rotten meat (unpleasant)'	dtsʔkxāla	'burnt veld odour'

Table 10 (continued)

ǂgúʔi	'pleasant odour, e.g., acacia inflorescence'	|áhʔni	'odour of unpleasant meat or blood (snake, flesh eaters or human)'
!Góhʔmi	'pleasant odour, e.g., acacia inflorescence or soap'	!àhʔla	'odour of unpleasant meat or blood (snake, flesh eaters or human)'
dzáʔa	'pleasant odour, e.g., orange'	tsáʔa	'badger secretion odour'
Qàhla	'Carallum Knobelii or Caralluma Lugardae odour, Asclepiadeacae Duvalia polita (unpleasant)'	‖qʔána	'dirt'
‖góʔba	'pounded tsamma melon odour (Cucurbitacae Citrullus lanatus)'	‖ája	'water with rusty odour (unpleasant)'
‖ála	'spicy odour of acacia eriobola'	tshāmi	'pure rainwater odour/taste'
‖gáa	'spicy odour of acacia eriobola'	‖luhʔi	'rain or wet grass odour'
G!qhùm	'inflorescence'	!Gūā	'semen'
|gàhʔa	'stench of faeces or very rotten meat (unpleasant)'	dzohʔa-te	'formic acid'

\| = dental click; ! = alveolar click; ǂ = palatal click; ‖ = lateral click

Odours hence are expressible in languages, as long as one speaks the right language (Majid and Burenholt 2014). What these and other examples from different lexical domains should also make clear is that languages do not vary without constraint, but our current knowledge of the human cognitive system does not allow us to make interesting predictions on these variant categorizations of taste or smells (or, to a lesser extent, colour). There is, again, no reason to interpret cross-cultural differences in lexical differentiations for smells, taste, or other lexical-semantic fields in evolutionary terms (Dimmendaal 1991). There may be regressions, as with terms for smells in many industrialized speech communities. But richer vocabularies may re-emerge, as with professionals producing new perfumes. Those involved in fashion and the development of new styles or colours for flowers also have a much richer vocabulary for describing colour than most other members of Euro-American societies do.

Storch (2014: 214) presents additional lexemes related to smells: *yòŋ* 'unbearable smell of rotten things', *kɔ̀th* 'sesame smell', *bʌ́dh* 'neutral, breath/saliva'. Furthermore, there are at least thirteen verbs related to the taste of food in Luwo, as shown by Storch (2014: 173).

Levitan et al. (2014) report on a research project in which 122 speakers of American English, Dutch, Chinese (the authors do not specify which varieties of Chinese were involved), German, and Malay were asked to associate 14 odorants (embedded in odour pens) with 36 colours. The aim of their research was to investigate crossmodal correspondences between colours (or colour terms) and odours (or odour terms, such as 'fruity', 'musty', 'fish', 'meat', 'woody' etc.). Not surprisingly, the fruity odour tended to be associated with pink or red colours by speakers, regardless of the primary language they spoke. However, as claimed by the authors, alongside such congruency there was also incongruency, in that there were statistically significant differences between these speech communities (or cultures, as Levitan et al. 2014 call them) with respect to the colour labels used for odour perception. Unfortunately, no lists of words in these languages are presented either for colours or for odours. Moreover, the authors do not spell out at least some of the conclusions to be drawn from their statistical figures, so that it is left to the reader to come to his or her own conclusions.

There are, of course, several additional lexical-semantic fields manifesting cross-linguistic and cross-cultural differences, for example concerning taste. With respect to the latter, it has been claimed that we distinguish between five basic tastes, 'sweet', 'sour', 'bitter', 'salty', and 'umami' (a savoury taste). But again, it is obvious that there is a lot more variation cross-linguistically than is claimed by universalists. Take Tima, a Niger-Congo language spoken in Sudan, which does not have a lexeme describing "umami", but does have terms describing other sensations (Dimmendaal 2015a: 138–139):

(10) -hín 'sweet'
      -dɛ́   'sour'
      -kɨk 'bitter'

In addition, there are reduplicated adjectival stems which synchronically at least appear to be basic, i.e., not derived from some other lexeme in Tima.

(11) -kààkààk   'bitter-sweet (e.g., tea with little sugar)'
      -həlɛ̀həlɛ̀m   'very sweet' (e.g., of sugar cane)'
      -hùlùhùlùm   'sweet-salty (e.g., of sourdough), sweet-sour (e.g., of a mango)'
      -dɛ̀kʊ̀dɛ̀kʊ̀k   'sourish'
      -lɛ̀lɛ̀lɛ̀   'calcium tasting'
      -hòòhòòk   'salty'

It should be kept in mind, as Hale (1986: 233) observes, that "establishing a connection between a philosophical postulate and a principle of grammar requires that the two be established independently". In other words, the impression that certain environmental phenomena are important in the daily lives of a specific community and that this should therefore be reflected in their language may turn out to be wrong, as the story of the "great Eskimo vocabulary hoax" by Pullum (1989) shows. Pullum bases his work upon earlier attempts by the anthropologist Laura Martin to debunk the myth about the "hundreds of words for different grades and types of snow, a lexicographical winter wonderland, the quintessential demonstration of how primitive minds categorize the world so differently from us", as Pullum (1989: 275) put it in his rhetorical masterpiece. Instead, there are four basic terms in the Inuit language, already identified by Boas (1911): *aput* 'snow on the ground', *qana* 'falling snow', *piqsirpoq*, 'drifting snow', and *qimuqsuq* 'a snow drift'. Pullum's point about the presumed highly ramified snow vocabulary of Inuit people is therefore well-taken.

A number of methodological lessons can be learned from investigations of lexical-semantic fields in a cross-linguistic perspective. First, there is the semantic dimension, involving the manipulation of meanings by speakers, and related to this, a potential translation problem for terms in a foreign language. Second, there is considerable differentiation between individual languages in some of these domains, for example for smells, but it is nevertheless possible at this point in time to establish inductively-based implicational relations within systems by starting out from prototypical systems, at least in several of these fields. Third, areal features (reflecting patterns of multilingualism between speakers) are relevant. Fourth, in at least a number of cases it can be shown that cultural selection has played a role. Fifth, there is also ritualized (conventionalized) behaviour, which, together with the lexical elaboration that goes along with it, may linger on without necessarily (still) being "functional". Specific numeral systems may be retained without necessarily maintaining their original function. From a phenomenological point of view, such behaviour may be compared to other types of ritualized behaviour, such as the habit of decorating a fir tree at Christmas, not only among Christians, but also among agnostics and atheists. The cultural origin of this custom is probably unknown to many 21st century citizens, as this process for them has simply become part of their habitualized behaviour. A purely functionalistic interpretation consequently fails, because the replacement of such systems need not be motivated by a loss of their original function, but because of the patterns of dominant regional or national languages may be replicated in all of these domains. Such globalization effects may also be observed with respect to colour, for example, when languages borrow terms like *blue* from influential lingua francas like English. Senft (2012) reports such a case from the

Trobriands. In countries in southern Africa where English plays a central role in the educational system, similar tendencies can be observed (Davies and Corbett 1997 mention *pinki* in Xhosa (South Africa) and *chabuluu* in Chichewa (Malawi)).

The investigation of different lexical domains discussed above shows that globalization is the new impetus causing the spreading of alternative systems associated with important regional and national or official (ex-colonial) languages, not necessarily because they are more "apt" or "functional", but simply because they have become dominant in the daily lives of people, for example as a result of new contacts and corresponding new social networks.

Alongside the inductive method with its corresponding implicational hierarchies, propagated primarily by Joseph H. Greenberg, the theoretical concept of prototypicality has been central in the discussion above. The intellectual inspiration for this latter approach comes from the pioneering work of the psychologist Eleanore Rosch (Heider), for example Rosch (1972a, 1972b, 1978).

Geeraerts (1988a) raises the question of where prototypicality as a cognitive notion comes from, and arrives at four types of explanations. First, there is the physiological hypothesis. Indeed, when studying colour it is clear that this dimension is relevant for our understanding of perception. The cells responsible for fundamental neural responses for hue and brightness can be related to lexical items in different languages – even if this is not the entire story.

A second hypothesis explaining the cognitive importance of prototypicality, namely reference, can also be shown to play a role cross-linguistically. The investigation of lexical-semantic fields such as bionomenclature shows that it is sometimes useful to distinguish between core and peripheral members, based on the number of attributes (features) they share.

A third explanation for the presence of prototypicality as a cognitive notion derives from a statistical observation (Geeraerts 1988a: 208), namely that the most frequently experienced member of a category is the prototype. At least, this is the simple form of the frequency model. It can also be combined with the family resemblance model; the weight of an attribute within a concept is then not only determined by its role within the family of applications constituting the category, but also by the relative frequency with which it is experienced. The present author prefers to treat this exponent of prototypicality as epiphenomenal, as it follows from the perceptual or referential significance.

This leaves us with the fourth explanation, Dirk Geeraerts' (functionalist) psychological hypothesis. As already argued by Rosch (1977), it is advantageous from a cognitive point of view to maximize the conceptual richness of each category through the incorporation of closely related nuances into a single concept, because this makes the conceptual system more economical. Because of the maximal conceptual density of each category, the most information can be provided with the least cognitive effort. The incorporation of beavers into the category "fish" during the late Middle Ages may be taken as an example here. "Prototypical categories maintain themselves by adapting themselves to changing circumstances and new expressive needs; at the same time, they function as expectational patterns with regard to reality: new facts are interpreted in terms of information that is already at the disposal of the individual" (Geeraerts 1988a: 223).

The rather traditional differentiation of lexical-semantic fields in the present as well as in the preceding chapter should show that in all these fields we find universal patterns based on shared human facts as well as aspects of diversity reflecting different social concepts. We owe these insights to contributions in the field of cognitive anthropology, as well as in cognitive linguistics. In addition, and as further shown in the next chapters, insights from cognitive-psychological as well as social-psychological studies continue to play a role in the development of anthropological linguistics as a discipline.

4 Spatial orientation

During a hiking tour in a remote area of southwestern Ethiopia in the 1990s with the aim of reaching speakers of Baale, Chai, and Tirma in the border area with (what is now) South Sudan, the present author and four students accompanying him arrived in Tum from Addis Ababa with Ethiopian Airlines, and asked the local teacher for directions in Amharic. The aim was to travel on foot towards the town of Maji and then towards the Suri (Surma), the area of the ethnic group whose three languages the team was interested in.

One point of confusion in the teacher's briefing on the hiking tour to the Suri area concerned the meaning of moving 'straight ahead' (*fit-lə-fit*) in Amharic. In this mountainous area in Ethiopia, this term apparently means 'staying on more or less the same height while walking along mountain edges', rather than moving 'straight ahead by going uphill and downhill' (as depicted in Figure 6).[20]

Figure 6: Moving straight ahead in southwestern Ethiopia.

But there was another interesting experience, related to Map 1 of southwestern Ethiopia below, which shows the approximate area where Suri people were assumed to live. The person explaining about route directions in the area was a primary school teacher in the region, who was well aware of cardinal directions and their role in topography or geography.

---

20 Aberra (2016: 88), in his study of the Amharic word for 'face', *fit*, translates *fit-lə-fit* as 'at/to the forefront (lit. face to face)'

https://doi.org/10.1515/9783110726633-004

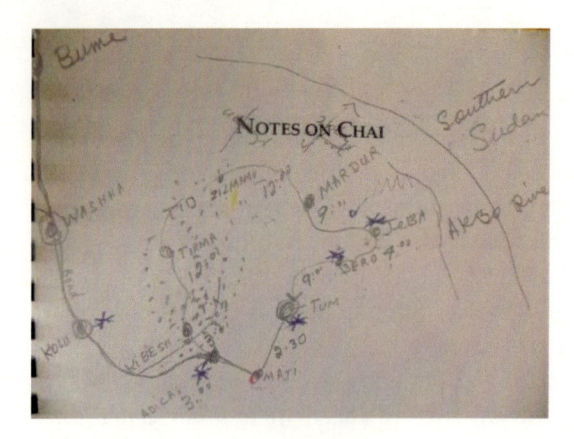

Picture 9: Front page of Lucassen (1994).

Nevertheless, these seemed to play no role in the mental representation and corresponding visualization of his route directions, as a comparison of Picture 9 with Map 1 shows. The drawing kindly produced by the local teacher was used by one of the students from the fieldtrip, Deborah Lucassen (1994), as the front cover of her MA thesis *Notes on Chai*, as shown in Picture 9.

Route knowledge hence sometimes constitutes a special kind of spatial knowledge. As the research over the past decades, reported on below, shows, spatial orientation as such is also subject to intercultural variation, which is reflected in linguistic structures as well. The classical assumption was that space orientation is egocentric and forward-looking. Moreover, for us as human beings, abstract space is argued to be constituted by three planes defined in relation to the human body: one vertical *up/down*, one horizontal *front/back*, and one horizontal *left/right* plane. As a secondary usage, we can transfer the centre of these co-ordinates onto any object, and assign an object a front, back, left, and right side, so that we can use that object, rather than ego, as a relatum. But cross-linguistic research by cognitive linguists and anthropologists over the past decades has shown that there are interesting alternative solutions to the conception of physical space. We may also view social space metaphorically along such spatial lines. Of course, this latter idea is not new; it goes back to Bourdieu's notion of spatially allocated forms of social structure (for example Bourdieu 1991: 13–29). Section 4.2 gives some further examples of this phenomenon, followed by examples of the co-evolution of culture and language, and more specifically the expression of space (Section 4.3).

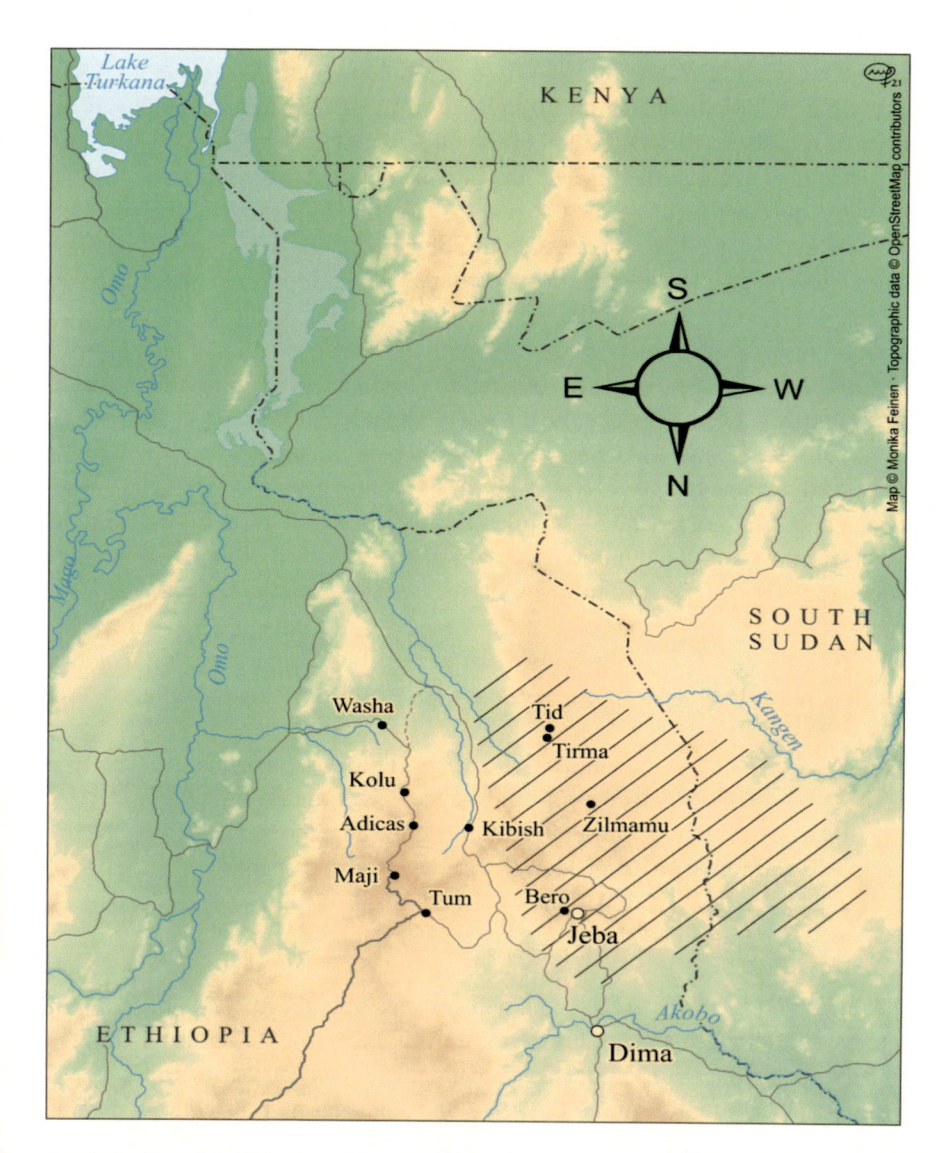

Map 1: Southwestern Ethiopia and the approximate home area of the Suri people (kindly produced by Monika Feinen).

4.1 Physical space

Traditionally, the conceptualization of space was assumed by western scientists to be a cognitive domain where little variation is found cross-linguistically. The influential "cognitive hypothesis" of the psychologist Jean Piaget (1896–1980) states that children take their prelingual egocentric understanding of topology or space as a basis for the acquisition of spatial semantic categories in the primary language they acquire, thereby learning, for example, that concepts like "front" or "back" may also be projected onto objects, and that these concepts depend on the position of Ego. The ontogenetic development of this latter type of relative space concept, i.e., learning that concepts such as "in front of" or "at the back of" are not absolute but defined in relation to Ego, follows the development of a cognitive egocentric perspective or orientation. The acquisition of tacit knowledge of this second type of spatial orientation, also known as "projective space", is apparently not completed before the age of six with children.

It has been known for some time now from cross-linguistic typological comparisons that some languages are much richer in their inventory of spatial terms than others. Amha (2001: 140–141) describes such a rich system for Maale, a language spoken in a mountainous region of southwestern Ethiopia. The basic demonstratives *ha-* (close to the speaker) and *ye-* (far from the speaker) are also used to express locative adverbs, *ha-ka* 'here (close to the speaker)' and *ye-ka* 'there (far from the speaker)', whereby *-ka* is a locative case marker. But in addition, Maale has the following distal locative adverbs expressing elevations:

(12) lé-ka 'up there (higher in altitude than where the speaker is found; from *lóó* 'up' plus the locative case marker)'
lí-ka 'down there' (lower in altitude than where the speaker is found; from *lúú* 'down' plus the locative case marker)'
sé-ka 'on level ground to the side of the speaker (from *sóó* 'there on level ground / distant but visible place)'

The adverb *ha-ka* may also be combined with *lóó* and *lúú* in Maale in order to express an altitude higher or lower respectively than where the hearer (rather than the speaker) is. In addition, Maale distinguishes between case forms involving direction and source (Amha 2001: 55–70). Languages may also have separate case forms in order to express such meanings as 'behind', 'inside', 'in front of', 'adjacent to', 'between', 'under', 'on top of', and various other semantic nuances by means of distinct case forms or adpositions.

Deictic systems where, similar to Maale, altitude in addition to proximity is important are described by Anderson and Keenan (1985: 292) for Dyirbal, an Australian language formerly spoken in northeastern Australia, where hills as well as rivers play a role in spatial orientation.

(13) baydi   'short distance downhill'
      bayda   'medium distance downhill'
      baydu   'long distance downhill'
      dayi   'short distance uphill'
      daya   'medium distance uphill'
      dayu   'long distance uphill'

(14) balbala 'medium distance downriver'
      balbulu 'long distance downriver'
      guya   'across the river'
      dawala   'medium distance upriver'
      dawulu   'long distance upriver'
      guya   'across the river'
      bawal   'long way (in any direction)'

Within the system of projective space, it is common cross-linguistically to use locative case markers, adpositions (prepositions and postpositions), or spatial nominals derived (synchronically or diachronically) from body-part terms (as discussed in 3.2 above), in order to express the relative positions of objects. Topological information may also be encoded in verbs. As shown by Ameka and Levinson (2007), there are two types of locative predicates involving verbs: (a small set of) posture verbs on the one hand, and (a large set of) positional verbs on the other.

Tima, a language whose location marking is discussed by Dimmendaal and Schneider-Blum (to appear) using the framework provided by Ameka and Levinson (2007), uses the positional verb hɨ́ndáná 'sit' in order to identify the ground regardless of axial properties, with a prepositional phrase (introduced by a preposition with a range of functions, in particular instrumental) describing the intrinsic frame of reference of the figure.

(15) kù-bɔ̀bɔ́k   ɲ́cɛ́=hɨ́ndáná   ŋ̀=k-ááh   áyín   líhì
      SG-bat   3IPFV=sit   INS=SG-head   towards   LOC:place
      'a bat hangs (lit. sits) upside down'

The West African lingua franca Hausa shows another rather common dimension of location marking listed above (alongside case marking and the use of adpositions), one in which body-part nomenclature as an axis of orientation tends to be used, namely in specifying the search domains for objects. Thus, the spatial nominals 'inside' and 'behind', derived from the nouns for 'belly' and 'back' respectively, are linked to the following modifying noun by means of the masculine genitival linker -*n*.

(16) cikĩ 'belly' ciki(-n) 'in(side)' ciki-n gidā 'inside the house'
      bāyā 'back' baya(-n) 'behind' baya-n gidā 'behind the house'

However, research initiated in the 1990s on a range of languages and cultures across the world by the Cognitive Anthropology Research Group at the Max Planck Institute for Psycholinguistics in Nijmegen, the Netherlands, provided us with another rather intriguing dimension of cross-linguistic variation in the spatial domain. As shown by Levinson (2003a), in his synopsis of the most important results from this research endeavour, languages use different frames of reference. Furthermore, non-linguistic cognition mirrors these alternative systems available in the language spoken by a community. According to Levinson (2003a: 55), three kinds of frames of reference can be identified cross-linguistically and cross-culturally in order to represent the location of objects; these are summarized in Table 11.

Table 11: Aligning classifications of frames of reference (Levinson 2003a).

INTRINSIC	ABSOLUTE	RELATIVE
Origin ≠ Ego	Origin ≠ Ego	Origin = Ego
Object-centred	Environment-centred	Viewer-centred
Intrinsic perspective		Deictic perspective
	Allocentric	Egocentric
Orientation-free	Orientation-bound	

The "egocentric" perspective is the default, and presumably innate or part of nature; only allocentric systems have to be learned, at least as suggested by the scientific contributions subsequent to Jean Piaget's contributions. If we start out from our own egocentric deictic perspective, we can divide the space around us into up and down, front and back, and left and right. However, nurture then sets in, and depending on where we grow up on this planet, we have to learn where and when so-called "allocentric" perspectives play a role. A number of languages have been reported to use an absolute frame of reference with an orientation involving an environment-centred perspective, such as cardinal directions *north, east, south* and *west* (e.g., in Guugu Yimithirr, an Australian language spoken in the North of Queensland) or *uphill* vs. *downhill* (e.g., in Tzeltal, a Mayan language).

With the other two types, intrinsic (object-centred) and relative (viewer-centred) dimensions such as *front* or *back* in English are projected onto objects, which then receive an intrinsic front, back, etc.[21] To which objects this can apply is something speakers have to learn, as the examples below illustrate.

Absolute systems of reference have been reported for Australian (aboriginal) languages. Clearly, such cognitive systems of spatial orientation also have consequences for grammatical features. Australian languages, apart from having a locative case, do not encode locative preposition-like or postposition-like concepts like 'behind' or 'next to', i.e., they have absolute systems. Hence, these languages use a system of absolute orientation which applies over both millimetres and miles; one finds expressions such as 'to the north of (your shoulder)' or 'to the south of (Brisbane)'. One of the earliest detailed descriptions of such a system is found in Haviland (1998) for Guugu Yimithirr (also Guugu Yimidhirr), a language of northern Queensland, whose speakers use absolute frames of reference. In such a system, morphemes describing spatial direction each cover quadrants of a hypothetical horizontal plane. These lexical roots, which correspond roughly to the English words *north*, *south*, *east*, and *west*, are relational terms which are not "egocentric" or "body-centric" but "earth-centric" or "geocentric".

(17) gungga- 'northern edge'
 naga- 'eastern edge'
 jiba- 'southern edge'
 guwa- 'western edge'

Speakers of Guugu-Yimithirr thus carry around a mental map of the area they live in with proper alignments of these quadrants. They usually do not employ body-relative locational descriptors like 'in front of', but rather "earth-centric" notions to describe positions, for example "facing south". As pointed out in Deutscher (2010: 168), there are words for 'left hand' and 'right hand' in Guugu Yimithirr. But these are used only to refer to the inherent properties of each hand, for instance to say "I can lift this with my right hand but not with my left hand". Whenever the position of a hand at any particular moment is to be indicated, an expression such as 'hand of the western side' is used.

Similar systems are attested in Australian languages like Djaru, Warlbiri, and Kayardild, but not, for example, in Jaminjung (Deutscher 2010: 169, 189). Deutscher makes the important point that this is not a decree of nature (environmental determinism) but an expression of cultural choice (Deutscher 2010: 189).

---

[21] Danziger (2010) has argued for a fourth type of frame of reference (alongside the absolute, relative, and intrinsic frames), called the direct frame, in order to accommodate the rotational sensitivity of spatial scenes.

Speakers growing up in such an environment and speech community acquire and develop a "mental compass", "a learned ability to maintain fixed bearings at all times" (Levinson 2003a: 169), as becomes clear from the following experiment.

Like speakers of other languages in Europe, speakers of Dutch generally do not use an absolute system when thinking or talking about space in daily interactions. In order to test and compare the differential recognition and recall of spatial orientation of objects between speakers of Dutch and Guugu Yimithirr, Stephen C. Levinson asked speakers of both languages to take part in an experiment depicted in Figure 7. This experiment, discussed in detail in Levinson (1992), involved a recognition test, with the subjects first facing north looking at two cards displayed in Table 1 of Figure 7. The first card had a square to the viewer's left or west side (marked grey here), and a rectangle to his right or east side (depending on one's cultural perspective). The second card in Table 1 was rotated 180 degrees, and therefore had the rectangle on the left/west side and the grey square on the right/east side.

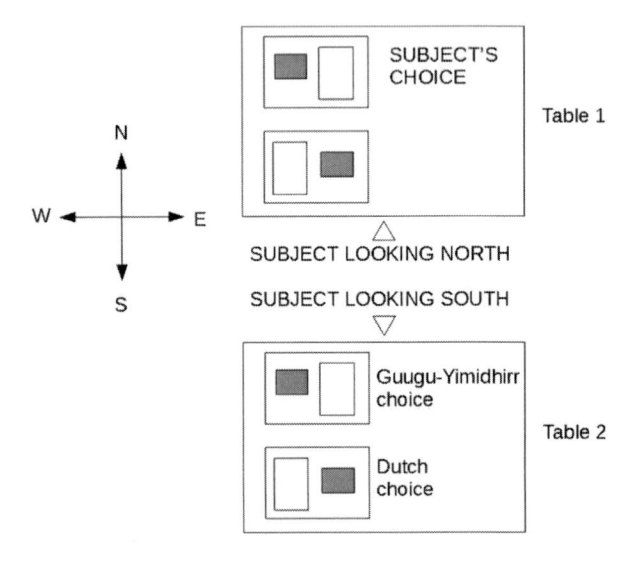

Figure 7: Spatial orientation in Dutch and Guugu Yimithirr (after Foley 1997).

Next, the participants in the test were asked to choose one card and remember it. They were then taken to another room, this time facing south. For speakers of languages with absolute systems, this of course is highly irrelevant. If the card with the square in the west (left) quadrant was chosen, it should still be in the same quadrant. And as a matter of fact, nine out of ten Guugu-Yimithirr speakers taking part in the test chose this option, thereby demonstrating that they were identifying the cards on the basis of absolutely aligned quadrants. All speakers of Dutch in the experiment rotated the map with them, thereby maintaining the left-to-right orientation (Table 2 in Figure 7).[22]

Levinson (2003a: 115–146) reports on further cognitive consequences of spatial thinking as reflected in individual languages, and also gives further examples of how language may influence the way people think, memorize, or reason about direction and spatial relations. One such cognitive experiment was conducted as follows, again involving the fascinating Guugu Yimithirr language of northern Australia. Members of the research team from the Max Planck Institute for Psycholinguistics, directed by Stephen C. Levinson, drove through the bush by different circuitous routes at night in a van together with ten speakers of Guugu Yimithirr, in order to find out how the latter orient themselves in difficult circumstances.

Picture 10: Mound of magnetic termites in northern Australia.

Speakers of languages in northern Australia use termite hills, amongst other cognitive hints, as landmarks, as shown in Picture 10. These mounds are built by so-called magnetic termites or compass termites (*Amitermes meridionalis*), which are endemic to northern Australia. Their wedge-shaped mounds with their thin edges always point south to north.

Speakers in Australia but also in other parts of the world also use additional navigation strategies (apart, obviously, from the position of the sun), as the following example should make clear. The anthropologist Thomas Widlok, who was involved in the same research endeavour at the Max Planck Institute for Psycholinguistics

---

22 In her study of spatial orientation in the Polynesian language Tongan, Völkel (2010: 105–154) argues for the use of a square and a triangle (rather than a rectangle), because the triangle shows differentiation along a second axis (in this case North-South and not only East-West). This dimension is important if a language has only one absolute axis (e.g., uphill/downhill) and no specified traverse (see also the Tzeltal example below).

in Nijmegen, reports on his investigation of topographic navigation strategies of Hai‖om people in Namibia, as representatives of San hunter-gatherers in southern Africa, who traditionally moved between permanent and non-permanent settlements in a local ecology consisting of bush and desert.

The ten individuals participating in the experiment were taken to a location along a bush road, and then walked some distance into the bush, between 15 and 40 kilometres from the base-camp, on a number of occasions. They provided an average of 19 accurate estimations of locations at a distance of between two and 200 kilometres (Levinson 2003a: 234).

Following the classification of Levinson (2003a), the spatial orientation system of Hai‖om is characterized by the dimensions "absolute" and "intrinsic". According to Widlok (1997), their topographical knowledge is built up through experience as well as co-operative training, and more specifically through "topographical gossip", involving prolonged social interaction in the community. Community members are also capable of pointing accurately to places they have never been to before, hence the experience of moving through the bush cannot explain this.

This competence may be explained by a "mental map theory", with individuals carrying a cognitive structure like a map which provides models for all possible routes, the sources being landscape categories and a good indication of the distance covered (i.e., the speed of travelling), rather than the position of the sun. Furthermore, "dead reckoning" of one's current position plays a key role, i.e., the ability to keep refining and updating the internal model of the external environment in the process of solving navigation problems as they arise. For further details on this strategy of keeping track of direction and also of distance, see Widlok (1997), and Levinson (2003a: 124–133).

Speakers of languages living in similar environments do not necessarily rely on the same coordinate system, as can be observed when comparing the conceptual systems of the Hai‖om and the Kgalagadi in the border area between Namibia and Botswana. Whereas the latter tend to take an egocentric perspective on spatial orientation, the former prefer geographic solutions (Widlok 1997, 2008). Such differences possibly are related to the fact that Hai‖om people were nomadic foragers until fairly recently, whereas the Kgalagadi live by a mixture of agriculture and livestock herding.

Bush and desert are part of the natural environment of ǂAkhoe Hai‖om speakers, and bush and rain forest in the case of Guugu Yimithirr speakers; sub-alpine forest as well as open fields constitute the natural habitat of Tenejapa Tzeltal speakers, whose spatial orientation system has also been investigated in detail. Levinson and Brown (1994) analyze spatial orientation as reflected in the grammar of this language spoken in southeastern Mexico. The mountainous area in which they live lies roughly from uphill (highland) south, referred to as *ajk'ol* in Tenejapa Tzeltal, to downhill (lowland) north, called *alan* in their language. In addition, there is a transverse axis orthogonal to these points of orientation, called *jejch*. These terms play a role not only in large scale orientation (kilometres) but also small scale. Example (18) illustrates the use of 'uphill'.

(18) waxal ta y-ajk'ol xila te limite
stand.of.vertical.cylinder PREP its-uphill chair the bottle
'the bottle is standing uphill (i.e., south) of the chair'

The uphill/downhill orientation is fundamental to the spatial systeme of Tenejapa Tzeltal speakers. They also use concepts like *slok'ib k'aal* 'the coming out of the sun' and *smalib k'aal* 'the spilling of the sun', "but this is an independent axis, not thought of as orthogonal to 'uphill/downhill' (nor indeed would it be geometrically related, since the one system is tied to a fixed terrain, and the other to the movement of the sun across the edges of the mountains from solstice to solstice)" (Levinson and Brown 1994: 23).

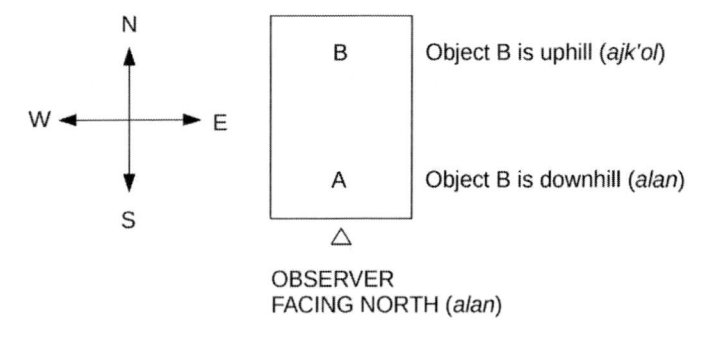

Figure 8: Spatial orientation in Tenejapa Tzeltal (Foley 1997: 224).

The terms may also be used for horizontal surfaces, the alignment being more or less consonant with the uphill/downhill layout of the country, reflecting proximity of two objects relative to the speaker (or observer) regardless of the geographical orientation, as in example (18).

The object which is further away from the speaker or observer is uphill, i.e., *ajk'ol*, and the closer object is downhill, *alan*. Foley (1997: 224) presents an elegant conceptualization of spatial description for objects and its corresponding terminology in Tenejapa Tzeltal, illustrated in Figure 8.

Thus in Tzeltal, and in several Meso-American languages, one also uses absolute angels of orientation, by virtue of reference to a fixed notional 'uphill/

Space

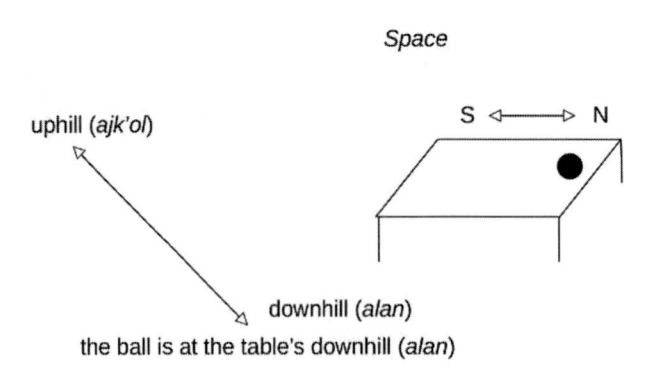

```
uphill (ajk'ol)              S ◄─────► N
        ↖                     ╱──────╱
          ╲                  ╱   ●  ╱
           ╲                ╱──────╱
            ↘   downhill (alan)
    the ball is at the table's downhill (alan)
```

Figure 9: Spatial description for objects in Tenejapa Tzeltal (Foley 1997).

downhill' inclined plane (Haviland 1992). The system corresponds to the overall fall of the terrain along a south/north axis; it is not essentially egocentric in character either. There appear to be no general terms like 'to the left of' or 'to the right of' in languages such as Tzeltal, except when designating the hands.

How does one carry out research in order to establish what kind of spatial orientation a specific community uses? Apart from participant observation and experiments of the type described above, further ideas about typological differences between languages may be derived from the monograph by Levinson (2003a), *Space in Language and Cognition: Explorations in Cognitive Diversity.* The companion volume by Levinson and Wilkins (2006), *Grammars of Space: Explorations in Cognitive Diversity*, also provides useful information about methods for the collection of data on space as expressed in grammar.

There is an additional tool originally developed to explore spatial reference in field settings within the MPI research endeavour, but which can also be used independently for the investigation of spatial orientation, called the *Man and Tree & Space Games* (Levinson et al. 1992). These Field Manual entries, and the accompanying stimulus materials, can be downloaded from the MPG Publication Repository.[23] The so-called "Space Kit" furthermore involves the use of plastic objects by means of which notions of relativity in spatial conception and description can be investigated, as illustrated next. It should be kept in mind that speakers taking part in investigations on spatial orientation in their language are not necessarily accustomed to looking at two-dimensional pictures representing objects situated in a three-dimensional setting, especially if they are not familiar with such objects from their own personal lives.

---

[23] See [https://doi.org/10.17617/2.2458804] (accessed 21 January 2021).

The Africanist Angelika Mietzner applied this method in her research on Cherang'any (Kenya), as illustrated below. She also integrated cognitive concepts going back to Heine (1997: 12–13), who proposes a paradigmatic contrast between two types of allocentric orientation.

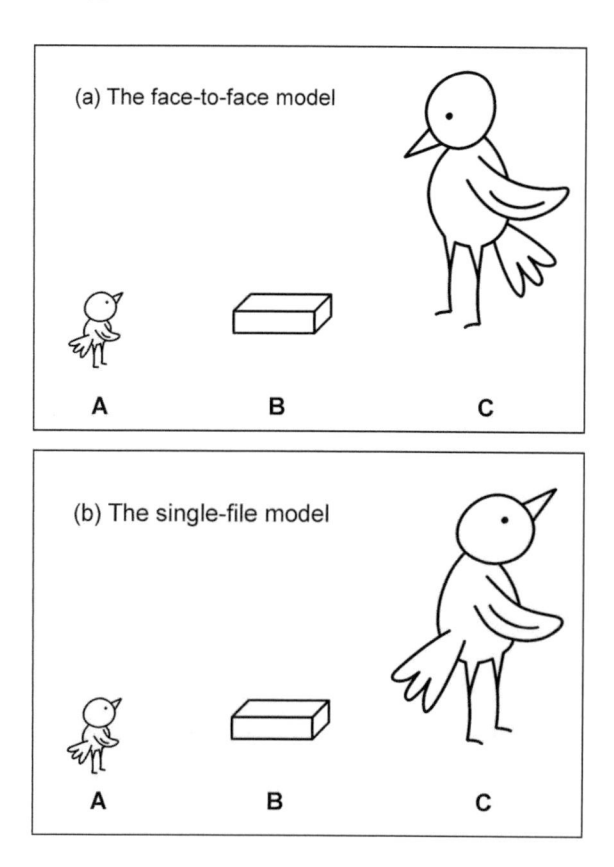

Figure 10: The face-to-face and single-file models (inspired by Heine 1997).

The two models are distinguished by their contrasting perspectives of spatial front-back orientation, as shown in Figure 10. In the single-file model, a landmark (C) also has an intrinsic front and back but is "looking away" from the speaker (A) so that the object (B), a box in this case, is located behind some landmark; this perspective is sometimes also sometimes referred to as the goose model.

With the alternative model, the face-to-face model, the box (B) would be in front of the object (C). It should be noted that in the model proposed in Heine (1997) these alternative allocentric orientations are not necessarily linked to cardinal directions. The findings resulting from these different research methods for spatial orientation, as tested among speakers of Cherang'any in Kenya and reported on in Mietzner (2016), also show that contextualization cues are important for the way in which speakers interpret the stimuli.

Descriptions by speakers vary depending on the importance which they attach to the objects in the space (Mietzner 2016: 263–264). Moreover, in contextless pictures the objects are described in an absolute frame of reference with the help of cardinal direction terms in the so-called single-file model. The educational background of Cherang'any speakers may also affect the use of orientation models or reference frames. English is important in Kenya, and consequently educated speakers may take recourse to a face-to-face model, in line with what is common in the latter language.

Picture 11: Man and Tree game (Mietzner 2016: 265; picture from Levinson et al. 1992).

Example (19) from Mietzner (2016: 265) illustrates a tree in front of a cow in the single-file model of Cherang'any speakers, as depicted in Picture 11 (from Levinson et al. 1992).

(19) mí kètìt táì
     COP tree front
     'the tree is in front'

Parallel to the system described for Tenejapa Tzeltal, Cherang'any speakers may also use cardinal direction terms in the allocentric description of objects:

(20) mi tètá kómósí pórè
     COP cow   side   down
     'the cow is on the lower side/south'

(21) mí   kètìt   kɔ́mɔ́s-á   tɔ́kɔ̀
     COP   tree   side-POSS up
     'the tree is on the upper side/north'

As for Tenejapa Tzeltal, the answers by Cherang'any speakers do not depend on the actual incline. The plastic figures in the test with Cherang'any speakers were positioned on a flat ground (or surface). The different strategies used in answering the question of where the figures are located depends on whether speakers imagine themselves to be in the actual territory from which the inclined plane is abstracted, or whether they are reacting to an elicitation. "If pictures tell stories, i.e. the objects/animated objects are in interaction, the perspective changes in a face-to-face model" (Mietzner 2016: 268); it is within this context that terms show up that are also used to express cardinal directions. Hence, for speakers of Cherang'any, one frame of reference can be converted into an alternative representation, which shows that an individual's perspective on what is seen in a situation influences the use of the spatial parameters.

In an earlier contribution on deictic organization in the related language Ateso (Teso, a language spoken in western Kenya and neighbouring areas of Uganda), Mietzner (2009: 230–236) discusses a system of cardinal direction terms used for spatial orientation similar to the system found in Cherang'any (as well as Tenejapa Tzeltal). In the following examples the interlinear glossing has been adapted to the general conventions used in the present study.[24]

(22) e-jei   ekikombe   kuju   k'amesa
     3-be   cup   top   PREP.table
     'the cup is on the table'

(23) e-jei   ataa   kuju   k'amesa
     3-be   lamp   above   PREP.table
     'the lamp is above the table'

(24) e-jei   epusi   kwap   k'amesa
     3-be   cat   under   PREP.table
     'the cat is under(neath) the table'

---

[24] Interlinear glosses are placed between the language of investigation and the free translation into another language, in order to be able to follow the structure of the source text. They may involve word-by-word translations or abbreviations for morphemes performing specific grammatical functions (whose translations are found in the list of abbreviations at the beginning of this monograph). The interlinear glossing system followed here is the Leipzig Glossing Rules.

(25) e-jei empira kwap k'ekicolong
    3-be ball under(neath) PREP.chair
    'the ball is under(neath) the chair'

Examples (22) and (23) also suggest that contact between the figure and the ground, or lack thereof, does not play a role. The terms for 'above' and 'under(neath) in these examples are the same as those used for 'north' and 'south' respectively in Ateso, as the following data kindly provided by David Barasa show (for additional information see Barasa 2017).

(26) kuju / ɲakoi   'north'
    kwap / agolotomei 'south'
    kɪdɛ   'east'
    tɔɔ   'west'

The terms for 'north' and 'south' are also used as object-centred terms with respect to homes. Thus, if the back side of the house faces south, the following topographical description is used in Ateso:

(27) kwap akai
    south house
    'back side of the house, behind the house'

Wassmann (1993) describes similar visual conceptualizations among the Yupno of Papua New Guinea, where the conceptual topography of the physical environment is also projected onto the homestead. The terms used for 'uphill' or 'downhill' appear to have no immediately obvious link to the actual cardinal directions in islands in the Pacific. On Ranongga Island in the Solomons, 'up' is used for south-east along the coast, and 'down' for north-west. The same directions are used at sea and probably relate to the direction of the prevailing wind from the south-east ('up' being against the wind) (Chambers 2009). This pattern seems to be found across the Austronesian-speaking Pacific. The uphill-downhill axis may correspond to north-south on one side of the island but east-west, south-north or west-east on other sides of the island because the up-down axis corresponds to inland-seaward (Völkel 2010).

The paradigmatic distinction proposed by Heine (1997) between the single-face model and the face-to-face model for spatial orientation can be applied to any object as part of the egocentric orientation. As illustrated by the following examples, these alternative orientations may lead to interesting, and sometimes funny, cultural misunderstandings.

A case of a face-to-face perspective on objects in the natural environment is found in the following examples, taking Picture 12 as a basis. When facing the direction in which the local school is to be found, one may ask about the exact route direction towards that school. A Tima speaker may tell you to turn right at the next crossing, where there are various buildings along the road, including the school. Here, speakers of Tima and English behave alike in that they use the words for 'left' and 'right' in the same way. However, if a Tima speaker is working in the field and a neighbour visits him in order to ask whether he can borrow this person's shovels, and the latter agrees, he may tell the neighbour that they can be found to the right of the house. A speaker of English would probably look in vain in such a case, because he would be looking on the wrong sight of the house, the side (s)he would call the 'left'. For speakers of Tima, the imagined house itself is taken as a reference point in such a case, having its own (inherent) front and back (with windows as "eyes"), and thereby a left and a right, in contrast to the intrinsic 'left' and 'right' attached to the home when approached by the Tima neighbour.

Picture 12: Going up/down the street and turning left/right at the traffic lights.

Just as 'left/right' or 'front/back' may reflect culture-specific conceptualizations, 'up/down' may also do so, when it comes to describing objects in the natural environment, as examples from German show. Whereas most parts of the city of Cologne are situated in a more or less flat landscape, speakers may still tell you to go *diese Straße hoch* 'up this street' or *diese Straße runter* 'down this street'. Whereas some speakers cannot explain when to use *hoch* versus *runter*, others relate their use to the house number signs; moving towards higher numbers means 'up', whereas moving towards lower numbers correlates with 'down', again showing that there is no immediate link with geography.

A further interesting example of the culture-specific way in which these terms may be used derives from one of the earliest experiences of the present author in intercultural differences concerning spatial orientation. Whereas speakers of English would refer to the side of an envelope on which the name of the addressee or receiver is written as the front, speakers of many African languages instead call this the back, since the front is where the mouth or opening of the envelope is found, as in Picture 13.

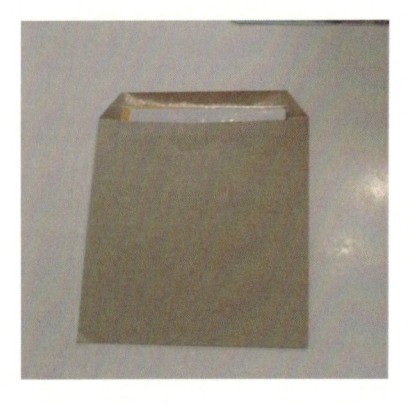

Picture 13: The front or back of an envelope.

When acquiring a language with an intrinsic or relative system of spatial orientation, speakers have to learn which objects the face-to face model is used for, and which the single-file model. Learning what a "prefix" or a "suffix" is in morphology is one such example of how these terms have come to be defined, based on the face-to-face model Western scholars operate with, as against the single-file (goose) model many African students grew up with. Take the following example from the language of wider communication, Swahili, which can build various prefixes and suffixes around lexical roots such as *-tak-* 'want'.

(28) ni-na-tak-a   ku-fahamu   jambo   hili
     1SG-PRS-want-F   INF-understand   matter this
     'I want to understand this matter'

If the verb is negated, the prefixes *ni-* and *na-* are replaced by a single prefix *si-*, whereas the suffix *-a* is replaced by *-i* (*si-tak-i* 'I don't want'). But for somebody who is used to a single-file model the morphemes *ni-*, *na-* and *si-* would be "suffixes", because they are found in a position from which one looks in a forward direction towards the front of the word, where a "prefix" *-a* or *-i* is found. In other words, the way in which labels like "prefix" and "suffix" are used, in scientific disciplines such as linguistics, in actual fact has an ethnocentric basis.

Interestingly, the egocentric perspective with corresponding terms for front/back, left/right, and up/down is commonly transferred onto landscapes in languages in order to refer to absolute (geocentric) directions, such as cardinal or wind directions. As shown by Brown (1983) in a cross-linguistic survey involving more than a hundred languages, languages frequently use the same three planes of spatial orientation, 'left/right', 'up/down', and 'front/back', including with respect to the expression of the cardinal directions 'north', 'south', 'east', and 'west'. Not surprisingly, the lexical encoding for 'east' may be derived etymologically from an expression such as 'where the sun rises', whereas the term for 'west' may be derived from an expression such as 'where the sun sets'. The relative position of the sun may also be used with respect to one of the other cardinal directions, as in the Amerindian language Seneca, where the term for 'north' means 'the sun is not there'.

But far more common etymological sources for 'north' and 'south' are the terms involving one of the three planes associated with the egocentric perspective. For example, in the First Nation language Mohawk 'down' also means 'east' and 'up' also means 'west'; in Fijian (Fiji Islands) 'upwards' also means 'east' and 'down, below' also means 'west'; in Cornish (Great Britain) 'left' is also used to express 'north' and 'right' is also used to express 'south' (Brown 1983: 128–130). The rationale behind this widespread tendency is the common (and presumably archaic) strategy in different speech communities to project oneself into a familiar landscape and to conventionalize this blending, for example in order to communicate maps.

These blending strategies consequently are "environment-centred" because they involve cardinal directions as absolute concepts, but at the same time an egocentric (rather than an allocentric) perspective is employed, in the terminology of Levinson (2003a), because of a conventionalized blending of the relative and viewer-centred terms left/right, front/back, or up/down onto fixed parts of a landscape, for example a mountain range or a river.

An example of the latter strategy is found in Bari, which is spoken in South Sudan (data from Spagnolo 1960).

(29) lɔ-bɔt '1. back; 2. north'
      yʊrɛ   '1. Morning Star, Venus; 2. east'
      kɪ   '1. above, over, up; 2. south'
      bwolu 'west'

The motivation for this system is to be found in the fact that the main point of orientation in the area, the Nile, comes from the south (in Uganda) and flows in a northward direction. Thus, upstream, towards the higher lands from where the Nile flows, coincides with the south. Consequently, the north represents the lower lands and the direction in which the Nile flows.[25]

Comparable strategies for spatial orientation are found among speakers of Koegu in southern Ethiopia, who live mainly along the Omo River, which flows southwards into Lake Turkana. While the terms for 'east' and 'west' are based on the expressions 'where the sun rises' and 'where the sun sets', *togu* means '1. south; 2. downstream', and *gaak* means '1. north; 2. mountain' (Hieda 1991; Dimmendaal and Rottland 1996).

Given the polysemic nature of words such as *togu* in Koegu, the question arises which of the two meanings, '1. south', or '2. downstream', is basic and which one is derived, especially given the existence of systems such as those described for Telejapa Tzeltal, Cherang'any, and Ateso above.

Solving this issue requires historical-comparative research on genetically related languages manifesting only one of the two meanings (as Brown 1983 shows for a number of languages), or language-internal research on etymological sources, as in the next example from Tima. Its speakers live at the western edges of the Nuba Mountains, in Sudan. When facing east, they see the higher elevations of these mountains, where the sun rises, or 'at the mouth', *lí-ŋéè*, as Tima speakers would say. By extension, the root for 'left', *dʊ̀-kwààlí*, is used to designate 'north', whereas the root for 'right', *dʊ̀-kɔ̀mál*, also means 'south'. While the etymology for 'left' is not known, the word for 'right' contains the lexical root *-mal*, which also means 'correct in a moral sense' (a lexical source which is quite common cross-linguistically). To the west of the Tima-speaking area, the mountains flatten out into a more or less flat savannah and desert area, reflected in the term for 'west', which is derived from the root for 'land, soil', *-hì*.

---

25 Additional examples can be found in Dimmendaal and Rottland (1996).

(30) dʊ̀-kwààlí   'north, left'
    dʊ̀-kʊ̀mál   'south, right'
    lí-ŋɛ́ɛ̀   'east, up (lit. at the mouth)'
    lí-hì   'west, down' (lit. on the ground)'

Tima thus operates with a vertically oriented (up/down) armature, rather than a front/back armature (Alamin, Schneider-Blum, and Dimmendaal 2012). As pointed out above, the word for 'east, up' is derived from the body-part term *kɪ-ŋɛ* 'mouth' (whereby the prefix *kɪ-* marks the singular). This example consequently contradicts the claim made in Heine (1997: 57) that terms for cardinal directions never derive from body-part terminology.

Lusekelo (2018) identifies seven sources of terms for cardinal directions in languages in eastern Africa belonging to the Bantu family. Names of ethnic groups are the most dominant source, followed by terrain (uphill, downhill), body parts, direction of sunrise and sunset, water bodies, winds, and lexical borrowing from the dominant languages of wider communication in the area. Additional examples for the expression of cardinal directions in languages belonging to the Ubangian and Nilotic families are found in Mietzner and Pasch (2007). Apart from cosmological, geographical, and atmospheric concepts, these languages use names for neighbouring ethnic groups or historical events as sources. Moreover, the authors also point towards the importance of body parts in the creation of cardinal terms, a feature attested in a range of other languages, as shown for Tima above.

Hock and Joseph (1996: 245–248) discuss the words for cardinal points in a number of early Indo-European languages, showing, amongst other findings, that the term for 'east' is frequently related to the rising sun, and 'west' to the setting sun. The corresponding north-south axis may be described by 'left' and 'right' in various Indo-European languages, as in Old Irish *tuascert* 'left direction/ north'; *descert* 'right direction/south'. An additional discussion of the etymology of terms for cardinal directions is found in Heine (1997: 49–58) and Comrie (2003).

Ameka and Essegbey (2006) give examples of such modifications in the meanings of spatial terminology in Ewe. In the Aŋlɔ dialect of Ewe (spoken in the coastal area of Ghana), the terms *dziehe* 'upside' and *anyiehe* 'downside' are used to refer to the southwest and northeast, respectively. In other words, in this dialect these terms no longer describe any inherent characteristic of the region, as the topography where these terms are used is flat. "One speculation on their etymology is, therefore, that they come from an era when the Ewes lived in a hillier region. The orthogonal axis is expressed by reference to the sea and the lagoon which are located on the east and west of the region respectively" (Ameka and Essegbey 2006: 382).

Something similar appears to have happened with Turkana in Kenya. While its speakers employ the same terms as speakers of the closely related language Ateso, educated younger people, especially, tend to use the term *kwap* in order to refer to 'south' and *kuju* to refer to 'north', presumably due to geography lessons in schools. The point is, however, that many Nilotic languages, including Turkana, have a basic distinction between 'east' and 'west' (where the sun rises and sets). On the other hand, the basic meaning of the two other terms seems to be – or rather to have been – 'up(hill), in/towards the sky or some elevation, where the water comes from', and 'down(hill), on/towards the earth or ground, where the water is flowing to'. Compare the following related Turkana forms and corresponding meanings from older speakers, which reinforce this (partly historical) interpretation:

(31)   kwap   1. 'south'; 2. 'under, down(ward), below, underneath'
      a-kwap   'land, country'
      kuju   1.'north'; 2. 'up, above'
      a-kuj(u) 'God'

It would appear that the primary sense of *kuju* historically was 'up(stream), above, where the water comes from', and this may have been linked to, or coterminous with, a cardinal direction; the primary sense of *kwap* in all likelihood was 'down(stream), where the water flows towards', a term again coterminous with a specific cardinal direction historically (in an environment from which the ancestral communities originated). Synchronically, the translations of 'north' and 'south' are also correct, as this is the sense in which these terms are used these days, for example in geography lessons in school.

The volume edited by Hickmann and Robert (2006) presents the reader with further interesting research on cross-linguistic variability in the conceptualization of physical space in grammar. As shown by Robert (2006) in her contribution on space in Wolof in the same volume, the use of deixis in this Senegalese language of wider communication goes far beyond the spatial location of an entity.[26] For a recent typological survey and a detailed account of the state of the art concerning physical and social aspects of deixis, interested readers are also referred to Levinson (2018). Some aspects of social space emerging from the available literature so far are discussed next.

---

[26] The same volume contains contributions supporting the hypothesis of a relative autonomy of the language faculty in the behaviour of patients with pathological disorders such as deficits in the ability to navigate in space or non-linguistic spatial impairments. Such studies again support the claim that language can – at least to some extent – be learned in non-interactive ways.

4.2 Social space

Related to allocentric and egocentric frames of reference in physical space, there is a domain which manifests itself in the social or cultural interpretation of spatial orientation. Moore (1986), in her study of space and gender among the Marakwet of Kenya, presents one of the first detailed accounts of "the anthropology of space", i.e., of the social-cultural meaning of space, in an African speech community.

Marakwet manifests interesting semantic extensions for the terms for 'left' and right', as shown in Table 12 (Moore 1986: 58). As is more common cross-linguistically, the term for 'left', *let* in Marakwet, is used for 'north', and *tai* for 'south'. But there are additional, rather intriguing aspects of deixis in Marakwet, involving the same two concepts. As shown by Moore (1986: 58–59, passim), these antonyms have several meanings in corresponding English translations:

Table 12: Metaphorical extensions of 'right' and 'left' in Marakwet (Moore 1986).

let	tai
'left'	'right'
'north'	'south'
'behind'	'front'
'future'	'past'
'lower part of the valley'	'upper part of the valley'
'going'	'coming'
'unborn'	'ancestors'

Map 2 shows the home area of the Marakwet in the Cherangany Hills in western Kenya. When the Marakwet are looking in an eastward direction to see the sunrise, they also see the Kerio River in front of them. When looking towards the right, i.e., the south, they see the upper part of the valley from which the Kerio River originates; when looking towards their left, i.e., the north, they see the lower part of the valley southwest of Lake Turkana. The south-to-north direction in which this river flows may consequently be associated with the beginning of life in the present and past (which includes the ancestors), whereas the north constitutes the future and, by metonymic extension, the unborn.

From a cognitive point of view, the conceptual integration of two domains consisting of a physical space and a (virtual) social space, and the metaphorical and metonymic extensions emanating from this merger, may be interpreted as another instance of conceptual blending in the sense of Fauconnier and Turner

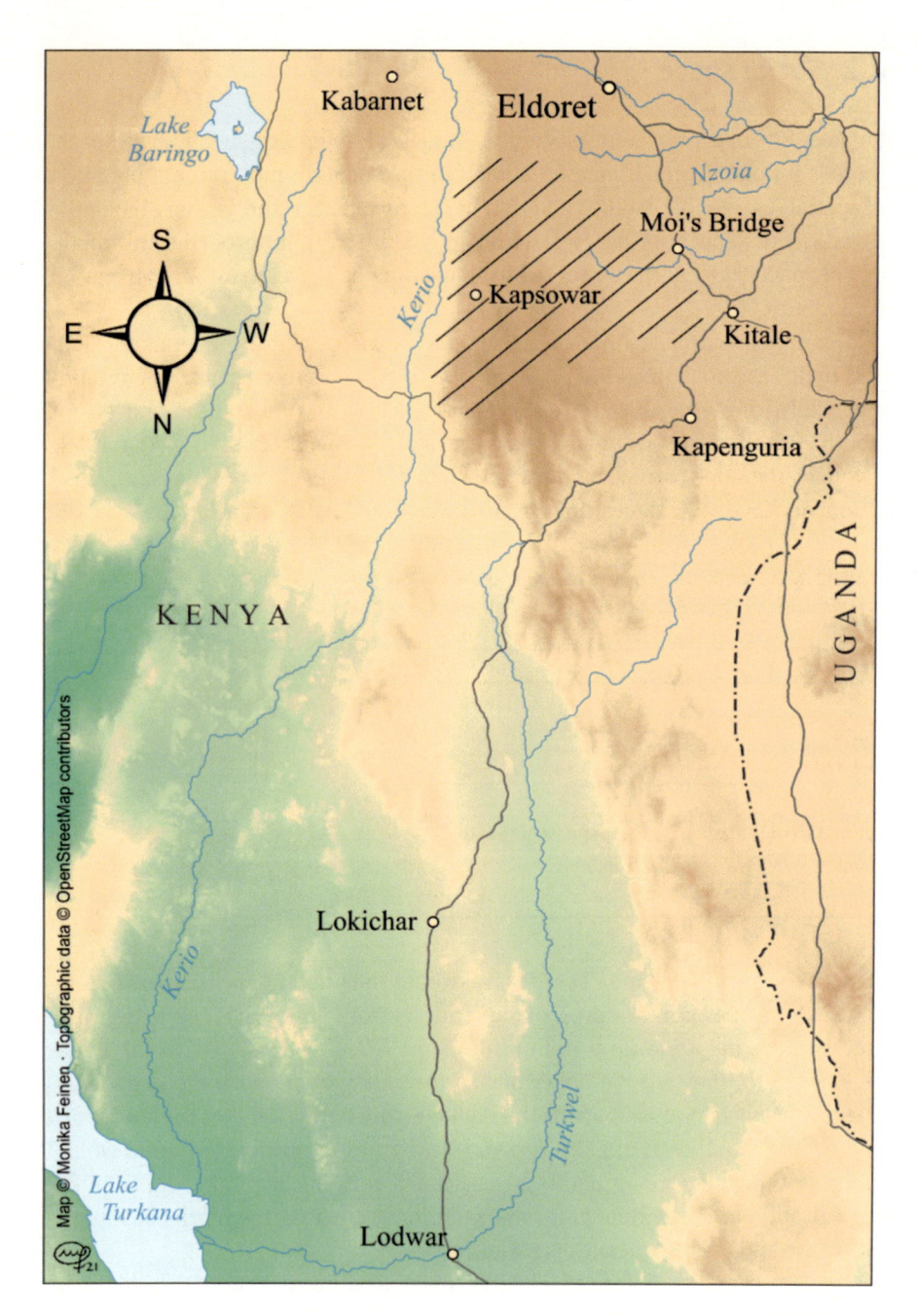

Map 2: The Marakwet area of the Kerio River, viewed from the north (kindly produced by Monika Feinen).

(2002). Initial examples of this process are given above in Section 3.1 on colour and Section 3.2 on body-part terminology. If we take space as a generic concept, there are two inputs, the physical space and the social space of the Marakwet speech community, as two mental spaces.

> Mental spaces are to be understood as small conceptual packets constructed as we think and talk, for purposes of local understanding and action. (. . .) [They] are connected to long-term schematic knowledge called "frames" (. . .). Mental spaces are very partial. They contain elements and are typically structured by frames. They are interconnected, and can be modified as thought and discourse unfold. Mental spaces can be used generally to model dynamic mappings in thought and language. (Fauconnier and Turner 2002: 40)

By projecting the temporal space (those who have passed away, those living now, and the unborn) onto the physical space, with the Kerio River as the most prominent landmark, a blended space emerges. The direction in which the Kerio River flows (from the south towards the north) symbolizes the flow of time and thereby of older and younger generations.[27]

The particular type of conceptual blending involved in the case described here, where time and space intersect and fuse, is what the literator and philosopher of language Mikhail Bakhtin (1895–1975) referred to as a chronotope (lit. 'time-space'), a unit of analysis denoting the semiotic configurations of time, space, and personhood as represented in language. If we take space as a generic concept, there are two inputs, the physical space and the personal space, as two mental spaces surrounding ego and other individuals in a society. The cognitive strategy of conceptually blending these domains allows members of a society such as the Marakwet to make time and the history of their people visible for human contemplation. Through this projection of a time axis onto a physical axis, they also shape images of themselves as links between the past and the future. The spatial dimensions frequently showing up in the expression of cardinal directions thus also play a role in social deixis, as the examples from Marakwet show.

The following are further examples showing how spatial concepts like 'left/right, 'up/down', and 'front/back' may be associated with social space. In his axiological investigation of the terms for 'left' and 'right' and their negative and positive associations, Foolen (2019: 152) points out that worldwide around 10% of the population is left-handed, and that this is a species-specific property of the lateralization of the human brain. Whereas 'right' tends to be associated with positive values (frequently derived from a word or morpheme for 'correct, right'), 'left' tends to be associated with negative values (it tends to be associated with

---

27 This conceptual blending in Marakwet is reminiscent of the ancient Greek credo *panta rhei* (πάντα ῥεῖ) 'everything flows (and nothing is forever)' (ascribed to Heraclitus).

cleaning activities, for example), although exceptions occur. As further observed by Foolen (2019: 154), there is also empirical evidence for the lateral distribution of the processing of emotions, which strengthens the axiological asymmetry between 'left' and 'right'. "The positive associations with the right side of the body related to handedness thus fit the general processing of positive emotions in the left hemisphere. In a similar way, the processing of negative emotions in the right hemisphere 'fits' the negative associations with the left side of the body based on handedness". An interestingly linguistic correlate is the frequent replacement of the word for 'left', due to its relationship with taboo and euphemism (Foolen 2019: 149).

In their investigation of pointing as a gesture in Ghana, Kita and Essegbey (2001) mention that left-hand pointing is not totally suppressed, for example when giving route directions ("you turn left"), although such gestures may be reduced in size and in the periphery. But as usual, there are exceptions to the common associations of left and right as concepts. Strecker (1993) reports on the words of a speaker of Hamar (or Hamer) in southern Ethiopia by the name of Lalombe, who points out that if he stumbles with his left foot, he will meet well-being, much food, and good fortune. If he stumbles with his right foot, on the other hand, this will lead him to suffering, lack of food, and misfortune.

'Right (hand)' is commonly expressed in African languages as 'male/strong (hand)', but also as '(hand used) for eating', as in the Bantu language Swahili, *mkono wa kulia*. But in Nilotic languages (which are spoken across eastern Africa, from Sudan in the north to Tanzania in the south), the root for 'eat' sometimes also figures in the term for 'left' (rather than 'right'), as in Dinka *cam* (Nebel 1979: 156). A partial answer to this at first sight somewhat enigmatic issue may be found in the fact that the meaning of *cam* 'eat' includes that of 'cheat' or 'bewitch' (Nebel 1979: 18). These latter senses, rather than 'eating (of food)', presumably formed the basis for this type of metaphorical extension in these Nilotic languages. The left hand may be used, for example, in cursing people, by throwing sand over one's left shoulder, a custom which can be observed among the Turkana in Kenya.

In their study *Metaphors We Live By*, Lakoff and Johnson (1980) also discuss cross-linguistic tendencies to associate "up" with corresponding positive connotations such as "high status", or "down" with more negative connotations such as "low status"; also "good is up, bad is down" (compare being *upbeat* with being *down* in English); further examples can be found in the abovementioned monograph.

Whereas for many people in the West, the past lies behind us and many of us still have a future ahead of us, this perspective is not universal. Evans (2010: 169–170) gives examples from Aymara, a language spoken in Bolivia, Chile, and Peru.

(32) *nayra mara   qhipa   pacha*
      front year   behind time
      'last year'   'future times'

These latter associations between "front" and "past", and "back, behind" and the (invisible) "future" are presumably common cross-culturally.

Social space manifests itself in different ways, one of which is social deixis. The linguistic anthropologist William F. Hanks is probably one of the most prolific scholars on spatial deixis as a research topic; see, amongst others, Hanks (1996, 2005, 2009). Deictic expressions, such as English *this*, *that*, *here*, *there*, are typically used to individuate referential objects in relation to the context in which these are used within an utterance. Hanks (2009) argues that the basis of deixis is not the spatial contiguity of the referent, but rather the access (perceptual, cognitive, social) that participants have to the referent. Hanks (2009: 4) also argues that "[i]n order to analyze socially situated speech, it is necessary to recognize that language is only one of multiple modalities of expression, all of which may be operant in communicative practice. These other modalities include gesture and posture, the spatial and perceptual arrangements of interactants" (Hanks 2009: 4). Further examples of verbal and non-verbal deixis are presented in Chapter 12 on non-verbal communication. The discussion hereafter serves to illustrate the point made by Hanks (2009) on the perceptual, cognitive, and social access participants have to a specific referent.

Gregersen (1974) lists several strategies for encoding social deixis. As he points out, apart from indirect ways of addressing others through the avoidance of certain linguistic forms, there is the use of special honorific pronouns (including plural forms to address a single person), or of titles; naming taboos and the use of special registers are further strategies. Mitchell and Neba (2019) present a survey of such special registers (more specifically, initiation registers, secret registers, ritual and spirit registers, royal registers, urban youth registers, and avoidance registers). The discussion below illustrates some of these strategies.

In line with Diessel (2012), a distinction is drawn here between participant deixis (serving the communicative function of presenting the speech participants and their social relationships to each other in terms of gender, social status, communicative role), and object deixis (elements used to orientate the interlocuters in the situational and discourse context, including the time and location of a speech event). Sometimes the two may merge, as already illustrated in the Marakwet examples above.

Encoding the social identities of speech participants or interactants in a speech event (as part of participant deixis), or the relationships between them, plays an important role in politeness and impoliteness strategies, as the following examples from Amharic (Ethiopia) illustrate. As shown by Hoben (1976: 287), pronominals as deictic markers are popular as in-group markers or, alternatively, when expressing social distance in Amharic. Table 13 summarizes the creative employment of second person personal pronouns in this language. Similar distinctions for gender, person and number are expressed on verb forms, although a number of formal neutralizations (known as syncretism in linguistics) occur.

Table 13: Amharic pronouns (Hoben 1976).

Person	Singular				Plural
	Insulting	Familiar	Intermediate	Honorific	
1st		ïne		ïñña (royal)	ïñña
2nd, male	anci	antɛ	antu	ïrswo	ïnnantɛ
2nd, female	anci		antu	ïrswo	ïnnantɛ
3rd, male		ïrsu		ïrsacccɛw	ïnnɛrsu
3rd, female		ïrswa		ïrsaccɛw	ïnnɛrsu

The independent pronouns in Table 13 are used for addressing others. The different forms manifest alternations in number (using a plural versus a singular form), gender (using a masculine versus a feminine form), and person (using a second person versus a third person form), as well as (lack of) respect.

While there were and still are fixed Amharic terms for institutionalized authority, such as for members of the ecclesiastical hierarchy of the Orthodox Church, courts of justice, or for the last emperor of Ethiopia, Haile Selassie (1892–1975), one could and still can play around with these pronominal reference markers as part of politeness and impoliteness strategies in this language. An honorific (polite) form such as *ïrswo* may be used among kin, depending on "religious purity, rank, education and age" (Hoben 1976: 285), for example between a girl and her parents-in-law. But if a warm bond of affection develops between the girl and her mother-in-law, *anci* may be used.

In order to express anger or an insult, the expected polite form *ïrswo* may be replaced by *antɛ* inside or outside kin relations, while the masculine second person form may be replaced by the corresponding feminine second person form *anči* when trying to insult a man. The polite form *ïrswo* may be used humorously or ironically for small children, relatives, or friends to express exaggerated respect (Hoben 1976: 287). There are also subtle differences between urban and rural areas; in the capital Addis Ababa, for example, some male friends use mutual *anci* to show affection. In the countryside parents may address a son by the feminine form *anci* and a daughter by the masculine form *antɛ*, in an effort to conceal their true identity from the evil forces that attacked their earlier babies (Hoben (1976: 287–288). Interested readers are also referred to Pankhurst (1992), which is another rich source on gender manipulations and their social ramifications in Amharic.

Whereas the Amharic deictic registers are the result of the "invisible hand" of generations of language users, sometimes changes are more rapid and abrupt, as was the case in Swedish. The sociohistorical context and dominant political ideology in the second part of the 20th century was important in the case of Swedish, where the social implications of the polite pronoun *ni* underwent reanalysis, being replaced by the informal *du* in many situations, although different social classes have different rules, according to Paulston (1976).

Something similar can be observed in modern Spoken Dutch, where the honorific second person singular form *U* is being replaced in more and more social domains, including more formal ones, by the informal second person pronoun *jij*. Correspondingly, using the *U* form in these social contexts is no longer interpreted as a sign of respect but instead of social arrogance and distancing.

A rather intriguing instance of social language manipulation for cultural purposes is described by Pasch and Mbolifouye (2011) for Zande, a language of wider communication spoken in the Democratic Republic of the Congo, the Central African Republic, and South Sudan, which was also the language of a centralized (Zande) state or kingdom until the end of the 19th century. The authors analyzed Zande texts collected and published by the anthropologist Edward E. Evans-Pritchard between 1954 and 1974, which they qualify as "excellent" (Pasch and Molifouye 2011: 2). In one text about a ruler claiming power at an intermediate level, as a regional governor, between his subjects and Gbudwe, the traditional king of the Zande, as the power superordinate to him, this ruler apparently uses the subject pronoun *mi* in object position, in order to refer to himself.

(33) Gbudue ki ni-mo ka fu mi ko-no
Gbudue SEQ X-begin SUB give 1S.1 DIR-here
'and then Gbudwe sent me here (lit. gave me to this place)'

The object pronoun expected here would have been the enclitic marker -*re*. While some Zande speakers consulted by Pasch and Mbolifouye did not recognize or accept example (33) as proper Zande, other language consultants recognized this strategy as somewhat archaic, and thus as reflecting the language of "the ruling class", as one speaker consulted by the authors phrased it (Pasch and Mbolifouye 2011: 5). Apparently, this type of construction with a subject pronoun in object position was a sophisticated way of expressing irrevocable rule, claiming "power of an intermediate level, more precisely that of a prince over a local population, a prince who himself is dependent on his superior, King Gbudwe" (Pasch and Mbolifouye 2011: 5).

4.3 Social deixis and the co-evolution of language and culture

Routine culture-specific patterns of usage can harden into language-specific morphosyntactic constructions which are "tailor made" to meet the communicative needs of the speech community, as argued by Dimmendaal (2000: 192) in a survey of morphological features in African languages, and as illustrated above. The present section discusses additional examples of the direct encoding of cultural meaning in the semantics or morphosyntax of languages, an endeavour sometimes referred to as "ethnosyntax" (Enfield 2002). For reasons of space, only two domains are discussed here, first social deixis related to the use of inclusory reference, and second, what is here called the egocentric perspective of speakers in com-municative interactions.

The ingenious Africanist and one of the teachers of the present author, the late Achiel Emiel Meeussen (1912–1978), identified a range of widespread lexical and grammatical features on the African continent which he labeled "Africanisms". Among these is a phenomenon Meeussen (1975: 4) refers to as "totalization", which these days is more commonly referred to as "inclusory" reference. It involves a grammatical form expressing incorporation, where the whole set of participants, the superset, and a subset of participants are expressed in a conjunctive form, as illustrated by the following example from Hausa (a major language of wider communication of West Africa): *su Audù* 'them including Audu, Audu cum suis (lit. them Audu)'. Here the third person plural pronoun functions as an inclusory marker denoting the superset, plus a proper name (a position which may also be taken by a noun) functioning as a subset. In languages with a separate inclusory (inclusive) construction, the latter is different from the union of two sets, as with coordination ('x and y'), or comitatives ('x with y'), as illustrated by the examples below.

Inclusory constructions are known from different language families across the world, for example from Oceanic and other branches of the Austronesian family (Lichtenberk 2000). But they are also common across Africa, as pointed out by Meeussen (1975: 4) in his list of "Africanisms". Khachaturyan (2019: 92) gives an example from Mano (a language spoken in Liberia and Guinea), which is structurally similar to the Hausa example above: *kò Pèé* 'Pe and I/we (lit. we [including] Pe)'. For the expression of inclusion, Mano uses a separate set of pronouns (distinct from the set of pronouns used for the object, possessives, etc.), which historically emerged from the fusion of a pronoun (probably used in focus constructions) and a comitative preposition, glossed as COORD rather than INCL in Khachaturyan (2019: 95), and glossed as "COM" below:

(34) wà   ē   nā
     3PL.COM 3SG.REFL wife
     'he and his wife (lit. [they] including his own wife)'

One of the most detailed analyses of inclusory constructions in an African language to date is found in Moodie and Billington (2020: 373–387) for Lopit (Lopid), a language spoken in South Sudan. In contrast with comitative constructions in Lopit (as in (35) below), inclusory constructions involve non-singular indexing. As is typical for inclusory constructions, they "show participant indexing between the verb and a superset comprising the subject and object NP [noun phrase]" (Moodie and Billington 2020: 373). The authors distinguish between normal and special inclusory constructions in Lopit. In the former, the subject noun phrase and a so-called oblique noun phrase (introduced by 'with') occur, but the verb takes plural subject marking (the latter expressing the superset (example (36)). In the third type, also involving plural indexing on the verb, the subject noun phrase is either topicalized, thereby preceding the main clause, or it is given or understood from preceding discourse, and therefore not expressed (as in example (37)). These three types are illustrated in the following sentences:

(35) á-réx-ó   náŋ   xò=ìjè
     1SG-be.close-IPFV   1SG.NOM   with=SG.ABS
     'I and you are close (lit. I'm close with you)'

(36) eí-fwò   náŋ   xò=ìjè
     1PL-go.PL-IPFV   1SG.NOM   with=SG.ABS
     'you and I are going (lit. we go with you)'

(37) x-í-ij:én   íjé   ìràsı   lìti   e: eì-ibóŋ   xɔ̀=nàŋ
     Q-2-know   2SG.NOM   brother.ABS   my.M   yes 1PL-meet   with=1SG.ABS
     'Do you know my brother? Yes, he and I met (lit. we-met with me)'

The difference between the conversational implicature in the listing strategy and with the use of inclusive constructions is that in the latter a kind of "togetherness" is expressed, as further illustrated by the following two contrasting examples (Moodie and Billington 2020: 378).

(38) á-pár   náŋ   xɔ̀=lɔ̀bɔ̀ŋ
     1SG-stand.N 1SG.NOM with=Lobong.ABS
     'I stand with Lobong'

(39) ɛí-pár   náŋ   xɔ̀=lɔ̀bɔ̀ŋ
     1PL-stand.N 1SG.NOM with=SG.ABS
     'I and Lobong stand (together) (lit. we-stand I with Lobong)'

As illustrated in Section 4.2 on social space, pronominal reference plays a significant role in social deixis. Evans (2003) describes rather spectacular examples of this from Australian languages. In a language like Adnyamathanha, kin-sensitive pronouns or other kinship-sensitive terms occur, all referring to the mother of the speaker and/or hearer, but triangulating the relationship between speaker, hearer, and a specific other referent. For example, different pronominal forms are to be used depending on whether "the one who is *your mother* and *my daughter*, given that I am your mother's mother" or "the one who is *your daughter* and *my mother*, given that I am your daughter's daughter" is involved (Evans 2003: 34). This kin-based morphosyntax (or "kintax"), which is obligatorily encoded in the grammar, is cognitively rather demanding and apparently not mastered before adulthood. Such languages force their speakers to pay attention to intricate kinship relations between participants in a discourse. In order to choose the correct pronoun, one must first work out whether the referents are in even- or odd-numbered generations with respect to one another, or related by direct links through the male line. Based on his experiences with languages such as Adnyamathanha, Evans (2003: 36) prefers to "refrain from overdetermining the set of possible linguistic structures through biological constraints". The problem is: to date, nobody knows where the borderline is between culture-independent categories and grammatical constraints and cultural selection leading to sometimes unique areal structurations, as in the case of Adnyamathanha and other Australian languages. As pointed out in the preface to this monograph, and as argued at various points in previous chapters, the present author does not adhere to either of these two extreme positions, as there is evidence for both universal (constraint-based) principles and the co-evolution of language and culture and the key role played by a "theory of mind"; in the present monograph the main focus is, of course, on the usage-based dimension (in the sense of Tomasello 2003, without, however, ignoring evidence for innate linguistic principles).

A second domain involving social deixis, discussed here in order to illustrate a further type of construal which appears to be motivated by cultural relevance, is the so-called "egocentric perspective". The notion of "perspective" plays a role as one of several aspects of construal in cognitive linguistics, alongside notions such as prominence (of specific constituents in an utterance) or background (involving such phenomena as presupposition, or given and new information; see Langacker (1991: 591–592) for a succinct summary.

Within the field of African linguistics, probably one of the best known grammatical phenomena with a wide areal distribution and involving perspectives is the marking of direction towards the deictic centre (usually the speaker), frequently referred to as "ventive" marking. More recently, the term "associated motion" has become popular, particularly in order to show parallel structures in languages spoken in South America or Australia (where the latter term is commonly used), as discussed in the volume edited by Guillaume and Koch (2021). The notion of "egocentric" reflects the fact that the deictic elements used are indexical of the position of ego as the origo or deictic centre of speaking (these latter concepts going back to Bühler 1934). Compare the following two sentences in Tima (Sudan), where the verb in the first example does not contain a ventive (VEN) marker, whereas the second example does.

(40) Kwʌ́kwʌ̀ŋ án-dʊ̀wà à-lì-ŋɛ́ɛ̀
 KwʌkwʌŋD 3PRF-go.down source-LOC-east
 'Kwʌkwʌŋ went down from the east/top (speaker neither at the starting point nor at the goal)'

(41) Kwʌ́kwʌ̀ŋ àn-dʊ́wá-y-íŋ á-líŋɛ́ɛ̀
 Kwʌkwʌŋ 3PRF-go.down-EE-VENT SOURCE-LOC.east/top
 'Kwʌkwʌŋ went down / came from the east (speaker is in the west)'
 'Kwʌkwʌŋ went down / came from the top (speaker is down)'

The absence of the ventive marker in example (40) implies that the person uttering the sentence (i.e., the speaker) was not there and consequently did not see Kwʌkwʌŋ coming down or going down. In other words, the conceptualizer (i.e., the speaker) is construed subjectively (as this perspective is called in cognitive grammar, which was originally was called space grammar), and remains implicit as an "offstage" reference point. (S)he construes herself or himself more objectively in the example with the ventive marker, as Kwʌkwʌŋ moves towards the speaker, who thereby observes this movement. For this latter reason, ventive marking in Tima is interpreted as part of evidentiality marking in Dimmendaal (2014a). Apparently, it is important for speakers of Tima to make clear whether the information reported on is based on something the speaker (or protagonist in a story) has witnessed herself or himself, or whether it derives from something (s)he heard.

But Tima goes beyond this cross-linguistically common pattern, as it also marks the egocentric perspective on prepositional phrases. Compare the following example from Alamin, Schneider-Blum, and Dimmendaal (2012), who provide a detailed analysis of locative marking in this language, with (40) and (41) above:

(42) Kwʌ́kwʌ̀ŋ   án-dʊ̀wà   á-nṯí-ŋɛ́ɛ̀
      Kwʌkwʌŋ   3PRF-go.down   source-EGO-east/top
      'Kwakwang went down from the east (speaker is still in the east)'
      'Kwakwang went down from the top (speaker is still on top of a mountain)'

The form *á-nṯí-ŋɛ́ɛ̀* is in paradigmatic contrast with the alternative form in this position, *á-lí-ŋɛ́ɛ̀*. The presence of – *nṯí*- implies that the speaker was on top of the mountain at the time of the event described in this sentence, and hence that the speaker witnessed the scene. Both the ventive (associated motion) marker and the prepositional marker for the egocentric perspective occur in the following example, where the speaker orders somebody to come to the place where (s)he him/herself is located:

(43) dí-y-ʌ̀ŋ   ǹṯə̂-lâh
      walk-EE-VENT   EGO-field
      'come to the field (where I am)!'

There are no separate verbs for 'come' and 'go' in Tima; instead a verb 'go, walk, move', *di-*, is used, and the direction towards or away from the deictic centre becomes clear from the verb or the prepositional phrase, as shown above.

The markers for the egocentric perspective in Tima, expressed by way of a ventive (associated motion) morpheme on the verb or a distinct morpheme on a prepositional phrase, depending on the syntactic structure involved, are so-called "shifters" (Jakobson 1957) or "referential indexicals" (Silverstein 1976: 24), as their propositional reference is dependent on the suitable indexing of the speech situation. This should become even clearer from the following example, where again some information is construed from the vantage point of the speaker, who constitutes the reference point. This sentence from Alamin, Schneider-Blum, and Dimmendaal (2014: 15) was uttered by a speaker looking at a picture in which he himself also figured, standing underneath a baobab tree.

(44) ìhwáá-y-ˇɛ́   hɪ́làk   n̂t̪-ʌ́hí   w-ʌ́cúk   kɪ́-pə̀rárʊ̀ʊ́k
     people-EE-FOC stay   EGO-ground   LOC2-baobab   NC.SG-hollow
     'the people are staying under the hollow baobab (where I am/was at the time this picture was taken)'

The concept of "index" goes back to the tripartite division of semiotics by Charles S. Peirce consisting of symbols, icons, and indexes (indices), which he started writing about from the 1860s onwards (see Atkin 2010 for a succinct discussion).[28] Let us take English as an example. When learning this language, one notices that for most of its lexical items or words (and for languages in general), the relationship between the entity signaled (the object, as reflected in the form of a word for that object) and the sign vehicle token (the perceptible phenomenon which does the representing, for example the meaning of a word) is arbitrary and therefore unpredictable. When reading this book one may be sitting on a *chair* in English, an object referred to as *kiti* in Swahili or *kujera* in Hausa, etc., the association between form and meaning being conventionalized. With iconic signs (words) on the other hand, the connection between form and meaning is motivated (non-arbitrary), as with onomatopoetic words for particular animals, like *cuckoo* in English. Finally, with indexes there is a connection of spatio-temporal contiguity to the occurrence of an entity, as with pointing towards an object and saying 'that one'.

The examples from Tima above show some more complex properties of indexes, as their proper interpretation depends on the context in which they are used, as a result of which they play a role as part of more general strategies of evidentiality marking in this language (Dimmendaal 2014a). As members of a speech community we may infuse specific distinctions with meaning and employ these in the course of "embodied practices" because they are relevant in our cultures. As such, these Tima examples, as well as the examples from Lopit, are instances of the co-evolution of language and culture.

---

28 Readers interested more generally in the philosophers of language quoted or referred to in this monograph, like Austin, Grice, Peirce, or Searle, may want to consult Clark (1996) for an informative survey of their ideas.

5 Language and habitual thought

> If there is a linguistic relativity, then it may create real dilemmas for the conduct of research because researchers themselves are not exempt from these linguistic influences.
>
> (Lucy 1992a: 2)

As a primary school pupil in the Netherlands, the present author was once asked by the teacher to go and collect the key for the library from the caretaker's office, so that the children from our class could have a look at specific books. When I asked the caretaker for the key because the library "is not *loose* yet," I was told I would need a screw driver. "But if it is not *open* yet, you need a key," the caretaker continued, with a smile on his face. It was the first time the present author became aware of the fact that in Standard Dutch, the language used in schools, there is a distinction between *open* 'open' and *los* 'loose', whereas in his local and primary language (Lower Saxon, a Western Germanic variety closely related to "Plattdeutsch", and spoken in the eastern and northern regions of the Netherlands and northern Germany), there is only one word, *lös*, expressing both the concept of being closed and of being fixed or locked. In spite of the fact that Standard Dutch later on became the present author's dominant language, interpreting cognitive experiences and describing these as either "loose" or "open" has remained somewhat problematic, especially when dealing with new situations.

McDonough, Choi, and Mandler (2003) report on a rather fascinating experiment with 9- to 14-month-old infants and adult speakers of English and Korean involving spatial orientation, which helps to explain such cognitive problems. Tight and loose containment are both expressed by *in* in English, and therefore not distinguished lexically, whereas *on* expresses loose support. Korean, on the other hand, distinguishes between *kkita* for tight containment or interlock (for example, when putting a letter in an envelope), and *nehta* for loose containment (for example, when putting an apple in a bowl), as well as *nohta* for loose support with respect to objects.

For the experiment, speakers of both languages were first familiarized through pictures with tight fit or loose fit objects. Next, they were shown a picture of a tight fit object on one screen and a loose fit object on another. While all the infants, involved in their nonverbal, preferential-looking tasks, and growing up with either English or Korean as a first language, categorized the contrast between the former two (tight and loose containment), suggesting conceptual readiness for learning such spatial semantics well before a language is acquired, the behaviour of adult speakers of English differed from that of adult Korean speakers. English-speaking adults looked equally long at the familiar and the novel scenes. Interestingly, Korean-speaking adults looked longer at the kind of spatial relations they had just been familiarized with. In another experiment, Korean speakers easily picked out the odd example showing loose fit among a set of pictures otherwise showing tight fit (or vice versa), whereas English speakers could not.

From this experiment it may be concluded that spatial relations that are salient during the preverbal stage with infants become less salient if the primary language they acquire does not systematically encode them. Phrased differently, the presence of certain lexical distinctions in the primary language we acquire helps us to dissect, filter, and channel cognitive experiences in certain ways and to ignore others, not because we are forced to do so, but because it helps us to focus our attention on distinctions which need to be expressed in the language (or languages, if one grows up bilingually) we grow up with. It is this "habitual thinking" which is essentially what linguistic relativism is about, in the present author's view.[29] For a proper understanding of what this means in concrete terms, it is convenient to break the hypothesis down into three subdomains: 1. lexicon; 2. grammar; 3. pragmatics. Hymes (1966) was probably one of the first authors to point out that the principle of linguistic relativity also applies to the third domain, the differential engagement of languages in social life. Hymes (1966: 116) points out that "[p]eople who enact different cultures do to some extent experience distinct communicative systems, not merely the same natural communicative condition with different customs affixed". The first two domains where linguistic relativity appears to play a role, the lexicon and grammar, are treated in the present chapter, whereas linguistic relativity in the (third) pragmatic domain is discussed in Chapter 10, as this latter phenomenon requires the introduction of a number of additional parameters in order to be properly understood by readers.

5.1 The roots of linguistic relativism

The hypothesis that our language competence and performance interact with our cognitive system in non-trivial ways has become associated with two American pioneers in this domain, Edward Sapir (1884–1939) and his student Benjamin Lee Whorf (1897–1941). Sapir, who was based at Yale University in New Haven from 1931, switched the focus of his academic interest from Germanic philology to the investigation of Amerindian languages under the influence of a senior colleague at Columbia University in New York, the anthropologist Franz Boas. He went on to elaborate upon a research hypothesis initiated by the latter, namely

---

[29] Readers are also referred here to the discussion of being bilingual and experiencing linguistic relativity in Wierzbicka (2013: 234–241).

that languages represent a classification of cultural experience to some extent. Edward Sapir also claimed that linguistic classifications and categories cohere into formally complete systems which may vary from language to language, and that organized linguistic classifications channel thought. As formally systematized abstractions from experience, linguistic categories guide the interpretation of experience or habitual thought, "that is, the habits of thought into which individual speakers routinely fall (what speakers actually think as opposed to what they are able to think)", as argued by Lucy (1985: 74).

Edward Sapir ranks among the most outstanding linguists of the 20th century because of his contributions on language, culture, and personality, amongst other topics. Darnell and Irvine (1997) present a detailed overview of the life of this eminent scientist, while Vermeulen (2009) presents a succinct survey of his academic accomplishments.

Edward Sapir's thoughts and ideas were elaborated upon by his student Benjamin Lee Whorf, who was a chemical engineer working for a fire insurance company before he started studying Hebrew, linguistics, and anthropology at Yale University, where he met Sapir for the first time in 1928. It may have been Whorf who coined the term "ethnolinguistics" for the discipline that is now widely referred to as anthropological linguistics (Lee 2009: 256). As somebody who was familiar with Einstein's relativity theory, Whorf referred to the cognitive phenomena described through the metaphor of the "linguistic relativity" principle, which Silverstein (1976: 25) characterizes as "the metaphorical idiom of the then beginning Atomatic age". In informal terms the concept implies that speakers of markedly different grammars are led towards different evaluations of externally similar acts of observation, and hence are not equivalent as observers but must arrive at somewhat different views of the world (Whorf, in the collection edited by John B. Carroll 1956: 221).

As pointed out by McWhorter (2014: 136):

> among the originators of the paradigm, such as Benjamin Lee Whorf, his mentor Edward Sapir, and pioneering anthropologist Franz Boas, the main motivation for their observations about language and thought was to demonstrate that peoples we thought of as primitive were anything but. That agenda was well intended and, in its time, urgent even among the intelligentsia.

Whorf's primary concern was with widescale cultural habits of thought that shape the thinking of both children and adults. He was not concerned primarily with perception, but rather with cognitive appropriation and conceptual content, as pointed out by Lucy (1992a: 82). His story of the "empty gasoline drum" (Whorf 1956: 135) shows that speakers of English may be led astray by the meaning of *empty* as 'null and void, negative, inert', i.e., no longer containing gasoline, but at the same time the drum may still contain highly explosive vapour, and so in this sense it is not "empty". This in turn may have disastrous consequences when somebody smokes a cigarette around such a drum. As an employee of a fire insurance company, Whorf was interested in reducing risks of explosions and fire, and experiences like this raised his interest in the question of how linguistic categories shape thought. Interestingly, space was one area where Benjamin Whorf apparently did not expect to find any relativity; instead, he assumed that "innate, probably biologically based, universals" (Foley 1997: 228) play a role. As should have become clear from the preceding chapter, research from the past few decades has proven Whorf wrong in this respect.

A number of scholars, on the other hand, have discredited Whorf's contributions on Amerindian languages. Malotki (1983) criticizes the latter's contribution on "Some verbal categories of Hopi", where it is claimed that this language contains no words, grammatical forms, or constructions directly related to time, and also that there is no objectification of Hopi time, that is, as a region, an extent, a quantity, of the subjective duration-feeling. As it turned out, Whorf's analysis of Hopi in this respect was flawed and misguided.

But in the same way in which the "great Eskimo vocabulary hoax" does not disqualify research in general on the rich lexical elaboration attested for culturally important domains in speech communities, it is useful to distinguish between Whorf's scientific contributions in this domain and the more fundamental question of the relationship between habitual thought and fashions of speaking, a research agenda initiated by his peers, Boas and Sapir.

The label "Sapir-Whorf hypothesis", sometimes used in the literature, is somewhat of a misnomer, as there was never any joint statement by these two scholars. Or, as Hill and Mannheim (1992: 386) phrase it: "just as the Holy Roman Empire was neither holy, nor Roman, nor an empire, the 'Sapir-Whorf hypothesis' is neither consistent with the writings of Sapir and Whorf, nor a hypothesis". Moreover, the exegesis of the "Sapir-Whorf Hypothesis" with a so-called "weak" version (assuming cognitive effects of linguistic categories) and a "strong" version (assuming a deterministic effect on cognition) was a fabrication apparently formulated by two opponents of relativism in the 1950s, Eric Lenneberg and Roger Brown; these scholars are best known for their work on colour terminology in (American) English and Zuni (as discussed in Chapter 3).

A range of publications have appeared over the past decades, trying to assess what exactly linguistic relativism encompassed for Sapir and Whorf. Foley (1997: 192–229) and Deutscher (2010: 129–156) present the probably most informed historical accounts of this line of thinking, starting with Wilhelm von Humboldt (1767–1835). One century later, Edward Sapir modified his own views on the structure of language through his interactions with Franz Boas and the latter's experience with different Amerindian languages. As a result of these newly required insights, Sapir developed his first ideas about the "relativity of concepts or, as it might be called, the relativity of the form of thought" (Deutscher 2010: 138–139).

Modern experiments involving cognitive tests carried out using methods that are widely accepted in the social sciences have reconfirmed the intuitively based hypotheses on linguistic relativity, as the following two sections should help to show. Nevertheless, the effects that have emerged from recent research on the question of whether a particular language is a lens through which we view the world are far more down to earth than Whorf apparently assumed. "They are to do with the habits of mind that language can instill on the ground level of thought: on memory, attention perception, and associations" (Deutscher 2010: 22), rather than "world view".

5.2 The name strategy

The lexical manifestation of linguistic influence on habitual thinking is referred to here as the "name strategy", after an experiment described by Kay and Kempton (1984) with speakers of Tarahumara, a language spoken in Mexico, and speakers of American English. According to the "name strategy" hypothesis, a speaker who is confronted with a task of classificatory judgment tends to take recourse to the *lexical* classification of the objects judged in his or her primary language. The language we speak best helps us to assess cognitive experiences in a manner that is meaningful to us (but not necessarily to others), not because we are forced to do so, but because it is convenient. As the introductory anecdote to the present chapter should help to illustrate, such assessments may lead to minor complications with bilingual or multilingual speakers, whose dominant language shifts.

Kay and Kempton (1984) report on interviews with speakers of Tarahumara and American English, who were asked to compare a total of 56 triads of colour chips with (what are referred to in English as) eight shades of blue and green (A to H), and to come up with similarity judgements. Whereas English makes a lexical distinction between *green* and *blue*, Tarahumara refers to these with one lexeme, *siyóname* 'grue'. According to Kay and Kempton (1984: 68), "[t]he Sapir-Whorf hypothesis (. . .) predicts that colors near the *green-blue* boundary will be subjectively pushed apart by English speakers precisely because English has the words *green* and *blue*, while Tarahumara speakers, lacking this lexical distinction, will show no comparable distortion".

Speakers of Tarahumara and English were asked to compare three colour chips at a time. The "name strategy", as a subjective cognitive strategy, predicts that for speakers of English – but not for speakers of Tarahumara – looking at triads of A, B, and C, the reasoning might be: A and B are referred to in my language as *green*, whereas C is called *blue*; therefore, I would say that C differs most from A and B.

Indeed, the presence of the blue-green lexical category boundary caused speakers of English participating in the experiment to exaggerate the subjective distances of colours close to this boundary ("C differs more from A and B, it is called *blue*, and A and B are more similar, both are called *green*"), whereas speakers of Tarahumara (as a language without a lexical blue-green contrast) did not show this distorting effect (Kay and Kempton 1984: 72).

In a second experiment, speakers of these two languages were shown two colour chips at the same time, for example A and B, and B and C, but never the three of them together. In this way, the speakers interviewed oriented themselves on the basis of their capacity to distinguish visual stimuli, and the structure of the task blocked the "Whorfian effect", so to speak.

Winawer et al. (2007) describe an experiment measuring speed of reaction carried out with speakers of Russian, a language with two basic colour terms for (what is called) *blue* in English, *siniy* 'dark blue' and *goluboy* 'light blue'. The average speed with which Russian speakers managed to press the button, whenever a new picture appeared on the screen, was shorter if the colours had different names in the language. In other words, shades with different names look more distinct to speakers.

Psycholinguistic experiments on colour are virtually non-existent with respect to the study of African languages so far. It would be interesting to carry out such tests with speakers of Tima and Sudanese Arabic, for example, in order to measure speed of reaction. Tima is a language with one term for what is referred to as *blue*, *green*, and *yellow* in English, namely -*hɛh* 'yeen' (see Section 3.1), whereas Sudanese Arabic makes a lexical distinction between these. Such experiments would shed light on the cognitive significance of such diverging systems, but no experiment of this type has been carried out so far for languages with the kind of system found in Tima.

It is important to keep in mind that specific concepts may exist in a speech community without a corresponding term in the language being used by the speakers, as shown by D'Andrade (1995) for Tzeltal; Section 3.2 on bionomenclature provides further details on this. The essential point is that the presence of a lexical distinction helps us in assessing cognitive experiences in a rapid manner. This is easy to understand, if one looks at a picture of the tropical forest in Amazon. Somebody growing up in this area, and speaking one of the regional languages, immediately has a rich bionomenclatural vocabulary at hand, which allows him or her to describe what can be seen in the picture, and also to recall afterwards what (s)he has seen. A speaker of English may only see "trees, shrubs, and plants". There is also empirical evidence that such relationships between labelled categories and cognition extend beyond the lexical domain, as argued next.

5.3 Grammar and cognition

Whereas developments in the linguistic sciences over the past decades at first glance appear to have cast doubt on any rampant "Whorfianism" in grammatical domains, instead emphasizing universal constraints on language structure, more recent results of cross-linguistic studies do in fact suggest a place for language influencing thought processes even in this domain. One of the most convincing studies in this respect is to be found in Lucy (1992a, 1992b), who reports on the effects of grammatical distinctions on habitual thinking by conducting cognitive tests with speakers of English and Yucatec, a Mayan language spoken in Mexico and Guatemala.[30] English makes a clearcut distinction between countable nouns (as in *banana/bananas*) and non-countable nouns (as in *beer*); while the former alternate between singular and plural, the latter do not. A language with numeral classifiers like Yucatec only makes a formal distinction between singular and plural with nouns referring to animate entities, not with nouns referring to inanimate entities.

When enumerating nouns in Yucatec, numeral classifiers are required (providing information about the shape and other perceptual qualities of the entity referred to), as in the following examples with the word for 'banana', *há'as*, which in English only refers to the fruit (examples taken from Lucy 1992a).

(45) 'un-c'íit   há'as   'one/a 1-dimens. banana (i.e., one banana fruit)'
      'un-wáal   há'as   'one/a 2-dimens. banana (i.e., one banana leaf)'
      'un-kúul   há'as   'one/a planted banana (i.e., one banana tree)'

Such non-alternating nouns in Yucatec primarily denote substance (for example 'banana-like substance') rather than some object, as in the corresponding English translation ('banana fruit/banana leaf/banana tree'). Speakers of English should therefore habitually attend to the number of various objects of reference more and for a wider array than Yucatec speakers should. Speakers of English are only capable of communicating useful information if they pay attention to the question

---

30 A related contribution is that of the Russian psychologist Vygotsky (Wygotski). In his 1934 monograph in Russian, which was translated into English and published in 1962, Vygotsky also examined the crucial role of language in mediating and developing thoughts.

of shape for nouns, as this determines whether one has to refer to, for example, *banana tree*, *banana leaf*, or *banana fruit*, including how many of them there are (because of the plural marking on nouns). In Yucatec, there is a fundamental orientation towards substance for nouns, as the separate grammatical category of numeral classifiers – if present – takes care of shape.

John Lucy points towards the importance of systematically attending to such local structural facts in languages and aiming at a formulation of an adequate formal-functional theory of lexical meaning. To this end he prepared various cognitive experiments in order to systematically assess three domains: observation (comparing triads), memorization (recall tests), and classification preferences among speakers of English and Yucatec Maya. The effects of grammatical distinctions on habitual thinking based on such tests with speakers of English and Yucatec are discussed in two monographs (Lucy 1992a, 1992b).

The first cognitive assessment task involved visual stimuli, whereby speakers were asked to describe what they saw in specific pictures. The picture stimuli represented scenes of everyday Yucatecan village life, such as a kitchen (or cooking area of a house), a field (where a forest is being cleared), or a truck (illustrated in Figure 11). With each triad the two alternative pictures differed from the original picture in the quantity (number or size) of one of the target objects. The same English and Yucatec speakers were asked to judge which of the alternate versions of each picture was most similar to its original. These tasks were "constructed to assess cognitive sensitivity to the *number* (i.e., one versus many) of various kinds of objects in the two language groups" (Lucy 1992b: 93).

The second type of cognitive test, the "recall test", involved a verbal report without the picture in view, "that is, on the basis of short-term memory" (Lucy 1992b: 97).

The third cognitive test, the "object triad sorting" test, involved the comparison, amongst other items, of a sheet of paper and a sheet of plastic, where one may observe that the material composition (substance) rather than the shape changes. If, on the other hand, one is comparing a strip of cloth and a shirt, the shape changes (compare Figure 12 below). The question then arises: Do English speakers attend more to the shape of objects, and Yucatec speakers more to the material composition of objects, as this reflects a fundamental distinction between the grammatical systems of these two languages?

While speakers of both English and Yucatec mentioned animals (as animate objects) more than implements and substances, there were also (statistically) significant differences between them, related to the divergent morphological structure of the two languages. Both the picture (verbal description) task and the recall task showed that "English speakers showed a greater sensitivity to changes in the number of an [a]nimal or [i]mplement than to changes in the number of a

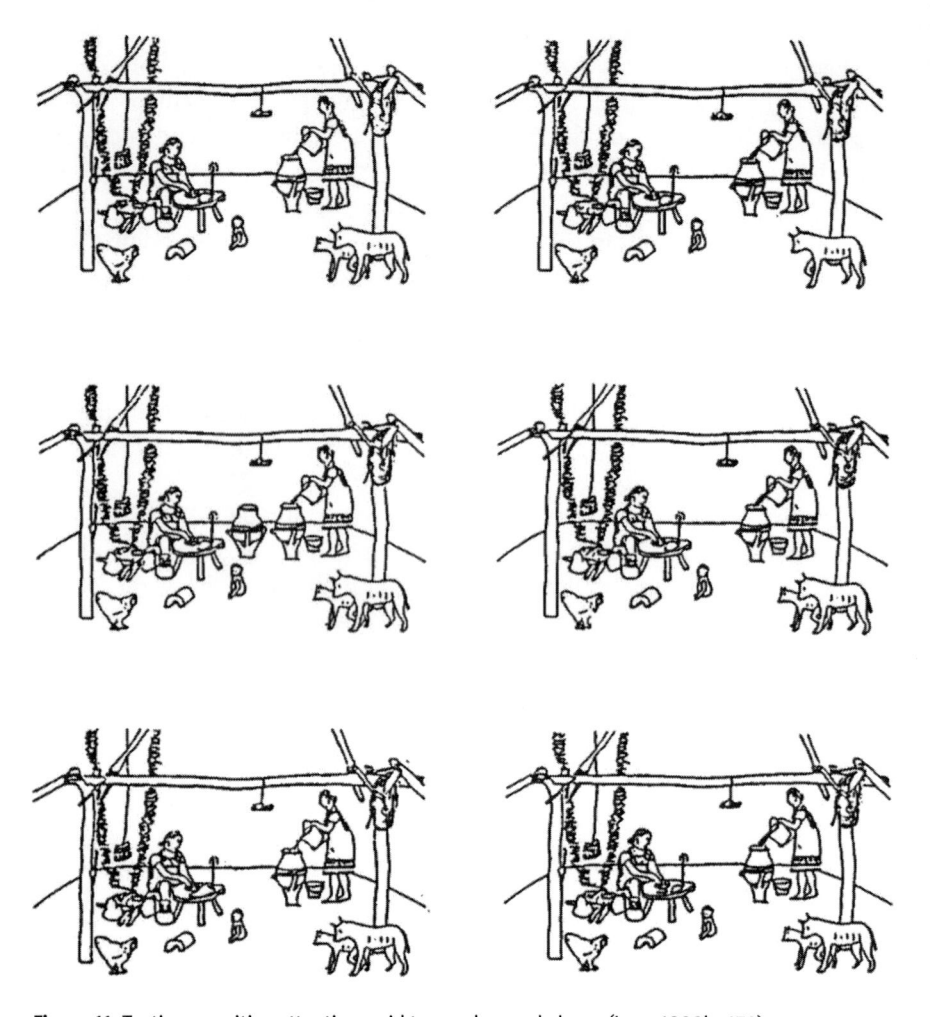

Figure 11: Testing cognitive attention paid to number and shape (Lucy 1992b: 170).

[s]ubstance, whereas Yucatec speakers showed a greater sensitivity to changes in the number of an [animal] than to changes in the number of an [i]mplement or a [s]ubstance" (Lucy 1992b: 135).

With respect to the third task, where speakers were asked to make judgments of similarity between triads of objects, shape was more significant than material as a basis for classification (thereby reflecting cognitive salience) for twelve speakers, and material was more significant for one speaker. For eight Yucatec speakers, on the other hand, material was more than significant, whereas for two speakers shape was (Lucy 1992b: 141).

Triad number	Triad objects		
	Original	Material alternate	Shape alternate
1.1	sheet of paper	sheet of plastic	book
1.2	strip of cloth	strip of paper	shirt
1.3	stick of wood	candle stick	block of wood
1.4	cardboard box	plastic box	piece of cardboard
1.5	length of vine	length of string	woven ring of vine
1.6	grains of vine	beans	tortilla
1.7	half gourd	half calabash	gourd with opening
1.8	ceramic bowl	metal bowl[a]	ceramic plate

[a] A plastic bowl was used with the English sample

Figure 12: Triad sets contrasting shape and material as a basis for classification (Lucy 1992b).

Languages differ essentially in what they *must* convey or say, and not in what they *may* convey or say, as Jakobson (1959: 236) has already observed. The obligatory inflection of nouns for number in a language like English forces speakers to pay attention to this dimension. As shown by the statistical results (Lucy 1992a: 89, 1992b: 144–45), English speakers attended relatively more to the shape of objects, in keeping with their ontological commitment to the primacy of "bodies", and Yucatec speakers attended relatively more to the material composition or substance of objects, again in accordance with the grammatical structure of this language.

There is at least one group of genetically-related languages in Africa with numeral classifier systems, namely the Cross-River language Kana and its closest relatives in Nigeria (Ikoro 1994; Dimmendaal 2011: 135–138). In Kana, there is no formal marking for number (plurality), nor is there a formal distinction between countable and mass nouns. One of a set of 16 numeral classifiers occurs whenever a noun is modified by a numeral. When a noun occurs in combination with a numeral, for example 'one', *zìì*, as in the following examples, an obligatory numeral classifier occurs between them. For most numeral classifiers there is a clear etymological source in the language. For example, *bēè* derives from *bēē* 'fruit', the tonal difference with the form below being due to the construction in which it occurs; *kpó* means 'heap', and *ápéé* means 'piece'.

(46) zìì bēè mṳ̀nṳ̀ 'one fist'
 zìì àkpò kpá 'one book'
 zìì àpéé zíá 'one piece/slice of yam'
 zìì ápéé mī́ī 'one splash of blood'

It would be interesting to repeat Lucy's experiment with speakers of Kana and speakers of historically conservative languages from the same language family (Cross-River), like KoHumono, which has a noun-class system expressing singular/plural alternations characteristic, in fact, of several branches of the larger family to which Cross-River belongs, Niger-Congo.

As a caveat, Lucy (1992b: 147) also points out that all exploratory or "experimental work is inherently problematic. One can never be sure to what extent the results stem from some unnoticed feature of the design itself rather than from some general disposition in the respondents". In order to make such studies comparable, researchers would of course have to pay attention to the question of whether the stimuli and instructions are identical (although this is a challenging task, especially if the classifiers or underlying shapes and the culturally familiar items differ, as pointed out by Svenja Völkel (personal communication)).

But no such experiment has been carried out to date; see also Lucy's directions for future research (Lucy 1992b: 158–161). Typological distinctions between languages with or without a count/mass distinction also raise the question of the extent to which the presence versus absence of a grammatical distinction between countable and mass nouns affects children's conceptual distinctions between "bodies" and "substances". On the basis on interviews with 2- and 2.5-year-old, i.e., "presyntactic" American children who were shown objects and non-solid substances, Soja, Carey, and Spelke (1991) conclude that children are endowed natively with these conceptual distinctions.

Imai and Gentner (1993) carried out tests with speakers of English and Japanese, the latter being another language which does not distinguish between objects or substances in its grammatical structure. While 90% of the English children taking part in the experiment showed a very strong object (shape or form) bias for simple objects in the "simple object trial" test, for example, the Japanese children in the experiment did not; the latter guessed 50% object, 50% substance. Imai and Gentner (1993: 183) conclude that the projection of word meanings is determined by an interplay between cognitive universals and language-specific factors.

Apart from number as a morphological category of words, gender has also been investigated in order to test to what extent formal grammatical distinctions between masculine and feminine nouns are linked to sex distinctions for humans. Boroditsky, Schmidt, and Phillips (2003) report on an experiment in which they asked speakers of Spanish and German to rate similarities between pictures of people and of objects (the names of which had opposite grammatical genders in the two languages) by using specific adjectives. According to the authors, both groups associated female properties more with grammatically feminine inanimate nouns and male properties more with grammatically masculine inanimate nouns. For example, for the masculine (inanimate) noun *der Schlüssel* 'key' in German, speakers tended to come up with adjectives like *hard, heavy, jagged* (in English, as the experiment was carried out in English); Spanish speakers on the other hand tended to associate the feminine (inanimate) noun for 'key', *la llave*, with adjectives like *lovely, shiny*, or *little*.

Mickan, Schiefke, and Stefanowitsch (2014) repeated this experiment with speakers of German and Spanish but apparently failed to replicate the above-mentioned results emerging from the "gender-as-sex" hypothesis. The authors using a word association task (asking speakers to write down the first three adjectives (in German or Spanish) that came to mind when thinking about the objects referred to by a specific word). In a subsequent lexical decision task, other speakers were asked to categorize the adjectives emerging from the first experiement as "female" or "male" if possible. Based on two statistical methods, Mickan, Schiefke, and Stefanowitsch (2014: 44) conclude that responses to grammatically masculine nouns on average have slightly more male ratings than responses to grammatically feminine nouns in both languages; however, the differences are very small and statistically non-significant. For further details, including on an additional experiment using response time, readers are referred to the actual article.

As Aikhenvald (2016: 127) points out in her discussion of such experiments regarding the question of whether linguistic gender affects cognition: "One should keep in mind that all such experiments are artificial – how many times in real life do speakers of any language have to bother with female or male names assigned to bridges and apples? They may, however, point towards an interesting direction: that some people may attribute 'male' and 'female' labels to inanimate objects in agreement with their Linguistic Gender assignment".

Feminine gender in Hamar (southern Ethiopia), for example, is associated with the importance of an object, and its larger size, whereas masculine gender in this language is associated with small size (Petrollino 2016: 77–92 for a detailed discussion). In Oromo, feminine gender is associated with something cute or affectionate, whereas the masculine linguistic gender has pejorative connotations, as shown in the following examples from Clamons (1993: 276–278).

(47) waan-ti   tun   jiidh-tuu
     thing-F.SU.TOPIC this:F wet-F
     'This (cute little) thing is wet'

(48) waan-ix   un   jiidh-aa
     thing-M.SU.TOPIC this:M wet-M
     'This (nasty) thing is wet'

Aikhenvald (2016: 99–119) quotes a range of such sources on grammatical gender reversal in languages across the world and corresponding negative or positive associations with men and women as social constructs, for example in order to express pejorative and insulting readings, endearment, or solidarity. What is more, one and the same expression may be insulting or endearing, depending on the relative age of the people and their social relationships; again, contextualization cues are crucial.

Clearly, grammatical gender systems in languages are not all of the same kind. The extent to which speakers consciously play around with gender depends on the nature of the gender system, and the degree to which the latter has drifted away from an original sex-based system. In languages where a formal (grammaticalized) system with obligatory marking of gender without any obvious link to natural sex, where consequently semantic transparency has disappeared, no such overt system actively used by speakers may be expected.

Dixon (2015: 43) points towards the importance of the perspective of speakers in this respect, and criticizes the interpretation of Lakoff (1987) in *Women, Fire and Dangerous Things: What Categories Reveal about the Mind*. The title of this monograph was inspired by the gender system of Dyirbal, a subsequently extinct language of northeastern Australia, as described by Dixon (1972: 306–311) and Dixon (1982: 159–183).

In ordinary speech in Dyirbal, a noun is preceded by one of four gender markers: *bayi*, *balan*, *balam*, or *bala*. According to Lakoff (1987: 92–96), *bayi* is associated with human males, *balan* with human females, and *balam* with non-flesh food as "central" members, and *bala* with everything not in the other classes. The title of Geogre Lakoff's influential book (which has been cited more than 32,000 times, according to Google Scholar) derives from the fact that women and fire, for example, both belong to the *balan* gender class, but also some snakes, most birds, and anything connected with water or fire. According to Lakoff (1987: 95), these grammatical facts can be explained by taking "typical" members as a basis, and linking other members (nouns) through "category chaining". Hence, the word for *sun* belongs to the *balan* gender class, because the sun is the wife of the moon in Dyirbal myth. And the hairy mary grub belongs to the same grammatical gender class because its sting feels like sunburn, which connects it with the sun. However, the notion of harmfulness in association with the *balan* gender class relates to a subset having an important property which was often – but not exclusively – 'harmfulness'. However, Dixon (2015: 43) criticizes authors putting forward speculative views which go against what speakers have said.

> I was explicitly told there was no implication that, because (say) women and certain harmful things are assigned to the same gender, there is any cultural association between

them (. . .) Lakoff is free to speculate, but when his speculations go against cultural beliefs, these speculations must be regarded as harmful. (Dixon 2015: 43)

Linguists differ on the question of whether one treats sex-based gender systems and noun-class systems as instances of "gender", i.e., on a par (contrasting with numeral-classifier systems of the type described for Yucatec or Kana above). Barasa and Dimmendaal (to appear) discuss the advantages and disadvantages of such dichotomies. In languages with noun classes of the type illustrated below, speakers sometimes play around with prototypical meanings of sex-based gender markers or noun classes in order to express "evaluative morphology". For noun classes, this involves modifying the structure of words expressing notions such as diminution (reduction in size or importance), augmentation (increase in size or value), contempt, or endearment. Thus, in languages with noun classes speakers sometimes create honorific as well as pejorative meanings through the substitution of these markers, as in the Zambian language (Chi)Bemba (Irvine 2009: 159). For example, a class 2 prefix otherwise used for plural nouns usually referring to human beings (with class 1 as the corresponding singular class prefix primarily for human nouns) may be used to express respect. The examples are adapted from Irvine (2009: 159, with noun class numbers added by the present author):

(49) aba-kaši '(respectable) wife' (honorific; class 2)
      umu-kaši 'derespectful; class 1))
      aka-kaši '(insignificant) wife' (insult; class 12)'
      iči-kaši '(gross) wife' (insult; class 7)'
      ili-kaši '(egregious [?]) wife' (a little derogatory; class 5)

The (presumed) semantic basis of noun classes in the language family to which (Chi)Bemba belongs, Bantu, has been subject to a lot of speculation in various publications, as shown by Palmer (1996: 126–141). However, evaluative morphology, as reflected in paradigmatic oppositions based on the differential use of noun-class prefixes, as in the Chi(Bemba) examples above, provides more solid empirical evidence for the semantic perspectives of speakers. Such alternations show that speakers are aware of semantic networks involving features such as singularity/plurality, diminutive/augmentative, animate/inanimate, honorific / pejorative, and the like. For additional examples illustrating the role played by gender (including the category of noun class systems) in evaluative morphology, the reader is referred to Di Garbo and Agbetsoamedo (2018).

Other grammatical domains have also been subject to speculation concerning their potential influence on cognition. McWhorter (2014: 94–101) discusses a thesis put forward by the economist Keith Chen (Chen 2013), that in countries with languages that do not mark future tense, the absence of such tense marking makes people pay *more* attention to futurity, and thereby to saving money or to preventative health practices. According to Chen (2013), future-marking languages cluster among the countries with lower saving rates. McWhorter (2014: 96) raises the rhetorical question of whether the statistics show the reality. "Sure – but only if the linguistic analysis is solid. And it happens not to be". This becomes clear, for example, from a comparison of two Slavic languages. According to the statistics, Czechs are good savers, while Poles are bad ones, and Slovaks are somewhere in between", i.e., they are spread across the grid. None of the three languages, however, has grammatical future marking.

Perspectives on time already fascinated Benjamin Whorf. More recently, Yu (1998) raised the question of whether the different metaphorical ways of expressing time in English and Mandarin Chinese are significant from a cognitive point of view. Time may be projected metaphorically along a front-back axis in the latter language, for example *qián* 'front' and *hòu* 'back', similar to English, where the bad past lies behind a person who may still have a bright future ahead. But the temporal dimension may also be expressed by means of the up-down axis, with earlier events being *shàng* 'up' and later events being *xià* 'down' (Yu 1998: 10). See also Boroditsky (2001) for similar conclusions based on various psycholinguistic experiments.

For further insightful discussions on modern cognitive experiments and their potential drawbacks, including the ecological validity and limits of such empirical methods, the reader is also referred to the overview in Senft (2012).

In his monograph *The Language Hoax: The World Looks the Same in Any Language*, McWhorter (2014) criticizes those who bring in "world view" in discussing the experiments described in Lucy (1992a, 1992b), a point well made, according to the present author:

> The question is what is meant by thought. Man seeks to read experiments like these as shedding light on larger issues: real life, the human condition. But what could that really mean from data of this sort? A difference in thought must be of a certain magnitude before it qualifies realistically as a distinct "world view". (McWhorter 2014: 24)

Indeed, "world view" implies deeply rooted philosophical principles, and the experiments so far certainly do not justify such far-reaching conclusions concerning cognitive effects.

Linguistic relativism in the present author's interpretation of the concept is more about dissecting day-to-day cognitive experiences, in particular related to perception, and the role played by language in this process, rather than "world views". Whereas research is notably complex (and controversial) in the second (i.e., the grammatical) domain, this complexity is still more obvious in the third domain, when it comes to the cultural interpretation of speech acts, as argued in Chapter 10.

Of course, we are capable of thinking or communicating without using (spoken) language, as case studies of language-less adults confirm. Schaller (1991) discusses the case of the deaf man Ildefonso, who was able to converse with the author after having been taught sign language. The point is that most of us do use verbal communication, and where this option is available to an individual it is clearly interconnected with a theory of mind.

5.4 On WEIRD people and cognitive tests

The epigraph at the beginning of this chapter, referring to Lucy (1992a: 2) and his sharp observation that "reflexivity" is a general problem in the social sciences, has not lost its relevance three decades later, as the following discussion should help to illustrate.

Cognitive experiments are probably best known traditionally from psychology (as the involvement of cognitive linguists is of more recent origin). Social scientists have assumed for too long that their methods are objective, rather than reflecting cultural biases, as argued by Henrich, Heine, and Norenzayan (2010) in their survey of psychological tests. These authors introduce the concept of WEIRD people, i.e., those from Western, Educated, Industrialized, Rich and Democratic societies, and point out (p. 1) that they are "among the least representative populations one could find among humans". In spite of this, samplings from a single sub-population from such societies figure prominently in many psychological tests on cognitive salience, and authors (often implicitly) assume that their findings are universally valid.

The famed Müller-Lyer illusion, first described by the psychiatrist and sociologist Franz Carl Müller-Lyer in 1889, is one poignant example of so-called illusions in visual perception, based on three stylized arrows (Figure 13).[31]

Segall, Campbell, and Herskovits (1966) report on an experiment carried out with speakers from 16 societies, including 14 small-scale societies, among them San foragers from southern Africa. Most subjects from industrialized societies, in this case American undergraduates, perceive the second line segment forming the shaft of the arrow with two tails as longer than that forming the shaft of the first arrow with two heads. In actual fact all the shafts of the arrows are of the same length, and speakers of San languages apparently were not affected by the

---

[31] See [https://commons.wikimedia.org/w/index.php?curid=1792612] (accessed 13 January 2021).

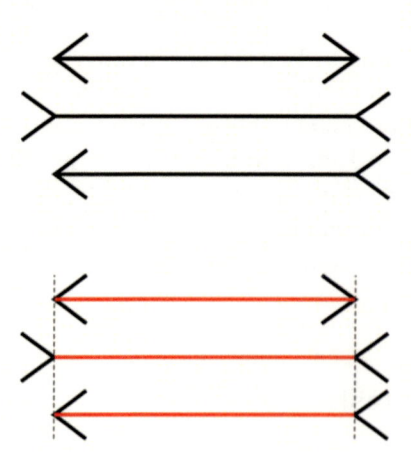

Figure 13: The Müller-Lyer illusion.

illusion. Henrich, Heine, and Norenzayan (2010: 4) consequently conclude that from a cognitive point of view "the visual system ontogenetically adapts to the presence of recurrent features in the local visual environment" of speakers.

Apart from visual perception, Henrich, Heine, and Norenzayan (2010: 7) also address claims on folk-biological reasoning. More specifically, they provide a natural explanation of why folk genera or generic species ('starling' and 'crow', or 'oak' and 'beech') are at the basic level and are the first learned by children in non-industrialized small-scale societies, whereas for children of (what the authors call) WEIRD parents, life-form taxa like 'bird' or 'tree' are more salient. Deficient input probably underpins the fact that children living in a culturally and experientially impoverished environment, in contrast to those of small-scale societies, tend to answer questions like 'what's that?' by 'that's a tree', rather than being more specific and more informative by answering 'that's a maple', for example.

The authors conclude that "we need to be less cavalier in addressing questions of *human* nature on the basis of data drawn from this particularly thin, and rather unusual, slice of humanity from the West (Henrich, Heine, and Norenzayan 2010: 1).

The discussion of spatial orientation in Chapter 4 teaches us a similar lesson: for quite some time spatial descriptions and orientation were regarded as being universally egocentric; and as argued in Chapter 3 on colour, the use of the Munsell colour chart also has its problems. Clearly, the way in which colour terms are or are not used says absolutely nothing about people's general cognitive ability to generate linguistic expressions for colours. This may be further illustrated with material from the widely quoted case of the Dani language of West Papua. In the early Berlin and Kay framework, the investigation of colour in this language by Rosch (1972a,

1972b) played an important role, as Dani is assumed to represent an "evolutionary early system" with only two basic colours, 'white' (WHITE) and 'black' (BLACK).

Rosch (1972a, 1972b) shows that the Dani terms *mili* and *mola* are not brightness terms with foci in 'black' and 'white', but categories best classified as 'dark-cool' and 'light-warm'; *mili* refers to 'dark, dull, dark-cool', and also 'bad'; *mola* refers to 'light, bright, light-warm', and also 'good'. These terms, however, comprise but a small subset of the resources of the Dani speech community in talking about concepts of colour. They may use expressions such as *gut*, the name for 'white heron', also used to describe albinos; *jagik*, 'cockatoes', a term also used for a white clay; *bimitet*, referring to 'mountain dove' or the rusty colour of some pigs; and *getega*, when referring to the bluish 'adze stone' as well as to a greenish feature.

In her book *The Invention of Basic Color Terms*, Saunders (1992) reports on her research among Kwakiutl (Kwa'kwala) speakers in Canada. While the collection of colour names for plants, animals, beads, and sequins was unproblematic, the introduction of the Munsell colour chart at the end of each interview caused discomfort, anxiety, and agitation among her language helpers. Apparently, all but one person was reluctant to continue, although there was no total refusal to cooperate (Saunders 1992: 147). In line with the present author's experience, Saunders came to realize that the meaning of a term cannot be attained or understood by asking speakers to provide a labelling response to some colour stimulus. Rather, it should involve all of the culturally meaningful relationships it activates.

This constellation may also be interpreted as a failure in the strict validation of the *basicness* of colour terms, at least for some speech communities, or, as Saunders (1992) has formulated it, in the invention of the notion of "Basic Color Terms". As should be clear from the discussion above, there is sometimes not only an imminent danger of subjectivism in our scientific endeavours, but ethnocentrism has already had its effects on the so-called objective investigation of different domains of interest to cognitive scientists.

This cultural myopia, or ethnocentrism, is also reflected, unfortunately, in the scholarly work of one of the most influential cognitive psychologists of our times, Steven Pinker, who has been propagating the primary role played by nature, rather than nurture, for example in *The Stuff of Thought* (Pinker 2007). Claiming that any remaining effects of language on thought are mundane, unsexy, boring, or even trivial ignores the serious effect such thoughts have had in scientific discussions. As shown in the discussion of so-called "WEIRD" people above, there is ample evidence that the perceptual categories of Western researchers have systematically caused them to misperceive or to fail to perceive entirely an element that is meaningful in another speech community.

In an earlier monograph, *The Language Instinct*, Pinker (1994: 32) claims that "[a]ll languages have words for 'water' and 'foot' because all people need to refer to water and feet". Again, the question arises: What causes authors like Stephen Pinker to make such claims? Those of us who do believe that our habitual thinking tends to be influenced by the language(s) we speak best would tend to conclude that English moulded his cognitive system and thereby his conceptualizations of reality. Speakers of different African languages (and people from other parts of the world) would immediately object and point out that in their language there is no separate word for 'foot'. In the East African language of wider communication Swahili, for example, the word *mkono* includes 'arm' as well as 'hand' (the same is true in modern spoken Hebrew, to mention but one other language); only for the digits is there a separate word in Swahili (*vidole*, singular: *kidole*).

Wierzbicka (2013) arrives at similar conclusions when criticizing Pinker (2007) for his strong claims about human nature: "The irony is that Pinker himself is arguably an example of someone whose thinking appears to be strongly influenced by his native language (English) – for example, when he interprets human evolution through the prism of the modern English concepts 'violence' and 'cooperation' (...), or when he characterizes the concept of 'story' – a highly culture-specific conceptual artifact of English (...) as a human universal and a product of evolutionary adaptation". Indeed, it seems that being multilingual – or at least bilingual – helps researchers to understand the potential impact of linguistic relativism.

The more general claim made by McWhorter (2014: 56) that languages do not develop via people applying their ingenuity or being creative, and that instead they develop via step-by-step driftings that operate below the level of consciousness, is at least partly wrong. While there is indeed "the invisible hand" of the language users, which results in languages drifting in specific directions (Keller 1994), there is also conscious language manipulation. One only has to think of the numerous cases of manipulated languages across the world at different points in time; see Storch (2011) for a detailed survey. The creation of urban (youth) languages in different African metropoles, discussed in considerable detail in Mc Laughlin (2009) and Nassenstein and Hollington (2015), shows that such language manipulation strategies are still alive and kicking in modern times.

McWhorter (2014: xiv) warns against the "Whorfian meme in public discussion (...). Crucially, a connection between language and thought does exist. The problem is how that connection has percolated into public discussion".[32] Of course, one can only sympathize with such statements. However, in his sharp and witty downgrading of linguistic relativity, McWhorter (2014: 50) also wonders

---

[32] The term "meme" was coined by the evolutionary biologist Richard Dawkins in his monograph *The Selfish Gene* (1976) as a shortening of "mimeme", expressing a unit of cultural imitation or replication (by analogy with "gene" in evolutionary biology).

whether "[i]t's all about the bubbles", and therefore uninteresting and trivial. The preceding discussion hopefully makes clear that it is not all about uninteresting trivialities. Moreover, his remark about the triviality of differences in reaction time, for example with respect to the colour discrimination tests described by Winawer et al. (2007) as "that study of blueness in Russian" (p. 25), like ". . .[i]t was – wait for it – 124 milliseconds!" (p. 14) ignores the important fact that this is one of the valued standard methods in modern psycholinguistics (along with eye tracking) for cognitive tests measuring the perception of visual or auditory information. See for example the experiment described in McDonough, Choi, and Mandler (2003) in the introduction to this chapter, and numerous other experiments in pycholinguistics. Indeed, they do not reveal anything about "world view", but they do reveal important properties about online accessing of cognitive systems programmed in the human mind and apparently using language as a channel.

Western scientific practices in which the knowing, non-situated "ego" peeks out at a world of objects and produces supposedly objective knowledge of those objects have been strongly criticized by the sociologist Ramón Grosfoguel in a number of publications (for example Grosfoguel 2007). This knowing observer is assumed to be able to know the world without being part of that world and (s)he is able to produce knowledge that is supposed to be universal and independent of context, rather than accepting that understanding tends to be situated. Grosfoguel focuses on post-colonial studies and political-economy paradigms in his academic writing.

Similar claims have been made by historians like Joseph-Achille Mbembe. According to Mbembe (2016: 33), this hegemonic tradition actively represses anything that is actually articulated, thought, and envisioned from outside of these frames. As the discussion and analysis of lexical-semantic fields above should have shown, the assumption that one can produce knowledge that is universal, independent of context, and timeless has also been around among anthropologists and linguists, who apparently forget that concepts and categorizations may also be the result of an understanding resulting from the language or languages the researcher speaks best. In this sense, the effects of European colonialism did not cease with the processes of decolonization and national independence of the 19th and 20th centuries, as they still persist in ways of thinking, or in epistemology more generally, as argued by Mbembe (2016).

6 Onomastics

When the great German poet Johann-Wolfgang von Goethe (1749–1832), himself a close friend of one of the pioneers of anthropological linguistics, Wilhelm von Humboldt, wrote his Magnum Opus *Faust*, the key figure in the play, Faust, uttered the phrase "Name ist Schall und Rauch [name is sound and smoke]", or 'What's in a name?' (in a free translation).

Personal names in the German (and more generally, in the European) tradition of those days consisted primarily of a conglomeration of Germanic, Greek, Latin, and Hebrew conventions. The poet's first name, *Johan*, for example, is a shortened form of the Hebrew name *Yəhôḥānān* meaning 'God is gracious', whereas his second name, *Wolfgang*, consists of the Germanic root for 'wolf' and the Old High German root *ganc*, 'move'. Knowledge among many people in Europe about the etymology of such Germanic first names apparently gradually vanished from the late Middle Ages onwards, when such names were often replaced by names emerging from a Christian tradition.

It was common in feudal Europe during the Middle Ages to add an epithet to a first name, particularly among the nobility (and clergy), as with *Alfonso X the Wise*, king of Castile, or *Charles the Bald*, emperor of the Franks. Outside these circles, it became common in cities to add an epithet or other attributive word or phrase to a name (later these came to function as surnames), probably from the 12th century onwards in Germany and somewhat later in the Lower Countries (now Belgium and the Netherlands), Apart from prestige, being able to distinguish between individuals with the same first name in a growing network of people living in urban areas was another motivation for the extension of names.

Surnames were based on the local or regional origin of a person in many parts of Europe, as with the ingenious Renaissance polymath *Leonardo da Vinci* (from Vinci, his birthplace in Italy; 1452–1519). His full name was *Leonardo di ser Piero da Vinci* 'Leonardo [son] of sir Piero da Vinci'. This alternative tradition, found across Europe, involves the use of a patronymicon for males, and is still used as such for example in Iceland, where the first name of the father is followed by *-son* 'son', as with the linguist *Stefán Einarsson*; the use of a matronymicon *-dottir*, 'daughter', is still found with females, as with the name of the linguist *Sigríður Sigurjónsdóttir*.

Historically, surnames in Europe evolved as a way of sorting people into groups by occupation, place of origin, clan affiliation, patronage, parentage, adoption, or physical characteristics. It was not until the early 19th century, during the Napoleonic era, that the use of surnames and their registration in a Code Civil became obligatory (in 1811) in the areas in Europe occupied by this French emperor (to which Iceland did not belong).

Even if the associated semantic content, in particular of first names, has vanished for many people in the Euro-American world, naming is still an instance of cultural or social indexicality, i.e., the expression of a relationship between some sign (token) and a putative object. This relationship may be one expressing co-presence or contiguity. Thus, somebody with a first name *Gerrit*, like the present author, is likely to be over 50 (as the name is no longer popular), with a more-than-chance frequency of originating from the eastern or northern parts of the Netherlands and adjacent areas across the former border with Germany.

The surname *Dimmendaal* goes back to the name of a farmhouse which still exists in a part of the Netherlands known in Dutch as the *Achterhoek* 'backcorner'. The first name *Gerrit* goes back to a Frisian and Lower-Saxon name *Gerhard* (compare this with the English variant *Gerald*), which etymologically derives from *ger-* 'spear' plus *harti* 'strong, tough', something the author's parents were not aware of; the present author was actually named after one of his uncles. In the area where the present author comes from, it also used to be customary to receive another first name (as a nickname) as well as a last name, based on the name of the farm or courtyard where one grew up (which is different from the farm where the first Dimmendaals grew up).

It now seems that in the global village surnames are disappearing again and tend to be treated as superfluous information, at least in the (social) media. Insiders appear to know which "Julia" from Springfield is calling in on a live show on TV, or which "Robert" is calling in on a radio programme, in order to express their opinion. After all, there are only a few hundred thousand of them.

How does all of this compare to naming traditions found on the African continent and in other parts of the world? The present chapter discusses aspects of onomastics, a term referring to the investigation of proper names, of which personal names are a part. In the following, the domain of personal names, which is also known as anthroponomy, is discussed first (Section 6.1), followed by observations on toponymy in an African context (6.2). The final section (6.3), on avoidance and endearment strategies, serves as a transition to the next chapter on language use, which focuses more specifically on conventionalized speech.

6.1 Anthroponymy

The study of personal names has been a popular topic in African studies, as already suggested by the following small selection of studies (Akkinaso 1980 and Oduyoye 1972 on Yoruba names; Arensen 1988 on Murle name; Egblewogbe 1984 on Ewe names; Essien 1997 on Ibibio names; Ferry 1977 on Bassari names; Lienhardt 1988 on Dinka names; Neethling and Neethling 2005 on Xhosa names;

Ntahombaye 1983 on Kirundi names; Suzman 1994 and Turner 2000 on Zulu names; Ubahakwe 1981 on Igbo names), as well as more general monographs (Asante 1995, Kimenyi 1989, Madubuike 1976, Obeng 2001, Tierou 1977, to mention but a few).[33] A selection of these and others are discussed below, in order to illustrate different naming traditions, including vanishing traditions and the effects of globalization.

Blount (1993) investigates names in Luo, a language spoken in western Kenya as well as in neighbouring zones of Tanzania and Uganda, and arrives at four categories or types: 1. names referring to circumstances of birth; 2. nicknames; 3. western names; 4. family/clan names. Names reflecting circumstances of birth, such as the time of the day, a specific event, or the location where the birth occurred, reflecting a widespread practice across the continent (and in other parts of the world), which Agbedor and Johnson (2005: 162) call the "Home Context Principle". Among the approximately 200 Luo names collected by the Blount, there are names like *Okoth* 'rain', which may be given to somebody who was born when it was raining, as for the late (*Duncan*) *Okoth Okombo*, a linguist from the Luo area in Kenya.

Family or clan names in Luo tend to come from the names of ancestors who acquired the names during their lifetimes. Hence, a Luo name such as *Oduor* 'mid-day' may serve referentially, to point to or identify the individual so-named, it may allow the assignment of contextualizing knowledge about time of day or birth, but it may also be an inherited family/clan name representing the birth, or nickname of an ancestor who bore it during his lifetime. Alternatively, it may be the family or clan name that an individual inherited when he was born and that he carried throughout his life (Blount 1993: 125).

Nicknames in Luo are either self-ascribed or assigned by others (Blount 1993: 135), and are used by intimates, serving to establish and strengthen bonds between individuals, as with the Kenyan politician *Tom Mboya* (1930–1969), whose nickname *Mboya* 'big stomach' was also used as a surname, and whose first name reflects influence from the language of the former colonizer Great Britain.

As is common across Africa and elsewhere in the world, names may also be selected (within the same "Home Context Principle") on the basis of specific events or circumstances predating the birth, for example when a couple has remained childless for a long period, or if a child is born at a time when a close relative in the homestead has passed away. The middle name of the linguist George Bureng Nyombe indicates that he was ill when he was a baby. The

---

[33] Several journals are dedicated essentially to this topic, for example *The Journal of Onomastics*; journals like *Sociolinguistic Studies* frequently publish articles on naming strategies as well.

name *Bʊrɛŋ* in Bari, a language of South Sudan, is one of a range of first names whose meaning is described by Spagnolo (1933: 443–448) in his Bari grammar. The examples in Table 14 illustrate more of the commonly found principles in Bari name giving, based on the existence of younger or older brothers or sisters, or of a twin brother or sister.

Table 14: Bari names (Spagnolo 1933).

	FIRST-BORN CHILDREN	
Kʊlaŋ	passing over, first, chief	(Male)
Köjijak	kraal queen	(Female)
	SUBSEQUENT CHILDREN	
Kɔsɛ	born after two sisters	(Male)
Dwökiden	born after two brothers	(Female)
	TWINS	
Bɔjɔ	despiser of her twin sister (name of elder)	(Two females)
Joré	enough, full (name of younger)	
Ulaŋ	a passerine bird (name of elder)	(Two males)
Lɔdʊ'	coming after (name of younger)	

Among Bari speakers, the firstborn is considered to be the older one with twins, whereas among Ewe speakers it is the lastborn which is considered to be the older one (coming behind the younger one, who goes in front; Agbedor and Johnson 2005).

Sagna and Bassène (2016) investigated more than 1000 proper names in Eegimaa, a language of southern Senegal, involving (what the authors call) both "meaningless" and "meaningful" names. "Meaningless" names are borrowed from English (like *Elizabeth*) or Arabic (like *Ibrahima*), and reflect the religious affiliation of the name givers or name bearers (Sagna and Bassène 2016: 45). In this respect, such names may still of course be seen as meaningful, because they are indexical of the parents' (or more generally, the relatives') stance, reflecting cultural influence from a globalizing world. But the so-called "meaningful" names described by the authors reflect naming strategies of the type discussed for Luo or Bari above, based on the bearer's physique, behaviour, or the circumstances prevailing at the time the child was born, including unfavourable ones. In Eegimaa, for example, a child may be called *Akkobeçet* (lit. 'he waits for death'). Agbedor and Johnson (2005) refer to this naming strategy as the "Philosophical Principle". Parents take recourse to this strategy with respect to newborns when they have been affected by high rates of child mortality. Names like *Kɔkɔli* 'garbage' or *Akagã* 'vulture' are further examples of this principle in Eegimaa.

Death prevention names of the type found in Eegimaa appear to be common across the continent, given their widespread distribution. Mietzner (2016: 191–202) presents a lucid account of naming and renaming strategies among the Cherang'any. In this speech community in western Kenya, death prevention names refer to "the death or deviating character of a child during birth and also during the first years of the child's life (. . .) because evil spirits are said to be the cause of the deviation from the norm, and cleansing ceremonies are held in order to prevent future attacks and protect the child from evil spirits" (Mietzner 2016: 197). The prefixes *che(p)-* and *ki(p)-* in the following examples refer to feminine and masculine names, respectively.[34]

(50) Chemoso / Kimoso   mósò 'baboon'
      Chepng'etuny / Kipng'etuny ŋétùiɲ 'lion'

Renaming ceremonies as death prevention strategies among the Cherang'any may be held either before a child is born, or for a child between the ages of three and fourteen, for example "when a child has lost its siblings due to sickness or accidents or for other reasons which are regarded as having been caused by an evil spirit, or when the child itself is always sick or behaves in a way that deviates from the social norm, such as stealing, lying or incessant fighting" (Mietzner 2016: 198).

Death prevention strategies have been reported for such geographically distant communities as the Luba (Democratic Republic of the Congo), Hausa (Nigeria and Niger), or Bambara (in Mali), and of course they are also attested in Asia and the Americas. But as Obeng (2001: 112) points out, "[i]n Akan society, it is rare to find anybody under forty years of age with a survival name. This most probably suggests that such names are no longer given in view of the fact that there is improved medical care and also people no longer believe in the potency of such names".

Personal names in Akan (Ghana) are also to be interpreted as "iconic representations of composite social variables that indexicalize and relate to the name and the person. They include sex, hierarchy in birth, circumstances surrounding the birth, the person's structure, power, status, etc." (Agyekum 2006: 209). A common strategy among the Akan as well as in neighbouring speech communi-

---

[34] In her autobiographical account of fieldwork among the neighbouring Tugen, the anthropologist Heike Behrend (2020) appears to have misinterpreted this death prevention naming strategy, which was also applied to her by calling her *Monkey*, not as an instance of "othering" and "alterity", but rather as a sign of ultimate concern and affection for an ethnographer interested in documenting their culture.

ties is to name children after the day they were born. Table 15 from Agyekum 2006: 214) presents this temporal deixis.

Table 15: Akan days and male and female birthday names (Agyekum 2006).

DAY NAME		MALE NAMES		FEMALE NAMES	
English	Akan	Twi	Fante	Twi	Fante
Sunday	Kwasiada	Kwasi	Kwesi	Akosua	Akosua/Esi
Monday	Ɛdwoada	Kwadwo	Kojo/Jojo	Adwoa	Adwoa
Tuesday	Ɛbenada	Kwabena	Kobina/Ebo/ Kwamena	Abenaa	Abenaa/Araba
Wednesday	Wukuada	Kwaku	Kweku/Kuuku	Akua	Ekua/Kuukua
Thursday	Yawoada	Yao	Ekow	Yaa	Aba
Friday	Efiada	Kofi	Kofi/ Fiifi/Fi	Afua	Efua/Efe
Saturday	Memeneda	Kwame	Kwame/Kwamina/Ato	Ama	Ama

Agyekum (2006: 217) describes the naming ceremony for his daughter as follows:

> Baby, you are welcome to this world. Have a longer stay, just do not come and exhibit yourself and return. Your mothers and fathers have assembled here today to give you a name. The name we are giving to you is Afua Ataa Boakyewaa Agyekum. You are named Afua because that is the day your soul decided to enter into this world. We are naming you after your grandmother Afua Ataa. Your grandparent is Ataa because she was born a twin. Her real name is Boakyewaa the feminine form of Boakye. Remember that your grandmother is a twin and therefore a deity and sacred figure that must be kept hallowed. In view of this, come and put up a good moral behaviour. Again we are attaching your father's name Agyekum to your name. Follow the footsteps of your father and come and study hard. When we say water, let it be water, when we say drink let it be drink [drunk]. (Agyekum 2006: 217)

A further variable, apart from names indicating whether one has older brothers or sisters, the day of the week on which a child is born, or death prevention names, is personal names indicating how many older brothers or sisters a person has. Such systems are attested in Tima (Sudan, as illustrated in Table 16); examples from Schneider-Blum (2013b):

Table 16: Female names in Tima.

Àká	'first born female'
Ìtʌ̀ŋ	'second born female'
Cɛ́cɛ̀ŋ	'third born female'
Cìŋʌ́ʌ̀	'fourth born female'

Table 16 (continued)

Kɔ́kɔ̀ŋ	'fifth born female'
Ńkîi	'sixth born female'
Ṭàhâŋ	'seventh born female'
Kànǒ	'eighth born female'

Similar strategies occur with names for males in Tima; see Meerpohl (2012: 167) and Schneider-Blum (2013b) for details. Quint and Manfredi (2020) point out that this naming strategy is more common in the Nuba Mountains, an area otherwise characterized by a tremendous degree of typological disparity and genetic diversity.

As elsewhere, Tima names may also be based on specific events, e.g., *Bókònà* as a name for a girl whose father died during the mother's pregnancy, or *Àmbɔ̀l* (alternatively *Àmbɔ́ɔ̀l*) for a person whose mother became pregnant after many years of being childless. In other words, different strategies may co-exist in one and the same community (which also includes the use of both Arabic and Christian names in the case of the Tima speech community).

Bashir (2015: 137) describes another variation on a theme, the use of skin colour (as part of somebody's physical appearance) as a basis for naming practices among speakers of Midob, a language spoken in Sudan. The following examples consist of an adjectival root fusing with a modifying suffix *-(i)cc/-(i)ʃʃ* expressing less intensity.

(51) kéʃʃi 'person of lighter red skin'
    úccí 'person of lighter black skin'

Bashir (2015: 144) also describes hypocoristic (endearment) names for Midob. These are usually based on "midobized" Arabic names, and are used among family members, peers, and close friends.

(52) pèrhó (< pèrhímì < ʔibraahim)
    sénábó (< sénábà < zeenab)

One and the same person may also have several names, as with speakers of Karimojong, a language spoken in northern Uganda. Novelli (1985: 187–190) lists six types of naming strategies for the language of the Karimojong, who are nomadic pastoralists traditionally. The first is the name given 'at the cutting of the umbilical cord', as Karimojong speakers call this strategy accompanying the birth of a child, and involving names linked with the events of everyday life, such as

Lokiru for somebody born when it was raining (after the word for 'rain' *akiru*). The second type involves intimate names related to the first names of individuals with whom there is a friendly relationship, for example *Limilìm* after the verb for 'drizzle', *-limilim*. A person may also receive a pet name or nickname, which is chosen in accordance with his or her physical or behavioural characteristics, for example *Náílókòp*, which contains the root for 'dew', *-kòpì*. This nickname may be given to a short person, "so short that the dew – *ŋákòpì* – will fall on his head if he passes in the grass at sunrise" (Novelli 1985: 188).[35]

Related to the pastoral traditions of the Karimojong and other (semi-)nomadic communities across Eastern Africa, two additional naming strategies can be identified with male community members. First, the use of so-called "ox names". A male may be called 'father of . . .', followed by the name of his favourite ox, the latter having been donated by his father. Moreover, as cattle raids were common among these agro-pastoral communities, the killing of an enemy might result in an additional battle name. Finally, the practice of referring to or addressing parents by the names of their children, 'mother of . . .', or 'father of . . .', a phenomenon known as teknonymy, is common across Africa and other parts of the world, and is also found among the Karimojong.

It would be interesting to plot the various naming strategies on a map of the continent in order to detect areal patterns or patterns related to the historical expansion of specific language families (as with kinship terminology and other lexical domains, like colour).

In his discussion of personal names in Hausa, Newman (2000: 338–346) distinguishes between birth names (SG: *sūnan yankà̃*) and everyday names (SG: *sūnan rānā*). In line with Hausa tradition, whispering the baby's name (*radà sūnā*) into its ear takes place seven days after its birth. As the overwhelming majority of Hausas are Muslims, these names tend to be derived from Arabic, e.g., *Mùhammadù* for a male or *Fādîmatù* for a female; they may also be used in a shortened form, e.g., *Mùhammàd* or *Fatī̃*, respectively.

Whereas birth names in Hausa are typically given in honour of a deceased relative, everyday names, as additional names (commonly referred to as *lakàbī* in Hausa), are based on the time or occasion of a birth, the appearance of the baby, or some conventional connection between the additional name and the Islamic name, as in the following examples:

---

[35] An interesting elaboration of nicknames among the Acholi, a neighbouring community, is described by Odoch Pido (2017: 17). Here nicknames may be presented in the form of riddles. *Malakwang*, the name of a vegetable, and the name derived from it, *A-malakwang*, may be given to a "Casanova".

(53) Kằka (from kằkā 'harvest season')
    Dōgo (from dōgō 'tall')

These names, as well as other naming strategies in Hausa, such as names related to birth sequence (e.g., *Gàmbo* 'boy born after twins', *Kànde* 'girl born after two or more boys'), reflect a pre-Islamic tradition, as do further strategies described by Newman, who also mentions nicknames (p. 347) as acquired mainly by young urban males as an additional naming strategy. Such names sometimes persist throughout the rest of a person's life, as with the famous Hausa poet, *Alh. Mūdī Sìpīkìn* (< *spic and span*; Newman 2000: 347).

Newman (2000: 347–348) discusses a related phenomenon, that of hypocoristics, in order to indicate attitudinal information about the affection of the speaker, usually an adult, towards the person referred to, usually a younger child, by means of different morphological strategies.

	Regular name	Hypocoristic variant
(54)	Bàla	Bàlēle
	Kànde	Kandalā
	Bằba	Bằbandi

Surnames, as such, did not exist in Hausa. But as pointed out by Newman (2000: 351), "[u]nder English (and French) influence, especially as applied in Western-style schools, Hausas have adopted a first-name last-name system" comparable to the development of surnames in Europe, e.g., based on an occupation (*Hasàn Mài Tūrằrē* Hassan the perfume seller) or as 'son of Y' (*Abdùn Bāwà* 'Abdu (son) of Bawa'); a person's hometown or district can also serve as a surname (as in *Àmīnù Kanò*, 'Aminu from Kano'). Females may take one of their husband's names as a surname, or may use a last name acquired earlier, e.g one of her father's names (as with *Hàdīzà Jùnaidù*; Newman 2000: 350). These newer developments hence parallel the historical development of surnames in Europe and other parts of the world, namely as a way of sorting people into groups by occupation, place of origin, clan affiliation, patronage, parentage, adoption, and physical characteristics.

Rapoo (2002) discusses a further dimension of naming strategies, the gender bias in traditional onomastic practices among the Tswana, whose language Setswana is one of the major languages of Botswana in terms of number of speakers. According to Rapoo (2002: 42), their naming system is "one of the ideological tools that their society implements to shape and maintain the ideological conceptions of male and female". The social stratification between the latter is reflected in a boy's name like *Mogomotsi* 'one who brings comfort' with the class 1 prefix *mo-*

used for nouns and prototypically referring to human beings. The suffix -*i* is used in Setswana and other Bantu languages to derive agentive nouns from verbs (as in English *comfort-er*). The female counterpart *Segomotso* 'the object with which I am being comforted' (or *Kgomotso* 'comfort'), is formed with the class 7 prefix *se-*, which is also used to derive instrumental (i.e., inanimate) nouns. The derivational suffix -*o* in Setswana (and other Bantu languages) tends to be used in order to refer to a place or action (as well as instrument). These affixation strategies are recurrent with other male versus female names. Their allocation in different noun classes with different derivational markers thus to some extent reflects cultural ideologies and the idealized traditional roles of males and females in a society.

Chala and Gutama (2019) describe changes in personal namegiving and renaming among Oromo speakers in Ethiopia since 1991, after the totalitarian Derg Regime fell and ethnic federalism was introduced. Rather than bestowing names on newborn children derived from Amharic, the dominant language of wider communication in the country, the social practices of parents changed and Oromo tended to be more popular. The following examples are from the Afaan dialect of Oromo (Chala and Gutama 2019: 21):

(55) Mo'eera   'I won, he won'
      Sabboona   'a nationalist'
      Bilisummaa   'freedom'
      Diinaa'ol   'superior to the enemy'

Self-renaming is allowed by the Ethiopian civil code, and so some adults also changed their Amharic names; hence, *Aberash*, 'you shine' was changed into Afaan Oromo *Ibsituu* 'one who shines', in order to mark Oromo identity. As further noted by the authors, names may also be changed "in a very opportunistic and instrumental manner to meet a certain personal goal. Our data indicated that academically weak students often change their names to the name of academically active students to sit next to them and copy examination answers to pass regional and/or national examinations" (Chala and Gutama 2019: 22).

Similar re-indexing strategies are attested for speakers of Akan in Ghana, replacing non-Akan names (Agyekum 2006), or for Afro-Americans taking African names (Benson 2006). The importance of political ideologies also becomes obvious when comparing naming strategies in mainland China with those in Hong Kong. Whereas in traditional Chinese cultures names reflect social values, modern English names in Hong Kong, such as *Cola* or *iPhone*, reflect a different language ideology, and, presumably, a different political orientation from those who are in power in the People's Republic of China.

A further interesting phenomenon, that of pronoun choice determined by the category to which a specific name belongs, is described by Bing (1993) for Gborbo Khrahn, a language spoken in northwestern Liberia and the Ivory Coast (where it is usually referred to as Wobé or Guéré). These Khrahn names are rarely used when addressing a person. Instead, a nickname, English name, or the corresponding terms for 'father', 'mother', 'older sibling', 'younger sibling' are used (Bing 1993: 121). The names in Table 17 from Bing (1983) present a small selection. The digits represent tonal levels on vowels (a system also used for tonal languages in South and East Asia); 1 represents the highest tone, 5 represents the lowest tone. The slashes represent the structural (phonological) representation of the pronoun; the square brackets represent its pronunciation (i.e., the phonetic level). In addition, there are other forms used for second and third person, depending on aspect (perfect versus imperfect), and on the syntactic role of the pronoun (as a subject, or expressing another syntactic function); in all cases, however, the distinction between the two name classes is maintained. The list in Table 17 is consequently incomplete. For further details the reader is referred to Bing (1993: 123).

Table 17: Gborbo Khrahn names and corresponding pronominal reference (Bing 1993).

O-class names	2nd person	3rd person	U-class names	2nd person	3rd person
Tia$^{3\text{-}45}$	en^4	/O/^{3} [ɔ]^3	Gbaia$^{4\text{-}2\text{-}2}$	a^3	/U/^{3} [ʊ]^3
Kai^{32}	en^4	/O/^{3} [ɔ]^3	Jlu^2	a^3	/U/^{3} [ʊ]^3
Lai^{21}	en^4	/O/^{3} [ɔ]^3	KwE^1	a^3	/U/^{3} [ʊ]^3

The forms associated with O-class names are also used when making reference to strangers or foreigners, unless that person is known to have an U-class name. The following examples illustrate these deictic principles.

(56) O^3 dba^2 jlu^1 [jru]^1
     3SG   kill   cobra
     'he (referring to Tia$^{3\text{-}45}$) killed a cobra'

(57) U^3 dba^2 jlu^1 [jru]^1
     3SG   kill   cobra
     'he (referring to Gbaia$^{4\text{-}2\text{-}2}$) killed a cobra'

(58) en^4 dba^2 jluu$^{2\text{-}1}$ [jru]^1
     2SG   kill   cobra.Q
     'did you (addressing Tia$^{3\text{-}45}$) kill a cobra?'

(59) a^3 dba^2 jluu$^{2\text{-}1}$ [jru]^1
 2SG kill cobra.Q
 'did you (addressing Gbaia$^{4\text{-}2\text{-}2}$) kill a cobra?'

Bing (1993: 127) surmizes that the most probable explanation for the binary distinction in Gborbo Krahn is its link with the spirit world, as names tend to be revealed in dreams by ancestors; a child is not only named after an ancestor, it is also considered the reincarnation of an ancestor, who always belongs to the same gender. These Gborbo names, therefore, are neither individualizing nor arbitrary.

The claim by Blundy (2016) that personal names serve to individualize persons, thereby assigning a unique identity to somebody, sounds straightforward and obvious on the first account. However, as the phenomena discussed above help to illustrate, from a cultural-historical perspective things are probably slightly more intricate – and more interesting, for that matter – than that.

As the kaleidoscopic survey of naming strategies above shows, many of these are embedded in a phenomenological approach by human beings whereby newborn children, as individuals, are seen as phenotypes of a specific genotype. Thus, a boy born in an Akan-speaking area in southern Ghana may be called *Kofi* if he is born on a Friday. The fourth girl in a row born into a Tima family in Sudan may be called *Cìŋʌ̀ʌ̀*. Many traditional names consequently reflect an individual's position in an existing social network, indexing different types of information about the time, location, social position, and other parameters. Those named *Kofi* consequently may be considered as phenotypes (or representatives) of a certain genotype (group), 'Those born on a Friday', and those named *Cìŋʌ̀ʌ̀* are phenotypes of the genotype 'Fourth girls amongst brothers and sisters' among Tima speakers.

While, in a globalizing world, such traditions are vanishing in the non-academic world, these naming traditions are still used when naming newly discovered animals, and as such they have been copied into modern science, for example by biologists and palaeontologists, when naming newly discovered (sub)species, whether extinct or "discovered" on our planet today. The world's largest shark, discovered some time ago, was named *Megalodon* 'Big-tooth/teeth' by palaeo-biologists, referring to a prominent phenomenological feature of this extinct species.

People living in the Annamite Range of Vietnam and Laos knew about a specific forest-dwelling bovine in their area. In one Thai language in Vietnam this beautiful animal (shown in Picture 14) is known as *Saola*, which means 'Spindle[-horned]', or 'Spinning wheel post-horn' in this language; its scientific (Latin) name is *Pseudoryx nghetinhensis*.

Picture 14: *Saola* as shown on stamps in Vietnam.

This tradition of naming animals after some prominent feature is widespread across the world. Vossen (2015) presents various examples from languages belonging to the Nilotic family, for example the following from Maasai (Kenya, Tanzania):

(60) o-le-n-tim
      M:SG-GEN:F:SG-bush
      'baboon (lit. the one of the bush)'

(61) ol-o-l-masi
      M:SG-GEN:M:SG-M:SG-hairdo
      'African hoopoe (lit. the one of the hairdo)'

(62) e-na-gor-kewan
      F:SG-REL:F:SG-strangle-REFL:SG
      'bat (lit. the one that strangles itself)'

The individualizing role of naming only becomes prominent with humans through the *combination* of different names individuals become associated with. In a range of languages belonging to an African language family which is spread over major parts of central and eastern Africa, Nilo-Saharan, this latter sociocultural feature of having more than one name has become grammaticalized. In his genetic classification of the languages of Africa, Greenberg (1963: 114–115, 124, 131–132) points towards an interesting syntactic property of the word for 'name' in different languages in this language family (established by him), namely that in several Nilo-Saharan languages the word for 'name' is inherently plural. Its plural (transnumeral) status is either marked formally on the noun (i.e., it is overt), or it becomes obvious indirectly when nominal modifiers such as demonstratives are added (its plural status being covert, i.e., not marked on the noun itself but only on modifiers such as demonstratives). Greenberg (1963: 103, 142) mentions the word for 'name' in the following Nilo-Saharan languages:

(63) Bari   ka-rın
     Dinka (Rek dialect)   rin
     Fur   kario
     Mangbetu   eru

In his Bari-English-Italian dictionary, Spagnolo (1960: 86–87) states that the word for 'name' in this language from South Sudan is invariably (feminine) plural, and that speakers differentiate between proper names, common names, nicknames and age-grade names. In some Nilo-Saharan languages, the original root has been replaced by another form. Jakobi (1990: 86) lists a different word for 'name' in Fur from Greenberg (1963: 142), but she also points out that in this Nilo-Saharan language (spoken in Sudan and Chad) the word for 'name' contains the plural deictic marker *k-* as well as a plural number suffix *-a*. This word functions as a syntactic plural parallel to a *plurale tantum* (i.e., a plural form without a corresponding singular or singulative form) such as 'blood' or 'water'.

(64) k-òn-à   'name, song'
     k-èw-à   'blood'

Interestingly, the new word for 'name' in the Nilo-Saharan language Baale (southern Ethiopia) also functions as a *plurale tantum* (author's data), as shown by the plural agreement marker:

(65) sára   g-aandí
     name   PL-my
     'my (collection of) name(s)'

From a sociological point of view, it may be argued that the individualizing function of naming in the case of human reference is rendered by its combination with additional strategies, such as nicknames and other naming strategies described above. The multitude of names inextricably linked with personhood has already been illustrated for the Nilo-Saharan language Karimojong (Uganda). Lienhardt (1988) describes similar phenomena for Dinka (South Sudan), for example with respect to a person by the name of *Macar Aciek Ader*. *Macar* indicates a birth late in the child-bearing life of the mother, while *Aciek* reflects the fact that this person's father is likely to have been born after a long delay, and *Ader* (the person's grandfather's name) implies that he was born after a previous child or children had died.

A second interesting phenomenon from a cultural-historical point of view is described by Brenzinger (1999) for speakers of Kxoe (most of whom live in Namibia, although there are also speakers in Angola, Botswana, Zambia, and South Africa). Apart from names borrowed from the neighbouring Mbukushu language, as well as from Afrikaans and English (which include biblical names entering Kxoe through these languages), there is the traditional Kxoe naming after an affine or kin (though never the father or mother) or a well-known person.

Importantly, the original bearer of the name (known to most if not all Khoe) remains the true owner, even after his or her death (the same names may be used for males and females). A further fascinating aspect of naming in Khoe is the fact that "Kxoe, when they have reached their early 20s, know most of the approximately 4000 adult Kxoe with their individual key names, despite the fact that Kxoe are scattered over five countries" (Brenzinger 1999: 10).

The official first names are not normally used in daily life among Kxoe speakers, and tend to be unknown to others; moreover, their surnames, which tend to be based on the "official" first name of the father, are quite frequently changed by the bearer, and a Kxoe may have different names, including nicknames and names given by age-mates. As pointed out by Brenzinger (1999: 8), "[t]he names which appear in the IDs reveal not seldom a total communication breakdown between the ID issuing officials and the Kxoe applicants. Some IDs are issued under the name of the wife or mother, names of both the husband and his wife may be listed in one ID (...)"

What the examples above from various regions in Africa should make clear is that naming only results in individualizing persons to a limited extent; in actual fact, it is only through the *collection* of names that somebody is individualized.

6.2 Toponymy

Place names denote or locate geographical sites such as human settlements, rivers, valleys or hills. The taxonomic study of such names, toponymy, usually involves an investigation of their geographical location and etymology, built, for example, on anthroponyms, ethnonyms, characteristics of a place, flora, or fauna (as stated by Newman 2000: 353 with respect to Hausa).

In the Turkana area of northwestern Kenya, one finds place names probably going back to Päkoot, whose speakers now live mainly south of the Turkana area and who are claimed by Turkana speakers as well as Päkoot to have lived in the Turkana area before the Turkana migrated from (what is now) South Sudan into (what is now) Kenya. Places introduced by *ka-* in the Turkana area, as in *Ka-bokok* 'place of the tortoise', are reminiscent of the language cluster to which Päkoot belongs, Kalenjin. Mietzner (2016: 202–207) describes this strategy with the prefix *ka(p)-* for another member of this cluster, Cherang'any, where it occurs as a location-marking preposition in place names such as *Kaptalamwa* 'place of locusts/ grass hoppers'; the consonant *p* in *Ka-p-* is an archaic possessive marker in Nilotic, the language family to which Cherang'any, Päkoot, and Turkana belong.

From a historical point of view it is important to keep in mind that it is often primarily languages rather than people which migrate (or expand). And rather than displacing communities when moving in, language replacement or shift towards the new dominant language is a common historical phenomenon, including in this part of the world. It has been observed by different anthropologists, particularly with respect to pastoral communities in eastern Africa, that identical clan names are found in communities speaking different, and frequently also genetically unrelated languages; see Schlee (1989) for one such source. Common clan names across distinct speech communities (at times speaking unrelated languages) in eastern Africa in general suggest that permanent processes of ethnic fission and fusion were part of their ethnohistory (and so some Päkoot speakers may have shifted their primary language of solidarity towards Turkana, rather than migrating to different regions, although the latter no doubt occurred as well).

Similar processes of ethnic fission and fusion probably occurred in southern Africa. Raper (2009) describes this phenomenon for areas in South Africa where Zulu has become the dominant language. San names based on natural features of the landscape such as *eNthubeni* (lit. 'at the pass'), which contains the lexical root *thub(a)*, which is cognate with stems with the same meaning in San languages like Naron *daubu* or Hietʃware *dhau* 'path'. Such toponyms point towards the presence of speakers of Khoisan (Khoe and San) languages (as an areal grouping) as earlier inhabitants of these regions. Speakers of these latter languages were not necessarily driven out of these areas. Research on the DNA structures of Zulu speakers and speakers of other Bantu languages in the area (as reported on by Herbert 1990) provides strong empirical evidence that intermixing occurred between the first inhabitants of the area and the newcomers. Place names consequently may be interpreted as instances of a "collective memory", reflecting practices through which groups create shared interpretations of the past.

Stolz, Warnke, and Levkovych (2016) analyze European colonial place names in Africa. Prototypically, such constructions consist of an anthroponymic constituent and a classifier (a morpheme or word indicating the ontological class to which the geo-object belongs). A colonial toponomasticon like *Port Harcourt*, a major city in Southern Nigeria, consists of the classifier *port* and *Harcourt*, after the British Secretary of State for the Colonies (1910–1915), Lewis Vernon 1st Viscount Harcourt, who was in charge of colonial policy when the city of Port Harcourt was founded in 1912. Such ideological naming strategies obviously reflect national pride personified in specific individuals. In this sense, they are not different from *Fort William*, in Scotland. However, as pointed out by Stolz, Warnke, and Levkovych (2016: 294), such ideological naming strategies were used far more frequently than in the home country, inscribing the colonizer's language and the appropriation of the territory on the map of the colony "by way of marking it with culturally / politically / historically loaded ANTHs [anthroponyms] of national significance" (Stolz, Warnke, and Levkovych 2016: 314).

Naming a place or area after a place or name in the home country was also common during colonial times. Compare, for example, Lagos, with a town of the same name in southern Portugal (as the Portuguese navigated along the African coast from the 15th century onwards). Alternatively, politicians, military leaders, explorers, or entrepreneurs gave their name to a town or area, as with Rhodesia, based on the surname of a major instigator of the British expansion in Africa, Cecil Rhodes (1853–1902), with a latinate derivational suffix.

Not unexpectedly, such colonial names were sometimes modified in postcolonial times, as with North Rhodesia, which was renamed Zambia, or South Rhodesia, which was renamed Zimbabwe. In the former Belgian colony the Democratic Republic of the Congo, the colonizers had practised similar naming strategies. Léopoldville (or Dutch: *Leopoldstad*), for example, was founded in 1881 in what was then called the Congo Freestate in honour of the Belgian king Léopold II; together with the "hinterland" it became the personal property of the latter in 1885 (until 1908). Six years after independence, the capital of the Democratic Republic of the Congo was renamed Kinshasa in 1966 (after the name of a village which became part of the capital) by the then president of the country, Mobutu Sese Seko.

Such renaming strategies are also known, of course, from Europe, for example in Russia, where cities were renamed after the dissolution of the Soviet Union. They show that names can become a resource of symbolic capital (after Bourdieu 1991), fulfilling the desire of a community to invert power relations and to (re)create its own heritage.

6.3 Names and avoidance or endearment strategies

During the "flower power" era (or what some have called the "cultural revolution") in Europe and North America in the late 1960s and 1970s, it became fashionable for some parents to let themselves be addressed in the same way in which they would address their children, namely by their first names. This conscious effort on the part of the parents to breach a code of conduct of older generations did not last very long, nor did it receive wide acceptance across societies in other parts of the world.

What it did illustrate, however, was that there were specific conventions which members of the society were aware of and which they wanted to break away from.

While the western tradition of parents addressing their children by their first names is quite common in different parts of the world, this is not necessarily so everywhere. In their discussion of avoidance strategies for addressing adults by their personal names among Fulbe (also known as Fulani, after the name of the language, whose speakers these days are found in an area ranging from Senegal to Ethiopia), Ameka and Breedveld (2004: 180) refer to a phenomenon called *yage* in Fulbe. This may be translated as 'shame', 'respect', or 'proper behaviour', which needs to be attended to depending on the nature of the relationship between two persons. In Fulbe society, relationships that evoke the highest degree of *yage* involve an extreme type of name avoidance. A person who is in a relationship with a person named *Hammadi*, for example, not only should never pronounce the name *Hammadi* to address or refer to this relation, but should also not mention any name that is a variant of or is derived morphologically or hypocoristically from this name. In the case of *Hammadi*, such a person consequently cannot say names like *Hamma*, *Hammadu*, and *Mohammadu*, which are variants of it. Addressing somebody as 'father of . . .' or 'mother of . . .' (i.e., teknonymy) is one way out as an avoidance strategy.

An alternative motivation for teknonymy may be the expression of affection, as Farghal and Shakir (1994: 250) illustrate in their investigation of Jordanian Arabic. As shown by the following examples adapted from Farghal and Shakir (1994: 243–244), the term for 'maternal aunt' can be used as an affectionate kin vocative without any kin or affinal relationship being implied.

(66) maraḥaba   yā   xālah
     hi   VOC   maternal.aunt
     'hi!'

(67) 'i.ā samaḫt-i   yā   xālah
     if   allow.2SG-F   VOC   maternal.aunt
     'if you allow, please'

Such semantic extensions become even more intricate when taking into account examples such as the following, where the denotational signification is reversed (Farghal and Shakir 1994: 246):

(68) 'a'tī-ni   may   yammah
     give-me   water   mother
     'give me water, son/daughter'

Semantic extensions of kin vocatives like these, as part of endearment strategies, help us to understand one reason for the non-biological use of kinship terms. The strategies enhance intimacy among relatives but also between acquaintances or strangers, where they function as politeness or affection enhancers, as illustrated in Chapter 2.

An early representative of British structural anthropology, Radcliffe-Brown (1940, reprinted 1952), pointed out that in ambiguous social relationships, i.e., those that are simultaneously disjunctive and conjunctive, one may find institutionalized forms of interaction. Avoidance languages as "stylects", or, more specifically, the omission of names when referring to or addressing others, appear to be one potential outcome of such ambiguous relationships. Treis (2005) describes a type of name taboo traditionally practised by married women speaking Kambaata (a language of Ethiopia) as a sign of respect towards their in-laws (including deceased ones), known as *ballishsha*. This special vocabulary is used exclusively by married women. These lexemes are acquired by the bride once she has moved to the husband's place of residence after marriage, the teachers usually being her sister-in-law and her husband's paternal aunt (Treis 2005: 297). Enculturation and the acquisition of a specific habitus thus is not necessarily something which is completed during childhood, as this tradition shows.

The social domain involves in-laws' names and any word starting with the same consonant-vowel sequence, a tradition also found among other speech communities in the area. Should a married woman make a mistake, she "spits out" the forbidden word and utters a fixed phrase. Treis (2005) describes a number of strategies that make up this *ballishsha* register, which consists of a more or less standardized vocabulary of around 200 words, created historically by borrowings and language-internal word-formation processes, such as the use of semantically similar words (synonyms) or antonyms. Semantic similarity can be observed in the word *kottí-ta* 'footprint, track', which is used instead of the common Kambaata word *lokká-ta* 'foot, leg'. Instead of *gal-* 'pass the night', *ballishsha* requires these women to use the antonym *hos-* 'pass the day'. Loanwords from neighbouring languages or from the important contact language in Ethiopia, Amharic, illustrate a further strategy; thus, instead of *kodá* 'turn', *tará* (from Amharic *tära*) is used. Paraphrases can be observed in the *ballishsha* term for 'water', *daadaamú* (instead of *wo'á*, the word for 'water' used by other community members), which is derived historically from a root *zaaz-* (< **daad-*) 'flow'. An alternative lexical strategy involves periphrasis. Thus, instead of using the taboo word *hizóo* 'brother', a periphrastic construction *ama'í beetú* 'the son of my mother' is used. The register is used when interacting with in-laws, but also when the latter are bystanders in conversational interactions.

6.3 Names and avoidance or endearment strategies — 143

According to Treis (2005: 315–316), *ballishsha* is becoming obsolete these days, mainly due to the influence of Protestant missions in the area. Other reasons for its abandonment are the fairly high school attendance rate among the Kambaata, the impact of the Derg (military junta) regime under Mengistu (between 1974 and 1991), and the declaration of women's rights after 1974.

Avoidance language among the Kambaata is but one example of an areal phenomenon of linguistic avoidance strategies starting in Ethiopia with speakers of Cushitic and Omotic languages, and extending southwards all the way to southern Africa, where languages belonging to the Nilotic and Bantu families are spoken. Kambaata belongs to the Cushitic language family, and in related speech communities such as that of the Oromo (in Ethiopia) there is a similar tradition, known as *laguu* (Mbaya 2002). Cushitic languages are found in Ethiopia and Kenya, but this family also extends into what is now Tanzania. There is linguistic evidence for areal contact between speakers of Cushitic languages and communities speaking Nilotic or Bantu languages in Kenya as well as Tanzania (Kießling, Mous, and Nurse 2008). The presence of avoidance languages in Nilotic and Bantu languages in Tanzania, but also further south, consequently, is probably not a coincidence, as argued below.

In her research on avoidance registers in Datooga, a Nilotic language spoken in Tanzania, Alice Mitchell came across specific properties of social deixis, those of allusive reference. Mitchell (2018: 8) describes how and why adult female speakers have an enregistered set of alternative words at their disposal in order to avoid having to use specific taboo words. These latter also result from the association of such words with names of in-laws. In the example below, the noun *nyabuul-da* 'cow' is an avoidance term used in place of the ordinary word for 'cow', *dee-da* (whereby the suffix *-da* is a specifier or selective marker in this language). The latter word "smells" (in Datooga parlance; Mitchell 2015b) like *Duudee*, which is the personal name of a male in-law. This personal name consists of the lexical root for 'black' followed by the lexical root for 'cow', *-dee*, and consequently should be avoided by this woman. By using the word *nyabuulda* instead of *deeda*, she indexes her relationship with this non-present other carrying the name *Duudee*.

(69) g-àj-ée-géanu gèesh-tá nyábùul-da àk-k-í-dàbí gìli
 AFF-FUT-1PL-take.CP leg-UR COW-UR SEQ-AFF-2SG-beat.IS thing
 'you take the cow's leg and then you hit it with this thing (...)'

The sentence above derives from an audio-taped scene where the woman is cutting up beef in the company of several other women; the in-law is not present but is nevertheless alluded to as a "third party" (present with speaker and hearers). By using such registers adult females indirectly take a stance towards such a person, expressing in a symbolic manner that they are mindful of that person's social identity, and hence showing deference (Mitchell 2018: 13). Through this "other-oriented stance" female speakers manifest an awareness of proper social distance and social obligations, as a result of which they are also respected members of the community.

Hollington (2019) describes a phenomenon called *muroora* 'daughter/sister-in-law (lit. the one that was paid dowry for/the one that was married)', a register found in in Shona (chiShona) in Zimbabwe which is associated with the prescribed and desired social roles of a wife with regard to her in-laws. Hollington (2019) also emphasizes that comparable behavioural rules apply to Shona men when addressing (older) in-law family members, including the avoidance of eye contact.

Avoidance language may be interpreted as a possible exponent of a wider cultural phenomenon, that of taboo as a "proscription of behaviour for a specifiable community of one or more persons, at a specifiable time, in specifiable contexts" (Allan and Burridge 2006: 11). As pointed out by the same authors, "[a]voidance speech styles help prevent conflict in relationships that are potentially volatile" (Allan and Burridge 2006: 9).

Given the widespread nature of taboos cross-culturally and, linked to this, of avoidance registers, it may be argued that the cases described above and hereafter are the result of "self-organization", the independent, parallel development of similar systems. It should be noted, however, that the use of special registers primarily by females has been reported for a range of communities in the area, for example in Bantu languages like Haya, Kerewe, and Nyakyusa in Tanzania (Sommer and Lupapula 2012). As shown below, this phenomenon is found in its most dramatic form in the Nguni language group (within Bantu) in southern Africa.

The areal spreading of avoidance registers does not necessarily imply a migration of speakers of Cushitic languages all the way to South Africa, although South Cushitic languages are found as far south as Tanzania (where Nilotic languages like Datooga also show taboo registers similar to Cushitic languages). There is linguistic and archaeological evidence for a southward migration from the Great Lakes area in eastern Africa of communities speaking Bantu languages over the past two millennia. This expansion of the Bantu family (also southwards from Cameroon and Gabon) is associated with a new technology, the introduction of iron working. Pastoralism probably also played a role in its southward expansion. Map 3 (kindly produced by Monika Feinen) is inspired by the genetic subclassification for Bantu and the corresponding historical spread as proposed by Nurse and Philippson 2003).

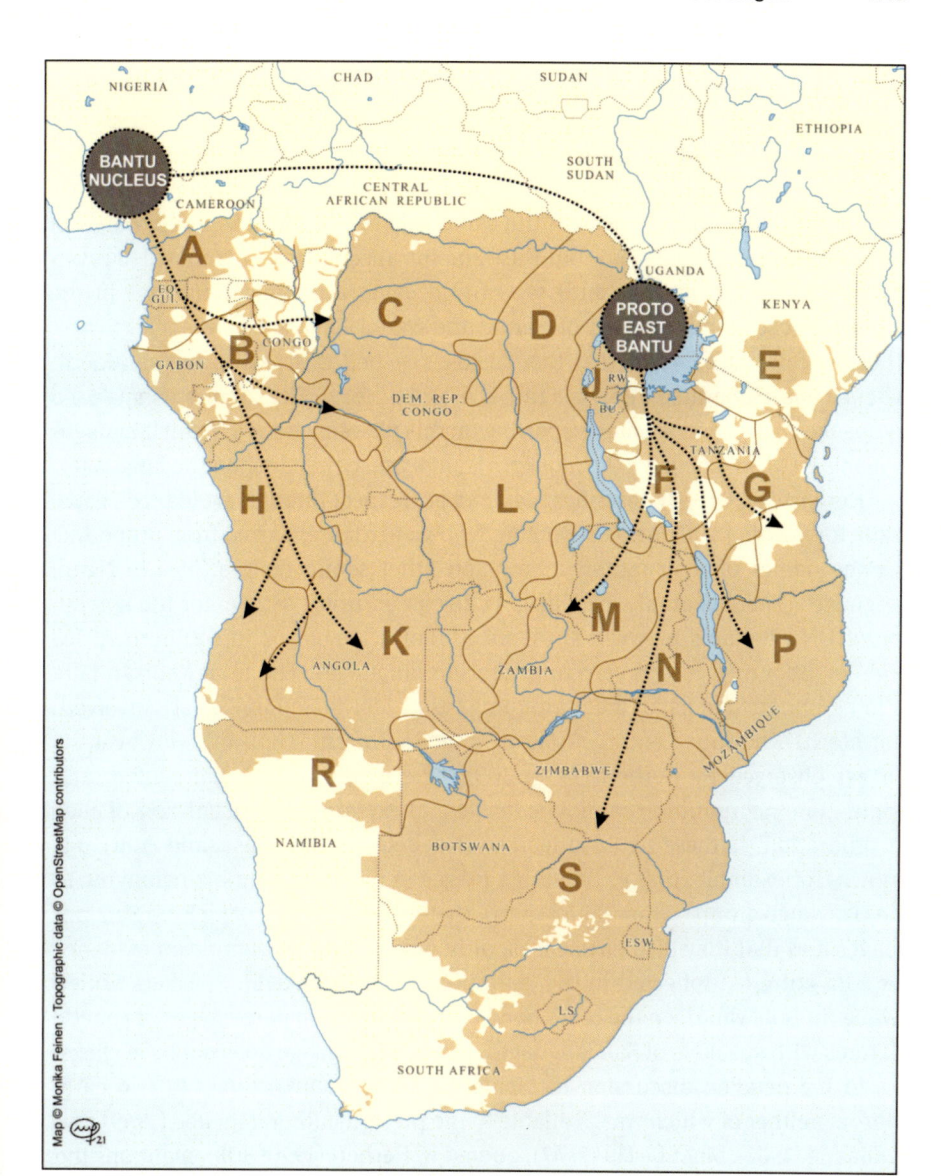

Map 3: The southward migration of eastern Bantu languages.

Fleming et al. (2019: 171) argue that any partial diffusion of in-law avoidance practices in this area "has been complemented by a complex of sociocultural factors motivating the emergence of this pattern at different times and places across the African continent. These factors include pastoralism, patrilineal descent ideologies and norms of patrilocal postmarital residence paired with cattle-based bridewealth exchange."

The slightly "patchy" areal distribution today of the phenomenon described here may also be due to the fact that these traditions disappeared in some areas before they were documented (in the same way in which clicks disappeared in some languages in this area). But this remains speculative, of course. However, the extensive distribution (until recently) of such avoidance strategies in the southernmost representatives of Bantu, the Nguni languages (Ndebele, Swazi, Xhosa, Zulu), makes clear that this custom reached this part of the continent, where it was elaborated upon in a rather dramatic form. The common name used by speakers as well as scholars reporting on this phenomenon in Nguni languages is *hlonipha* (also *hlonip(h)(i)a, hlonep(h)a, hlompa,* depending on the language).

Herbert (1990: 303) describes *hlonipha* as 'respect through avoidance', especially for married and engaged women, who were (or are) barred from pronouncing the names of their fathers-in-law and other senior male affines in Nguni languages. There is ample evidence, as discussed in his article, for the spreading of DNA features between speakers of Bantu languages in southern Africa and neighbouring groups speaking Khoisan languages. The term Khoisan here is to be understood as an areal grouping, as in fact three families are involved: North(ern) Khoisan, Central Khoisan, and South(ern) Khoisan). However, as further observed by Herbert (1990: 303), "the extent of physical contact and population incorporation cannot be invoked to explain the unusual case of click incorporation" in these Nguni languages (Ndebele, Swazi, Xhosa, and Zulu). It is known, for example, that in Bantu languages in northern Namibia belonging to the Okavango group (rather than Nguni), there is lexical borrowing from San languages and that they also have clicks, although there is no significant evidence for admixture (as reflected in the gene pool of the speakers). Speakers of Setswana (in Botswana), on the other hand, share significant percentages of genetic features with speakers of San languages, but their language does not have clicks.

In his detailed discussion of *hlonipha*, Herbert (1990) refers to two early sources neither of which was available to the present author, Mncube (1949) and Mzamane (1962). Mncube (1949: 47), quoted in Herbert (1990: 308), mentions the custom among Xhosa and Zulu speakers of young girls practising syllable avoidance so that they could comply with the custom after marriage, when addressing or referring to specific in-laws. Mzamane (1962: 256) points towards the standardization of specific *hlonipha* words within larger areas where Southern Nguni languages (Zulu and Xhosa) are spoken, an issue taken up again below.

A third important source is Kunene (1958), who translates *hlonipha* (or *hlonepha,* as it is called in his contribution) as 'respect, honour', or 'avoiding certain words', showing similarities to names of certain kinship, more specifically by married women with respect to their male in-laws, among speakers of Southern Sotho. This custom was apparently already on its way out in the 1950s, when Daniel Kunene collected his data. Interestingly, when avoided words are written down, they lose their taboo character (Kunene 1958: 165).

Avoidance strategies in Southern Sotho may be rendered by using teknonymy, for example *Ra-* 'father of . . .', *Ramponeng* 'father of Mponeng', *Mponeng* being the person's oldest daughter. Alternatively, morphemes forming the core of a word (usually called "radical" in Bantu studies), and expressing a name, may be replaced by corresponding *hlonipha* morphemes: the marker *mo-* below is a noun-class prefix (commonly used with words referring to human beings):

	Name	Corresponding *hlonipha* form and name	
(70)	Mojalefa	Mofutaletlotlo	
	-ja	-futa, -kos(ol)a, -maea	'eat'
	-lefa	-letlotlo	'inheritance'

The different linguistic strategies used by speakers of Southern Sotho are very similar to those described by Treis (2005) for *ballishsha* in Kambaata, i.e., borrowing or metonymy; words related to or derived from the radical or root form are also to be avoided.

The article by Kunene (1958), which is rich in data, is also rich in observations important for our understanding of how standardized *hlonipha* words may have come about in Southern Sotho (as well as in other Nguni languages). Kunene (1958) presents a comprehensive list of *hlonipha* terms "which have gained universality and performance, becoming part of the language" (p. 159). As observed by the author (p. 163), children hear these words and so may start using them, even though they do not have to abide by the avoidance strategy themselves (p. 163). This is presumably also the reason why basic words with a high frequency of usage in the language have been affected as a spin-off effect, as with the word for 'river', *noka*, originally a *hlonipha* word for *molapo*.

There are also usually several substitute forms (synonyms) available as well, as with the verb *-ja* 'eat' above, for example if a substitute form resembles another form a specific individual is supposed (or was supposed) to avoid given the family network of which this person is part. Such examples show that speakers master several repertoires in order to observe avoidance.

Doke and Vilakazi (1958), in their Zulu dictionary, also give several examples of *hlonipha* terms in this Nguni language. The following examples are derived from this dictionary and quoted in Irvine (2009: 163):

	Ordinary	Hlonipha	
(71)	aluka	acuka	'graze, weave'
	jaba	gxaba	'be dejected'
	indaɓa	injušo	'affair'
	imvuɓu	incuɓu	'my father'
	-ithu	-itšu	'our'
	inkosi	inqoɓo, inqotšana (dim.)	'chief'
	nenga	cenga	'annoy'
	lenga	cenga	'swing'

Note that in Zulu orthography the consonant *c* represents the dental click (IPA symbol: [|]), *q* represents the palatal click (IPA symbol: [ǂ]), and *x* represents a lateral click (IPA symbol: [‖]).

Finlayson (1995: 146–149, as well as earlier studies by the same author) also describes how basic Xhosa vocabulary came to be affected by *hlonipha*. As shown in the following examples, these "standardized" Xhosa words include words related to food and eating, domestic animals, people, and body parts, replacing the whole lexical item in order to avoid specific syllables. This constellation can be explained by taking into account the sociolinguistic observations made by Kunene (1958), discussed above.

	Core hlonipha	Xhosa	English
(72)	ukumunda	ukutya	'food/to eat'
	imvotho	amanzi	'water'
	ibetha	inja	'dog'
	incentsa	indoda	'man'
	iphoba	intloko	'head'

In more recent times, English and Afrikaans words have been used in order to avoid the tabooed syllables, along with neologisms and circumlocutions (Rudwick 2008: 155). The custom of syllabic avoidance originally applied to "the names of the father-in-law, mother-in-law, father-in-law's brothers and their wives, and the father-in-law's sisters (...). This process extends back in time usually as far as the great-grandfather-in-law" (Finlayson 1985: 141). But as pointed out by Rosalyn Finlayson, *hlonipha* (the abbreviated form of *isihlonipho sabafazi*, 'the conscious avoidance in the woman's everyday speech of the syllables occurring in the family names of the husband'), is gradually disappearing as a custom.

Hlonipha must have "primed" Nguni languages, so to speak, to be receptive to click incorporation (Faye 1923–5). Unadapted borrowing of words containing click sounds and related to the natural environment presumably entered these southern Bantu languages as a result of contact during their southward migration with people speaking Khoisan (Khoe and San) languages, who are widely assumed to have been the original inhabitants of the area. In addition, lexical borrowing occurred in socio-economic and ritual spheres. Common clan names found in Bantu speech communities and communities speaking San languages suggest that these relationships primarily involved symbiotic interactions.

As argued by Irvine (2009: 163), the clicks were (in the early years of the process) quintessentially 'foreign' sounds. One could well imagine that the customization of words with clicks provided creative new ways of language manipulation (*hlonipha*). Thus, a widespread root for 'extinguish (fire)', which is cognate with a widespread root found in Bantu languages like Sotho, *-tima*, or even the distantly related language Swahili, *-zima*, is *-cima* in Zulu (whereby "*c*" is the orthographic symbol used for the dental click [|] in the language). Furthermore, inherited Bantu roots may occur next to a form with a click, carrying a slightly different meaning. Herbert (1990: 300) gives the following examples: *-chela* 'sprinkle (ceremonially)' and *-thela* 'pour (out)' (whereby "*h*" represents aspiration of the preceding consonant).

Khoisan borrowings in Xhosa and Zulu (Herbert 1990: 309) for words such as 'egg', 'knee', 'name', 'navel', and other basic vocabulary itemes not only suggests a strong impact from language ideology (the importance of avoidance registers), but probably also another sociolinguistic phenomenon, already mentioned above: fixing or "standardizing" certain terms, in particular those with a high frequency, has the advantage of avoiding confusion between interactants, those who are supposed to abide by the custom and those who are not necessarily expected to do so. Kunene's (1958) sociolinguistic observations discussed above hence provide important motivations for the spreading of such basic vocabulary. If females in the homestead were frequently speakers of Khoisan languages, and used the *hlonipha* register containing clicks in their interactions with their children, the latter would easily pick up the corresponding forms, turning them into "standard" forms as used in the speech community. Because of their high frequency as basic words, confusion can also be avoided if these very same words are used by as many speakers as possible. One side effect, of course, is that such words no longer constitute a special gender-based register, as males also use such words, which thus become part of the language in general.

No doubt there are also other reasons for the wider spreading of certain *hlonipha* words. Thus, the pronunciation of names associated not only with in-laws but also prominent members of the speech community needed to be avoided, like *Shaka* (also known as *Shaka Zulu*), the name of an influential Zulu monarch in the 19th century, as a name taboo for an entire community; consequently, forms that sounded similar, like -*shaya* 'hit' or -*shanela* 'sweep', needed to be avoided (Herbert 1990: 306). The Zulu word for 'chief', *inkosi*, was replaced by *inqoɓo*, whereby *k* is replaced by the palatal click [ǂ](*q*). Once such clicks occur in a range of words (both basic and non-basic), they may spread like a "virus" across grammatical systems due to language-internal mechanisms. For example, if a verb root (or radical in Bantu terminology) containing clicks is used to derive new words, the latter also contain clicks.

The result was a rather dramatic restructuring and increase in the consonant systems of Nguni languages, particularly in Xhosa and Zulu. Due to the incorporation of clicks, which are often combined with other consonants, Zulu and Xhosa added 17 and 25 consonants, respectively. No influence from Khoisan languages is found on the vowel systems of these southern Bantu languages.

Of course, taboos on the pronunciation of names do not only apply to human beings. The circumscriptions found cross-linguistically for animals feared by human beings are a reflection of this. In fact, this may be one reason why descriptive terms are developed for animals in the wild. Thus, among the Turkana, the actual word for 'buffalo', *ekosòwan(ì)*, may be avoided and instead this ferocious and dangerous animal, known for its surprise attacks by standing in wait in a concealed position, may be referred to as *lɔ-ŋarab à è-kumè* 'rough-nosed one (lit. the one which is rough-of-the-nose)'. In Hausa, *snake* may be referred to by the circumscriptive term *macìjī* (lit. 'biter'), or the euphemistic term *àbin ƙasà* 'thing of the land/ground'. Leslau (1959: 106) lists *äsa'ar wädärä* 'rope of the grass' for snake in Gurage, and *'are mədri* 'beast of the earth' in Tigrinya (both in Ethiopia).

The great sociolinguist John J. Gumperz wrote in the 1970s that "[m]ost discussion in the area of ethnographic semantics has so far centered on such areas as kinship terminologies, botanical classification, zoology, etc., in which facts are easily obtainable" (Gumperz 1975: xvii). But as the preceding chapters should have made clear, theories are sometimes cheap whereas empirical facts may be harder to come by. Gumperz (1975: xvii) continues, "some scholars, notably Frake (1964, 1972) and his students, have begun to apply similar techniques to the study of terms for speaking. Their analysis here focuses on the isolation of verbal categories for differing kinds of speaking, examining local meanings of terms like *discussion*, *argument*, *chat*, and the like. The goal, as Frake puts it, is "to formulate the conditions under which it is congruous, neither humorous nor deceitful, to state that one is engaged in the speech activity in question. These conditions constitute the semantic characteristics of the activity" (Frake 1972).

The following two chapters introduce models that were developed from the 1960s onwards in order to describe and analyze such language practices, starting with the "ethnography of speaking" (or "ethnography of communication"), initiated by Dell Hymes, and followed by a discussion of "interactional sociolinguistics", initiated by John J. Gumperz. As we shall see, much of what has been described and analyzed with respect to these domains so far can be explained through common properties of human cognition. But at the same time, there is again plenty of space for culture-specific structurations.

7 The ethnography of communication

During a visit in the 1980s to the United States, the present author took part in a linguistics conference and also had the opportunity after the conference to stay with an American colleague in New York for a couple of days. As a country boy from the Netherlands, he felt intimidated by the size of the city, of course, but also by the people's behaviour, for example when addressing somebody on the street with a naïve question like "Excuse me, do you happen to know which direction Broadway is?", and then being completely ignored by the addressee. Also, observing that people avoid eye contact on the street or in the tubes, or that they start to feel uncomfortable whenever somebody behind them walks with the same pace over any distance, gives an outsider the feeling that he or she has just landed on another planet. Before leaving the Big Apple, the present author decided to buy some wine for his wonderful host, a dear colleague who unfortunately decided to leave the field of linguistics a few years later. While taking the elevator down from the flat in order to try and find a liquor store in the neighbourhood, the elevator stopped and a woman entered, of course avoiding eye contact and pretending there was nobody else in the elevator. Out of habit, the present person greeted this woman. But her reaction was: "It's only because it's such a beautiful morning, otherwise I would have hit you right in your face!" So much for greeting strangers in elevators in New York City.

Conversational routines such as greeting and parting strategies have been a popular topic in anthropological linguistics because of their ritualized nature, which turns them into easier objects of investigation than "once in a lifetime events". Moreover, there are sometimes intriguing intercultural differences between them, as the small anecdote above should help to illustrate. These ritualized speech events, as frequently recurring sequences of verbal behaviour, are taken below as an illustration of an influential descriptive framework, introduced by Hymes (1962) with the label "the ethnography of speaking". Gumperz and Hymes (1964) subsequently gave the label "ethnography of communication" to this descriptive model, which aimed to delineate cultural patterns of language usage.

7.1 Hymes' etic framework

Linguistic investigations in the 19th century centred primarily around the historical development of languages and the genetic relationships between them. The initiation of the synchronic investigation of languages is often associated with Ferdinand de Saussure's posthumous publication of his *Cours de linguis-*

tique générale (1916). While scholars like Franz Boas had propagated the study of languages as windows into the culture of communities one was interested in, linguistics as a science in the 20th century also started developing its own scientific questions, delinked as it were from culture, for example by investigating the nature of sound systems, as in the work of the influential linguist Nikolai Sergejewitsch Trubetzkoy (1890–1939) and others.

While Edward Sapir made his own important contributions on structural differences between languages, for example in the way in which words are structured, he also maintained a clear interest in the interaction between language and culture. Contemporaries like Leonard Bloomfield (1887–1949), often seen as the "father" of descriptive (structural) linguistics in the United States with his classic *Language* (1921), initiated a research tradition that was – and still is – concerned primarily with the formal structure of languages rather than with situated discourse.

This research tradition received a new impetus with the first publications of Noam Chomsky, probably the most prominent protagonist of formal schools of linguistics, from the second half of the 1950s onwards. Chomsky and his followers, in what is sometimes called the "Generative Enterprise", prioritize(d) the "ideal speaker-listener" in a homogeneous speech community, whose competence, or, more specifically, whose tacit knowledge of grammatical rules takes a central place. The interested reader may want to read the insightful survey by Kroskrity (2004: 498–500) of "language ideologies" among linguists in this respect.

It was this diminution in the role attached to culture in mainstream linguistics in the United States which appears to have motivated the anthropologist and linguist Dell Hymes (1927–2009), through his seminal article "The ethnography of speaking" (1962), to try to bridge the widening gap between linguistics and anthropology at the time, with the following statements:

> In one sense this area fills the gap between what is usually described in grammars, and what is usually described in ethnographies (...). The ethnography of speaking is concerned with the situations and uses, the patterns and functions, of speaking as an activity in its own right. (Hymes 1962: 16, 1968: 101)

Hymes also saw this as an opportunity in anthropology for comparative studies of the patterning and functions of speech, for which he proposed the term "ethnography of speaking". In a slightly modified programmatic statement published in 1968, Hymes repeated the goals and central notions of his publication from six years earlier. As speech and language vary in function cross-culturally, the speech activity of a community is the primary object of attention (Hymes 1968: 132). The

model known as the "ethnography of speaking" contains four central notions, which are as follows:
1. speech community;
2. speech events;
3. constituent factors of speech events;
4. functions of speech.

In the original (1962) contribution, a "speech community" was defined as a group of people who often use common signs. Because they communicate in a particular way, they are different from other groups. According to Hymes (1974: 54) a "speech community" involves "a community sharing rules for the conduct and interpretation of speech, and rules for the interpretation of at least one linguistic variety". In other words, for him "speech community" does not refer to a community defined by a common language, but rather by common linguistic norms. This definition moves its conceptualization away from questions of grammar (and grammatically possible utterances) to language use and the question of whether interactants share ideologies about proper language use.

An important part of the investigation of "speech events" (events with a beginning and an end) as an ethnographic or anthropological-linguistic technique is formed by the identification of words which name them in the speech community one is interested in as a researcher. An elegant application of the notion "speech event" in Hymes' descriptive model is found in Katriel (1985) in her description of a "verbal ritual" known as *kiturim* or *kuterai* in colloquial Israeli Hebrew, which may be translated as 'griping' in English. It involves socializing, typically among middle-class Israeli friends, through face-to-face oral engagements and joke telling. Primary topics are the expression of discontent about issues of public life, with the purpose of relieving pent-up tensions and frustrations among the group, especially at Friday night gatherings in private homes.

Katriel's contribution already illustrates a number of additional features which are part of Hymes' model, namely the additional two notions "constituent factors" and "functions of speech". Hymes (1968: 111) lists seven "constituent factors":
1. Sender (Addresser)
2. Receiver (Addressee)
3. Message Form
4. Channel
5. Code
6. Topic
7. Setting (Scene, Situation)

In the speech event described by Katriel (1985), sender and receiver are friends meeting in private homes (as a setting) on the evening before the Sabbath (the day of rest), where they discuss topics related to public life in the country. Rather than using social media, they use oral communication as a channel. The message form is the conversations of people socializing on a Friday evening. The code used in such settings is rather informal, as the participants are friends.

With respect to the fourth component of the model, that of "function of speech", Hymes (1968: 117) lists seven types of functions, six of which go back to Jakobson (1960) and his semiotic model of language. The first three concepts from this list, the expressive, the directive, and the poetic function, in turn go back to Bühler (1934).

1. Expressive (emotive)
2. Directive (conative, pragmatic, rhetorical, persuasive)
3. Poetic
4. Contact (phatic)
5. Metalinguistic
6. Referential (denotative, cognitive)
7. Contextual (situational)

Additional terms between parentheses in the list of functions indicate terms also found in the literature with basically the same meaning or function. These types of functions do not necessarily operate separately from each other, as already pointed out by Jakobson (1960: 353). Directives, for example, involve orders, prohibitions, instructions, suggestions, permission, and the like, as in *One should open the window in order to ventilate this room*. However, several features of a message may participate in all functions, sometimes in a covert (rather than overt) manner. Thus, the referential value of a message may be understood, but not the expressive or directive notion implied; for example, if a speaker of English asks *Could you open the window?*, the referential function may be clear (*Yes, I can*), but its directive role (as a polite request) is only understood through socialization in the English language.

The fourth function of speech in Hymes' model, that of phatic communion (involving the establishment of contact), can be observed with infant-directed speech as the first verbal function acquired by infants, as the latter are not able to send or receive informative communication yet themselves. For Laver (1992) it seems to have three functions in the initial phase of conversation.

> The first of these is to defuse (...) the potential hostility of silence in situations where speech is conventionally anticipated (...). Secondly, it (...) has an initiatory function, in that it allows the participants to cooperate in getting the interaction comfortably under way, using

> emotionally uncontroversial (...) material, and demonstrating by signals of cordiality and tentative social solidarity their mutual acceptance of the possibility of an inter-action taking place (...) Thirdly, (...) phatic communion has an exploratory function, (...) in that it allows the participants to feel their way towards the working consensus of their interaction (...), partly by revealing their perception of their relative social status. (Laver 1992: 301)

Metalinguistic function revolves around "speaking of language", rather than speaking a language or investigating language as an object. Jakobson (1960: 356) observes that "aphasia [the inability to comprehend or formulate language] may often be defined as a loss of ability for metalinguistic operations". Metalinguistic awareness, or knowledge about metalinguistic functions of language, is at the heart of language ideologies and of understanding other people's minds, as further discussed in the next chapter.

Hymes (1968) adds another parameter, number 7 in the list, that of contextual or situational function. He thereby initiated an important dimension picked up at a later stage by cognitive linguists (as discussed below), by pointing towards the importance of exploring the contexts of speech events. "The contextual frames must be sought not in the usual linguistic corpus, but in behavioral situations" (Hymes 1962: 104), for example when looking at a set of greetings in English ranging from "Hi" to "It's a damned good thing you got here when you did, Jack". Examples of contextual frames and their social implications are found in the next two sections of the present chapter, as well as in subsequent chapters.

A further crucial feature of Hymes's (1962, 1968) model is the distinction between "etic" and "emic" approaches. The four main components or notions of his "ethnography of communication" model together constitute an "etic grid", i.e., a framework or network whereby not all features are necessarily relevant in describing and analysing specific speech events. The distinction between "etic" and "emic" goes back to a central distinction in linguistics between "phonetics" and "phonemics". The latter term, which was popular in American structural linguistics in the 20th century, has the same meaning as "phonology" in European linguistics. Whereas "phones" (represented between brackets in linguistics, [ ]) refer to sounds, "phonemes" (represented between slashes in linguistics, / /) refer to sound units, i.e., abstract units which may encompass one or more sounds. Hence, there is not necessarily a one-to-one relationship between phonemes and phones in a language (i.e., between the phonemic/phonological level and the phonetic level), as the following examples help to illustrate.

English and Korean are both languages with stops (i.e., consonants produced with a closure of two articulators in the oral tract, for example the upper and lower lip, or the tongue and teeth ridge, as with [p] versus [t]). In both English and Korean these two sounds may be aspirated, i.e., pronounced with an exhalation of breath ([p^h], [t^h]). In English it is predictable when aspiration will occur with stops, namely at the onset (beginning) of a stressed syllable, as in [pə tʰeɪtəʊ] 'potato'. As shown in this example, there are standardized phonetic symbols for every sound attested in human languages, the so-called IPA (International Phonetic Alphabet) symbols.

The slight burst of breath accompanying the pronunciation of these stops is absent in other positions in English (as in *span, stan, map, mat*). Similar phonetic distinctions occur in Korean. However, in contrast with English, the distinction in Korean is not predictable, for example because both the unaspirated and the aspirated "*p*" can occur at the beginning of a word (or syllable):

(73) pul   'fire'
      pʰul   'grass'

In other words, while English and Korean are phonetically identical in this respect, phonemically (or phonologically) they are not. Because in English the stop produced with the upper and lower lip is unaspirated in most positions, this may be argued to be the norm, the aspiration at the beginning of a stressed syllable being the exception. Hence, the phoneme /p/ is normally pronounced as a phone [p] (i.e., phonetically), with the phone [pʰ] being a predictable variant, i.e., an allophone. A phoneme may thus be viewed as a prototypical representation of a set of phones. In Korean, on the other hand, there is a phoneme /p/ and a phoneme /pʰ/, each with its own phonetic realization.

This abstraction also reflects the (sometimes tacit) knowledge which speakers have of the language (or languages) they speak, i.e., they may not be aware of such distinctions but they would immediately recognize a foreign accent if somebody were to fail to make this distinction in the proper places. From a linguistic point of view, languages may have the same sounds, but the phonemic/phonological status of these sounds may be different, as the contrast between English and Korean shows.

It was these important distinctions between phonetics and phonemics which inspired the linguist Kenneth Pike (1912–2000) to draw a fundamental distinction between "etic" (parallel to "phonetic") and "emic" (parallel to "phonemic") standpoints for the description of human behaviour in his magnum opus (Pike 1967: 37–72).

Etic (or phonetic) units are available in advance and are based on prior broad sampling or surveys (for which the International Phonetic Association provides symbols in the case of languages), i.e., before one begins the analysis of a particular language or culture. This preliminary work results in a specific analysis that subsequently provides an internal (emic) perspective on that language or culture.

Where is the parallel to etic and emic approaches in anthropological linguistics? Let us take "proverbs", a popular topic given the social wisdom usually reflected in them, as shown by the numerous publications on "proverbs in language X or language Y" from different parts of the world; see, for example, the collection of studies by Baumgart and Bounfour (2004). According to Hymes (1962: 24), one crucial technique in order to arrive at an emic understanding of phenomena investigated by a researcher is through words which name them. An important question from an emic point of view, therefore, is the question of whether this channel (in Hymes' terminology) or form of speech called "proverb" is also recognized as a taxonomic "category" in speech events by speakers of the community one is interested in. In actual fact, in quite a few languages there is no word or phrase that could be translated as 'proverb' in English; these utterances are simply part of oral communication. It is still possible that speakers attach a special status to such idiomatic constructions, but if a language does have a separate word or phrase to characterize these, one can be reassured that one has identified a taxonomic category which is also relevant from an emic perspective.

"Etic outsiders" may treat specific linguistic phenomena in a foreign language as a distinct genre, but this may be the result of an ethnocentric move (influenced by the structure of the outsiders' primary language). Pike (1967) also points towards the difficulties in learning to react emically to an alien emic system: "The general problem can be summed up in the words of Goodenough (1957: 173), who affirms that '[t]he great problem for a science of man is how to get from the objective world of materiality, with its infinite variability [an etic view of the world], to the subjective world of form as it exists in (. . .) the minds of our fellow men' [through the discovery of their emic units]" (Pike 1967: 55), This is a rather interesting warning, especially in light of the discussion in earlier chapters of the present monograph on the potentially ethnocentric bias of some cognitive tests in science.

Readers are encouraged to read Hymes' original contribution (1968), but additional examples are presented below, first through the introduction of a slightly modified model, called "the ethnography of communication", following a suggestion for a terminological modification by Gumperz and Hymes (1964), in order to emphasize the intersubjective dimension of verbal communication and also to accommodate non-verbal communication. The same descriptive and analytical framework as in the original contribution by Hymes (1962, 1968) has been represented in a slightly alternative manner, summarized by the mnemonic acronym SPEAKING, from Hymes (1974: 53–62). The latter relates to the third dimension of his model, that of "constituent factors", containing eight divisions covering sixteen components. The acronym stands for Situation, Participants, Ends, Act, Key, Instrumentality, Norms, and Genre.

S(ituation)	1. Setting (time and place of a speech act)
	2. Scene (cultural definition of a setting)
P(articipants)	3. Speaker, or sender
	4. Addressor
	5. Hearer, or receiver, or audience
	6. Addressee
E(nds)	7. Purposes – outcomes
	8. Purposes – goals
A(ct sequence)	9. Message form
	10. Message content
K(ey)	11. Key (clues that establish the spirit of a speech act)
I(nstrumentalities)	12. Channel
	13. Forms of speech
N(orms)	14. Norms of interaction
	15. Norms of interpretation
G(enres)	16. Genres

The first constituent factor, *Situation* (covering setting and scene), involves descriptions of the social context in which specific speech events occur or play a role. They are the subject of traditional ethnographies describing ritualized behaviour after the birth of a child, marriage, burials, and other occasions involving specific conversational routines. From an analytical point of view, the advantage of rituals for the insider is their repetitive nature, and thereby their (partial) predictability in terms of their structuring, which reduces the complexity of social interaction for insiders. Sections 7.1 and 7.2 serve to illustrate two such rituals, greeting and parting, from an anthropological linguistic point of view.

Participants primarily involve dyadic relations between speaker or sender and receiver or audience, alternatively labelled "addressor" and "addressee", as illustrated with greeting and parting strategies below; triadic communication is discussed in Chapter 8, whereas more complex (polyadic) interactions are discussed in Chapter 11, as part of the presentation of conversation analysis as a model.

The concept of *Ends* involves purposes, outcomes, or goals of communicative interactions. Scholars disagree as to the role of greeting strategies in this respect, namely in terms of whether they just involve ritualized behaviour (phatic communion), or more than that, as further illustrated in the discussion of greetings below. Senft (2009) presents an informative discussion of the status of phatic communion in scientific discussions.

Act sequence is another constituent factor potentially relevant for a description of speech events in a given community concerning the message form and order of speech events. This feature is illustrated below in the discussion of greeting and leaving strategies, and analysed in more detail from an intercultural perspective in Chapter 11 on conversation analysis.

Key, i.e., the manner or spirit in which a speech act is realized, governing speaker's intent, primarily relates to intonation, change in volume, or voice quality. For example, Loveday (1981) describes the use of high pitch in speech among Japanese females, who thereby separate themselves acoustically from Japanese male speakers more than speakers of English would do, and hence stereotypically highlight sexual differences. Japanese males may emphasize their masculinity "by adopting a deep-voiced, guttural mode of speaking which is often accompanied by stern faces and stiff postures" (Seward 1968: 111, quoted in Loveday 1981: 86). In the same contribution, Loveday (1981: 86) points towards parallel behaviour among males from the Wolof nobility, who thereby express dignity. This observation is in line with the claims made by Albert (1972: 77), who describes the use of a special tone of voice and its modulation together with "a suitable elegant vocabulary, graceful gestures with hand and spear for deflecting the anger of a superior, or when serving as an intermediary between a petitioner and one's feudal superior in traditional Wolof society".

A final example illustrating the importance of prosody in the establishment of roles in social interaction comes from the Turkana gender trope *o-ityoo-koy* 'oh mother oh my', typically used by women to express amazement or excitement. However, men also sometimes use this expression with a falsetto voice, repeating it several times in order to imitate female amazement or excitement.

The "key role" played by prosody even in intercultural communication becomes clear from the following case. Gumperz (1982a) shows how different sets of extra-linguistic knowledge may lead to misinterpretations and miscommunication. Indian and Pakistani women working in a staff cafeteria at a major British airport were perceived as surly and uncooperative due to the fact that they used an intonation pattern that differed from British English, something they only became aware of after some discussion and teaching sessions (Gumperz 1982a: 173). Further examples of the role played by the notion of "key" can be found under the heading "key" in the index of the present study.

Instrumentality involves channels, styles of speech, or repertoires in a speech community, but also verbal but nonvocal (or spoken) communication in its various forms, through alternative media of transmission such as writing, whistling, drumming, or sign language as against non-verbal communication (the latter being discussed in more detail in Chapter 12). With oral communication, there is also a gamut of options, as the discussion of performance in Section 8.4 illustrates.

The description of constituent factors such as the setting for specific speech acts presupposes the presence of a researcher observing, describing, and possibly participating in the events. It is sometimes assumed that in an etic approach the cultural perspective of the scientist in his "participant observation" does not interfere. But being "culturally neutral" or limiting the cultural bias of the scientific observer is more easily said than done, as the discussion of "WEIRD" people in Section 5.4 should also have made clear.

Observation attained by participating in social events (a building stone of research in the social sciences probably first proposed by the anthropologist Bronislaw Malinowski) may be complemented by quantitative research (usually involving the use of questionnaires) as well as qualitative research (through interviews, ideally in the language of the speakers whose language behaviour one is interested in, or, alternatively, in the contact language of the area). This latter strategy is particularly valuable as a "discovery procedure" for the identification of emic perspectives of speakers.[36]

Each of the elements from the "etic grid" is illustrated below in Sections 7.2 and 7.3 on the basis of two types of access rituals: greeting and parting. This is followed by a survey of more recent approaches (in Section 7.4) inspired by Hymes' descriptive model, but also involving elaborations upon his model: first, the frame-and-scenario model, and second, speech act theory.

The access rituals discussed below are instances of what have come to be known as "schemas" or "schemata", or more specifically "event schemas". "Schema" as a concept goes back to the philosopher Immanuel Kant, or specifically to Kant (1781), and refers to a procedure for generating an image of a concept. "Event schema" was already used in cognitive psychology by authors like Bartlett (1932) as an organizing principle in interpreting events. Such event schemas in human memory networks are activated in response to external stimuli, for example when meeting somebody. As the examples of greeting and parting strategies in Sections 7.2 and 7.3 show, such event schemas are subject to intercultural variation. The interested reader is also referred to Palmer (1996: 177–185) for a discussion of additional schemas, such as sequencing schema, more or less corresponding to "scenarios" in the present study, or perspective schemas; here, the analysis of the egocentric perspective in Tima, as discussed in Section 4.3, may serve as an example.

---

[36] The textbook by Völkel and Kretzschmar (2021) contains useful exercises sensitivising investigators to biases resulting from the researcher's own experiences as well as emphasizing the importance of emic perspectives.

7.2 Greeting strategies

Inspired by Hymes' descriptive model, numerous studies appeared in the 1980s and 1990s on greeting and parting strategies in different speech communities on the African continent, for example Adegbija (1989) on greetings strategies in Ogori, Yoruba, and Nigerian English; McIntyre (1980) on Hausa; Naden (1980) on Mampruli; Morton (1988) on Beja; Akindele (1990) on Yoruba; Nwoye (1993) on Igbo; and Yahya-Othman (1995) on Swahili, to mention but a few. One of the earliest studies applying Hymes' descriptive model to greeting strategies in an African language is the investigation by Ag Youssouf, Grimshaw, and Bird (1976) of such strategies in Tuareg (Tamāshaq), a Berber language spoken in Mali, with closely related varieties spoken in Niger and Algeria. The authors distinguish between routinely performed formulaic expressions by these nomadic groups in the desert and in camps in the Tuareg dialect spoken between Timbuktu and Gao. Although similar in form, the functions (and meanings and interpretations) of greetings in these two settings are quite different, as summarized in Table 18 (using Hymes' acronym SPEAKING, as the authors of the article do).

Table 18: Greeting in Tuareg (Ag Youssouf, Grimshaw, and Bird 1976).

Hymes' categories	Location of Encounter	
	Camp	Desert
Setting	Routine, familiar	Potentially dangerous
Participants	Usually known	Frequently unknown
Ends	Summons; politeness; validation of inter-personal access, etc.	Summons; identification of interlocutor; validation of access for purpose of obtaining survival-relevant information
Act characteristics	Formulae (religious invocation/ inquiring on well-being	Formulae (religious invocation/ inquiring on well-being)
Key	Usually unattended to (will be monitored if situationally relevant or if status of interpersonal relations is hostile or unclear)	Carefully monitored (key need not be carefully attended to if participants are known *and* friendly)
Instrumentality	Speech (Special Code) Arabic and Tamāshaq	Speech (Special Code) Handshake
Norms	Visitor begins/turns standardized	"Newcomer" initiates/High status first interlocutor
Genre	Greeting	Greeting

The visitor or newcomer is required by Tuareg rules to initiate the interaction during an encounter. When people meet far away from the nomadic camps, there is a complex interplay of variables such as perceived age, status, and other factors.

> This assignment of roles as visitor and host has further implications for subsequent rights of interrogatory priority. The assignment, moreover, is influenced not only by the perceived attributes of the participants themselves but also by such additionally complicating factors as the relative status of the participants' tribes and of their status within their own tribes. Finally, even such factors as numbers are important; one person meeting a group will initiate greetings. (Ag Youssouf, Grimshaw, and Bird 1976: 803)

Such diverging strategies between familiars and nonfamiliars also show that greetings tend to be indexical. Initial greeting typically involves three stages, followed by a stage whereby actual informational questioning occurs. At Stage One, when A is a newcomer, using the Arabic greeting is common; speakers may pronounce the pharyngeal fricative ʕ (signalling more Arabic influence), represented by an apostrophe ('), as a velar fricative ɣ instead; the macron on the vowel indicates a long vowel.

(74) A. salāmu   {'/ɣ} aleykum   'peace be on you'
      B. aleykum   ɣ   sālam   'on you be peace (too)'

This tends to be followed at Stage Two by handshakes, after which either A or B takes the role of interrogator depending on age, social status, and/or sex. Older persons with higher status and males are more likely to assume interrogator roles.

(75) Q mā   d   tolahad   'what do you look for?'
      R alxer ɣas (al {ḥ/x} amdulillahi)   'only peace (praise be to Allah)'

The optional form expressing 'praise to Allah' indicates stronger Islamic influence when the glottal fricative ḥ is used, but may also be pronounced as *alxamdulillah*. After these opening routines the responder is generally required to take the role of the interrogator.

(76) Q mā   d   tolahad   'what do you look for?'
      R alxer ɣās   'only peace'

Stage Three expresses the transition from a formulaic or non-referential greeting to a referential exchange of information (without a limit on recursiveness).

(77) Q. mā   iɣshādan   'what has gone wrong?'
         mā   ijān   labāsan   'what bad has occurred'
    R.   kalash   'none (nothing)'
         kala, wer deɣshas ofraya   'none, not that I have heard'
         alxer ɣās   'only peace'
    Q   mā   d ishrāyan   'what is new?'
         isalān   'the news?'
    R.   kalash   'none (nothing)'
         alxer ɣās   'only peace'

At Stage Four, questions can be asked by either person:

(78) hār   n-dake   'where are you going (lit. up to where)?'
     n-dake s-ihal   asīkel   'where does travel take you?'

Although one does not necessarily know the other person when meeting in the desert, there is no obligation at any point to introduce oneself, nor is it considered appropriate to ask for identification among Tuareg speakers meeting in the desert, according to the authors. As shown in Table 18, the desert as a setting contrasts with an encounter in a Tamāshaq camp.

Anthropologists interested in symbolic behaviour, like Victor Turner, have pointed out that greetings as linguistic routines are potentially "threshold" or "liminal" events, as they involve the status of individuals as perceived by others or by themselves (Turner 1969). The importance of liminality becomes particularly clear from a pioneering study by Irvine (1974) on greeting strategies and strategies of status manipulation among speakers of Wolof in Senegal. From a sociological point of view, the society whose greeting strategies are described by Judith Irvine may be characterized as "patronage", involving a hierarchical structure characterized by inequality as a cultural ideology, which is also enacted in greetings. The Wolof saying "When two persons greet each other, one has shame, the other has glory" (Irvine 1974: 175) presumably reflects this social experience. "The principal criteria for ranking people in a Wolof community are age, sex, caste, and achieved prestige (which may consist of wealth, or of an exceptional moral character)", according to Irvine (1974: 169).

Greetings in Wolof are dyadic, i.e., one greets members in a group individually, rather than a group as a whole. A typical greeting in Wolof consists of a salutation (sal), questions (Q) concerning the state of the other person and that of the other person's family and friends (optional), followed by praising God (P), as shown in Table 19, reproduced from Irvine (1974: 174).

Table 19: Greeting in Wolof (Irvine 1974).

Sal		1.	A.	*Salaam alikum.*	Peace be with you (Arabic)
			B.	*Malikum salaam.*	With you be peace (Arabic)
		2.	(A.	A's name)	[A. gives own name]
			(B.	B's name)	[B. gives own name]
		3.	A.	B's name	[A gives B's name]
			B.	{A's name / *Naam*, A's name}	{[B gives A's name] / Yes, A's name}
QP					
Q₁		1.	A.	*Na ngga def?*	How do you do?
			B.	*Maanngi fi rek*	I am here only.
		2.	A.	*Mbaa dyamm ngg' am*	Don't you have peace?
			B.	*Dyamm rek, naam.*	Peace only, yes.
Q₂	(a)	1.	A.	*Ana waa kïr gi.*	Where/how are the people of the household?
			B.	*Nyu-ngga fa.*	They were there.
		2.	A.	*Ana* [name]?	Where/how is X?
			B.	*Mu-ngga fa.*	He/She is there.
	(b)	1.	A.	*Mbaa {tawaatu / feebaru} loo?*	Isn't it that you aren't sick?
			B.	*Maanggi sant Yalla*	I am praising God
		2.	A.	*Mbaa kenn {feebarul? / tawaatul?}*	Isn't it that anyone isn't sick?
			B.	*Nyu-nggi sant Yalla*	They are praising God
P		1.	A.	*H'mdillay.*	Thanks be to God. [Arabic]
			B.	{*H'mdillay.* / *Tubarkalla.*}	{Thanks be to God. [Arabic] / Blessed be God.}
		2.	A.	{*H'mdillay.* / *Tubarkalla.*}	{Thanks be to God. / Blessed be God.}
			B.	{*H'mdillay.* / *Tubarkalla.*}	{Thanks be to God. / Blessed be God.}

The analysis presented in Irvine (1974) is based on participatory fieldwork as well as on interviews with speakers and their emic perspective on greeting strategies. According to Judith Irvine, ideally, the lower-ranking person greets the person of higher social status first; however, "[a]cceptance or refusal of the role of initiator is of major importance in how one handles the greeting situation" (Irvine 1974: 169). Thus, although greetings in Wolof are ritualized, they are not necessarily fixed, for example in that interactants may try and manipulate their status and thereby adapt the corresponding kind of greeting strategy. A higher status implies more power, but the other side of the coin is social (i.e., financial) responsibility or obligations towards those considered to be lower in the social hierarchy. This may lead to situations such as the following:

> It is possible (...) that the two parties to a particular encounter do not so readily fall into a tacit agreement on their relative positions (...) For this reason each party must enter the greeting equipped with some strategy as to which role to take. The two strategies of role position, which for convenience I shall call Self-Lowering and Self-Elevating, refer to attempts to take the lower-status or the higher-status in the greeting (I[nitiator] or R[epondent]) respectively. (Irvine 1974: 175)

Strategies or tactics for "self-lowering" include initiating greetings and ignoring questions of the type illustrated above. Avoiding initiating the greeting, as part of self-elevating strategies, is less common than mutual deference as a choice of role. Speakers have a number of other strategies to hand. In terms of Hymes' SPEAKING model, the key may also be modulated, in order to communicate one's self-image as part of a self-lowering strategy. Thus, higher pitch, louder voice, and more rapid tempo are associated with lower status, and lower pitch, softer voice, and slower speech tempo are associated with higher status as features of speech demeanour. The quantity of speech also matters; a verbose style is associated with low status, while a terse style is associated with high status, according to Irvine (1974: 176–177).

The Wolof greeting strategies above illustrate a specific type of schema, that of "role schema" (also sometimes referred to as "participation schema"), which Augoustinos and Walker (1995: 3) define as "knowledge structure that people have of specific role positions in a cultural group". As pointed out by Sharifian (2011: 9), "people across different cultural groups construct different categories and schemas about the same role. Among Aboriginal Australians the word for 'mother' evokes a role category, which would extend well beyond the biological mother and among certain Aboriginal people it may even include some male members of the extended family (...)".

Such greeting strategies can be described as situational *frames*, i.e., conceptual representations of the collection of factors determining specific language behaviour. These frames stand in paradigmatic contrast to each other, i.e., speakers may activate a particular frame when intending to speak or when speaking. During social interactions, such frames may also change, as shown in Irvine's (1974) discussion of greeting strategies in Wolof.

While ritualization or conventionalization is involved to some extent, the schemas should not be interpreted as rigid and fixed conceptualizations. Rather, as the discussion of Wolof greeting strategies shows, agency plays a significant role. Duranti (2004: 453) defines this notion as the property of those entities (i) that have some degree of control over their own behaviour, (ii) whose actions in the world affect other entities' (and sometimes their own), and (iii) whose actions are the object of evaluation (e.g., in terms of their responsibility for a given outcome).

In an early contribution on intercultural miscommunication resulting from the activation of differential event schemas and role schemas of participants, Van Jaarsveld (1988) describes the different greeting strategies of speakers of Afrikaans, Zulu, and other languages of South Africa. A greeting exchange in Afrikaans may take the following structure, for example:

(79) Goeiemôre Jan   'good morning John'
     Môre Piet. Hoe gaan die? 'morning Pete. How are you doing?'
     Goed en met jou   'fine, and you?'
     Goed, dankie   'fine, thanks'

From an intercultural perspective the question arises: Does the more junior person greet first, as is common in Afrikaans and English, or the more senior person, as is common in languages like Zulu? Van Jaarsveld (1988) describes additional points of variation, such as whether eye contact is involved during the exchange of greetings; consider the Zulu greeting by the more senior person: *sawubona* 'I see you', to which the common reply is: *yebo* (*sawubona*) 'indeed (I see you)'. Social space is another potential point of variation. A junior Zulu speaker is supposed to sit down without necessarily being invited to do so, in order not to find himself or herself in a position elevated above the more senior person. In post-Apartheid South Africa, there has been mutual cultural adaptation to some extent, presumably, but no research appears to be available on this yet.

One question which researchers have asked is to what extent such ceremonial greetings simply involve routines and thereby non-referential speech events just involving phatic (from Greek *phatos* 'spoken') communion, i.e., "small talk", which serves to establish bonds of personal union between people brought together by the mere need for companionship and not by any purpose of communicating ideas (as claimed by Malinowski 1923: 316, 1936: 319). Based on an analysis of greeting strategies in Samoan, however, Duranti (1997b) argues that greetings are not necessarily devoid of propositional content. For Felix K. Ameka, himself a speaker of the Ghanaian language Ewe, phatic communion is also about displaying cultural values such as inclusiveness and harmony (Ameka 2009: 129). And, as pointed out by the same author, they are not only about courtesy but also about genuine inquiries about the well-being of others.

Malinowski's claim has also been contradicted by researchers from other speech communities where extensive greeting strategies occur, as pointed out in Ameka (1999). This issue is also addressed by van Jaarsveld (1988: 88). While 13 out of 74 speakers of Afrikaans took the question 'How are you doing' to be a sincere question, 51 out of 59 speakers of languages such as Zulu interpreted it as sincere. As argued in Ameka (2009), there is usually a sincere commitment or interest involved, serving to establish bonds of personal union between people, or to cement social relations.

Some readers may assume that from a cross-cultural perspective greetings are standard ("ritualized") procedures, themselves validating one's personal accessibility. But this is not necessarily so. Strecker (1988: 73) states that among the Hamar of southern Ethiopia the right to hospitality is an open question for those who are not closely related. Ivo Strecker relates this to the "individualistic pattern of Hamar social organization, where small domestic groups are on perpetual guard against each other". Avoiding verbal greeting can be observed in different scenes in the *Hamar Trilogy*, a brilliant documentary by Jean Lydall and colleagues on the Hamar speech community. In one scene, relatives of one of the main characters come to collect their share in a brideprice that was agreed upon at an earlier point. Instead of being welcomed, these visitors sit down outside the homestead, waiting for an audience, so to speak. Here the liminal ("threshold") status of greetings is probably manifested in its purest form. Strecker (1988: 73) also reports on such an experience among the Hamar: "No one in the homestead will seem to notice him at this stage (an irritating experience, by the way, for a European visitor who has been culturally conditioned to expect his face wants to be attended to immediately)".

The present author had similar experiences while living in the Turkana area, northwestern Kenya, for a total period of 18 months. Although the languages of the Hamar and Turkana are not genetically related (they belong to Omotic and Nilotic, respectively) and their speakers are not neighbours either, their pastoral culture and habitus appears to be rather similar. In fact, neighbouring groups like the Turkana or the Karimojong tend to describe the two speech communities, Hamar and Päkoot, as being "the same" (Quincy Amoah, personal communication 2020). As is the case among the pastoral Hamar, one is not necessarily met with great hospitality expressed through mutual greetings on one's first arrival at a Turkana homestead. On the other hand, Turkana speakers do have extensive greeting strategies. There is, for example, the informal exchange of greetings, which may be followed by additional questions on the well-being of others:

(80) A :   ɛ-jɔ́k=ắắ   'is it (everything) good/fine'
             3-be.good=Q
       B :   ɛ-jɔ́k   'it (everything) is good/fine'
             3-be.good

But in addition there are ceremonial greetings, for example between two adults (A and B), as in the following brief set of turn-taking exchanges (which may be followed by another ten or so exchanges of so-called "allo-bono" expressions):

(81) A: maatá   'hail!'
      B: maatá   robó   'hail alright'
      A: maatá   na-wúy(e)   'hail to the homestead'
      B: maatá   robó   'hail alright'
      A: maatá (à)   ŋíkílyók   'hail to the people'
      B: maatá   robó   'hail alright'
      A: maatá (à)   ŋáátúk   'hail to the cattle!'
      B: maatá   robó   'hail alright'

The particle *robó* is a discourse marker belonging to the realm of expressive speech acts, showing empathy with the interactant. The same exchange of greetings and wishes for well-being may also be used in public assemblies, for example between members of generation sets or territorial sections (which are part of the social organization of the Turkana people).

Greeting strategies are often seen by speakers in different parts of the world as indexical or emblematic signs of both their own and other communities' local, regional, or ethnic origins. Ameka (1987: 306) points towards such areal differences within the Ewe speech community with respect to the use of specific fixed expressions in linguistic routines. Such differences, for example with respect to greeting or parting strategies, may be explained as the result of regional variants of frames, as well as schemas which are more common in the area. Such routine formulae must be learned as a unit, and hence provide a script for greeting as one type of scenario. The latter express generalized knowledge about the sequence of speech events in specific contexts. Thus, while still engaging in the same discursive practices of greeting, alternative elaborations on inherited common cultural knowledge index regional origins.

7.3 Parting strategies

Those of us who have visited Australia may have wondered about the common formula heard in shops and elsewhere when parting: *See you later*. It is one of those idiomatic phrases showing that there may be a mismatch between the literal meaning and the actual cultural meaning of some ritualized utterances.

Ameka (1999) presents an elegant discussion of areal conversational routines and leave-taking strategies in a southern Ghanaian context. Closing of social contacts here tends to consist of three stages: "The first, the pre-closing, is the phase in which an interactant asks permission from the other party to leave. The second, a leave-taking phase, may comprise a gesture of formal closure and/or a seeing off strategy, and the exchange of farewells. The third, the departure phase, is when parting finally takes place" (Ameka 1999: 262).

Ameka (1999: 263) quotes the following excerpt from an Ewe play by Frank K. Nyaku, *Hogbedede* ('Visiting Hogbe'), between a visitor (Tsiami) and a host (Bokɔ), in order to illustrate the first phase of such ritualized parting strategies.

(82) Tsiami: ... fífiá mía-bíá mɔ́
 ... now 1PL-ask way
 Lit. now we will ask the way
 '(...) Now, we will ask permission to leave.'
 Bokɔ: mɔ́ li faa
 way be:PRES:3SG freely
 mia-de aƒéme nyúíe
 2PL-reach home well
 Lit. There is way. Reach home well.
 'You may go. Have a safe journey home.'
 Tsiami: yoo
 'OK.'

Ameka (1999: 264) observes that the parting strategy *[o]n va demander la route* (lit. 'one will ask for the road/route'), as a forewarning followed by an exchange of farewells accompanying leave-taking and the final departure, is common across West Africa. Ameka (1999: 264) mentions a funny anecdote about a student from Mali in Paris who apparently transferred this strategy to French after having been invited for dinner by a French lady. When he said "On va demander la route", the French host understood this as a request for a route description of how to get back home. This pre-closing strategy is referred to in Ewe as *mɔ́bábíá* 'way asking/permission seeking'. The next phase, negotiating leave-taking, consists of "(i) a physical gesture marking the closure of formal and ceremonial encounters; (ii) the seeing-off activity; and (iii) the exchange of farewells" (Ameka 1999: 266). Accompanying a departing visitor beyond the bounds of the home is common among Ewe speakers, but it is also widespread across the continent. The departure phase may be accompanied by hand shaking and/or waving. As further pointed out by Ameka (1999: 279), farewell expressions among Ewe speakers tend to obey the "Pollyanna Principle, stressing the positive and favorable aspects, e.g., blessing, reciprocal good wishes, plans for future contacts and remembrances to people at the departing person's destination".

In an earlier, more general contribution on ritualized speech, Ameka (1987) described such linguistic routines or formulaic expressions for Ewe. According to him, these fall into two categories: "allo-bono recognitive expressions" and "allo-malo recognitive expressions" (from Greek *allos* 'other, different', and the lexemes for 'good' and 'bad', respectively), a terminological distinction proposed by Matisoff (1979) in his monograph on psycho-ostensive expressions in Yiddish. With respect to the cultural background of these expressions, Ameka (1987) observes that in Ewe the praise for good things happening to somebody goes to supernatural beings (God, divinities, ancestors) and not to the individual, as in the Anglo-Saxon world. Moreover, the range of contexts in which such expressions are used in the two speech communities also differ.

Farewell expressions are subject to quite a bit of intercultural variation, although they never seem to involve interrogatives (Ameka 1999: 274). In the same way in which greeting strategies may be avoided among speakers of Turkana when meeting others (as discussed above), there is not necessarily any distinct closing phase in social encounters, nor any formal signaling of departure by boundary markers either. Such a scene may again be observed in the ethnographic documentary by the McDougalls, *Lorang's Way* (1977). David and Judith Mac-Dougall produced an impressive trilogy, *Turkana Conversations*, consisting of *A Wife among Wives*, *Wedding Camels*, and *Lorang's Way*. In the latter, a prosperous Turkana herdsman by the name of Lorang is the key figure, reflecting upon his life experiences based on his travels and contact with people from different cultural backgrounds.[37]

Pastoral communities such as those of the Turkana tend to be characterized by social scientists as gerontocracies, i.e., communities where social authority is associated with age. The McDougalls show one such meeting of elders in *Lorang's Way*, where they are discussing Harambee, a fundraising tradition in Kenya intended to strengthen community building. In this meeting the Turkana elders are discussing the question of whether they should contribute financially (by donating animals) to this initiative or not, because of misappropriation by government officials. When the group dissolves, virtually all participants go without exchanging any verbal or non-verbal greetings, a kind of ritualized behaviour which is common with group meetings (Picture 15). The main protagonist of the

---

37 Screenshots of *Lorang's Way* as found in the present monograph are taken from a version of the film on the internet which can be accessed under https://archive.org/details/lorangsway/. The importance of this and other ethnocinematographical contributions for language documentation and anthropological linguistics is discussed in Dimmendaal (2010).

ethnographic documentary, Lorang, uses this opportunity to rebuke another person in public who has apparently not returned a loan in time. The debtor replies and explains the reasons for the delay, and then walks off, as most other participants at this meeting do. Greeting and parting strategies, whether verbal or non-verbal, may thus be seen as enactments which help to (re)confirm and also to (re)negotiate identities.

Picture 15: Leave taking among Turkana after a meeting (*Lorang's Way*).

Speakers of Turkana and other pastoral communities in the area are far from unique in this respect. Ag Youssouf, Grimshaw, and Bird (1976: 817, fn.7) refer to a personal communication with Dell Hymes, where the latter explicitly challenged the universality of farewells, based, for example, on knowledge about the Wasco First Nation speech community in Oregon. Here, interactants may also simply leave without formally signaling departure. Leaving without signaling departure is something which may also be observed at linguistics conferences and other scientific meetings where hierarchical ranking on the one hand and personal sovereignty on the other is at stake. Conventionalizing such behaviour results in a minimization or at least a reduction of the risk of face loss, in case somebody does not reciprocate a greeting. It is these shared sociological conditions, presumably, which result in similar patterns of behaviour in different parts of the world.

Goody (1972) claims that extensive greeting strategies are found in complex hierarchical societies. But as Morton (1988) shows with respect to the Beja in Sudan, whose society is claimed to be strongly egalitarian, extensive greeting ceremonies are also common in this society. Common areal strategies in social interaction have been reported for Ethiopia by Yimam (1997). The author shows that cultural practices as embodied actions in specific contexts, such as greeting, felicitation, and condolence, also manifest common features in three languages historically belonging to different language families (although these are all distantly related to each other, as members of the Afroasiatic family): Amharic (Semitic), Oromo (Cushitic), and Wolayita/Wolaitta (Omotic). Strategies found in these speech communities differ from those found among the Nuer, who live in southwestern Ethiopia and across the border in South Sudan, and whose language belongs to the Nilo-Saharan family. While Nilo-Saharan languages in northern Ethiopia, such as the Kunama cluster and Nara, also converged towards Afroasiatic languages in the country, presumably as a result of multilingualism over a long period, Nilo-Saharan languages in southern Ethiopia are probably of more recent origin (Dimmendaal 2022a).

7.4 Elaborating upon the SPEAKING model

The four domains proposed by Hymes (1968) as part of his "etic grid" for language use, speech communities, speech events, constituent factors (of speech events), and functions of speech, have been subject to modifications and elaborations in subsequent decades, as shown next. Since the set of constituent factors involves so many components, and as several of these have received so many new impulses in recent times, new insights can be found throughout this monograph using the index entries related to the acronym SPEAKING (setting, scene, speaker etc.). Below, Dell Hymes' concepts are also taken as a basis for the introduction of additional theoretical concepts inspired primarily by cognitive linguistics and the philosophy of language, namely the frame-and-scenario model and speech act theory.

There is, first of all, the notion of "speech community", for which different definitions can be found in the literature. Alongside Hymes' definition (quoted in Section 7.1 above), there is a similar conceptualization in Labov (1972: 120–121), namely a community which "is not defined by any marked agreement in the use of language elements, so much as by participation in a set of shared norms".

The linguistic anthropologist Michael Silverstein (1945–2020) adhered to slightly different notions. Silverstein (1972: 622–623, and subsequent publications) distinguishes between "language community" and "speech community". For him, language was the collective attribute of a language community, embracing "variation from the very get-go" (Silverstein 2014: 19). A speech community is seen as a social group, generally a primary reference group, the members of which are, by degrees, oriented to a denotational norm, however much within its compass they recognize situated variation (Silverstein 2014: 4).

The term "language community" is avoided in the present monograph, as the concept of "language" is used for the abstracted system, whereas the term "speech" refers to language use. As pointed out by Morgan (2004: 8), the work of the sociologist John J. Gumperz (e.g., 1968) "revived the concept of the speech community by considering it a social construct". And this brings us to a second concept, that of "community of practice". The latter concept originated in the field of social learning (Lave and Wenger 1991), and was then transferred to linguistics, where it is probably best known through contributions of the sociolinguist Penelope Eckert (e.g., 2000). Eckert and McConnell-Ginet (1992: 96) define this concept as an "aggregate of people who come together around mutual engagement in an endeavor". Communities of practice, consequently, are not necessarily linguistically and physically located; instead, they may be bound by social conditions and values, as well as by attitudes about language use, for example through social media. Moreover, individuals may belong to different communities of practice, and the latter again may also cut across language boundaries, i.e., individuals often experience multiple communities of practice. This concept allows for such refinements both within a community sharing the same primary language but speaking different sociolects and in communities with different primary languages but interacting on a regular basis, for example by using a third language, or (in a diglossic situation) the (dominant) language of one of the two communities as a contact language.

De Fina (2007) describes such a situation where people belong to different communities of practice and engage in multiple identity practices. More specifically, she describes code-switching from English into Italian among immigrants in the United States, the setting being a card-playing club. The community itself consists of people with different social backgrounds, origins, and language competence, but participants apparently create an association between good card playing and the ability to speak some Italian. Based on her study of these immigrant communities, De Fina (2007: 389) also dispels the idea that ethnic identities are fixed properties existing in abstraction from concrete groups and their practices; she shows that it is only within those practices that they can be defined and qualified.

Many extensions and modifications have been proposed over the years with respect to the list of constituent factors. "Norm", for example, has been the subject of an influential monograph by Brown and Levinson (1987) on politeness strategies, to which an entire chapter is dedicated here (Chapter 10). Rather than listing these various modifications here, therefore, the reader is encouraged to check the list of terms associated with the acronym SPEAKING (above) through the index.

The fourth pillar in Hymes' model, that of "function of speech", has also been subject to closer scrutiny. With respect to the emotive function, for example, it is observed by Palmer (1996) that a direct indexical link to the emotional referent can be observed at different levels in languages, ranging from their sound structures, or the lexicon, to morphological and syntactic phenomena. With respect to sound structures, Palmer (1996: 280) gives examples from the First Nation language Ipai (United States), where the consonant ł (a lateral fricative) signifies largeness or neutrality with respect to size, and *l* (a lateral approximant) signifies smallness, as in *cəkulk* '(large) hole through something' versus *cəkulk* 'small hole through something'.

There is a rather large bulk of literature, in particular from the 1980s and 1990s, on African languages illustrating phonaesthetic processes illustrating the so-called "frequency code", i.e., the link between size or intensity and the position of the tongue root (phonaesthesia or sound symbolism). The following examples from Blench (2011), from Ịzọn, Nigeria, show the interaction of phonaesthemes and templatic structures in Kolokuma Ịjọ ideophones.

(83) fiyoo 'hollow (of large hole in a tree trunk)'
      fịyọọ 'hollow (of small hole in a tree trunk)'

The emotive dimension of language also manifests itself in what has come to be referred to as evaluative morphology. Elsewhere in the present study (Section 5.3.) examples are given from Bemba (Zambia). But Di Garbo and Agbetsoamedo (2018) present a range of other examples expressing semantic modifications such as diminutive and augmentative, thereby encoding differences in size (generally with a derogatory effect), as in Maasai (Kenya, Tanzania), based on Payne (1998):

	Inherent		Pejorative	
(84)	ɛnk-anáshɛ̀	'sister'	ɔnk-anáshɛ̀	'very large sister'
	F.SG-sister		M.SG-sister	
	ɔ-aláshɛ̀	'brother'	ɛnk-aláshɛ̀	'weak brother'
	M.SG-brother		F.SG-brother	

The emotive function of language is also manifested in the use of attitude markers and interjections (as discourse markers), as in English *gee* as an expression of regret; see the index under these terms for examples in the present monograph. In English and other languages, specific phrases may also be used as interjections, such as *the hell* in *Why the hell does he write a book like this?*

With respect to the poetic function of language, Banti and Giannattasio (2004) propose to broaden the category to "poetically organized discourse", in order to include prayers, blessings, or ritualized speech, as they all potentially involve musical and quazi-musical formulizations of speech, metrics, style, and other features. This is indeed a useful integration, not only for linguistic purposes (for example, because they may contain archaic features of a particular language, or show what kinds of metrical structures that language uses), but also because they reveal additional channels of speech used for sociocultural purposes.

Poetry may also be "instrumentalized" politically or in legal cases, as in Somali, where it is deeply rooted in nomadic culture. Samatar (1982: 57) states that "[p]oetry has the force of ritual among the Somalis and it is resorted to in the formalization and execution of almost every public act of importance: a man explains his behavior towards others in poetic oration; marriages are contracted and terminated through the use of verse; verse is chanted to fight wars and perpetuate feuds as well as to put an end to wars and feuds; and blame and praise are spread most rapidly through this medium. In short, poetry for the pastoral Somalis is a principal vehicle of political power".

The study by Taluah (2021) presents an elegant analysis of the performance of panegyric poetry in Dagbani in northern Ghana, a phenomenon found as part of the repertoire of speech styles in various speech communities across West Africa, but also in other parts of the continent.

Taluah (2021) gives examples of metaphors, such as the king being a lion, but he also points towards speech styles such as the use of irony, hyperboles, allusions, or rhetorical questions, all of which require a deep understanding of the conversational implicatures triggered by their use in Dagbani.

Across Eastern Africa, pastoralists traditionally compose and perform so-called ox songs, and they still do so today. Deng (1973: 96–158) is an early, pioneering investigation of this genre as well as of a range of other types of songs (cathartic songs, initiation sings, age-set insult songs, war songs, women' songs, hymns, fairytale songs, children's game songs, and school songs) among the Dinka in South Sudan. As pointed out by Deng (1973: 97–98), "[o]x songs are not about oxen only but include reference to diverse social situations (. . .) in ox songs a man combines the courage and virility of a bull with the gentleness and the submissiveness of an ox". Francis Deng gives English translations of texts composed in the Ngok dialect of Dinka, in which poets describe the shape of horns, the complexity of the colours of oxen, their styles of bellowing, the chiming of their bells, or their aggressiveness. And, as is usual in ox songs, accounts of the singer's social position are associated with the oxen (Deng 1973: 99).[38]

In the ethnocinematographic documentary *Lorang's Way*, produced by the McDougalls (1977), one can observe a scene where Lorang's son Lokatukan "raps" about his favourite ox, describing features such as coat colour, horn shape, ear shape (including ear markings), brand marks, and its beauty (Picture 16); see Ohta (1987) for a description. Such songs may also be used as a channel for social criticism. Dioli (2018: 1) calls it "an essential tool for a [Turkana] man to establish

---

[38] Interested readers may also want to consult the following link for the CD entitled *Songs of the Dinka of South Sudan* (2012): See [https://www.cambridge.org/core/journals/yearbook-for-traditional-music/article/abs/diet-ke-jieen-ne-cueny-thudan-songs-of-the-dinka-of-south-sudan] (accessed 15 January 2021).

his own concepts of aesthetic and to visibly express his own personal identity and social relationships among his people".

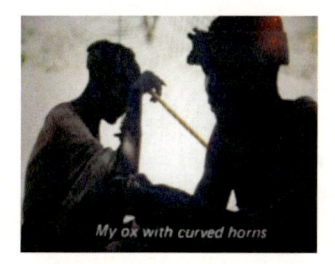

Picture 16: Lokatukan performing an ox song (*Lorang's Way*).

Hymes (1968) introduces a seventh factor into his list of speech functions, namely the context or situation in which a speech act occurs or is assumed to be appropriate (or not). Interestingly, Hymes (1968: 105) makes use of an important concept within this context, namely "frame", when he writes that the "description of semantic habits depends on contexts of use to define relevant frames". This concept, which goes back to Bateson (1972), is valuable for our understanding of language use and the role played by cognition, as discussed next.

Frame has also been used along similar lines as a concept in artificial intelligence models, where it is intended to contribute to the goal of providing computers with organized methods of interpretation in situations of incomplete knowledge (Minsky 1975, 1986). Frames serve computers to understand discourse, and humans to interpret the verbal intentions of others given typical and frequently occurring settings or event types. Fillmore (1975b: 127) defines frame as "the specific lexico-grammatical provisions in a given language for naming and describing the categories and relations found in schemata".

In the present monograph, this cognitive model, capturing metalinguistic knowledge of speakers about settings and corresponding adequate interactional conduct in relation to these settings, is referred to as the frame-and-scenario model. "Frames" are defined here as stereotyped representations of situations. A "scenario" represents "memory organization packets", involving the blending of different schemas, for example for events, roles, or participants (as illustrated with greeting and parting strategies in the preceding sections). As a concept it is thus comparable to Hymes' notion of "act sequence". How such schemas are programmed in our cognitive system is a point in our understanding we have not reached as yet. Because schemas, particularly for ritualized types of language behaviour, are culture-specific to some extent, they may also be called "cultural schemas", which is the label proposed by Sharifian (2017a).

"Scenes" are interpreted in the present study as exponents of scenarios, the latter involving processing structures that help speakers to infer what will come next, i.e., act sequences associated with different speech events. "Script" as a concept derives from cognitive science, and expresses a cognitive event schema. It has also been used in cognitive anthropology by authors like Casson (1981, 1983), from where it entered anthropological linguistics. Schemata, for Casson (1983), express knowledge structures, "but they are also referred to as 'frames' (...), 'scenes' (...), 'scenarios' (...), 'scripts' (...), 'gestalts' (...), 'active structural networks' (...), and 'memory organization packets'" (Casson 1983: 429). These various labels correspond, in the present author's view, to what Mey (2010: 2884) calls "pragmemes", which are defined as "general situational prototypes of acts that are capable of being executed in a particular situation or cluster of situations". The corresponding term "practs" is then used for the realizations of pragmemes, parallel to phonemes and phones, or morphemes and morphs.

In a review article on linguistics and cross-cultural communication, Verschueren (1984) argues that a theory of meaning capable of incorporating a "prototype-and-frames semantics" is what is needed for the study of communication. Barsalou (1992) refers to the same conceptualization as the "frames-and-prototypes" approach. As these "labelling strategies" should illustrate, terminologies have been developed by different authors for what seem to be closely related, or sometimes identical, cognitive phenomena. In other words, the label "frame-and-scenario" model simply represents the present author's preference for specific terms because of their conceptual status in different academic disciplines. What is more important, of course, is the question of what such abstractions bring us in terms of descriptive and explanatory adequacy for our understanding of language use. The following discussion should help to make such discussions more concrete.

Tannen and Wallat (1987) are among the first authors interested in the role played by language in social interaction, and also advocate the relevance of concepts such as frames and schemas. For them, schemas refer to what is going on in interaction, without which no utterance (or movement or gesture) could be interpreted. The authors illustrate the distinction and interaction between two types of schemas, interactive schemas and knowledge schemas. Knowledge schemas "refer to participants' expectations about people, objects, events and settings in the world (i.e., multiple knowledge schemas), [which] are continually checked against experience and revised. The interactive notion of frame (...) refers to a sense of what activity is being engaged in, how speakers mean what they say" (Tannen and Wallat 1987: 207).

First, such frames need to be activated, the triggered structure being based on earlier experiences, as argued in Tannen and Wallat (1987), who use the analysis of a medical examination of a child by a pediatrician in the presence of the mother as a basis (with such medical investigations themselves taking place at regular intervals). The interaction between the three individuals involved is characterized by shifting frames, as reflected in the use of different registers, for example between the two adults, or between the pediatrician and the child. But apart from the use of different speech styles, for example by the pediatrician when talking to the mother or the child (when examining the latter), there are also shifts in the interactive frames between the pediatrician and the mother. Tannen and Wallat (1987: 211) describe a shift in "footing" when the pediatrician establishes rapport with the mother. While using a "clipped style", i.e., short words, initially, the style used by the pediatrician in talking to the mother changes when they come to a more serious medical problem.

Goffman (1981) is probably the first author to use the term "footing" in the analysis of participation frameworks in conversations. Changing registers (as a signaling device) is an example of a change in footing, i.e., a change in the participant's stance to a particular utterance a speaker takes up to himself/herself and others (1981: 227). Issues of footing occur whenever the "participant's alignment, or set, or stance, or posture, or projected self is somehow at issue", as argued by Goffman (1981: 128). As a result, re-framing may occur on behalf of interactants. By changing the footing, the interpersonal relationship is "re-negotiated", so to speak. Thus, rather than being fixed during interactions, frames (or participant frameworks) are dynamic, and are checked against the background of existing knowledge schemas, which in turn may require a shift in footing. The case study by Tannen and Wallat (1987) also shows that there are no active and passive roles in conversation, as the recipient may also influence the interaction process through his or her reactions, which the speaker in turn may take into account.

A second source of inspiration for an elaboration upon the SPEAKING model of language use comes from the philosophy of language, and more specifically from speech act theory as developed by Austin (1962) and Searle (1969, 1976, 1979). Hymes (1962) lists different functions of speech, among them that of directives. Those of us interested in learning foreign languages sooner or later become aware of the different ways in which we may express a request. One of the most obvious speech acts from an intercultural perspective is presumably commands and imperatives; Aikhenvald (2010) gives a detailed survey of typological and cross-linguistic variation in this respect. In English somebody may tell you: *Close the door!*, or *Close the door, please!* If there are several people around, that person may also say: *Could somebody close the door (please)?* While interacting on a regular basis with speakers of Turkana in Kenya interested in acquiring English during the late 1970s, the present author learned that they found this latter utterance rather superfluous: *Of course all of us can close a door – unless we are handicapped*. This suggested they still had to learn that what looks like a question is an indirect way of summoning somebody to close the door (sometimes referred to as a "whimperative") in British English. And things would get even more complex from an intercultural perspective if a speaker of English were to say *It's kind of draughty in here*, thereby hinting at a suggestion that somebody should close the door (because it is cold outside).

Examples like this show that speech acts can be intricate, and need to be analysed from different perspectives. Austin (1962), in his classic *How to Do Things with Words*, makes a fundamental distinction between locutionary, illocutionary, and perlocutionary acts. This tripartite distinction is maintained by the philosopher of language and John Austin's student, John Searle, for example in Searle (1969), but with further refinements of the model which should not concern us here.

Locution or locutionary acts concern the performance of a meaningful utterance, or speaking. Speech acts are "the basic or minimal units of linguistic communication" (Searle 1969: 16). Taxonomic categories such as representatives (assertives, characterized *inter alia* as true or false), directives, commissives, expressives, and declarations are instances of illocution or illocutionary acts (Searle 1976). In other words, one speech act can be performed by means of the performance of another, as in the English question *Could somebody close the door?* This is where perlocution or perlocutionary acts, as acts directed to a hearer or listener in order to influence his or her thoughts and actions, come in: getting the hearer to realize something, and, where relevant, to act in a specific way.

Language use can thus be extremely complex and intricate, especially from an intercultural point of view. An illocutionary act in English such as a request for information may apparently also have a perlocutionary function, namely that of an indirect request. There may thus be a difference between what a speaker says and the (culture-specific) force of the utterance. Studies on language acquisition confirm that such subtleties are acquired by children during language socialization. As argued by Mackie (1983), Japanese children become aware of preferred conversational strategies, for example specific hedging strategies, before they have fully acquired the complex system of honorifics (reflecting morphosyntactic features emblematic of social positions) around the age of five. Thus, instead of using imperatives (as one type of illocutionary act), a peer may use the following conditional statement (no interlinear glossing available) in Japanese:

(85)   hora ijit-tara dame yo   'if you touch it, it is not good'

In other words, in Japanese a conditional statement may also function as a perlocutionary act, aimed at empathy training, which would turn it into an "indirect speech act", according to Searle (1979). Such strategies are part of language socialization strategies known as *omoiyari* '(empathy) training' in Japanese, involving the anticipation and understanding of other people's needs or feelings without using explicit verbal communication; see also Nakamura (2001). As we shall see in Chapters 10 and 11, indirect speech acts are quite common cross-linguistically. Misunderstandings emerging from cross-cultural differences in the use of different illocutionary acts can be humorous, as in the anecdote above about the student from Mali in Paris asking for permission to leave. But of course, these differences may also have nefarious effects of miscommunication, leading to stereotyping and resentment, as examples in the next chapters will show.

The volume edited by Gass and Neu, *Speech Acts Across Cultures* (2006), is one of the earliest contributions on intercultural differences in the way illocutionary acts may be used in order to trigger perlocutionary effects. The volume also contains methodological discussions on the gathering of relevant speech act data, including in second language acquisition, and practical applications both within and across speech communities. Readers interested in intercultural communication are encouraged to consult this volume.

The discussion on discourse markers below, which, in the terminology used in the present study also includes attitude (or modal) markers as well as interjections, serves as an illustration of what appear to be universal instances of perlocutionary acts. They are more or less easy to recognize as such by somebody not familiar (yet) with the sometimes intricate pragmatic structure of a foreign language. From an analytical point of view, it is usually easy to identify discourse markers because of their (often – though not always) independent syntactic status in a language, and because they usually consist of a small and closed set in a language. Describing and understanding their pragmatic roles, on the other hand, can be rather intricate, as the rather extensive literature on such markers in Indo-European languages shows. It should also be kept in mind that understanding the intersubjective structure of a language usually goes way beyond the investigation of such discourse markers. A corresponding compartmentalization in the study of language use between pragmatically relevant discourse markers and other grammatical features would be rather misguided, as the remaining chapters help to show. This is also the reason why "pragmatic markers" as a cover term is avoided in the present study, because a range of other grammatical features in languages can be pragmatically relevant.

The first type of discourse marker, attitude markers, involves epistemic particles affecting modality in an utterance. The term "attitude marker" was probably first used in Dimmendaal (1983) for a closed set of five particles in Turkana expressing attitudinal information on the part of the speaker in illocutionary acts (i.e., utterances produced by the speaker: *bo, ca, karɛ, mono, robo* (some of which may also be combined); the tones following the vowels in the examples below, rather than being carried by the latter, indicate so-called "floating" low tones triggering a register lowering on the following high toned vowel. The attitude marker *cà*, for example, "expresses the speaker's wish that a proposition be clear and evident, and that the addressee should think so likewise" (Dimmendaal 1996: 258). When adding this particle to an imperative verb 'wait!', the speaker shows that (s)he is losing his/her patience, for example by repeating the command. If, on the other hand, *robo* is added to the same imperative verb form, the speaker indicates that (s)he is asking for some understanding.

(86) kìdàrɔ(ù)   cà
     wait   ATT
     'just wait (I'm losing my patience)!'

(87) kìdàrɔ(ù)   ròbó
     wait   ATT
     'just wait, please'

In her analysis of conversational strategies in Acholi, Rüsch (2020a: 202–217) also gives a range of examples of what are referred to here as attitude markers. They are called modal particles by Maren Rüsch, and "add to the negotiation of interpersonal relationships within conversations" (p. 203). They consequently play a key role in our understanding of conversational strategies in Acholi. In line with a number of other authors, Rüsch (2020a: 203) distinguishes modal markers from discourse markers; the latter "have textual functions, such as textual coherence and discursive organization" (p. 203). Discourse markers in turn are divided into reception markers (referring to prior talk) and presentation markers (introducing subsequent talk), according to Rüsch (2020a: 205). The following two sentences in Acholi are drawn from a situation where "the vendor at the market encourages his customer to negotiate the price that he offered and he emphasizes this encouragement with the discourse marker *bá*. The customer himself uses *bá* (. . .) with the connotation 'you really need to make me understand so that I will continue negotiating with you'" (Rüsch 2020a: 209):

(88) Vendor: lăr   bá
                save.IMP   MP
                'negotiate!'

     Customer: níáŋ-à   bá   'mégò
                understand.1MP-1SGO   MP   brother
                'make me understand, brother!'

Additional examples from other languages in the same family (Nilotic) can be found in Dimmendaal (2014b).

The second type of discourse marker, the interjection, tends to involve prosodically and syntactically independent words. Like attitude markers, interjections are instantiations of what Jakobson (1959) calls the emotive function of language. But as shown in a classic contribution on this phenomenon, Ameka (1992a), interjections have not only an emotive function, although they do express this communicative purpose (as when a speaker says *wow!*), but also cognitive functions (*aha!*), or conative functions (related to the speaker's wishes). Phatic interjections are used in establishing contact, for example when saying *sh!* if one wants silence, or with respect to domestic animals (as shown by Amha 2013 for the Ethiopian language Zargulla); they are also common as backchanneling devices in conversations.[39]

Ameka (1992a) draws a distinction between primary interjections and secondary interjections. The former are used only as interjections, moreover they do not have addressees, and usually constitute a complete utterance (constituting an intonation unit by themselves). They may also be phonologically and morphologically anomalous. Note that the latter are not defining features, as interjections do not have to be "anomalous" from this perspective. Moreover, ideophonous words (usually, though not always, belonging to modifying categories such as adverbs or adjectives) may also manifest unique properties in this respect. Secondary interjections are words or phrases which have an independent semantic value, but which come to be used as interjections by virtue of their notional semantics (Ameka 1992a: 105, 111), such as *damn!* or *hell!* in English.

Ameka and Wilkins (2006) provide further examples of the distinction between primary and secondary interjections. While the primary ones do not enter into constructions with other word classes, secondary interjections are items used in two domains; a referential one, as with *hell* (a place contrasting with *heaven*) in English, whereas the non-referential, interjectional reading occurs if someone screams *Hell!*, for example when something bad happens (Ameka and Wilkins 2006: 5). Primary interjections may contain sound units which are rare otherwise in a language, and one usually cannot modify their morphological structure. Ameka and Wilkins (2006: 13) also note that sociolinguistic variables such as age or gender may be relevant in determining who the users are. As the following examples should help to illustrate, interjections are

---

[39] See also a public lecture on this topic and other phenomena (sometimes claimed by linguists to be marginal to human language) by Felix K. Ameka: https://www.youtube.com/watch?v=-zyxuW3Za8Kk

attested in a wide range of languages in different parts of the African continent (and of course elsewhere).

Amberber (2001: 42–42) lists twelve such expressions for Amharic (Ethiopia), for example *eč'č'* 'expression of disgust, of impatience', *gud* 'exclamation of (positive) surprise, of amazement, of awe, of wonder, of shock', and *ahe* (Figure 14), as an exclamation for surprise or sorrow. No examples of the uses of these expressions are given, but the author does give two descriptions of the polysemic interjection *ahe*, using semantic primitives as developed by Anna Wierzbicka and other scholars working within the frame of the Natural Semantic Metalanguage.

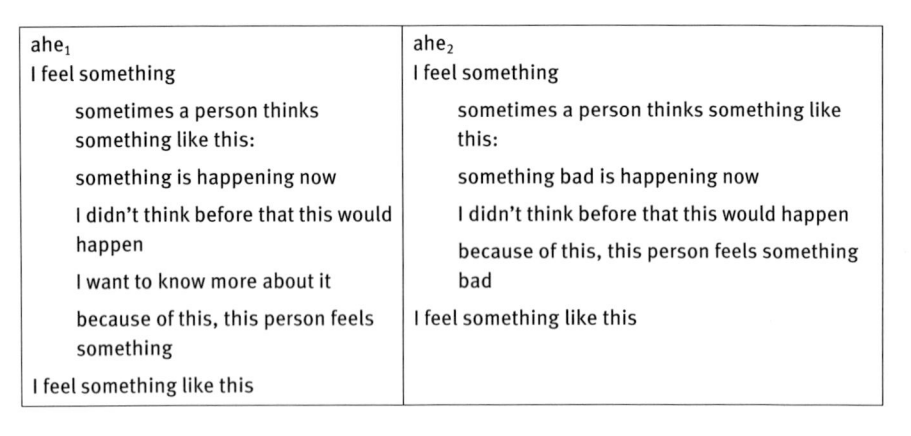

ahe_1 I feel something	ahe_2 I feel something
sometimes a person thinks something like this:	sometimes a person thinks something like this:
something is happening now	something bad is happening now
I didn't think before that this would happen	I didn't think before that this would happen
I want to know more about it	because of this, this person feels something bad
because of this, this person feels something	I feel something like this
I feel something like this	

Figure 14: The interjection *ahe* framed within Natural Semantic Metalanguage (Amberber 2001).

In his contribution on interjections in ǂAkhoe Hai//om (Namibia), Widlok (2016: 135) points out that these words are "rich entry points (. . .) into embodied experience" for anthropologists (and anthropological linguists) trying to understand social interaction in the communities they are interested in. "If interjections are midgets with regard to their linguistic form, they may be said to be giants of contexts" (Widlok 2016: 140), as with the interjection *hana* in ǂAkhoe Hai‖om, which has a high frequency and is used in a wide set of contexts, which of course makes understanding its role very elusive.

Roulon-Doko (2017: 84–86) lists several interjections used to express emotions in Gbaya (Central African Republic), for example *hó* 'oh!', expressing amazement, *hɛ̂ɛ̂* 'eh!', expressing disappointment, and *ʔòí* 'misère!', expressing complaint. The examples from different parts of the continent (and elsewhere) confirm the widely held view that interjections as pragmatic particles are accorded an important emotive function (in the parlance of Jakobson 1960) by speakers in social interaction. Obviously, understanding the function and meaning of interjections in these languages requires the investigation of their occurrence in different frames, but also of different scenarios in order to understand their perlocutionary effects.

Prosody also plays a role in interpreting the role of such markers, as with ǂAkhoe Hai//om *etse*, which may be translated as 'blimey'. The form itself is probably derived as a vocational form from the second person masculine singular *-(t) se-* (Widlok 2016: 141). As a declarative statement, *etse* may express something like '(blimey), that is really remarkable'. But when used as an exclamative *etseee* it may mean something like 'hey, stop what you are doing!' When pronounced as an interrogative/evocative *etse*, the English translation might be 'are you serious about this?' (Widlok 2016).

Discourse markers (which, in the terminology used in the present study, include interjections, as well as attitude markers) allow the subject-utterer responsible for the speech content "[t]o share feelings and attitudes about things with others", one of three elements constituting human sociality, according to Tomasello (2008: 86). The other two elements are: "Requesting: getting others to do what one wants them to", and "to offer help without being requested to – especially, by informing others of things" (Tomasello 2008: 192, 217). As instances of perlocutionary acts, they are usually easy to recognize for second-language learners, because they tend to constitute separate syntactic and prosodic units. However, as shown in particular in Chapter 10 on politeness and impoliteness strategies, and in Chapter 11 on conversational analysis, verbal interaction is far more complex, particularly from an intercultural perspective. These chapters introduce theoretical models whose aim it also is to come to grips with such intercultural differences in speech norms.

Before discussing these latter models, inspirational ideas and concepts from interactional sociolinguistics relevant to the field of anthropological linguistics need to be discussed first. The next chapter also serves to illustrate situational and cultural constraints on forms of language use. In this way, it is argued, criticism of Austin's and Searle's speech act theory can also be accounted for.

8 The contribution of interactional sociolinguistics

> To scorn diversity is antithetical to egalitarianism. However, to fetishize it, while perhaps seemingly progressive, can be equally elitist. (McWhorter 2014: 148)

The visit to New York City reported upon in the introduction to the preceding chapter was completed with a small shopping trip in order to express a big "thank you" to my host. A bottle of wine as a present seemed like a good idea, but inspecting the different options behind bulletproof glass, as shown by the person running the neighbourhood liquor store, was a new experience. While I was paying for the bottle, a young man – obviously an acquaintance of the employee or owner of the liquor store – walked in and started paying compliments to the latter. Apparently, she was not interested in his flirtations, whereupon he walked out again, saying "uuh honey, you're walkin' on high heels this mornin'". For a few seconds I felt like I was watching a third rate American movie where all cultural stereotypes about Afro-Americans were being fulfilled. Nevertheless, this "scene" was real. Living among Turkana people in northwestern Kenya for some time, a few years before my first trip to the United States, had already made me aware of significant cross-cultural differences in social interaction and corresponding conversational styles. But this interaction in a quarter of New York made me realize that I too was caught in an arena in which style on the part of "Whites" is rendered normative, while the linguistic behaviour of members of other communities of practice, for example of Afro-Americans, was interpreted as hilarious.

The investigation of speech styles or performance has become one of the four central "pillars" of interactional sociolinguistics. Bucholtz and Hall (2004: 380) argue that three more research themes play a key role within this field of research: *identity*, involving different semiotic acts of identification producing identities such as practice (repetitive or habitual social activity), *indexicality* (one entity or event pointing to another), and *ideology* (how language accrues sociopolitical meaning). These "pillars", of course, also play a role in anthropological-linguistic studies, as they all play a role in the creation of social identities. "Identity" is not discussed in a separate section, but interested readers can find information on this issue through the index; this also applies to the notion "indexicality". "Language ideologies" and "performance", however, are addressed below. Performativity as a concept goes back to the classical contribution by Austin (1962), *How to Do Things with Words*, where it refers to the function of utterances not simply to describe, but to change, social reality. Performance, as a deliberate and self-aware social display, in particular through marked speech events, has also been explored in relation to gender issues by Butler (1990), and is illustrated as a cross-culturally relevant phenomenon in Section 8.3 on style.

The close link between the ethnography of communication and interactional sociolinguistics, at least during their initial stages, is also reflected in the monograph *Directions in Sociolinguistics: The Ethnography of Communication*, edited by Gumperz and Hymes (1972). This chapter therefore starts with two phenomena, language socialization and dyadic and triadic motions of communication, using concepts emerging from Hymes' model while at the same time introducing concepts from interactional sociolinguistics as developed by Gumperz and others. In Sections 8.3 and 8.4, more recent debates within interactional sociolinguistics on language ideologies and corresponding conceptualizations of language as well as performance are introduced.

8.1 Language socialization across cultures

The concept of "nurturing" is frequently used in combination with the development of skills of small children. And language socialization plays a crucial role in this respect. This should already become clear from Chapters 2 and 3, on lexical-semantic fields in languages. The study of colour terminology, for example, has long served – and still serves – as a central topic where "universalists" have tried to argue that there are strong cognitive (biological) constraints on the way we human beings perceive the colour spectrum; hence, the role played by nurture (culture) is epiphenomenal.

Hymes (1968), in his descriptive and analytical model of the ethnography of communication, in fact dedicates quite a few pages to language socialization (pp. 124–129), thereby emphasizing its important role in socialization processes. Acquiring tacit knowledge about the social impact of specific speech strategies, the frames-and-prototypes scenarios, and the corresponding sociocultural implications that go along with them are central to such processes.

Children become aware of frames and schemas associated with ritualized speech such as greeting strategies at an early age, either through instruction from their peers, or through observation by inferring situational frames and corresponding schemas from the same peers. This applies to the most obvious instances of institutionalized behaviour, such as greeting and parting strategies, but also to other types of interactional practices, as shown in an early collection of studies on language acquisition from a cross-cultural perspective edited by Schieffelin and Ochs (1987). In the same volume, Katherine Demuth, who has become a prominent scholar on language acquisition, presents initial results on linguistic routines as part of her longitudinal investigation of the social development of children growing up with Sesotho in Lesotho (Demuth 1987). As shown by a comparison of her studies with those of other authors reporting on their investigation of language socialization in such different parts of the world as Japan, Samoa, and New Guinea, it is clear that there is significant variation with regard to caregiver-child interactions and corresponding language socialization activities. Schieffelin (1987) describes how Kaluli parents may tease or challenge their children in order to prepare them for a potentially hostile world. In this way, children socializing in Kaluli (spoken in Papua New Guinea) acquire routines for being assertive towards others.

Other sources on the investigation of language acquisition in speech communities outside the Euro-American zones include research on the socialization of Luo-speaking children in Kenya by Ben Blount (e.g., Blount 1969, 1970). In more recent investigations of language socialization studies, additional African languages have also started to feature. In the volume edited by Duranti, Ochs, and Schieffelin (2011), there are studies on speech communities such as the G|ui and G||ana (Central Kalahari San communities in Botswana) by Akira Takada. Takada (2011) argues that San caregivers avoid gazing at the infant and do not pause while nursing to attend to a fussing infant, bowing to a San preference for a continuous flow of rhythmic engagement, supplemented by songs and sounds.

These various studies provide further support for the claim that there is considerable cross-cultural variation "in the amount of interaction with infants, the positioning of infants as interlocutors whose 'utterances' are taken to be intentional communications (. . .), amount of eye contact (. . .), turn-taking practices (. . .), and the kinds of participant structures into which infants are drawn (. . .), as well as in interlocutors' tendency to respond to the child's initiatives and for example to label the objects that infants point to" (Brown and Gaskins 2014: 198).

Language socialization may be interpreted as socialization through language. Early sources on preferred speech styles have already shown that language acquisition as a cultural device is not immune to cultural variation, but rather, is usage-based through social interaction. Such sources may also be found within an African context. Thus, Traore (1965) reports on medicine, often in the form of charms, used to ensure appropriate speech among speakers of Bambara in Mali.

As observed by Hunter (1982: 390) in her study on language attitudes among Hausa speakers, "[t]here may be a cultural difference in assessing the relative importance of the form and the content of speech. Misarticulation of s or r̲, metathesis, stuttering, are all viewed in America as disorders requiring treatment. Among Hausa speakers these variations are recognized, but are considered identifying characteristics like being fat or having a space between the front teeth. There are treatments for stuttering ranging from prayers to herbs (to uvulectomy), but they are all regarded as cosmetic. What is more important to seek treatment for is speech without content, for garrulous, tactless, disrespectful speech" (Abdalla, 1981, personal communication to Ismail Abdalla Hussein by Linda Hunter). As further observed by Hunter (1982), the emphasis on content is probably not limited to Hausa alone but extends to much of Africa. One suggestion to explain the relative unimportance of form is that in multilingual societies people are both more aware and more tolerant of the considerable variation in pronunciation and grammar. The premium is on communication. This contrasts with the strongly normative thinking with which children in industrialized societies with one dominant national language prescribing what is or is not correct grow up.

Hunter (1982) shows that Hausa provides a rich lexical source for describing speech behaviour. Among the more than three hundred Hausa terms with negative and positive connotations all related to speaking, Hunter (1982: 398) also lists a form *fìtsārā*, which she translates as 'public humiliation of a person, with foul language'. Bargery (1951: 327), in his extensive dictionary of this language, translates the noun *fìtsārā* as "public humiliation of a person; exhausting every kind of abusive epithet to a person in front of others". The etymological connection with the noun *fìtsārī* 'urine' is not immediately obvious. But if one takes the corresponding intransitive and transitive verb into account, the link does become clear. *fìtsāra* means 'urinate what one has drunk, be shameless, care nothing for the feelings of others, have no respect for anyone', whereas the corresponding transitive verb means *fìtsārā̀* 'publicly humiliate a person with abuse.'

While understanding metaphorical expressions in a particular language frequently involves knowledge of the cultural background of its speakers, one is also struck again and again by specific parallels. In Dutch, for example, the verb *afzeiken*, lit. 'pee down (somebody)', is also used to express 'have a dump on somebody, bully'.

The cognitive linguist Charles ("Chuck") Fillmore developed a "scenes-and-frames-paradigm" in a series of publications (starting with Fillmore (1975a), in particular in order to explain how we understand the meaning of communicative acts. Scenes involve "not only visual scenes but also familiar kinds of interpersonal transactions, standard scenarios defined by the culture, institutional structures, enactive experiences, body image and, in general, any kind of coherent segment of human beliefs, actions, experiences or imaginings (. . .) The word frame [stands] for (. . .) any system of linguistic choices – the easiest cases being collection of words, but also including choices of grammatical rules or linguistic categories – that can be associated with prototypical instances of scenes" (Fillmore 1975b: 124).

Scenes also play a crucial role when it comes to the memorization (or the production) of mental maps related to visual information, spatial orientation, or situations one has observed. Or, as Levinson (2004: 133) formulates it, "[conceptualization] is not part of thinking similiciter, it is rather part of the process of regimenting thought for language production, or in Slobin's (1996) felicitous phrase, 'thinking for speaking'."

In line with this "Fillmorean paradigm", and bearing in mind one particular claim made by Fillmore (1975b: 114) about associations we as speakers of particular language tend to make once we hear certain words, "[w]hen you pick up one of these words, you drag along with it a whole scene", the present author carried out a small experiment. Several of the words or expressions listed in Hunter (1982) in relation to insults were presented to Dr. Muhammad Muhsin Ibrahim, Hausa lecturer at the University of Cologne, himself a prolific author on Hausa language cinematography. The present author would like to express his deeply felt gratitude to Malam Muhsin for agreeing to participate in this experiment. When hearing the Hausa word *fìtsā̀ ràrrū* 'shameless, without any decency (plural participle form)', which is linked etymologically to the above-mentioned word *fitsārā* 'public humiliation of a person, with foul language', scenes from so-called "Kannywood" movies (as a frame) were immediately triggered in his mind.[40] Kannywood movies are produced in the city of Kano, northern Nigeria, and are hence a blend of Kano and Hollywood, also by analogy with the film industry associated with Mumbai (Bombay), and known as Bollywood. Actors and actresses appearing in these movies are sometimes characterized by Hausa speakers as *fìtsā̀ ràrrū* 'shameless, without any decency (plural participle form)'. Activating this particular frame thus resulted in the activation of memories of scenes and scenarios (dialogues) from such movies for Muhammed Muhsin Ibrahim (personal communication), in the same way in which the Dutch word *afzeiken* does with the present author whenever this word comes to mind. Hearing the latter word brings back personal memories, in particular of situations where somebody abused his power to verbally humiliate the present author or other persons (particularly in the presence of others).

Whereas the Kannywood film industry immediately provided a frame or context for the Hausa word *fìtsā̀ ràrrū* for a speaker of Hausa who lived in Kano (northern Nigeria) for many years, the link (in Hausa) with the word for 'urine' *fitsārā* triggered different frames and scenes (as well as corresponding verbal scenarios) for the present author. The qualificatory term *fìtsā̀ ràrrū* may be used by Hausa speakers in order to talk about what, in their eyes, is the far too liberal and promiscuous behaviour of female Nigerian actresses, who are considered to lack

---

[40] See [https://www.researchgate.net/profile/Muhammad_Ibrahim155] (accessed 10 February 2022).

any decency, based on scenes from the movies these speakers saw (Muhammed Muhsin Ibrahim, personal communication). The present author associated the word *afzeiken* (which popped up when hearing this Hausa word and its corresponding meaning) with highly disliked social behaviour involving the humiliation of somebody in public, and particularly the abuse of this person's position in the social hierarchy (as a boss). This is also one reason, presumably, why speakers with a similar cultural background and speaking the same language tend to find it easy to "connect" to each other, just by mentioning one word related to a (dis)preferred habitus and corresponding social values.

As pointed out by Muhammad Muhsin Ibrahim (personal communication), at least eight additional terms from the list presented for Hausa in Hunter (1982) are associated with abusive language and used in different contexts as such, among which two are probably borrowings from Arabic: *asharu* 'foul-mouthed' (although this probably should be *ashararru*) 'foul-mouthed, evil-living', is a (plural) past participle form related to the noun *àshâr̃*, which Newman (1977: 6) translates as 'abusive, obscene language'; another term from the same semantic field, *jafa'i*, is translated by Newman (1977: 56) as 'slander, abusive language' (*jàfa'i*), to which Bargery (1951: 412) adds a further translation, 'refusal to accept judgment of the court'. As many speakers of Hausa are Muslim, these words presumably entered the language through the influence of Islam.

Manifestations of intersubjective capacities such as those described for Hausa and Dutch above provide further evidence for the claims made in Chapter 7 that speakers of languages tend to operate with a frame-and-scenario model, which itself is strongly inspired by the work of one of the great linguists of the 20th century, the late Charles Fillmore and his "scenes-and-frames" model. This (mostly tacit) metalinguistic or metadiscursive knowledge is acquired through primary language acquisition, but also at later stages in life, for example when acquiring knowledge about additional communities of practice, and in the case of multilingual individuals, about additional languages, something which is not uncommon in an African context.

Gumperz (1992: 233) also uses the concept "frame", which for him "signals what is expected in the interaction at any one stage". This knowledge of frames and prototypical scenarios which members of a specific community of practice possess helps them to come to grips with inferential understanding in a rapid and efficient manner. Gumperz (1982a: 153) defines the notion of conversational inference as "the situated or context-bound process of interpretation, by means of which participants in an exchange assess each other's intentions, and on which they base their responses".

A related relevant concept, also emerging from studies on interactional sociolinguistics, is that of contextualization cue, a feature of message form "by which speakers signal and listeners interpret what the activity is, how semantic content is to be understood and how each sentence relates to what precedes or follows" (Gumperz 1982a: 131). The intercultural dimension consists of the proper expression and interpretation of such cues by speech interactants.

Features of linguistic form contributing to the signalling of contextual presuppositions cover verbal as well as non-verbal signs that help speakers to hint at, or clarify, and listeners to make contextually appropriate conversational inferences, as argued by Gumperz (1992), who furthermore points out that such cues may involve different levels of speech production: 1. prosody; 2. paralinguistic signs (such as speech tempo and other indications); 3. code choice; and 4. choice of lexical forms or formulaic expressions. According to Levinson (2003b: 27), such a cue "denotes an encoded or conventional reminder, like a knot in a handkerchief, where the content of a speech act is inferentially determined. Thus the "cue" cannot be said to encode or directly invoke the interpretative background, it's simply a nudge to the inferential process".

It is not only linguistic knowledge, but also factors such as physical setting, participants' personal background knowledge and their attitudes towards each other, sociocultural assumptions concerning role and status relationships, and social values associated with various messages, which also play a role, according to Gumperz (1982a: 153). These should be seen as dynamic, in that social presuppositions and attitudes may shift in the course of interaction between individuals.

8.2 Dyadic and triadic modes of communication

Speech acts may involve monadic, dyadic, triadic, or polyadic communication. The notion of "hearer(s)" in a dyadic speech participation frame may be interpreted in a number of ways, depending on how they are positioned within an encounter. There are "ratified" hearers (addressed recipients and unaddressed recipients) and "unratified" hearers (bystanders, eaves-droppers, or overhearers). But there is another widespread type of speech participation, that of "multi-party talk", which may also be conventionalized or institutionalized. Ameka (2004) discusses the use of intermediaries as an institutionalized instance of "indirection" within the triadic mode of communication, particularly in traditionally centralized societies along the coastal regions of West Africa.[41]

---

[41] The term "triadic communication" is also sometimes used for the communication involving speaker, hearer, and the entities talked about.

Terms of royal distance in these kingdoms are reflected in formal situations, for example in that a traditional Akan chief or king does not speak directly to an audience in his presence; he speaks only through his *okyeame*, who relays or repeats his words. The cultural influence of the Akan on neighbouring communities is reflected in naming strategies, as illustrated in Chapter 5, but also in similar patterns of triadic communication, for example among the Gã, whose language has a cognate word for the mediator, *tsiame*, also found in Ewe (*tsiami*).

Yankah (1995: 16) describes such triadic modes of communication for the Fon (in Togo and Benin), where the *meu* speaks from the king to the people, and the *migan* speaks from the people to the king. More specifically, a principal may speak, and the mediator transmits the message in embellished form, either through artistic elaboration or paraphrasing. Alternatively, the principal speaks and the mediator literally repeats the words spoken or part thereof. The principal may also speak and the mediator ratifies his message by means of affirmative formulae. An orator may also reproduce the principal's message while the principal is present, but the principal does not speak himself. Alternatively, the principal is absent from the scene of discourse and the orator speaks on his behalf (Yankah 1995: 13). As further pointed out by the same author, this strategy not only involves (or involved) royal oratory, "it permeates all formal encounters involving face-to-face communication" (Yankah 1995: 182).

Tarr (1979: 204) describes this phenomenon for the Mossi speech community in Burkina Faso as follows: "The message to be communicated originates with the source. He whispers it up to his friend, who in turn whispers it to a lesser chief, who in turn whispers it to the big chief's main spokesman who then finally brings the message in an audible voice to the chief's hearing".

Irvine (1990: 145) describes the reverse strategy for the Wolof community, where a noble may say something quietly to the intermediary, who repeats the message loudly and more elaborately, relaying it to its intended receiver. Not only chiefs, but high ranking Wolof villagers in general rely heavily on intermediaries (or even double intermediaries), usually griots, i.e professional verbal artists, in situations they consider formal or important (such as a birth, death, or religious celebration), and when they must address a message to the public, to a stranger, or to someone of equally high rank, for a number of reasons. The intermediaries protect the nobles from displaying emotion in public, and thereby from shame (Irvine 1990: 145). The distancing strategy also preserves the royal sanctity, for example, in that the royal surrogate becomes not only a mouthpiece, but also a buffer against which all dangerous words are deflected, as observed by Yankah (1995: 19) in his study of Akan royal oratory.

In these indigenous state systems, professional orators are not a separate caste, and chiefs are also supposed to have verbal skills, although still using intermediaries. Special honorific registers, such as the esoteric Akan "palace speech", are used in the chief's court (Yankah 1995). Further north in the Sahel region, these social hierarchies traditionally involve a division of labour in a complex system of ranked castes and orders with griots as praise orators who are professional experts in the arts of language and communication.

The channel chosen may also take on the form of music or poetry produced by groups of professional orators, a phenomenon found as part of the speech styles in various speech communities across West Africa. Taluah (2021) gives a detailed analysis of praise orators delivering panegyric poetry for their patrons in one the traditional kingdoms of West Africa, that of the Dagbani in northern Ghana. While the Arabic script has been used as an orthography for the language for quite some time, poets and orators prefer not to write down the texts, as oral presentations allow performers to improvise. Here, a social hierarchy is created between the audience and the patrons (chiefs as well as the king or paramount chief) and expressed through intermediaries.

Irvine (2017) presents a detailed survey of the role of such intermediaries or "translators" in oral communication in West Africa. Triadic communication as a channeling strategy appears to be particularly common in this part of the continent, where some of the (former) centralized states date back around one thousand years (as documented in Arabic sources produced by visitors to the region). While these states had very pronounced social hierarchies with intermediaries, similar structures also occurred or occur in more egalitarian, small-scale societies. In such societies, the (putative) interactants may include an authoritative spirit represented by a mask, the mask's bearer, a "translator", and an audience (Irvine 2017).

In an eastern African context, Pumphrey (1937) is an early source on the use of royal registers in the former Shilluk kingdom (South Sudan). Among the neighbouring Dinka, who are traditionally pastoral agriculturalists without chieftaincies, the *Agamlong* ('acceptor, repeater of speech') is a person who repeats in a high-pitched voice (in terms of instrumentality or key) the whole or part of each sentence said in court, prayer, or in a public speech (Leonardi 2013). Similar institutionalized roles are found in other speech communities in the area, characterized by age sets and gerontocracy. Novelli (1985: 22–23), in his description of the Karimojong language in Uganda, for example, refers to a term ɛ-kɛsɛran 'spokesman', an agentive noun derived from the verb -ɪsɛr 'explain, interpret'.

8.3 Language ideologies

Duranti (2003) refers to three paradigms within the field of linguistic anthropology, starting with the Boasian conception of anthropology at the end of the

19th century, followed by the initiation of sociolinguistics and the ethnography of communication primarily by John Gumperz and Dell Hymes in the 1960s. Although the ethnography of communication was also intended to be(come) part of anthropology at large, in retrospect one has to conclude that this approach marked an intellectual separation from the rest of anthropology, as observed by Duranti (2003: 328). Fortunately enough, one may want to add, the new (third) paradigm, that of interactional sociolinguistics, which was initiated in the 1970s, had a tremendously positive effect on the description of language as social practice, and on our sociolinguistic and anthropological-linguistic understanding of language, and particularly of language ideologies and performance. These latter two domains of language practices are discussed below.

Language ideologies involve thoughts about language by their speakers. In one of the earliest studies on the subject, the linguistic anthropologist Michael Silverstein gives a more refined definition of language ideologies, namely as "sets of beliefs about language articulated by the users as a rationalization or justification of perceived language structure and use" (Silverstein 1979: 193). Kroskrity (2004: 505) adds an important observation, namely that "*members may display varying degrees of awareness of local language ideologies*" (italics in the original text); in other words, ritualization or conventionalization may play a role here as well, without all speakers necessarily being aware of specific ideologies.

Woolard and Schieffelin (1994) present an initial survey of literature on cultural conceptions of language, more specifically on its nature, structure, and use, and, as pointed out by the authors, "on conceptions of communicative behaviour as an enactment of a collective order" (p. 55). The volume edited by Schieffelin, Woolard, and Kroskrity (1998) contains critical approaches to language ideologies which also explore the capacity for language and linguistic ideologies to be used as strategies for maintaining social power and domination.

Research on the way people conceive of links between linguistic forms and social phenomena has boomed over the past decades. In this context, the classic contribution by Irvine and Gal (2000) on ideologies of linguistic differentiation, which readers are encouraged to read, deserves special attention. The authors identify three semiotic processes for the construction of language ideologies: iconization, fractal recursivity, and erasure.

Iconization refers to the ideological representation of a given linguistic feature (as an iconic sign) as formally congruent with the group with which it is associated. The association of specific greeting or parting "rituals" is often seen by speakers as characteristic (indexical) of their own cultural identity, as against that of others. Greeting strategies, as described in the preceding chapter, are therefore prototypical examples of iconization. But this may equally well apply to other overt discourse or grammatical features seized upon by speakers in order to distinguish themselves from others.

The second notion, that of fractal recursivity, refers to the fact that the differences which are treated as iconic are used in the creation of an "other". Fractal recursivity can both create an identity for a given group and further divide it; "the myriad oppositions that can create identity may be reproduced repeatedly, either within each side of a dichotomy or outside it" (Irvine and Gal 2000: 38).

The third process, that of erasure, is the process by which these distinctions are created and maintained. Erasure is integrally intertwined with both iconization and recursivity, as it is the erasure of any differentiation which is, according to the given ideology, inconsequential. "Facts that are inconsistent with the ideological scheme either go unnoticed or get explained away" (Irvine and Gal 2000: 38). Consequently, ideological outliers are either discounted as being anomalous or disregarded altogether and ignored. Erasure therefore determines what can become iconized and also what then becomes recursive within a given group.

In their contribution on language and identity, Bucholtz and Hall (2004: 371) give the example of a social grouping in school based on language skills in order to illustrate erasure. They show how a multicultural community in the United States, of people from different backgrounds and ethnicities, connected over their language skills; these people invented similarity by downplaying differences by erasing features that did not fit in.

Along lines identified by Irvine and Gal (2000) as part of the strategy of fractal recursivity, speakers may pick up on differences, thereby creating social distances in social interaction, as the following examples from the Euro-American spheres as well as Africa help to show.

An example of language ideology through the elevation of whiteness among Anglo-Americans can be observed in their use of "Mock Spanish" in the media, where until recently former President Trump occasionally referred to Mexican-Americans as *hombres* '(gentle)men', thereby using a strategy referred as indirect indexicality, as the relationship between the linguistic form and the social meaning is indirect; direct indexicality on the other hand relates to such phenomena as the phonetic features of a person's voice that define that person uniquely. Speakers usually have a high degree of conscious awareness of lexical phenomena, which makes them likely candidates to be seized upon as a locus for conscious reflection or manipulation. The use in English of a word from Spanish like *hombres* or *mañana* 'tomorrow' may superficially seem to index a jocular stance. But as Hill (1999) shows in her account of "Mock Spanish", such discourse strategies tend to involve a covert racist discourse, serving to construct a white public space for varieties of incorporated Spanish in English in the United States, where, for example, a heavy English accent in the Spanish of whites would be considered perfectly acceptable. As argued by her, such strategies serve to portray racialized stereotypes of Mexican Americans as being disorderly or stupid, thereby triggering associations with corruption, or sexually loose life styles. As such they are the practices of a racializing hegemony, in which whites are normal and in which racialized populations such as the Puerto Rican community in New York City are marginalized.

A further example of "othering" is discussed by Nortier and Dorleijn (2013) with respect to a variety of German which emerged in multilingual urban spaces in parts of the capital of Germany, Berlin, in the 1990s, known as *Kiezdeutsch*. This register was and is used by younger people whose parents or grandparents came to Germany as migrant labourers from Turkey, Morocco, and other countries. But it is also used by those whose parents or parents were born and raised in Germany, including those growing up with Standard German as their primary language, and hence is part of a repertoire. Such new sociolects of German (or other languages in Europe) are sometimes referred to as "ethnolects", a misleading (and, in fact, erroneous) labeling, as they are usually not associated with one "ethnic" group, or with one region or quarter.

The notion of "othering" goes back to psychoanalytical investigations by the psychiatrist Jacques Lacan (1901–1981), in particular his monograph published in 1978, in which the concept of "*Autre*" 'Other' plays a central role. The philosopher Slavoj Žižek picked up this notion and introduced "Otherness" in his postmodern writings.[42] Stigmatization through "othering" (of those who are not like us) is also a central theme in the work of Edward Wadie Said (1935–2003), for example in his foundational contribution to post-colonial studies, *Orientalism* (1978). The title reflects a central question of the monograph, namely how "The West" perceives "The East" or Orient, whereby "Orientalism" is seen as a Western style of dominating, restructuring, and having authority over the Orient.

"Othering" has been an issue in colonial history, but also in anthropological writing, as shown by Fabian (1983). In the writings of anthropologists from "The North" and their anthropological Self, one may also learn about "The South" and the ethnographic Other, as Johannes Fabian observes in *Time and the Other*. Banishing "the Other" to a stage of lesser development as spatially and temporally distanced groups, rather than emphasizing their coevalness, is what links colonial history and the history of anthropology to some extent, as shown in the contributions by Said (1978) and Fabian (1983).

---

42 Readers may also want to check the following link for an interesting instance of "othering" by a leading linguist of our times concerning postmodern "Paris intellectuals" like Jacques Lacan: See [http://www.critical-theory.com/noam-chomsky-calls-jacques-lacan-a-charlatan] (accessed 20 February 2022).

An extreme case of "othering" in sociological writings on intercultural encounters is found in the scholarly work of one of the most frequently quoted authors in the Social Sciences Citation Index, the controversial sociologist, Geert Hofstede. As the title of his 1991 monograph *Cultures and Organisations: Software of the Mind* already suggests, culture involves a collective programming of the mind, which members of a group or category of people separate one from another. Geert Hofstede started his research on corporate cultures among employees of the multinational company IBM (with extensions to other companies later on), in order to test notions such as the degree of individualism or collectivism in the company. His findings on cultural differences are usually assigned to nations (Japan, the Netherlands, etc.), or with respect to certain parts of the globe, even to large geographical regions such as "East Africa", without any further differentiation. A thorough criticism of his frequently quoted monographs on intercultural styles and social values is found in Behrens (2007), who argues, amongst other issues, that Geert Hofstede's analyses suffer from ethnocentrism in that the questionnaires which formed the basis for much of his research are modelled after the American conceptualization of freedom, and the degree to which other countries deviate from these norms.

Of course, "othering" is not unique to macro levels such as (imperial) governments or geographical zones such as "the West" or "the North"; it is equally widespread at the micro-level in different parts of the world, where it is applied to individuals as well as social groupings. Although the ultimate impact on world politics, and thereby on the number of persons affected, differs, they are ultimately all instances of the same phenomenon affecting individuals, as illustrated next.

Across eastern Africa, several smaller speech communities (often consisting of 500 persons or less), referred to as "Ndorobo" in older anthropological sources and frequently treated as "submerged" foreign groups by an economically and demographically dominant neighbouring group, either speak the language of the latter group, or a closely related language. Dimmendaal (1983: 3) makes reference to such a group in the southern Turkana region in Kenya, sometimes discriminated against by pastoral Turkana, who refer to them as *ngikebootok* 'people without cattle / poor people', as the latter are agriculturalists and hunters who also speak a slightly different variety of Turkana. These people may be the descendants of a community known as the Oropom, whose language probably constituted a genetic isolate; see Dimmendaal (2020) for a discussion of such communities sometimes speaking languages constituting linguistic isolates (i.e., the last representative of an otherwise extinct language family).

In southwestern Ethiopia, which constitutes a residual area (i.e., a zone manifesting a high degree of genetic and typological diversity), a linguistic isolate known as Ongota (or Bira(y)le), is still spoken by a few people (Fleming 2006; Savà and Tosco 2003). Shabo (Mikeyir) may be another such language in the same area, probably constituting a linguistic isolate. It is spoken by a small community of people who are now tending to abandon the language in favour of dominant neighbouring languages such as Sheko or Majang. More recently, Yigezu (2018) identified another such language spoken in a community of around 1500 individuals who call themselves Ngaalam, and who until recently lived mainly in the forest belt of south-western Ethiopia. Their language is also known as Majir, Ngidini, Olam, or Tama among neighbouring groups.

For some of these communities in eastern Africa there is literature stating their usually marginalized social status. But only for very few of them do we have data on their language use and speech styles. Leikola (2014) is a rather unique source in that it describes one such submerged group, the Manjo, among the Gomaro in southwestern Ethiopia. The Manjo now only speak the language of their dominant neighbours, the Gomaro, namely Kafa. Leikola (2014) describes the social status and language behaviour of the Manjo, and arrives at the conclusion that differential discourse styles or cross-group communicative skills play a key role in their stigmatization and marginalization by the Gomaro. One member of the Manjo community of practice (a concept also used by Leikola 2014) describes the marginalized status of his caste as follows (only the English translation is given here):

> In previous times we who are called the Manjo lived outside. The Gomaro told us not to be among them, so we lived outside. However, now in the times of the present EPRD [Ethiopian People's Revolutionary Democratic Front] government the Gomaro have come a little closer to us (. . .) As we were called Manjo before, we are outside even now as we are (still) called Manjo. The spirit mediators are the ones who have put us outside. They said that if a Manjo gets inside the house someone will die. So they told us to live outside.   (Leikola 2014: 41)

Inspired by Coupland's (2007) study on language variation and identity, Leikola (2014) shows how diverging speech styles and corresponding language ideologies are used in the Gomaro and Manjo communities of practice in order to construct social identities, in particular in the interests of the dominant social group, the Gomaro.

In spite of the fact that the Manjo and Gomaro speak the same (Kafa) language, the two groups claim to have distinct discourse strategies. The author, who spent around twenty years in these communities and who investigated a range of Manjo and Gomaro speech styles, arrives at the conclusion that "being Manjo" as opposed to "being Gomaro" involves the use of different registers and ways of speaking. Manjo style figures include "Elder rich style", "Being weak style", "Others speak style", and "Being strong style". "Elder rich style", for example, is characterized by the repetition of a verb to express that the action is continued for a certain time (Leikola 2014: 138); "Being weak style" involves the use of a special tone of voice (Leikola 2014: 138), etc. The Gomaro community practises style figures such as the use of honorifics in deictic reference not only with respect to 2nd person addressees, but also when talking about somebody who is not present, as with *niheeno* 'father (+honorific)' versus *niha* 'father (–honorific)' (Leikola 2014: 166).[43]

What one observes here is what Irvine and Gal (2000: 138) refer to as schismogenesis, or the creation of differences as part of the ideological process of fractal recursivity within one and the same speech community, essentially speaking the same language but consisting of two communities of practice. Not only are social differences (the presence of castes) seized upon, but the (presumed) use of different speech styles (as icons of the two groups) also serve to create separate groups, including through the erasure of shared features such as the common use of the same (Kafa) language, as this would be inconsistent with the ideological schema.

The investigation of different registers and the presence of two communities of practice speaking the same language nevertheless suggests that Kafa should not be treated as a monolithic unit. Studies such as Leikola (2014) and those of various other linguistic anthropologists and anthropological linguists over the past decades have resulted in the deconstruction of the notion of "language" as an autonomous system. "Rather than working with homogeneity, stability and boundedness as the starting assumptions, mobility, mixing, political dynamics and historical embedding are now central concerns in the study of languages, language groups and communication", as Blommaert and Rampton (2011: 3) put it.

Blommaert (2015) argues that the "paradigm shift" towards "superdiversity" in sociolinguistics takes phenomena such as codeswitching and multilingualism as the norm, rather than as being exceptional. Whether one should view this approach, propagated by the late Jan Blommaert (1961-2021), as part of a "paradigm shift" (Blommaert 2010: 197) is presumably a matter of definition, as such approaches are not entirely new. The linguistic anthropologist Michael Silverstein made reference to "superdiversity" in his account of Chinook Jargon (Silverstein 1972), which was used as the means of trade communication on the Pacific Northwest Coast of indigenous North America between speakers of languages belonging to the Athapaskan, Salishan, Penutian, and Wakashan language families.

---

[43] As argued by Irvine (2009: 166), the claim sometimes made that such systems are found primarily in complex, hierarchical societies "is vulnerable to several objections [...] as Worldwide, then, honorific systems inhabit many different kinds of societies and participate in different kinds of social dynamics". Examples from Kafa support her claim.

When European traders appeared on the scene from the 18th century onwards, new varieties based on Indo-European languages like English and French, as well as Spanish and Russian, were added in trading contacts with these coastal peoples, resulting in "superdiversity".

Then there are also innovative approaches by earlier scholars such as Mikhael Bakhtin (1895–1975), whose work was first published in English in 1986. Bakhtin also argued that the linguistic homogeneity assumed by some researchers is an ideological construction, itself strongly linked to the emergence of European states and national languages. In practice, polyglossia, i.e., the hybrid nature of language as a reflex of the use or coexistence of two or more languages (or varieties of a language) in the same community (alongside heteroglossia, i.e., the presence of many different varieties or voices) in one and the same language, tends to be involved. In practice, many different voices are involved, a phenomenon he refers to by the Russian label *raznorecie*, 'heteroglossia' (a term also used by Blommaert 2010).

What is new in the approach propagated in Blommaert (2010) and related publications by the same author is his critical approach towards the hegemony qua language communities of monoglot ideologies in European nation-states with standardized languages, which has increasingly come to be seen, by members of those very states, as perforated by the recalcitrantly "diverse" practices of their nonstandard speech communities and their mobile (rather than static or fixed) resources, as the attitudes towards English as spoken by Mexican-Americans or Kiezdeutsch in Germany described above illustrate.

This approach towards language as a potentially heteroglossic phenomenon conflicts with the way reference is made in preceding chapters to language X spoken by community Y, which assumes the existence of a rather unified structure instead. Of course, much of descriptive linguistics is based on this latter conceptualization of language, and this approach has its merits for our understanding of a language's formal properties, as it would hardly be possible to arrive at generalizations about the grammatical structure of languages otherwise. Moreover, it would be impossible to explain how language structures (grammar) could be transferred from one generation to the next.

Parallel to (misguided) notions of linguistic homogeneity, the idea of cultural homogeneity has been criticized by authors like Bhabha (2004), who also criticizes the representation of societies or cultures as closed containers. Colonialism as a result of Western expansion over the past centuries resulted in the emergence of new multilingual societies and new conversation styles and thereby of a "third space" (Bhabha 2004: 55). As a result, there has been and still is an active exchange of material and ideas within this "hybrid space".

Anthropological linguists and sociolinguists have always been more interested in language as an activity. Authors like Maturana and Varela (1987) were among the first to talk about "languaging", i.e., viewing language as a dynamic rather than a closed system. Again, the idea itself is not entirely new, as it is already reflected in von Humboldt's concept of *Enérgeia*, which may be translated as 'being at work'. The latter contrasts with *Ergon* 'work', which corresponds to *langue* (in French) as a formal system in the Saussurean tradition, whereas the former corresponds to *parole* or language use in the same tradition (see the preface to this volume). Of course, it is this latter domain which has been the focus of attention in anthropological linguistics and sociolinguistics.

García and Wei (2014: 2) define the concept of "translanguaging" as an approach that considers the language practices of bilinguals not as two autonomous language systems as has traditionally been the case, but as one linguistic repertoire with features that have been societally constructed as belonging to two separate languages. Moreover, their focus lies on the fluid nature and dynamicity of "languaging".

Cysouw and Good (2013) take actual documentary records attesting to the existence of some language variety, called a "doculect" ("documentary lects") by the authors, as a basis for the definition of the concept "languoid". Language-like objects, like dialects, sociolects, languages, genealogical groups, or areal groups, are to be defined by referring to a collection of doculects on which they are based. "Languoid" then refers to the superset of all those language-like entities. A crucial aspect of this conceptualization is that the grouping traditionally called 'language' does not have an inherently preferred or basic status in this model for classifying the world's linguistic variation.

Within the field of African linguistics, the monograph by Friederike Lüpke and Anne Storch (2013) on repertoires is the most detailed available survey showing the importance of repertoires on a day-to-day basis for polylectal and multilingual individuals. A linguistic repertoire may be defined as the totality of the linguistic resources a speaker has access to, and that (s)he has over time acquired (Gumperz 1982a: 20–21). Repertoires reflect speakers' flexibility as well as their creativity in linguistic practices, often involving multilingualism, as shown in the case studies by Lüpke and Storch. Corresponding social identities "are not defined in linguistic terms and allow for alliances beyond linguistic affinities and shared identities based on multiple factors in multilingual societies" (Friederike Lüpke, in Lüpke and Storch 2013: 47). These factors include "established connections between categories of which speaker and addressee are members – particular kin categories, clans, patronyms, 'castes' or professions, age groups, 'ethnic' groups or shared identity languages" (Friederike Lüpke, in Lüpke and Storch 2013: 47).

"Multilingual speakers do not have several complete language inventories, but tend to associate different languages (and registers therein) with different contexts and functions" (Friederike Lüpke, in Lüpke and Storch 2013: 76). A similar observation is made by Blommaert (2010: 102), who points out that multilingualism should not necessarily be understood as the acquisition of the normative grammar of different languages by individuals, as for several languages no "normative" grammar (as used, for example, in writing) exists, but instead as a complex of specific semiotic resources.

While multilingual individuals speaking a range of languages, regardless of whether they have had any formal education or not, may be found across Africa, multilingualism is not always the case. Moreover, it would be wrong to assume that speech communities are always characterized by social stratification and the corresponding use of different sociolects (based on social group, age, gender), dialects, or repertoires and the corresponding use of a multiplicity of registers. Some speech communities in the Nuba Mountains in Sudan were essentially monolingual until Sudanese Arabic appeared on the scene as the language of wider communication over the past seventy years or so (and extensive sociolinguistic investigations in fact confirm this claim; Dimmendaal 2022b). This constellation does not necessarily imply that these speech communities constitute static, monolithic units. On the contrary, there is good empirical evidence that these languages are best characterized as "patchwork languages", manifesting typological features shared with various languages spoken in the area – though not necessarily in the Nuba Mountains (Dimmendaal (2022b), as briefly discussed next.

Once speech communities such as those of the Tima in the western zone of the Nuba Mountains got established, territoriality (and ritual places associated with the area they live in) became important for these agriculturalists. The same community is also characterized by a low degree of bilingualism (as are other communities in the Nuba Mountains, the strong influence of Sudanese Arabic being a relatively recent phenomenon). What is more, speakers of Tima, for example, have an oral tradition according to which their ancestors manipulated the language, so that the neighbouring Katla, who speak a closely related language and with whom they were in conflict, could no longer understand them. This language ideology, whereby the language is treated as a unique property of a community, is also found in other parts of the world, and has come to be known as esoterogeny. For further details, including an analysis of this oral tradition of language manipulation as a *post hoc* rationalization by Tima speakers, as well as for an alternative explanation of the observed structural differences between Tima and Katla in terms of shift-induced interference, the reader is referred to Dimmendaal (2015a: 64–81, 2022b).

Everett (2012) uses the label "contingency judgments" to describe such processes, where a belief is formed about the relationship between two or more objects. He furthermore claims that there is a human predilection towards contingency, i.e., "[an] ability to see links of causality or correlation between objects" (Everett 2012: 166). Everett also claims that our ability to theorize, particularly our ability to theorize about other minds, is dependent on contingency. The latter phenomenon is interpreted in the present study as a further instance of conceptual blending, in the case of the Tima between their oral history and the observed disparity between the grammatical structure of their language and that of the Katla, whose language is very close to theirs lexically, as several speakers seem to know. Blending consequently occurs at all levels, including at the metalinguistic level.

Verschueren (2012) provides useful practice and training materials for the investigation of language ideologies as well as for the use of different tools, methods and theories of pragmatics and discourse analysis. For a practical application of notions playing a role in understanding language ideologies, particularly within an African context, readers are referred to the chapter on language and ideology by Anne Storch (Lüpke and Storch 2013: 123–179).

8.4 Performance

Different authors have emphasized the important role played by the enactment of agency in language use. As argued by Duranti (1997a: 14–17), performance involves not only the use of the linguistic system, thereby doing things with words (to paraphrase Austin 1962) with special attention to the way in which communicative acts are executed and evaluated by others, but a notion of creativity may also be involved.

Individuals become aware of or learn about preferred speech styles in early childhood in tandem with the grammar of the language(s) they acquire while growing up in a specific community, in the same way that language-specific features prime children to pay special attention to particular phonological or morphosyntactic features during language acquisition. We may define "style" as the meaningful deployment of language in order to achieve particular communicative effects or social meanings. Analyses of styles revolve around the totality of linguistic forms employed by speakers in the course of conversational interaction, and also encompass ways of organizing social interaction.

Style as a multimodal practice plays a central role in translanguaging, extending to speakers' choices of clothes, fashion accessories, or gestures as additional instances of semiotic strategies, and their context of use. Understanding language as stylized practice is also increasingly applied in other contexts, when for instance analyzing European "multi-ethnolects"; see Nortier and Svendsen (2014), among other sources. The term "multi-ethnolect" itself is somewhat unfortunate, as it associates the notion of "ethnolect" with the use of a specific linguistic register.

The selection of case studies discussed below, all addressing styles in language practices, serve a number of purposes. First, they show that the creation of new speech styles, and specifically youth languages, that is often associated with urbanization, constitutes a continuation of language manipulation as known from anthropological-linguistic studies. These latter, which are discussed first, show that different social parameters may play a role. Apart from different functions, different linguistic strategies employed by speakers can be identified, as illustrated below. As there are at least two extensive publications on the subject of registers and performance in an African context, namely Storch (2011), and Lüpke and Storch (2013), readers are also referred to these. The case studies below thus further illustrate the categories identified by these authors by listing older sources not discussed by them, as well as more recent publications.

Storch (2011: 19–45) differentiates between five types of derived or manipulated languages: 1. play languages; 2. honorific registers; 3. hunting and blacksmithing special-purpose registers; 4. avoidance languages and word tabooing; and 5. spirit languages. As it is not always easy to distinguish between some of these, this categorization is slightly simplified below: 1. "special purpose" languages; 2. avoidance languages; 3. (urban) youth languages. The various linguistic and social parameters (or features) motivating this tripartite division and the corresponding conventions of usage are summarized after these three categories (which necessarily involve abstractions) have been introduced.

"Special purpose" languages are characterized by the use of lexical and grammatical registers serving different purposes, such as a secret language, a spirit language, or a special register for initiation rites. In traditional Nandi culture (in western Kenya), male and female initiands are put through an ordeal whereby abusive language is used against them as part of the initiation. Langley (1979: 42) observes, with regard to these *rites de passage*, that the language of the songs during initiation is archaic and veiled, while the content is esoteric by intent. The songs often originate from Maasai, a related neighbouring language spoken by people whose habitus influenced other speech communities in the area.

The next examples of "special purpose" languages show one distinguishing feature, namely the question of whether the source for the special register observed is endogenous (i.e., originating from within the language system), or exogenous (originating from outside). This distinction is also found with the other two types discussed below (avoidance languages and youth languages), and is indexical of the language ideologies involved in the emergence or creation of such language varieties or repertoires. The other motivation for presenting these additional examples is to show that it is not useful to distinguish between tradition and modernity, as we find a continuity of strategies.

Among pastoral communities in eastern Africa, such as the Nandi in Kenya, cattle raids among neighbouring groups were common before national states were created. Related to these traditions, one may find euphemistic expressions for imminent or successful cattle raids in these languages. In his study of moral concepts among another such pastoral community, the Karimojong in Uganda, Amoah (2020: 554) mentions the word *agero* 'gathering' for 'cattle raid', a word which is otherwise used for the gathering or harvesting of agricultural products or wild fruits in this language.

Apart from euphemistically coded language, one may also find dysphemism. De-humanizing the enemy through dysphemism is a phenomenon known from many violent social conflicts or wars in different parts of the world, for example from the genocide against the Tutsi in Rwanda in 1994. Supporters of the Hutu militia referred to their Tutsi enemies or political opponents as *nyenzi* 'cockroaches', whereas the verb *gukora* 'to work' was used as a euphemism for eliminating Tutsi and their Hutu supporters (Rivet 2016). Here the use of endogenous sources (from Kinyarwanda) is associated with the creation of ethnic boundaries, erasing the fact that Tutsi and Hutu (whose "ethnic identity" was listed in their passports or identity cards) speak the same language. As Allan and Burridge (2006: 230) phrase it in their monograph *Forbidden Words: Taboo and the Censoring of Language*, "[t]he language of warfare provides a heaven for hypocrisy; it is a kind of political language which, as George Orwell said, 'is designed to make lies sound truthful and murder respectable, and to give an appearance of solidity to pure wind.'"

The second type of manipulated language briefly discussed here, that of avoidance languages, has already been discussed to some extent in Section 6.3. Such registers may be related to social categories such as gender or age, as well as others. Mitchell (2015a) discusses an avoidance register known as *gíing'áwêakshòoda* among the Datooga in Tanzania. In their patrilocal society, women must abide by an avoidance register after marriage at all times, avoiding the names of their husband's senior male relatives for three ascending generations, the mother-in-law and her sisters, as well as the sons of the husband's paternal aunts. Phonologically similar words are also to be avoided. While women's vocabularies in Datooga vary, depending on the household in which they are based (each with its own set of avoided names), there is also an overarching avoidance register, an areal phenomenon attested in a range of languages stretching from Ethiopia towards southern Africa, and probably resulting from areal contact, as argued in Section 6.3.

The formal techniques applied in Datooga are commonly found in manipulated languages. In the case of this language they centre around avoiding any word which begins with the same phoneme or sequence of phonemes as a tabooed name. The most common strategies, lexical substitution and consonant replacement, are illustrated below.

(89)
	Standard	Avoidance strategy
	gèeshta 'leg'	qóròoqta 'shin' (lexical replacement)
	uchúbòoda 'snake'	dìyéedágeaw 'long animal' (lexical replacement)
	uhùuda 'head'	ságànda (adapted borrowing from Iraqw *saga* 'head')
	sàbúuni 'soap'	nàlúuni (consonant replacement in a borrowing from Swahili *sabuni*)

The kind of taboo discussed in Mitchell (2015a) differs from cross-linguistically more common patterns observable in avoidance languages, as discussed by Allan and Burridge (2006). These authors point towards semantic fields related to sexuality, body parts, disease, and death, although the latter type of taboo of course is also widely attested across Africa. Moreover, the psychological rationale may be comparable. These may all be interpreted as redressive actions derived from conscious or unconscious self-censoring on behalf of the speaker, so that (s)he may not be thought ill of, as this might result in loss of face or worse. Ignoring such taboos may also have the potential effect of embarrassing or offending others.

The third type of manipulated language distinguished here is that of (urban) youth languages, and is only discussed briefly here, for two reasons. First, as a phenomenon it does not differ in terms of the linguistic techniques used by speakers, as these are quite similar to those described for the first two types above; second, an in-depth discussion requires the discussion of sociolinguistic variables such as age, gender, or social networks, which is beyond the scope of the present volume. The main distinguishing factor from the other two phenomena discussed above is the link with urbanization, and the frequent role played by national (African) or official languages (introduced from Europe during colonial times).

While these new varieties have generally been created in multilingual urban contexts in African metropoles (for example Nouchi in Abidjan, Ivory Coast, Sheng in Nairobi, Kenya, Randuk in Khartoum, Sudan, etc.), the widespread use of mobile phones on the continent has turned them into additional varieties of existing languages that are found in both urban and rural areas (such as French in the Ivory Coast, Standard Swahili in Kenya, or Sudanese

Arabic in Sudan).⁴⁴ The classical contribution by Kießling and Mous (2004) on urban youth languages in Africa, which triggered a still expanding interest in the linguistic consequences of urbanization on the continent, not only gives a list of such newly created varieties of existing languages, it also discusses the different formal strategies used by speakers to manipulate language; these are similar to those discussed for avoidance languages in, for example, Datooga above (based on Mitchell 2015a). But the social conditions of course are different. In the volume edited by Nassenstein and Hollington (2015), a range of authors give additional examples of such new varieties from different metropoles on the continent. Moreover, a number of studies in this volume show that such youth languages are not necessarily linked to criminality or a tough street image.

In a special issue of *Sociolinguistic Studies* on the dynamics of youth language in Africa, Nassenstein (2016a) discusses a variety of Swahili commonly referred to as Yabacrâne, as used primarily by younger people in Goma, a major city in the eastern part of the Democratic Republic of the Congo. As pointed out by Nassenstein (2016a: 235), this special register of Swahili is no longer limited to urban spaces in the area due to the presence of new media such as mobile phones. Moreover, several so-called "urban youth" languages date back to the 1960s (or earlier), as with Yanké, although they may sometimes still be part of the repertoire of the first users, many of whom are "oldies" now; hence, the labels "urban" and "youth" are also potentially misleading. Yabacrâne lexicon as illustrated in Table 20 derives, apart from inherited Swahili lexicon (and grammar), from a range of languages, particularly from regional contact languages like the Lingala-based youth language from Kinshasa, Yanké, as well as from the related (Lingala-based) variety called Langila, from Swahili-based youth languages such as Sheng, as well as from Kinyarwanda (spoken across the border in Rwanda), French, and English. The use of this register involves fluid practices (subject to replacement of vocabulary) rather than fixed entities, inspired by the creativity of its speakers, who may borrow from different languages in the media. Examples from Nassenstein (2016a: 246–250) include the following:

---

44 The term "metrolingualism" (after Pennycook and Otsuji 2015) is sometimes used for language practices in the city. Nassenstein (2016b) presents a discussion of this phenomenon for the city of Kampala (Uganda).

Table 20: Sources of Yabacrâne lexicon (Nassenstein 2016a).

Word	Source
djo 'guy, man'	From Yanké, after the male first name Joe, hence involving a semantic strategy know as onomastic synecdoche
bunga (Standard Swahili *unga*) 'flour'	Metaphor
joker 'girl who has slept with more than five guys'	Hyperbole
demu 'young girl'	Borrowed from Sheng (Swahili-based)
mère ya palais 'female fiancé' (lit. mother of a home)	Borrowed from French (with a Swahili connective *ya*)
masta/mista 'buddy, close friend'	Borrowed from English via Yanké

While codeswitching as a structural pattern actually *does* occur in the communication of primarily adolescent Yabacrâne speakers/users, especially since speakers are multilingual and share a set of languages that are intertwined, the structural component of "switching" languages leaves out some essential factors, such as ludic (playful) language use, the role of deliberate concealment/secrecy in speech, aspects of arranged performance, and the multimodality of semiotic means (by taking gestures, landscapes, and para-verbal communication into account).

In her contributions on South African urban youth languages, commonly referred to in the country as "tsotsitaals" (*taal* meaning 'language' in Afrikaans), Hurst and Mesthrie (2013) use the convenient label "stylect(s)" to characterize these varieties of regional languages.[45] In her in-depth investigation, Ellen Hurst also came across a so-called "floating lexicon", denoting terms spreading across different "tsotsitaals" via media or peer groups, and contrasting with other terms that remain specific to peer groups or particular geographical "tsotsitaal" varieties; the reader is also referred to Hurst-Harosh (2020) for an updated study of these types of manipulated languages in the area.

The compartmentalization of types such as those above necessarily involves abstractions (as with all taxonomic efforts). It is also important to keep in mind that individuals may be involved in all three types (using special purpose registers, avoidance registers, and urban youth languages, depending on the social arena in which they are operating). Lüpke and Storch (2013) use a concept from dialectology, that of "polylectality", for the use of several varieties and registers of a language by individuals; "being a fluent, complete speaker very often means being a competent speaker of various registers and speech styles" (Lüpke and Storch 2013: 121).

---

45 In his detailed analysis of Sheng varieties in Kenya, Wairungu (2014) also talks about "styles".

Not only may speakers be polylectal in an African context, quite often they are also bilingual or multilingual. Reda (2015) is a study on trilingual code-switching between the Ethiopian Semitic languages Tigrinya and Amharic, and English. The author points out (p. 121) that out of the 552 transcribed utterances in her database, only 45 instances contained Tigrinya, Amharic, and English, the remaining instances comprising either Tigrinya and English, or Tigrinya and Amharic. Reda (2015: 157, passim.) also concludes that the different constituent order of Tigrinya (as a verb-final language) and English (subject-verb-object) is not a barrier to codeswitching.

Sebba (2012: 52) states, quite rightly so, that "[t]he assumption that CS [code-switching] is the product of two monolingual grammars can be seen as a consequence of studying CS from the viewpoint of a monolingual norm, and a reluctance to deal with linguistic variation". Similar observations are made by Storch (2014: 269–280) in her anthropological-linguistic approach to the grammar of Luwo, a language spoken in South Sudan. "Luwo is one language in a repertoire of several available to its speakers", according to Storch (2014: 270). These languages include primarily Juba Arabic, Sudanese Arabic, and languages of the area, such as Bodho, Bongo, Dinka, or Shilluk, as well as other languages. In other words, the language ideology of the Luwo people acts as a selective force resulting in sociolinguistic diversity, and thereby, in the long run, in reconfigurations of linguistic structures in Luwo.

Storch (2014: 269) furthermore points out that Western concepts of ethnicity are closely linked to ideologies of linguistic purism, "as they imply that a community such as the Luwo 'has' or 'owns' a language of its own that exists as an unmixed, pure language, which acquires quantifiable elements from other languages only through discernible contact with these other languages". Whereas such views are not uncommon among Australian aboriginal communities, they often do not apply in the African context, although exceptions do occur, for example in the Nuba Mountain area in Sudan (Dimmendaal 2018).

The western perspective on language produced in the Global North, which was often proclaimed and spread within colonial systems and bound to missionary activities of promoting, documenting, and standardizing languages, is to some extent deconstructed by the translanguaging approach; this is what is referred to as "disinventing language" by Makoni and Pennycook (2006), even before the actual "translanguaging turn" took place. This view on languages as separable entities, which the authors see as antiquated, is therefore rejected by them whenever multilingual language use is analyzed from a translanguaging perspective. Instead, concepts like "fluidity", "anti-standardization", and "anti-fixation" are favoured.

9 Emotions and the sounds of silence in a cross-cultural perspective

Anybody who has lived in another part of the world for some time has probably wondered occasionally why his or her fellow human beings react in such an emotional manner when it comes to certain issues but not to others, especially when differences in character are apparently not the main reason. When the present author lived in the Turkana area in northwestern Kenya in the late 1970s, in order to collect data for his doctoral dissertation, he had such experiences a couple of times, one of which involved the following anecdote. One day, when travelling by car as a passenger across the vast semi-desert towards the district capital of the Turkana area, Lodwar, a Turkana herdsman appeared beside the road, with his herd consisting of goats, sheep and a few donkeys. As the car was about to pass by, all of a sudden a number of goats left the herd and crossed the road. The driver of our car tried to use his brakes, a dangerous venture on a sandy road, but he could not avoid hitting one of the goats with the front bumper of his car. When the Turkana man saw that one of his goats had been hit by the car, he became outraged and immediately searched for a big stone with which he could smash one of the windows of our car, so the driver accelerated his speed and dashed off. All of this happened within seconds. For the driver, somebody from "down country" in Kenya (i.e., the southern part of the country), the Turkana herdsman was to blame because one is supposed to keep one's herds away from main roads. But for the infuriated Turkana herdsman, the driver of the car was to be blamed because the latter had intruded into his territory and caused damage to his most precious property, so he wanted to retaliate.

Turkana people who observed European or American expatriates living in the Turkana area sometimes told the present author, when he lived there, that they had often been shocked by the manner in which the children of these foreigners sometimes spoke to their parents, which in their view was aggressive, emotional, and therefore disrespectful.

Of course, all of this is about cultural perspectives, which we learn about when growing up in a particular community. Kövecses (2000: 187), in his monograph on the linguistic expression of emotions, states that "feeling states are also, in part, culturally determined. This is because events that evoke parallel emotions in different cultures are unlikely to induce them in precisely the same way". As Wierzbicka (1999: 240) observes in one of her ground-breaking contributions on cross-cultural pragmatics, "although human emotional endowment is no doubt largely innate and universal, people's emotional lives are shaped, to a considerable extent, by their culture" – and this of course also includes researchers with their own cultural background.[46]

9.1 The expression of emotions

Scientific interpretations of emotional behaviour oscillate between biological reductionism (i.e., emotions arise from human biology) and social constructionism (i.e., emotions are products of culture). This "oscillation" between nature and nurture mirrors differences of opinion in other disciplines, for example criminology, where the origin of crime and deviant behaviour is explained or claimed to be conditioned by social factors like poverty or a genetic predisposition; again, there is evidence that both factors play a role.

Anthropologists like Margaret Mead (1942) were among the first to point out that children may undergo different types of socialization depending on the culture they grow up in. According to her, Balinese parents teach their children to avoid expressing emotion in ordinary interpersonal relations. In his description of Javanese culture, Geertz (1973) refers to similar preferences for a restrained and controlled behaviour. And, to mention some other case studies, Levy (1973) describes how Tahitian parents socialize children for "low affect", whereas Goldschmidt (1976), in his study of social interaction between parents and children among the Sebei in western Kenya, refers to "absent eyes and idle hands" as metaphors for the lack of (obvious) involvement of mothers with their children in situations where somebody from his own cultural background would presumably have interfered. Again, such observations on avoidance or "lack of involvement" as a presumed component of the "Other's" habitus are primarily true in the eyes of the beholder, reflecting the researcher's own experience as an exponent of another culture, for example when growing up in Japan or the United States of America.

The conceptualization of emotional states and neurophysiological changes arising from physiological changes, themselves due to some external stimulus, has come to be known as the James-Lange theory of emotions (after two 19th century investigators of emotions, William James and Carl Lange). Interestingly, the psychologist James (e.g., 1890: 485) also assumed that feelings are differently categorized in different cultures. According to more recent views defended in Els-

---

[46] More recent cognitive-psychological literature, as referred to for example in the volume edited by Mackenzie and Alba-Juez (2019) on emotion in discourse, draws a potential distinction between emotion, affect, and mood.

worth (1994), emotion is more complex than a mere physical sensation; moreover, physiological experiences have been shown not be a prerequisite for the experience of emotion. But again, as with colour perception or smells as discussed in Chapter 3, we are less concerned here with the physiological side than with the way speakers communicate information about emotional states, and more specifically with the way they talk about what they are feeling and the expressions they use.

Biological (or clinical) dimensions of emotions are reflected in English nouns such as *anger, disgust, empathy, fear, grief, hope,* or *love*. But as soon as one starts comparing words from other languages, which at first sight appear to present direct translations of these terms in English (as the metalanguage), it turns out that they do not necessarily cover the same emotional domains, as the following examples help to show.

Amberber (2001) discusses lexical and grammatical expressions related to emotions in the Ethiopian language of wider communication Amharic. The author shows that words like *sadness* and *disappointment* reflect different emotional states in English, whereas in Amharic they are covered by the same verb, *azzənə*. The author discusses the meaning and use of a range of lexemes related to positive and negative emotions in Amharic, again pointing out that the English translations only represent rough approximations.

(90) tə-dəssətə   'be happy/joyful'
      azzənə   'be sad, disappointed'
      fərra   'fear'
      tənbok'əbbok'ə   'be terrified'
      tənaddədə   'be angry, distressed'
      arrərə   'to be extremely angry, furious (lit. to be over-cooked)'
      dəbbənə   'be infuriated (lit. to be over-roasted)'
      tə-k'at't'ələ   'be furiously angry, livid (lit. burn (intr.))'
      tə-k'ot't'a   'rebuke, express verbally vented anger'
      affərə   'be ashamed, embarrassed'
      fəgəg alə   'smile'
      sak'ə   'laugh'
      alək'k'əsə   'cry'

Ekman et al. (1987) report on an investigation of reactions of speakers from ten different countries and eight languages to a set of posed and spontaneous photographs of facial expressions. These portrayed anger, disgust, happiness, sadness, fear, and surprise. The authors conclude that there was considerable cross-cultural agreement in the judgment of facial expressions, directed by our shared cognitive system as humans. At the same time, they also found cultural differences in the management of facial expressions, and corresponding differences in judgments of the absolute level of emotional intensity displayed on these pictures. Speakers of South Fore in New Guinea did not distinguish portrayals of fear and surprise, although another group from New Guinea, members of the Dani community, did, as already shown by earlier research (Ekman et al. 1987). As shown in the latter study, Dani speakers did not distinguish anger from disgust. Such blends or overlaps appear to be common. The close association between anger and disgust can be observed in a language like Dutch (the primary language of the present author), which makes a lexical distinction between 'anger' (*woede*) and 'disgust' (*walging*), but at the same time speakers also link the two emotional concepts through direct association, as shown by the following examples.

(91) godverdomme 'may God damn it (expressing anger)'
      gadverdamme 'damn it (expressing disgust)'
      gedverdemme 'damn it (expressing repulsion)'

As shown by these examples, one may play around in this language with vowels in a compound word functioning as an interjection containing the word for 'God' (*god*) as the agent or subject of a subjunctive verb form expressing 'may x damn', *verdomme*, hence 'may God damn (it)' in the primary form. The second and third "derived" forms of this swear word (involving vowel modification) suggest that anger and disgust or repulsion are closely related, involving conceptual blending or overlap for speakers of Dutch; as with speakers of Dani, being annoyed about something or somebody may also result in feelings of disgust, causing revulsion or repugnance.

Emotion labels have also been described in terms of prototypes, since the defining characteristics of the categories vary in their probability of being present in any given episode of an emotion. For example, with respect to feeling fear in a specific situation, Niedenthal (2003: 1119) contrasts the pounding of the heart when seeing a bear and running away with jumping off a high diving board, due to variables such as agency, familiarity, and outcome.

The perception of emotional states of course does not require lexical categories, as already argued for bionomenclatural terminology in Chapter 3. The experiment by Ekman et al. (1987) discussed above also makes clear that the perception of emotions does not require lexical categories. However, as shown on the basis of the "name strategy" discussed in Chapter 5 on linguistic relativity, lexical categories in a language clearly do help when assessing and categorizing cognitive experiences, or memorizing and reporting on them in a rapid manner in a specific speech community or community of practice.

This also applies to the assessment of emotions, as shown by Sauter, Le Guen, and Haun (2011). These authors discuss an investigation into the perception of emotional facial expressions in two speech communities, first with speakers of German, whose language makes a lexical distinction between disgust (*Ekel*) and anger (*Wut*), and second, with speakers of Yucatec Maya (Mexico, Belize, Guatemala), a language which does not make a lexical distinction in this respect. Their research results show that the perception of affective signals is not driven by lexical labels, "instead lending support to accounts of emotions as a set of biologically evolved mechanisms" (Sauter, Le Guen, and Haun 2011: 5). However, one should like to add, as with other lexical domains, that lexical distinctions – regardless of the semantic domain to which they belong – help us in assessing and recalling cognitive experiences in a rapid manner. The frame-and-scenario model accounts for the fact that when speakers are asked to reflect upon specific words related to emotional states, they are usually able to describe scenes or anecdotes where the use of these words would be appropriate as a characterization of what is or was going on.

The role of figurative language in the conceptualization of emotions has been a popular topic in cognitive linguistics (as one theoretical approach towards the study of language). Some authors working within this paradigm have propagated an analytical approach which considers the embodied conceptualizations of organic reactions in terms of "force dynamics", a cognitive model advocated by Leonard Talmy in a range of publications. Talmy (1988) dissects causation as a force into a range of "primitives" with opposite forces, such as "shifting" versus "steady state" (as in 'the ball kept rolling' vs. 'the shed kept standing') or "physical" versus "psychological" forces. Examples of the latter type of "force dynamics" are given below.

Amberber (2001) presents several grammatical constructions, alongside lexical forms, expressing emotional states in Amharic, thereby showing that metaphorical expressions involving "force dynamics" are part and parcel of such expressions; it should be pointed out, however, that Amberber (2001) does not analyse his examples within this framework.

(92) hod-e təmbboč'abboč'ə
stomach-POSS.1 move.PFV.3M
'I felt sorry for someone (comparable to 'sympathy/compassion')
(lit. my stomach moved)'

(93) fit-u aməd məssələ
face-3M.POSS ash be.alike.PFV.3M
'his face became ashen (with fright)'

Amharic also uses words like 'heart' or 'stomach' as metaphors for the expression of emotional states (examples adapted from Amberber 2001: 59):[47]

(94) lɨb-e   tɨr tɨr alə
      heart-POSS.1 IDEO say.PFV.3MS
      'my heart was pounding (with fear or anxiety)
      (lit. my heart was saying tɨr tɨr)'

Noonan (1992: 189–190) presents a discussion of such "body-part imagery" in Lango (Uganda), where emotions and personal characteristics are attributed to both the stomach/belly and the liver, as shown by the following examples.

(95) yì-ɛ́   yòm
      belly-3SG 3SG:soft:HAB
      '(s)he is happy'

(96) cwíɲ-é   yòm
      liver-3SG 3SG:soft:HAB
      '(s)he is happy'

One of the richest sources on the expression of emotion in African languages is to be found in a collection of studies edited by Batic (2011), with contributions on Akan, Botatwe, Dogon, Hausa, Igbo, Nigerian Pidgin English, Tupuri, and Wolof. In his cognitive-linguistic contribution on Akan in the same volume, Ansah (2011) argues that anger is both a physiological and a sociocultural phenomenon. The word *bo* 'chest' in Akan (Ghana), as the outer cavity protecting the heart, frequently occurs as a conceptual metaphor in expressions related to patience and tolerance, as well as in the expression for 'anger', *a-bo-fuw* (lit. 'chest growing', whereby *a-* is a nominal(izing) prefix, and *fuw* is 'to grow weed', as in the following example, adapted from Ansah (2011: 124):

(97) ne-bo   fu-i
      his/her-chest grow.weed-PST
      '(s)he was angry (lit. his/her chest grew weeds/became weedy')

---

[47] Kilian-Hatz and Schladt (1997) claim that 'heart' and 'belly/stomach' tend to be associated with positive emotions, and 'liver,' 'kidney', and 'bile' with negative connotations. But this claim is not corroborated by the data.

While anger is associated with boiling or heat, patience is associated with coolness in Akan, as in the following examples (Ansah 2011: 130–131):

(98) ɔ-wɔ   a-bu-fuw   hyew
      3SG-POSS   NOM-chest-weedy   hot
      '(s)he is hot tempered (lit. (s)he has a hot, weedy chest)'

(99) me-bo   a-dwo
      my-chest   COMPL-cool.down
      'my chest has cooled down'

In his extensive investigation of expressions for mental states in South-East Asian languages, Matisoff (1986) coins the notion of "psycho-collocation" or "psi-collocation", or simply "psis" (also "psys") as a polymorphic construction expressing a mental process, quality, or state. An example is a psycho noun like 'belly' or 'spirit', as one morpheme in English, and a verbal or adjectival "mate" (or "complement" in linguistic terms) constituting a second morpheme, as in the Akan word for 'anger', *a-bo-fuw*, above. From a conceptual point of view the Akan word involves the blending of a concept otherwise associated with horticulture (weeding) with the state of a particular body part. In addition, a metonymic extension or transfer occurs from physical symptoms to psychological effects. Additional examples of the use of "the body in the description of emotion" can be found in the special issue of *Pragmatics and Cognition* by Enfield and Wierzbicka (2002). In her rich and detailed survey of figurative meanings related to emotions, terms of endearment, or swearwords, Kraska-Szlenk (2014) also discusses organs such as heart, liver, or stomach functioning as the locus of emotions and the construction of figurative meanings in languages across the world.

In another informative monograph on the role of metaphors in the expression of emotions, Kövecses (2000) also points towards the importance of the visceral organs, e.g., the heart or stomach, in the activation of emotions. These smooth-muscle organs are innervated by the autonomic nervous system. The nerves and the brain in turn have the ability to receive and react to stimuli such as light or sound, amongst others. The frequent use of these or body part terms susceptible to physiological arousal, such as the liver, in metaphorical expressions for mental states including emotional conditions, is of course well known from a range of studies. But according to Schaefer (2015), there is little evidence in Safaliba and other northern Ghanaian languages for the presumed universal metaphors listed in Kövecses (2000). Instead, imageries involving body parts such as eyes or the chest show up in such metaphorical expressions in Safaliba.

(100) nimbikpɛɛne̱   'pitiless (lit. eye-hard)'
      nyɛmaare̱   'happiness (lit. chest-coolness)'

Languages like Tima (Sudan) show that other corporeal sites, such as bones, may also play a prominent role in the metaphorical expression of emotional states. The noun *kúùh*, primarily referring to 'bone', is also the locus of emotional states, and is used in a metaphorical sense to express 'soul, spirit' interior'; consider this etymon in the Tima-English dictionary by Schneider-Blum (2013b: 310–311).

(101) k-úùh   à-hín-yɛ̀ɛ́n
      SG-bone PRED:SG-sweet-LOC.1SG
      'I am happy (lit. the bone is sweet to me)'

(102) k-úùh   à-líl
      SG-bone PRED:SG-cold
      'be calm, deliberate, considerate, harmless (lit. the bone is cold)'

(103) k-úùh   à-kík
      SG-bone PRED:SG-bitter
      'be furious (lit. the bone is bitter)'

As shown by these examples, embodiment as an image schema may be invoked, not only by a container-like soft object such as the heart, liver, stomach, or belly, but also by a body part providing a framework or structure. For Palmer (1996: 66), image schemas are "schemas of intermediate abstractions that are readily imagined, perhaps as iconic images, and clearly related to physical (embodied) or social experience". As the examples above show, there are common patterns, but sometimes (as in the case of Tima) these image schemas are also subject to more culture-specific elaborations.

The bone also functions as a culture-specific metaphor for the Tima community in general. Thus, *Lúúh Kɔ́ɔ́*, literally 'at the bone of the family', is the name of the central area where the Tima live, which is formed by a valley basin surrounded by mountains, as illustrated in Picture 17.

Hence, *k-úùh* 'bone' represents an "embodied cultural metaphor", as this cognitive phenomenon is called by Sharifian (2017a), which allows Tima speakers to represent their sociocultural and emotional concepts. For further discussion of different semantic domains covered by 'bone' in Tima, the reader is referred to Schneider-Blum's (2013b) dictionary and Dimmendaal (2015a: 187–193).

Picture 17: Central area of the Tima (picture kindly provided by Gertrud Schneider-Blum).

Ameka (2002: 34) discusses body image constructions in Ewe (Ghana), describing notions similar to 'jealousy', 'envy', and 'covetousness' in English, as in the following example.

(104) é-fé ŋkú biã
 3SG-POSS eye red
 'he is covetous; he is downcast, sorrowful; he is revengeful'

The same bodily symptom of 'red eyes' is involved when speaking about being anxious or panicky in Ewe (Ameka 2002: 38).

(105) ŋkú-biã
 eye-read
 'anxiety, envy, covetousness, desperation'

The association of emotional concepts with 'red eyes' in Ewe is widespread in West Africa, according to the author (Ameka 2002: 51). This metaphor (resulting from metonymic extension) also extends into East Africa. In their analysis of adjectives in Shilluk (South Sudan), Remijsen and Ayoker (2020) point out that *kwáaaɽ̀* means 'angry' in addition to 'red', as in *ɲíŋ-áa kwáaaɽ̀* 'I am angry (lit. my eyes are red / my face is red)'.

The anthropological linguist Felix Ameka frequently uses a metalanguage with semantic primes for a systematic paraphrase of anthropological-linguistic phenomena, as in his contribution on phatic and conative interjections (Ameka

1992b: 257), where the meaning of the interjection *ú:ru*, used to draw someobody's attention, is described as follows:

> I want to say something to you
> I can't see you (here)
> I think you are in a place where you can hear me
> I want you to say the same kind of thing to me if you can hear me
> I say: [ú:ru] because of this

This metalanguage with semantic primes is inspired the Natural Semantic Metalanguage theory developed by the linguist Anna Wierzbicka and her followers over the past decades, and developed in an attempt to avoid ethnocentrism in the description and analysis of meaning. This model relies on around 60 (presumed) universal semantic primes. By using words which are assumed to exist in all languages of the world as semantic primitives (and constituents of a metalanguage), so-called "cultural scripts" of the type presented in the description of the interjection *ú:ru* are provided.[48] A partial problem with this approach is the fact that not all of these lexical concepts appear to be universally lexicalized. For example, the presumed universal concept FEEL, which is part of the Natural Semantic Metalanguage used in order to carry out cross-cultural analyses, does not appear to be attested in all languages. In Hausa, for example, the verb *ji* may be translated as 'feel', but it covers a number of other meanings in English, and consequently may be translated more properly as 'perceive'; see also the discussion on other African languages below.

Payne (2003) discusses the use of colour terms in relation to emotion in Maa, which is spoken in Kenya and Tanzania; the name Maa is used as a cover term for the dialect continuum Maasai-Camus-Samburu. Among around 30 colour terms and nearly 20 terms for colour plus a particular design (e.g., 'spotted black with white on underside'), essentially three ('be red', 'be dark/black', and 'be white/light') are used to describe human propensity and sentient-being (personality) concepts. Speakers used the verb (infinitive) *a-dɔ́(r)* 'be red' in order to characterize somebody as 'dangerous' or 'fierce'.

(106) á-tɔ́-dɔ́r-ɔ̀
 1SG-PFV-be.red-PFV
 'I have become angry'

---

[48] See also Goddard and Wierzbicka (2014) for a more recent state of the art concerning Natural Semantic Metalanguage.

The verb *a-rɔ́k* 'be dark/black' is associated by speakers with negative human-propensity concepts such as 'sad', 'bad', 'forgetful', 'stupid', 'unreliable', 'having no cattle', 'poor'.

(107) a-rɔ́k ɔ́shɔ́kɛ̀
 INF-be.dark belly
 'to be hard-hearted, unkind, unforgiving, uncaring, stingy, stubborn'

The verb *-ɪbɔrr* 'be white' and the adjective *-pʊs* 'blue' are associated with compassion and mercifulness, or "''favor' at one pole of cognitive associations for both 'white' and 'blue', and 'dislike' or 'moral/social rejection' at the other" (Payne 2003: 196).

(108) e-ná-ɪbɔ́rr-alɛ́m
 F.SG-REL-be.white-knife.ACC
 'interceder, mediator (lit. that which is white-knife)'

One also finds interesting instances of calquing of constructions characteristic of West African languages in creolized Indo-European languages in the Caribbean. Hollington (2017: 85) gives parallel examples from Jamaican English:

(109) red yai wi get yu ina chrobl
 red eye FUT get 2SG LOC trouble
 'envy will get you in trouble'

(110) im red yai di man fi im moni
 3SG red eye DEF man for 3SG money
 '(s)he envies the man for his money'

This type of conceptual transfer (or "relexification") through parallel structures in English constitutes further evidence for substrate phenomena in creolized varieties of Indo-European languages in the Caribbean (see Dimmendaal 2011: 223–230 for a discussion of some of the relevant literature).

Cases of conceptual transfer with respect to sensory experiences may also be observed in Eastern Africa. In many African languages, verbs translated as 'hear' in English in fact tend to cover a wider range of meanings. For example, the Swahili verb *sikia* may be translated as 'hear', but also as 'smell' (as in *ku-sikia samaki* 'to smell fish'). The polysemy of this verb is also found in West African languages like Hausa, where *ji* not only expresses 'hear' but also 'feel', 'sense', or 'smell' (as in *nā ji kanshinsà* 'I smell its fragrance'). This "Africanism" is also attested in Ethiopian Semitic languages, which adapted to Omotic and Cushitic languages in the country, not only only in their sound structure and constituent order, but also in terms of lexicalization patterns. As shown by Amberber (2001), the Amharic verb *(tə)səmma* also covers the meanings 'feel' and 'hear'.

(111) min   yi-ssəmma-h-al
       what   3M.IMP-feel-2M-IPFV
       '1. how do you feel? 2. what do you hear?'

However, when nominalized, i.e., when expressing a mental state rather than a process or event (as expressed by the verb), a formal as well as semantic difference occurs:

(112) simmet   'feeling'
       məsmat   'hearing'

Additional uses of the verb in Amharic show that it also covers meanings expressed by verbs like 'taste' or 'smell' in English (Amberber 2001: 58), which makes its semantic range similar to what is found in other African languages. An example is Swahili *sikia*, which covers taste and olfaction as well as hearing or feeling. However, as in Amharic, the noun derived from 'hear' in Swahili, *siki-o*, refers to 'ear', and not to other body parts.

Swahili developed over the past millennium as a contact language along coastal areas from Somalia down to Mozambique, as the name of the language (from Arabic *sawaaḥil* 'coastal areas') already suggests, primarily between speakers of Bantu languages and Arabic (and Persian) traders.[49] One reflection of this external influence from a predominantly Islamic culture on the habitus of (coastal) Swahili speakers can be found in words related to emotion, which are all borrowed from Arabic.

(113) hasira   'anger, wrath, passion' (Arabic: 'oppression of heart')
       ghadhabu   'rage, fury, passion, anger, exasperation' (Arabic: 'be angry')
       kasirani   'anger, bitterness of heart, vexation' (Arabic: 'cast down one's looks')
       ghaidi   '1. anger; 2. determination, resolution, exertion' (Arabic: 'wrath, anger, ire, exasperation, fury, rage')

---

[49] The inland expansion into what is now the Democratic Republic of the Congo dates back to the 19th century.

Hasira is a noun expressing a feeling that one should hide, as McGruder (2014) concludes in her study of emotions in Zanzibar (e.g., *hasira ni hasara* 'anger is loss'). The same lexeme may also function as a verb.

(114) a-me-iva   ku-hasira
      3SG-PFV-ripen INF-be.angry
      '(s)he is totally cooking with rage, anger'

Whereas Swahili terminology related to emotional states tends to involve early borrowings from Arabic, colloquial Swahili, particularly as used among younger speakers in Kenya or Tanzania, these days manifests another feature, which ultimately may be African in origin, but which reached East Africa through Anglo-American popular culture. A common answer to a question about the other person's mental state, *Namna gani?* (lit. 'which sort/kind?'), as part of a greeting, may be *poa* (lit. 'cool/cooled down'). The term *cool* also spread across Europe and is found in languages like German or Dutch, where it also appears to be Anglo-American in origin. Across Africa, there is a widespread tendency to treat being "hot" as a negative attribute of somebody's habitus. In a language like Turkana (Kenya), for example, it expresses absence of empathy and grumpiness.

(115) ì-mɔ́nà   íyòŋ
      2SG-hot.SG 2SG:NOM
      'you are stingy'

It is possible then that these conceptualizations of "coolness" and "hotness" travelled with the slaves transported from West Africa to the Americas, as a part of Afro-American culture, and from there to Europe.

Treis and Doyiso (2019) present a detailed analysis of temperature as a parameter in Kambaata (Ethiopia). This language makes a tripartite distinction (as reflected in different constructions) between the temperature of personal feelings (inner temperature) as against temperature related to weather (the ambient frame), and temperature connected with the sense of touch (the tactile frame). Inner temperatures are associated through metaphorical extensions, not only with emotions, but also with degrees of freshness, intensity of action, degree of spiciness or thirst, as well as other notions in Kambaata, as the following examples from Treis and Doyiso (2019: 252, 255) show:

(116) ís   san-úta   iib-a-a
      3M:NOM   nose-F:ACC   warm/hot-M:PRED-M:COP2
      'he is hot-tempered (lit. nose-warm/hot, warm/hot with respect to the nose)'

(117) gid-á íkk-o-kke
       non_tactile_cold-M:ACC become-3M:PFV-2SG:OB
       (congratulations) 'you are healed (lit. it has become non-tactile cold for you)'

Further studies on the role played by temperature in different languages can be found in Koptjevskaja-Tamm (2015).

Lakoff and Johnson (1980) also mention the cross-linguistic association between emotional states such as 'up' and being 'happy', or 'down' and being 'sad', as well as 'high status' as 'up', and 'low status' as 'down'. In other words, spatial markers may also form the source for metaphorical extensions not necessarily involving a physical displacement, as in *feeling down*, or *talking about somebody* in English.

Lakoff (1987: 267) defines image schemas as "relatively simple structures that recur in our everyday bodily experience: containers, paths, links, front-back, part-whole, center-periphery, etc." As pointed out by Geeraerts (1988b: 674), this cognitive-semantic approach is not entirely new, but "rather a partial return to the methodological position of the prestructuralist, historical-philological tradition of semantic research [of the 19th century]".

There is a lot more to be said about emotion from a cross-linguistic and cross-cultural perspective. Apart from older sources on the link between language and emotion, such as Athanasiadou and Tabkowska (1998), there is also the more recent handbook edited by Pritzker, Fenigsen, and Wilce (2020), which the interested reader is referred to here. Fleisch (2020) discusses a range of sources addressing links between language and cognition in relation to emotion, as well as other domains, such as spatial orientation, propagating "the advantages of a data-driven, fine-grained descriptive approach" (Fleisch 2020: 785).

9.2 The meaning of silence

> "Am schönsten sind die Kölner beim Küssen, weil sie dabei schweigen müssen" ('Cologne people are most agreeable when they are kissing because then they are forced to keep silent') (Kremer and Di Massi 2008)

Silence can be far more than a boundary marker delimiting the beginning and ending of an utterance in conversations, instead reflecting decisions by individuals on non-vocal as opposed to vocal channels. Saville-Troike (1985: 16–17) presents a kind of etic grid or taxonomy of types of silence by distinguishing between 1. institutionally-determined silence, 2. group-determined silence, and 3. individually-determined/negotiated silence.

Individually-determined silence, of course, does not always operate entirely separately from the other two types. Correspondingly, it does not always seem to be easy to distinguish between types 2 and 3 from an analytical point of view, although in principle the tripartite distinction is useful, and therefore maintained below. In institutions such as temples or libraries visitors may be required to be silent, while the professional code of conduct of physicians as a group usually includes doctor-patient confidentiality, thereby safeguarding patient confidences within the constraints of the law; finally, individually-determined silence is a common part of meditation in different religions. There are, of course, lots of other reasons why an individual might be silent.

In the volume edited by Tannen and Saville-Troike, Nwoye (1985) describes institutionally-determined silence rituals in Igbo society in relation to death. In this region in southern Nigeria one visits bereaved persons four days after the death of a family member without speaking a word, thereby marking or indexing the solemnity. After that, the embargo on speech may be lifted. Mourning or grieving sometimes involves a temporary or permanent change in personality, as many of us have experienced in our own personal environment. The widespread distribution across the world of silence in association with death as a strategy to control deeply felt emotions presumably reflects this observation about human psychology; ritualizing such behaviour makes it predictable – at least to some extent – in social practices. Of course, an individual who is seething with anger may also be silent as a strategy for the management of a tense situation, particularly within the family, because the family is an important network for survival and estrangement in family relations may be problematic.

As individuals socializing through language, we also learn to build proper frames with corresponding scenarios through contextualization cues as part of the language acquisition process. Language acquisition research over the past decades further shows that we are internalizing schemas in line with the emic perspective of community members for different contexts in which social interaction and corresponding language behaviour occurs. For example: Who is interacting? How are they communicating? Where are they interacting? What are the verbal and non-verbal signs functioning as meaningful contextualization cues?

There are interesting examples of such cues in the relevant literature. Hogan (1967, quoted in Saville-Troike 1985: 12), points out that "Ashanti children learn to observe silence at meals from an early age under threat that speaking would cause their father to die (. . .). This relates to the prescription which that society has for silence during some of its rituals, including when the spirits eat".

Hall (1959) is an early but still highly informative monograph on cross-cultural differences in "the many ways in which people 'talk' to one another without the use of words", as announced in the blurb on the cover. In another early source on cross-cultural differences in the meaning of silence, Samarin (1965) gives an example of individually-determined silence. The author reports on ritualized behaviour among speakers of Gbeya in the Central African Republic and observes that there is no obligation to talk in social contexts where from an American perspective this behaviour would be considered inappropriate. Related to this habitus, apparently, is "the shared wisdom" of Gbeya speakers that speech, not silence, is what gets a person into trouble. A further interesting case study is that of Bauman (1983) on the role played by silence in 17th century Quaker communities in the United States, who viewed noise as an imposition, and something which may also be interpreted as a sign of arrogance or presumed superiority.

In her contribution "Silence is also language: Hausa attitudes about speech and language", Hunter (1982: 393) claims, with regard to this speech community and its language ideology, that silence is regarded as a positive attribute. Gardner (1972), in his investigation of speech styles among speakers of Paliyan in southern India, claims that after the age of 40 people talk as little as possible. This attitude contrasts in a cross-culturally significant way with conventionalized behaviour as described for Cuna speakers in Panama, for example. Sherzer (1974), on the other hand, observes with respect to this speech community that being quiet is taken to be a sign of stress. Strecker (1976: 596) also observes that "societies differ significantly in the frequency of the speaking activities of their members. If one would plot all known societies on a continuum from quiet to talkative, the Hamar would probably be located close to the talkative pole". The author relates this emphasis on speaking to the absence of any institution of centralized social control. Inasmuch as the latter is achieved, this is never done without extensive speaking in this society. Additional early sources on silence are found in Muñoz-Duston and Kaplan (1985). Jaworski (1997) is another thorough source of information on this topic.

These and other case studies show that sociolinguistic variables such as age, gender, or the different communities of practice a speaker may belong to should be specified in order not to end up in a trap of stereotyping, even if speakers themselves propagate such a perspective. A popular view in Cologne (where the present author worked for two decades) among citizens speaking the local dialect is that Cologne people are easy-going and witty individuals, who like to socialize a lot. Outsiders' views include the stereotype of people in this metropole being *geschwätzig* 'talkative' in German (as reflected in the epigram above); they also prefer to help their close mates or friends first, hence the expression in Standard German *kölsche Klüngel*, 'Cologne clique'.

What these examples – in spite of their at times stereotypical nature – hopefully show is that silence, or refraining from verbal interaction, in all three domains, the institutionally determined, the group-determined, and the individually-determined, may be a sign or index of proper behaviour, or exactly the opposite, thereby reflecting rather divergent language ideologies. Examples of intercultural misunderstandings and miscommunications resulting from this variable status have been described, for example, by Basso (1970) with respect to the First Nation community of Apache in the United States. Keeping silent in Western Apache culture is a response to uncertainty in social situations in which participants perceive their relationships vis-a-vis one another to be ambiguous and/or unpredictable, whereas refraining from speech is sometimes interpreted by members of the White Anglo-Saxon community as indolence (Basso 1970: 225).[50]

The examples above reflect differential proposition schemas, as abstractions acting as models of proper verbal behaviour within communities of practice or speech communities. Such different patterns of verbal and non-verbal interaction across groups as instantiations of differences in proposition schemas (as well as other schemas, such as event schemas or role schemas, as proposed in cognitive linguistics) allow one to come to grips with intercultural misunderstandings in a more systematic manner when combined with two further analytical approaches, namely on (im)politeness strategies and conversation analysis. These are discussed in Chapters 10 and 11, while non-verbal communication is analyzed in more detail in Chapter 12.

The strategic use of silence in order to express disagreement or disapproval towards others, or "snubbing", as Thompson and Agyekum (2015) call this custom, is also described by Agyekum (2002) for southern Ghana. The author notes that if somebody remains silent when an older or a more powerful person is angrily interrogating this person, it is considered polite behaviour. However, in contexts where the former is expected to give answers to a question or pass a comment, silence is regarded as disrespectful.

Shunning, or group-determined silence towards individuals, as an extreme measure of ostracism for social deviants in order to bring offenders to repentance, is a language practice widely held to be the strongest form of social punishment, from the Inuit in Arctic regions to the Igbo of southeastern Nigeria. Social isolation is a serious matter, particularly in pre-industrial societies, as the absence of a social network may even threaten one's existence. In the form of excommunication, it became institutionalized in the Catholic Church in Europe,

---

50 Examples of intercultural miscommunication between white Anglo-Saxon authorities and members of a First Nation community can be observed in the movie *Three Warriors* (1977), with Kieth Merrill as the director. In one scene, a sheriff tries to investigate a case of horse theft, but it is only after he learns to use the proper greeting strategies from members of a local First Nation community that the latter are ready to communicate with him and help him solve the case.

and was applied, amongst others, to the founder of Protestantism in Christianity, Martin Luther (1483–1546).

In line with Hymes' ethnography of communication, one anthropological-linguistic research method thus involves the search for terms in a speech community referring to different speech events, to which wordless communication also belongs. An emic approach requires the search for words, or more complex expressions such as constructions, as reflected in idioms in the language expressing these key notions. The Japanese concept *haragei* (lit. 'stomach art'), for example, refers to an exchange of thoughts implied in a social interaction and involving wordless communication (which may also include facial expressions).

But as observed by Majid (2012: 441), focusing on descriptive emotion words fails to "do the job", as emotion is relevant to every dimension of language. Storch (2017: 4) makes a related methodological observation in this respect, particularly relevant for those interested in cultural dimensions of emotions: "even though linguists have prepared collections of emotion words and expressions, they very often have not provided any information [about] whether publicly discussing emotions in a particular language and community is an option at all". The following example is an attempt to bridge such a gap.

Bourgeot (2009: 107) gives examples of concepts associated with the habitus of speakers of Tamaschek, the language of the Tuareg people, a community with a nomadic lifestyle traditionally spread over countries like Algeria, Burkina Faso, Libya, Mali, and Niger. The author mentions three substantial social values as reflected in lexical concepts in the language: *tchighurad* 'strength', *tchileqqawin* 'weakness', and *takarakayt* '(being) reserved /restrained'. The latter concept reflects proper social behaviour, such as the containment of emotions. In a documentary on the exploitation of salt mines in Mali shown on *National Geographic* in the 1990s, there is also the story of a small group travelling hundreds of kilometres on camels to visit the mineworkers at this site. The caravan of adult men is accompanied by a young boy, who intends to visit his father in these salt mines. When the two meet after having been separated for about six months, they do not greet each other verbally. Moreover, rather than scolding his son for his irresponsible behaviour for coming along on this long and dangerous trip across the desert – or showing positive emotions because of his joy at being reunited with his son – the father keeps quiet and does not show any emotions. Instead, he puts his right hand on the forehead of his son for a few seconds as a sign of intimacy; see Picture 18, which is a screenshot from this documentary showing how father and son meet. Instead of expressing their feelings verbally, they choose silence as a channel within this public setting. Among speakers of Tuareg, containing one's emotions and being silent is also honour-related and characterized as showing *ashek* 'dignity', as it is referred to in Tamaschek.

Picture 18: Screenshot from a National Geographic documentary.

From the *National Geographic* documentary it is not clear whether the protagonists are in fact speakers of the Berber language Tamaschek or Tadaksahak, an unrelated language belonging to the Songhay family, whose structure as well as the habitus of its speakers have been strongly influenced by Tuareg Berber speakers (Souag 2015). If the protagonists shown in the documentary are indeed speakers of Tadaksahak, they would here manifest a transfer of speech styles (including the role played by silence) characteristic of Tuareg language ideologies. The Dutch subtitling in Picture 18 means: "It [silence] is a kind of politeness, of adulthood."

As pointed out by Carlos Benitez (personal communication), a scholar who knows the area and the languages involved well, it is difficult for non-specialists to tell whether somebody is Tuareg, Tadaksahak, or Tagdal (whose speakers live in Niger) on the basis of their dress style. Similarly, the Tagdal speakers in Niger participate in the larger Tuareg milieu in terms of dress style. Moreover, to non-specialists the two Songhay languages Tadaksahak and Tagdal sound like the Berger language Tamaschek.

Such migrations of language ideologies, or "travelling conceptualizations", as Andrea Hollington calls this phenomenon in her analysis of African linguistic and paralinguistic features in Jamaican English (Hollington 2015), are common. They either occur in situations where languages are maintained but where speech styles are copied from other speech communities (or communities of practice), or as part of a process of language shift.

Group-determined silence, known as *omertà*, apparently was and still is part of the behavioural code of the Italian mafia, which also migrated to the United States along with other immigrants. Salvatore Lucania, shown in Picture 19 and better known as "Lucky Luciano", was an American mobster or crime boss with Italian roots (and apparently one of the 100 most influential people of the 20th century), who had a mummified fish with an open mouth above his entrance door, symbolizing what would happen to those who would break this code of silence.

Picture 19: Cover of the monograph by Ovid Demaris (2019) on Lucky Luciano.

Group-determined silence has been observed with respect to secret societies in an African context; such societies are frequently – though not uniquely – male, bound by secrecy and the enforcement of laws, and appear to have a long history in some parts of the continent, as shown by the abundance of literature, especially from colonial times. But there are also interesting more recent, fresh perspectives on "secret societies" in a global perspective, as argued in the cover story of *New African* 470 by Ankomah (2008), "Secret Societies: Africa's Way Forward". Here, prominent figures in politics, religion, or industry are involved, doing their "work behind the scenes" to serve the parochial interests of their members. In this respect, their roles are not different, it would seem, from what has been described for more traditional secret societies by colonial officers and anthropologists.

This habitus and corresponding performance is of course not uncommon elsewhere in the world. It has been described for First Nation communities in the United States by Basso (1970), and may also be observed among the Freemasons in western society or among Paleo-Siberian groups in Russia. One psychological reason for this behaviour is presumably that one cannot know what the other feels or thinks, and so one has to be careful in showing feelings.

As with other anthropological-linguistic topics discussed in the present contribution, there is a lot more to be said about the role played by silence. Interested readers are therefore referred to an early source on silence as a cultural phenomenon, Muñoz-Duston and Kaplan (1985). Jaworski (1997) is a more recent rich source of information on this topic.

The following two chapters illustrate two additional research models (in addition to the ethnography of communication, introduced in Chapter 7, and interactional sociolinguistics in Chapter 8). The first one, discussed in Chapter 10, addresses notions of "face" and impoliteness as well as politeness models; the second model, on conversational analysis, introduced in Chapter 11, was initiated in the 1970s for English. However, it was not until the 1990s that this latter model was applied to other languages across the world. These two models form the transition towards a discussion of non-verbal communication, which is central to the final chapter.

10 Cultural conceptions of face

When the present author was about to graduate from Leiden University in the Netherlands in the late 1970s, he had written two theses (as part of the requirements), one of which was on a historical-comparative subject. Following an invitation from the *Centre National de la Recherche Scientifique* in Paris, some of the results of the second master's thesis were presented there. The central topic of the talk was the fortis/lenis contrast between consonants in a group of languages spoken in southern Nigeria, known as the Cross-River family. Those of us who attend conferences know that laymen sometimes show up at such meetings because they happen to be interested in (some of) the presentations. During the present author's talk, there was an elderly person sitting at the back of the room, who asked some questions after the presentation. Not being aware of who this person was, the present author started explaining some additional phonetic properties of such consonants. However, the gestures (more specifically, the repeated downward movement of the hand) of some of the attendants in the front row indicated that this explanation was considered superfluous. As it turned out, the "interested layman", a wonderfully friendly person, was the great linguist, anthropologist, and botanist André-Georges Haudricourt (1911–1996), and so this was like explaining relativity to Albert Einstein.

In his monograph *Interaction Ritual* (1967), the sociologist Erving Goffman analyses different types of social encounters and the so-called "facework" involved. Goffman (1967: 5) defines "face" as "the positive social value a person effectively claims for himself by the line others assume he has taken during a particular contact". This notion of "face" has been taken up and elaborated upon by Brown and Levinson (1987) in a highly influential contribution on speech norms entitled *Politeness: Some Universals in Language Usage*. Speech norms refer to judgments of proper interaction and interpretations, from grammaticality judgements to the proper use of registers. These are central to the present chapter, first from the perspective of politeness strategies (Section 10.1), and second from the perspective of impoliteness strategies (Section 10.2). In the third and final section, criticism expressed on aspects of these models is discussed.

10.1 Politeness strategies

Facework, in Goffman's (1967: 15–23) model, involves avoidance processes, namely avoiding potentially face-threatening acts, and corrective processes, performing redressive acts.[51] Brown and Levinson's (1987) model is the most detailed and influential account of speaking norms in a cross-linguistic perspective, strongly influenced by Goffman's academic contributions.

Apart from Brown and Levinson (1987), other authors have made valuable theoretical contributions on politeness strategies as well. These are compatible with the model developed by Brown and Levinson, e.g., Lakoff (1973 and subsequent publications), or Leech (1980, 2014, amongst others). Because of this and for reasons of space, only part of this body of work is referred to below. For a succinct summary and comparison of these various models, the interested reader is referred to Lavandera (2004).

"Losing face" may also be part of academic interactions, as the anecdote above illustrates. As pointed out by Brown and Levinson (1987), this notion of "face" as social image is used in a metaphorical sense, not only in English but also in other languages across the world, thereby reflecting its key role in social interaction. Mao (1994: 457) mentions two Standard Chinese words, *miànzi* and *liǎn*, both of which have the denotative meaning 'face, front of the head' and the connotative meaning 'public image'. Whereas *miànzi* is associated with prestige or reputation achieved through getting on in life, *liǎn* refers to "the respect of the group for a man with a good moral reputation", although the latter connotative meaning tends not be mentioned in Chinese-English dictionaries.

Similar expressions for *face* or "public self-image that every member wants to claim for himself" (Brown and Levinson 1987: 61) occur not only in other parts of Asia (compare Japanese *mentsu o tateru* 'save face'), but also in different African languages. Agyekum (2004a) refers to the concept of *anim* 'face' in Akan, southern Ghana, as a metaphorical expression for public image in communicative interaction. Nureddeen (2008) gives examples of apology strategies in Sudanese Arabic involving *washiy* 'my face' (Standard Arabic *wajhiy*) as a metaphor, as in 'my face is on the ground'.

In addition, the scholarly contributions of the philosopher Paul Grice play an important role in Brown and Levinson's model. Grice (1975) formulates the four maxims listed in Table 21 as behavioural codes contributing to a maximally efficient information exchange between speakers and hearers.

---

51 A succinct discussion of the sociological contributions of Erving Goffman on personal interactions can be found in O'Driscoll (2009).

Table 21: Conversational maxims (Grice 1975).

– The maxim of quantity	Try to give as much information as is needed
– The maxim of quality	Try to be truthful
– The maxim of relation	Try to say things that are pertinent to a situation
– The maxim of manner	Try to be perspicuous.

These maxims, which are part of the so-called "Cooperative Principle", are assumed to enhance effective communication in common social interactions.

Readers may wonder about these maxims and counter that one does not necessarily try to be as clear and as orderly as one can in what one says, for example because one may hurt the other person's feelings. This is exactly the point. When flouting these maxims, i.e., whenever one does not attend to these conversational maxims, there must be a reason, either a personal reason or a reason related to specific social values in the community to which one belongs. Brown and Levinson (1987) show how this social aspect can be incorporated into a model of politeness.

According to their model, the risk of face loss in relation to a conversational interaction within a particular speech community is conditioned by a number of factors:
– Model Person (MP) who has positive-face and negative-face wants
– The social distance (D) between the speaker (S) and the hearer (H) (a symmetric relationship)
– The relative power (P) of the speaker versus the hearer (or addressee) (an asymmetric relationship)
– The absolute ranking (R) of imposition; this factor is related to the question of who is entitled to "face protection" in a particular community

With respect to the notions of P (power) and D (distance), it is important to keep the following statement by Brown and Levinson (1987: 74–76) in mind, namely that it is "not intended as *sociologists*' ratings of *actual* power, distance, etc., but rather as *actors*' assumptions of such ratings, assumed to be mutually assumed, at least within certain limits". In other words, what matters is the emic perspective of speakers, not the outsider's etic assessment.

The authors had primary experience of conversational strategies in three languages: English (the primary language of Penelope Brown and Stephen Levinson), Tamil (spoken mainly in India, where Levinson did research), and Tzeltal (spoken in Mexico, where Brown did research). They assume that a so-called "Model Person" (MP) as a rational agent has specific positive-face and negative-face wants.

1. Positive politeness: "the positive consistent self-image of 'personality' (crucially including the desire that this self-image be appreciated and approved of) claimed by interactants" (p. 61).
2. Negative politeness: "the basic claim to territories, personal preserves, rights to non-distraction – i.e. to freedom of action and freedom from impositions" (p. 61).

Certain speech acts intrinsically affect these personal needs or desires of the hearer or speaker, i.e., they are face-threatening acts or "FTAs", as Brown and Levinson (1987: 65–68) argue. Thus, ordering somebody (H) to do some act potentially affects the negative-face needs of the hearer (H). The speaker's (S's) negative-face needs may also potentially be threatened by some speech act, for example when expressing thanks, thereby accepting a debt or humbling him/herself (Brown and Levinson 1987: 67). The hearer's positive-face wants may be threatened when the speaker criticizes H. The speaker's positive-face wants may be affected if he/she is ignorant of something that S is expected to know (Brown and Levinson 1987: 68). Speech acts may thus affect the hearer (H) as well as the speaker (S).

Brown and Levinson (1987: 69) make a binary distinction between different strategies, as shown in Figure 15. As there are no interesting linguistic reflexes of the strategy "don't do the FTA" (avoidance of unequivocal impositions), the latter is ignored in their discussion. A face-threatening act (FTA) can be done either "on record" or "off record".

Do the FTA
- on record
  - 1. without redressive action, baldly
  - with redressive action
    - 2. positive politeness
    - 3. negative politeness
  - 4. off record
5. Don't do the FTA

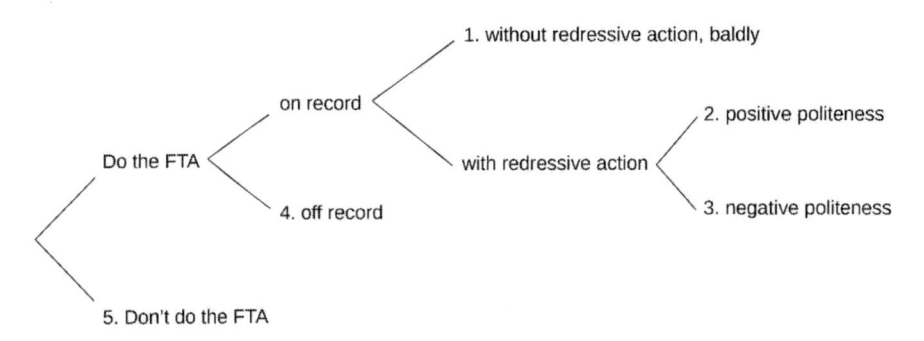

Figure 15: Possible strategies for doing FTAs (Brown and Levinson 1987: 69).

An actor goes on record "in doing an act A if it is clear to participants what communicative intention led the actor to do A (i.e., there is just one unambiguously attributable intention with which witnesses would concur)". When an actor (speaker) goes "off record" on the other hand, "there is more than one unambiguously attributable intention so that the actor cannot be held to have committed himself to one particular intent".

As shown in Figure 15 from Brown and Levinson (1987: 69), the on-record strategy bifurcates into speech acts carried out without redressive action or baldly, and speech acts involving either positive politeness or negative politeness strategies. With bald-on(record) strategies, positive and negative-face redress strategies do not play a role. Bald-on statements may be found in situations where face-protecting strategies are avoided, because security does not allow any redressive action or ambiguity in interpretation (as with interactions between medical staff in a task-orientated interaction such as a surgery in a hospital). Apart from efficiency, Brown and Levinson (1987: 95–101) discuss a range of situations where a face-threatening act (FTA) may not be considered as such, for example where H has high power over S, and the D factor is low, as in caste societies in India. This type of speech behaviour would be in conformity with Grice's maxims discussed above.

By using factors such as power relations (P) and social distance (D), Brown and Levinson (1987: 250) also arrive at different types of dyads (i.e., operators consisting of these two parts, P and D), and corresponding social contexts where specific FTAs are likely to be found. A low D value combined with a high P factor may be found in parent-child relationships. A low D value combined with a low P value is characteristic, for example, of relationships among age-mates. A high D factor combined with a low P factor may be found between buyers and sellers in marketplaces. Social interactions involving bureaucracy with government officials usually involve high social distance (D) combined with high power relations (P).

A full list of the speech acts associated with positive and negative face strategies, as well as off-record strategies such as redressive actions, is given in Appendix III, from Brown and Levinson (1987). Each of the concrete speech act strategies listed there is illustrated with rich sets of examples from English, Tamil, and Tzeltal by Brown and Levinson (1987: 94–283). Readers are therefore strongly encouraged to also consult Brown and Levinson's (1987) monograph, which is full of additional observations and suggestions for future research as well.

Rather than quoting examples from Brown and Levinson (1987), a selection of examples is presented below illustrating positive-face, negative-face, and off-record strategies based on the present author's interpretation of speech acts in Turkana. These in turn are derived from the interpretation of politeness strategies among speakers of this language in Kenya during a period of immersion fieldwork between 1978 and 1980. In addition, examples are drawn from the pioneering monograph by Strecker (1988) on speech acts, collected by Strecker over several years of fieldwork among the Hamar of southwestern Ethiopia, whose language belongs to the Omotic language family. However, unlike speakers of most other Omotic languages, who focus on agriculture as a means of subsistence in the mountainous areas in southwestern Ethiopia, the Hamar have a predominantly pastoral culture, and live mainly in the drier savannah country further south. Both in their material and immaterial culture, the life conditions of the Hamar show a lot more affinity with the pastoralists to the west and southwest, who speak Nilotic languages like Turkana or Päkoot in Kenya, than with the agricultural highlanders. Strecker (1988) also formulates a critique on the model and some of the assumptions made by Brown and Levinson (1987); as similar issues related to the discursive nature of politeness strategies have been raised by other authors, these are discussed separately in Section 10.3 below.

Strecker (1993: 124) argues that the Hamar concept of the *persona* is grounded in the concept of 'continuous creation', *barjo*, with physical and social well-being being a direct expression of one's *barjo*. Strecker (1993: 138) contends that in stratified (Western) societies the concept of "face" is linked to a sense of honour (thereby referring to Bourdieu 1979), whereas in egalitarian societies such as that of the Hamar there is a tendency to be less concerned with the self than with the other.

Several of the (numbered) speech act types listed below can be grouped together in that they flout one specific conversational maxim as formulated by Grice (1975), and as discussed below.

Positive politeness strategies

Strategy 1 (Notice, attend to H): Greeting, as a predominant way of showing that one has noticed the other person's presence or validates his or her presence, has been discussed as part of conventionalized speech strategies in Chapter 7. The different registers discussed there (including the absence of greeting) make it clear that greeting strategies play a key role both as positive-face and negative-face strategies.

Strategy 2 (Exaggerate): According to Strecker (1988: 78), "fully integrated and socially secure persons in Hamar will not employ strategy 2 but abhor it". The present author had similar experiences among Turkana speakers, for whom compliments, for example about a person's outfit, were thought of as something typical of *ŋimusungui* 'white people' (from Swahili *mzungu* 'European, white person'). Exaggerating one's own bad situation would be seen as a desperate act, although they had learned that foreigners often had a different attitude. The present author was once approached by an old Turkana man, who tried to obtain empathy and gifts such as tobacco and salt with the following statements:

(118) kà-nyam-it   akòrò
      3>1SG-eat-AS   hunger
      'I am hungry (lit. hunger is eating me)'
      à-nyàm-ɪ   ŋalùp(u)   bon(i)
      1SG-eat-AS   earth   only
      'I have only been eating soil (lately)'

As it turned out, he was the owner of numerous camels, as well as goats and sheep (herded by his relatives in the area). As the present author was told by the language helpers, he wanted to test how weak or strong the author's character was, and how easily this stranger to the culture would give out precious commodities just like that.

Strategy 3 (Intensify H's interest): Intensifying the hearer's interest by "echoing", i.e., repeating what the speaker just said in order to show support or agreement, is a popular strategy in the Hamar community (Strecker 1988: 80), and elsewhere in the region; it is discussed in more detail in Chapter 11 on conversational analysis. For somebody with a Euro-American background, on the other hand, this backchanneling strategy is easily interpreted as insulting – as if the other person is trying to pull one's leg.

Strategy 4 (Use in-group identity markers) has already been discussed in Section 4.2 on social deixis and pronominal reference and Section 6.3 on naming and terms of endearment, for example in Karimojong, whose language and culture are closely related to those of the Turkana.

Strategy 5 (Seek agreement) Brown and Levinson (1987: 112–113) mention repetition (echoing) as a strategy here. "Safe topics" such as weather conditions are another example.

Strategy 6 (Avoid disagreement): Being somewhat vague about one's own opinions, for example by using hedging strategies, would be an example here. In Turkana, the attitude markers discussed in Section 7.4 above would be instances of this positive-face strategy.

Strategy 7 (Presuppose/raise/assert common ground): Strecker (1988: 91) mentions a Hamar strategy whereby an attempt is made to absolve oneself of responsibility for what is happening. "By saying 'I have been wounded, I have been killed', when others rather than he himself have been hurt, the speaker indicates his concern for the others" (Strecker 1988: 91).

Strategy 8 (Joke): Strecker (1988: 92–93) describes the situation of a joking relationship between himself and the wife of a close friend. A more detailed discussion of this cultural phenomenon is given in Section 10.3 below on discursive perspectives on politeness strategies, as for outsiders the kind of interaction observed between interactants standing in a joking relationship towards each other may be reminiscent of impoliteness, whereas in actual fact joking is an exponent of close affinity and positive politeness.

Strategies 9–14 (Convey that S and H are co-operators) are treated together by Strecker (1988: 94–96). They may be observed in the Turkana speech community where social distance and power relations are relatively low, for example between community members from the same territory who are age mates and know each other's background well. Such a scenario, involving self-irony, can be observed in the documentary about the Turkana in Kenya, *Lorang's Way* (McDougalls 1977).

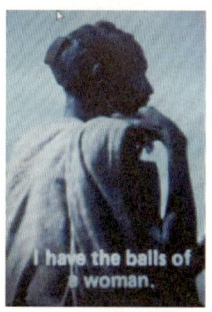

Picture 20: Lorang scolding at Abei. **Picture 21:** Lorang chuckling on hearing Abei's reply.

On one occasion, the protagonist Lorang expresses his disrespect for people who are not more assertive in defending their personal interests. While standing and looking down upon his age mate Abei, the latter sitting on his wooden stool (headrest), Lorang questions the latter's generosity in giving out livestock without being reimbursed at some point, just to be popular. Lorang asks Abei: "What kind of balls do you have?" (Picture 20). Whereupon Abei replies: "I have the balls of a woman". Picture 21 shows Lorang chuckling a little at this brilliant act of self-irony, as a result of which he decides to keep quiet.

Strategy 15: Give gifts to H (goods, sympathy, understanding, cooperation). Here the following Turkana custom may be mentioned. When going on a journey, one may be blessed by an elder. The performance involves spitting on another person's forehead (for example, a close relative) as an act of ritual purification, and expressing the following blessing:

(119) kàpé tó-búcár(-ì)
      go   2-bless-PASS
      'go and be blessed!'

Negative politeness strategies

Strategy 1 (Be conventionally indirect): Strecker (1988) does not give any examples from Hamar, but the following example from Turkana would seem to fall within this category. In utterances expressing statements in Turkana, first and second person singular and plural pronominal objects are expressed on the verb, if they occur, as in the following example. The initial *k-* shows that a speech participant (a first or second person singular or plural pronoun) is involved as an object, and a third person ((s)he, they) is the subject, hence 3>1):

(120) kà-ìnák(ì)   ŋákílé
       3>1-give   milk
       '(s)he has given me milk'

However, in imperative (command) constructions (referring to a second person as the subject), it is not possible to add a formal marker for the first person singular or plural. Instead, a passive or impersonal active marker (depending on the terminology one prefers to use) is required.

(121) nàkìn-áé   ŋákílé
       give-PASS   milk
       'let there be given milk'

The conversational implicature of such passive constructions is that the action is directed towards or for the benefit of a first person singular or plural ('me' or 'us'). In this way, the speaker obscures explicit agency and responsibility for an action, while the receiver or beneficiary is also implicit. Hence, the actual meaning of the sentence above is 'let me/us be given milk by someone'.

Strategy 2 (Question, hedge): Strecker (1988: 100) notes that this strategy does not seem to be frequently used in Hamar. In English, on the other hand, it is quite popular, as shown by the extensive discussion in Brown and Levinson (1987: 145–172). Questioning may be used in English as an indirect request, as in *Would it be possible to pass me some milk?* The hedging may be encoded in tags like *in a way,* or *it seems to me.*

Strategy 3 (Be pessimistic): Brown and Levinson (1987: 174) give sentences like *I don't suppose there'd be any chance of you (...)* as one such strategy. Strecker (1988: 101) notes that similar strategies may be used in Hamar, with the difference that 'anyone' would be used rather than 'you'. This corresponds to the Turkana example in negative-face strategy 1 (be conventionally indirect) above.

Strategy 4 (Minimize the imposition, R_x, whereby the latter symbol expresses the intrinsic seriousness of the imposition): Brown and Levinson (1987: 177) argue that in "Arabic, Indian, and Mexican cultures, a sentence like (. . .) 'Come again *tomorrow* and I'll have it fixed' is likely to mean 'in a few days' (. . .)". No corresponding examples from Hamar or Turkana appear to be available.

Strategy 5 (Give deference): In Hamar, the use of the honorific term *geshoa* 'master (lit. the one who is old and is bringing up others)' is used in situations where face threats are particularly prominent, for example in addressing ritual leaders or ancestors (Strecker 1988: 104–105).

Strategy 6 (Apologize): Lydall and Strecker (1979: 94–95, 195–197) mention a ritual form of face redress, known as *kash* in Hamar, which involves a reconciliation.

Strategy 7 (Impersonalize S and H): As stated by Brown and Levinson (1987: 191), commanding, in its direct expression, is one of the most intrinsically face-threatening speech acts. The conventionalized ("grammaticalized") use of the Turkana passive, or impersonal active as it is called in Dimmendaal (1983: 134, 182, passim), in the imperatives discussed under strategy 1 above, is presumably an exponent of a hedging strategy redressing negative-face needs. Strecker (1988: 108) mentions the use of the plural pronoun *wossi* 'we' instead of *inta* 'I' as a strategy of speakers at public meetings or on ritual occasions among the Hamar. This confirms the statement on the cross-linguistic tendency towards the pluralization of the 'you' and 'I' pronouns in order to indicate deference (P) or distance (D) by Brown and Levinson (1987: 198–204).

Strategy 8 (State the FTA as a general rule): Making such a statement by backing it up with the power of tradition is common in egalitarian societies such as that of the Hamar, as illustrated by Strecker (1988: 108–112).

Strategy 9 (Nominalize): Apart from using passives, another strategy to switch attention from the actor who is doing a face-threatening act is to nominalize a verb or adjective. Strecker (1988: 113) notes that "[i]n Hamar nominalizations abound, especially in requests, criticisms, admonitions etc.; that is, in situations involving an FTA". By using nominalizations one can obscure agency and responsibility for an action.

Strategy 10 (Go on record as incurring a debt, or as not indebting H). "Such redress is likely to have special force in cultures preoccupied with debt (such as the Japanese), but is probably relevant in any culture for doing large FTAs," according to Brown and Levinson (1987: 210), who give examples from Tzeltal (Mexico) and English, as in *I'd be eternally grateful if you would (. . .)* No comparable examples from Turkana come to mind for the present author, and Strecker (1988: 113–114) does not give any examples from Hamar either. Presumably, this is one such politeness strategy which did not become conventionalized in these languages.

Off-record strategies

The fourth approach in Brown and Levinson's model is to invite conversational implicatures by using off-record strategies or indirect message constructions, to achieve the aim either of social distance or of intimacy (as illustrated in Section 10.3).

Strategies 1–3 (Giving hints, giving association clues, presuppose): These strategies are particularly common cross-linguistically if risky phenomena or taboo areas are touched upon.

As pointed out by Strecker (1988: 119), most personal invitations in Hamar are made indirectly, for example by saying 'There is some more coffee in my house'. Euphemisms constitute another exponent of this strategy (violating Grice's maxim of relevance), and are common with taboo themes such as death, or cattle raiding, which traditionally was part of the culture of many pastoral communities in (north)eastern Africa (including the Hamar). "Thus a raid may be called a 'talk', a raider a 'hunter', and death may be referred to as a 'bleeding nose', etc." (Strecker 1988: 126).

Strategies 4–6 (Understate, overstate, use tautologies). Strecker (1988: 133) mentions the "lavish use" of onomatopoeic words in Hamar, referred to in the present study as ideophonic words. Quite frequently, such words are adverbs modifying some predication and intended at emphasizing a particular sensorial experience (something one smells, sees, experiences). An example from Turkana (Dimmendaal 1983: 381–384):

(122) è-lòs-í   cɛɛɛm cɛɛɛm
       3-go-IPFV IDEO
       '(s)he walks with pride'

Symbolic statements in myth, ritual, song, or poetry also belong in this category, flouting Grice's maxim of quality, according to Strecker (1988: 132), as a proper interpretation of their meaning often requires or presupposes socialization in the speech community involved.

An essential part of British humour also appears to involve flouting Grice's quality maxim.[52] Brown and Levinson (1987 217–221) also give such examples

---

[52] For a hilarious stereotypical enactment (or "interesting presentation", depending on one's cultural perspective) between somebody from Great Britain using off-record and negative-face strategies in combination with bald-on statements and somebody from the United States using positive-face strategies, readers are encouraged to watch the YouTube clip *John Cleese introduces Tina Turner*; see [https://www.youtube.com/watch?v=ENg2hApIL7k] (accessed 20 March 2021),

from English, for example: *That car looks as if it might go!*, referring to a flashy sports car with the conversational implicature being a complement on its quality.

Strategies 7–10 (Use contradictions, be ironic, use metaphors, use rhetorical questions). As argued for Hamar by Strecker (1988: 135), "[In] a whole range of criticisms, admonitions, reprimands, etc., a deliberate inversion of truth may be involved,"; Strecker further observes that only those with authority are granted such rights.

> The flood in the river beds flows downstream when it rains, may it turn back upstream, may it turn" (...) Of course, the Hamar know that the flood can't turn back. Yet they say it should. This gives their statement the cryptic and mysterious quality which elevates it above ordinary language and triggers off a set of evocations about the conditions under which it would be true that the floods turn back. (Strecker 1988: 134)

A further interesting example, taken up again in Section 10.3 below in order to explain the advantages of a discursive (as against an objectivized) perspective on (im)politeness strategies, is the following incident described by Strecker (1988: 136). During their fieldwork among the Hamar, Ivo Strecker and Jean Lydall experienced the case of a boy from the neighbouring Nyangatom (called Bume by the Hamar) who, driven by hunger, came into Hamar territory, where he was taken to an elder by some young Hamar men. After calling in all the young men from the neighbouring area, the elder made the contradictory statement 'kill him', referring to the boy. In actual fact, he meant 'don't kill him!', thereby emphasizing the taboo on killing him.

Strategies 11–15 (Be ambiguous, be vague, overgeneralize, displace H, be incomplete, use ellipsis). Idiomatic expressions and proverbs in languages frequently belong in this category, as in the English euphemism *I'm going down the road for a bit* (Brown and Levinson 1987: 226), the conversational implicature here being that somebody is going to the local pub. For the proverb *People who live in glass houses shouldn't throw stones*, in spite of the fact that its interpretation is conventionalized (meaning that one should not criticize others for bad qualities one has oneself), this "factual reading" needs to be learned separately. Brown and Levinson (1987: 227) state that "displacing H(earer)" is often delivered deviously in a Tamil village, for example when a speaker moans about his needs to a bystander in the hearing of the intended target of the request.

At this point, some readers may already be wondering whether it is possible or useful to classify or categorize speech acts as inherently affecting positive-face or negative-face needs. Before addressing this important issue (in Section 10.3 below), a number of related issues need to be discussed, first that of data gathering (below), and next the paradigmatic counterpart of politeness strategies, that of impoliteness strategies (Section 10.2).

Much of the data presented by Brown and Levinson (1987) on English, Tamil, and Tzeltal are based on fieldwork methods such as participant observation and interviews with speakers. Alternatively, quantitative methods, usually involving questionnaires, may be used in the humanities and social sciences.

Nureddeen (2008) discusses politeness strategies in Sudanese Arabic based on the latter method. By using a corpus of 1082 responses to a so-called *Discourse Completion Test* from 55 female and 55 male college-educated adults in Khartoum, she investigated verbal apologies in ten different social contexts, aiming at reestablishing social relation harmony. Arabic in Sudan is of a diglossic nature, with a formal variety (*Fuṣḥa*) which is similar to Modern Standard Arabic, and a colloquial variety (*'Āmmiyya*), which is used in everyday communication. Subjects were encouraged to write in the latter, i.e., the low variety. To put the participants in the required mood, the situations themselves were written in the colloquial variety Sudanese Arabic.

In their answers to the questionnaire, participants attempted to preserve their positive face by avoiding the use of apology strategies, for example by taking responsibility or promising. Instead they relied on "less dangerous" strategies, i.e., IFIDs (Illocutionary Force Indicating Devices). IFID is a category encompassing the explicit use of apology expressions such as 'sorry', 'forgive me', and the like. The latter concept goes back to Blum-Kulka and Olshtain (1984: 206) in their description of the Cross-Cultural Speech Act Realization Pattern Project, which involved participants who were native speakers and non-native speakers of American English, Australian English, Canadian French, Danish, German, Hebrew, and Russian, who were asked to take part in a (written) discourse completion task revolving around requests and apologies as speech acts.

For each discourse sequence in the data analysed by Nureddeen (2008), a short description was presented of the setting, the social distance between the interlocutors and their status relative to each other, followed by an incomplete dialogue. Informants were then asked to complete the dialogue, thereby providing the speech act they thought would be appropriate.

Informants used IFIDs in all ten social contexts, with frequencies ranging from 30% to 95%. Moreover, they used unthreatening – or face saving – strategies (humour, minimization, denial, and opting out) most frequently in five out of the six serious offense contexts. The author concludes that, when dealing with an event that requires apologizing, subjects were to a considerable extent aware that apologies damage their positive face, and this clearly affected their choice of apology strategies.

Nureddeen (2008) is fully aware of the potential limits of the method used in her study, for example the small sample size, and the fact that sampling needs to be extended to social groups other than college students. Even more importantly, Nureddeen (2008: 296) points out that more reliable results could have been obtained if natural data were collected and analyzed. Before addressing this important methodological issue, one further aspect of human interaction is discussed. As human beings we do not always try to keep social interactions friction free, as we all know from personal experience. More recently, there has therefore been much interest in another significant property of human social interaction, the conventional aspect of impoliteness or face-aggravating behaviour.

10.2 Impoliteness strategies

In one of his contributions on social interaction, Goffman (1971: 33) makes reference to so-called "virtual offence", in that, for example, the non-communication of the polite attitude will be read not merely as the absence of that attitude, but as the inverse, the holding of an aggressive attitude. With this observation on conversational implicatures, the author in fact had already initiated research on impoliteness strategies, the "poor cousin" of politeness studies, as Bousfield and Locher (2008: 2) call this phenomenon in the introduction to their collection of studies on conflictive talk. The study of impoliteness strategies is less popular among scholars than research on its "rich cousin", as becomes obvious from the number of publications on these topics. Nevertheless, intentional face attack is also a widespread phenomenon cross-culturally, as a number of pioneering researchers have already made clear over the past decades.

One of the prominent theoreticians on impoliteness strategies, Culpeper (2005), arrives at a typology of super-strategies similar to Brown and Levinson's (1987) typology of politeness strategies. However, these impoliteness super-strategies are characterized by the fact that a speaker does exactly the opposite of what would have been culturally appropriate in a specific context.

(1) Bald-on impoliteness
(2) Positive impoliteness
(3) Negative impoliteness
(4) Off-record impoliteness

A bald-on impoliteness strategy occurs when the face-threatening act "is performed in a direct, clear, unambiguous and concise way in circumstances where face is not relevant or minimized" (Culpeper 2005: 41).

Positive impoliteness consequently involves "the use of strategies deployed to damage the recipient's positive face wants" (Culpeper 2005: 41). In its most obvious form, this strategy occurs when a speaker does the opposite of what (s)he is expected to do in order to show low social distance or low power.

Negative impoliteness involves "the use of strategies deployed to damage the recipient's negative face wants" (Culpeper 2005: 41), for example by ignoring deference towards a person otherwise entitled to this register.

Off-record impoliteness as a meta-strategy is performed by means of a conversational implicature whereby the actual meaning of what is said is hidden under the surface, so to speak. Innuendos related to somebody's character or reputation are examples of this strategy, which consequently should be interpreted as a flouting of Grice's maxim of quality.

From an analytical point of view, it is useful to distinguish between ritualized and non-ritualized impoliteness strategies; this also shows that the speech act needs to be contextualized or situated. The actual strategies used may also be overt or covert, except with bald-on(record) impoliteness. An example of the latter can be observed in the documentary *Lorang's Way* by the McDougalls (1977), when the protagonist Lorang scolds a young boy called Eriyet for trespassing on his territory, and commands the boy to leave the area which Lorang considers to be his. Lorang also uses the opportunity to criticize his son's friends, whom he characterizes as "good-for-nothing friends" (Pictures 22 and 23).

Picture 22: Lorang scolding a young boy.   **Picture 23:** Lorang criticizing his son.

While visual or written documentations of such bald-on impoliteness strategies appear to be relatively rare in the literature, one finds quite a few case studies of ritualized or conventionalized impoliteness strategies, primarily involving positive-face impoliteness and negative-face impoliteness. The patterns of behaviour themselves are conditioned by such social parameters as liminal stages in the life or time of the year, kinship relations, gender, age, and others. They all share the fact that their ultimate aim is not to damage the other person's positive-face or negative-face needs permanently.

One such type of ritualized, and thereby legitimized, face attack (where positive-face strategies are otherwise the norm) is reported on by Irvine (1992), who describes a ritual impoliteness strategy among Wolof women in rural areas of Senegal, known as *xax(a)ar*, or insult poetry, as part of a Wolof wedding. A proper understanding of such verbal abuse requires an understanding of cultural systems of moral judgment, and situational specifics. As argued by Irvine (1992: 109), "[a]mong Wolof villagers, Islam, kinship, and caste (as the stem of social ranking found in the eastern Sudan is called in the ethnographic literature) dominate the moral framework of social interaction". Women in the family to which a new bride has come hire griots to chant outrageous poems insulting the bride, her relatives, and other members of the community. Griots, who rank low in the caste system, are spokespersons or intermediaries for others.[53]

Since this is a tradition inherited from the ancestors, with an aesthetic (poetic) dimension, no one has to assume immediate responsibility, particularly because one does not necessarily assume authorship of the poem. Moreover, since all in-married women make a financial contribution to make the performance possible, there is a joint rather than individual responsibility. It is these situational specifics, as well as the identities of speakers and hearers (for example, whether they are members of the same caste or not), which flow into the interpretation of such speech acts as being innocuous or not. In spite of its ritualized character, "being insulted in *xaxaar* matters. To be the subject of discussion in *xaxaar* poems is not only to be demeaned in public but also a guarantee of being talked about in private as well" (Irvine 1992: 120). Judith Irvine collected her data in the 1970s (as stated on p. 132), but this ritualized behaviour is still practised today (Saliou Mbaye and Fatou Cisse, both speakers of Wolof from Senegal, personal communication 2019).

While for visitors to Senegal from the Euro-American parts of the world such rituals may seem somewhat "outlandish", visitors from Senegal may be shocked by a ritual found in parts of Germany and the Netherlands where the Roman Catholic tradition of carnival was established. Although carnival parades are also found in the Caribbean or South America, politics does not seem to play a significant role in these regions. However, showing unmitigated, negative impoliteness

---

[53] Hale (1998) presents a detailed account of this tradition of griots and griottes in West African cultures. Like minstrels in medieval Europe, these troubadours or bards perform as praise singers or story tellers (including political comments or gossip) on specific occasions.

strategies, particularly towards politicians, during such parades in Germany and the Netherlands is part of the ritual of the inversion of power relations. Whereas normally (outside the carnival season) negative politeness, or at least mitigation, would be required, the pageant taking place on the Monday before Ash Wednesday (after which the fasting starts) allows those not in power to mock national and international politicians (or church leaders). Picture 24 shows one such parade float or truck, with the former Prime Minister of Great Britain, Theresa May, after Great Britain's decision to leave the European Union (which eventually took place in 2021). The picture was taken at the parade in the city of Düsseldorf (Germany) in 2020, with the concept (as usual) developed by the carnival float designer Jacques Tilly.

Picture 24: Great Britain's former Prime Minister Theresa May.

The advantage of ritualized impoliteness strategies, of course, is that they are known to end at some fixed point, which makes them predictable, and consequently those affected by them usually have to accept them, in order to maintain their position within the communities where they are based.

Descriptions in the anthropological literature of overt (non-ritualized) strategies for face damage are not really copious, but they do nevertheless occur. Novelli (1985: 186) describes common ways of offending in Karimojong (Uganda), for example by using the interjection òmɔɛ 'diarrhoea', followed by names of various diseases, thereby implying that the addressee as "the object of one's attention" is like that or as bad as that; for example:

(123)   òmɔɛ, lɔ́ɔkɔ́tᵘ
        'diarrhoea with blood'

Samarin (1969) gives examples of the art of insults in Gbeya, a language spoken in the Central African Republic. Such expressions contain a number of features which are more or less unique to the category of insults. One feature concerns intonation. In the following sentence, the word *oro* 'like' introducing the simile may be left out, and the phrase expressing 'an elephant's anus' (Samarin 1969: 328) acts as a separate sentence without being linked intonationally to the main sentence. (No interlinear glossing given by the author.)

(124)   nṹ mɛ́ ɔ́ wãɓuu (oro) nṹ gede-́fɔrɔ gá
       'your mouth is flabby (like) an elephant's anus'

Apparently, William Samarin collected around 3,000 ideophonic adverbs for Gbeya. While these normally modify verbs or verb phrases, they may also be combined with nouns when used as an insult.

(125)   kpuyuru nṹ
       'huge mouth'

Unfortunately, Samarin does not provide information on the cultural settings in which such insults are used by speakers of Gbeya. For another language in the Central African Republic, Zande (Azande), Raymond Boyd managed to collect such information. Boyd (2017) appeared in a collection of studies on "the language of emotion", edited by Tersis and Boyeldieu (2017), where various authors raise questions of universality, but also about whether talking about emotions involves specific syntactic constructions or discursive strategies. For reasons of space, only one contribution, involving impoliteness strategies, is discussed here, that of vituperation in Zande by Raymond Boyd. His study may be seen as an extension of a pioneering study by Evans-Pritchard (1956/1962) on verbal abuse known as *sanza* in the Zande speech community, characterized by the use of metaphors and other off-record strategies.

Strategies aiming at damaging somebody's social identity among Zande speakers are attested not only as part of a public display of anger, but also in songs accompanying public dances (Boyd 2017: 58). One subtlety of oblique speech (or covert impoliteness strategies) in Zande is indeed that the object of the insult is not necessarily overtly specified. "A person can thus be insulted in his own presence without being aware of it" (Boyd 2017: 59). The author distinguishes between non-attributive and attributive personal insults. An example of the first category is *ngbá dá ró (yò)* 'at the entrance to your anus' (Boyd 2017: 63). With attributive insults a speaker intends to associate a person with animals (*kúmbúsú* 'chimpanzee'), repetitive antisocial behaviour, physical defects, or reprehensible behaviour, such as not being circumcised or having an evil character.

Mitchell (2020) shows that in Datooga (Tanzania), the kin terms for 'mother' and 'father' can also function as terms of abuse. This abusive potential is pragmatically conventionalized. A mother may express a highly negative stance towards an addressee, which may be her own child, by using the phrase *géamádu* 'your mother'. The male form *gwêanu* 'your father' may be used as an interjectional phrase, or more specifically as an invocation, thereby expressing that some object is unexpected. As shown in example (126), these forms are in a paradigmatic contrast with non-abusive forms expressing the same referential (though not indexical) meaning.

(126) Abusive   Non-abusive
      gwêanu   qwáandáang'u   'your father'
      géamádu   qáamáttáang'u   'your mother'

The same forms may also be used in combination with first person singular possessives ('my') in oaths, in order to swear on the truth of a statement, in which case they are anchored to the speaker (Mitchell 2020: 85).

Cross-linguistically, it is more common to use the "mother theme" as a basis for impoliteness strategies, but as shown by Mitchell (2020), the "father theme" is equally common in Datooga, and both may be resumed under a more general "kinship theme", as other kin terms may also be used in Datooga. Data from Datooga also show that contexts are crucial in understanding the intended conversational implicature when kin terms are used.

Off-record impoliteness is of course more difficult for outsiders to observe or notice, as it tends to require deeper knowledge about contextualization cues. Agyekum (2010: 91–92) discusses seven types of institutionalized thanking routines in the Ghanaian language Akan, among them one aimed at blaming the addressee by using an ironical remark such as *wo, meda wo ase pa*, 'you, thank you very much.' This type of irony is of course widespread cross-culturally; consider English *thanks for nothing!*

Impoliteness strategies may be directed at individuals, but also at entire groups, as is typical with the stigmatization of specific social groupings. Mashiri (2005) discusses antagonistic relations and ethnic slurs between Shona speakers in Zimbabwe and immigrants from Malawi who speak (Chi)Chewa. The labels reflect these groups' disapproval of and stereotypical attitudes towards each other, resulting from "intergroup struggles over resources, cultural influence, and status" (Mashiri 2005: 2).

In their most obvious form (also to outsiders), impoliteness strategies are designed to attack face. But social conflict and disharmony may be caused not only when the speaker communicates a face attack intentionally. Intentionality carries some problems with it. Foremost is the fact that we can never know for sure whether someone intended to insult a target, as we have no direct access to his or her thoughts; moreover, people use indirect evidence to arrive at the conclusion that somebody probably had such an intention, primarily through contextualization cues, as a result of which the hearer perceives or constructs behaviour as intentionally face-attacking (Culpeper 2005: 38).

In his typology of impoliteness strategies, Culpeper also refers to so-called "mock politeness" or sarcasm, which however he does not take to be the counterpart of off-record politeness (Culpeper 2005: 44), as it involves a meta-strategy of using politeness for impoliteness. According to the author, an opposite impolite assumption is implicated if somebody says *DÒ help yoursèlf (won't you?)*. But examples like this provide strong indications for the claim made in Section 10.3 below that discourse needs to be situated, and that the proper interpretation of discourse strategies as polite or impolite is ultimately only possible by taking into account the contexts in which they are uttered. What is called "mock politeness" by Jonathan Culpeper is therefore referred to here as off-record impoliteness.

We need to study situated discourse in combination with corresponding contextualization cues in order to arrive at the intended interpretation. This latter aspect has become one of the main points of criticism of politeness and impoliteness models discussed above. Before going into details in the next section, one other phenomenon well known from anthropology, that of "joking relationships", is discussed first, again in order to show that without situating a discourse a range of strategies found cross-culturally remain unexplained and rather enigmatic.

The anthropologist Radcliffe-Brown (1940, reprinted 1952) was among the first to point towards a phenomenon called the "joking relationship", "a relation between two persons in which one is permitted by custom, and in some instances required, to tease or make fun of the other, who in turn is required to take no offence" (Radcliffe-Brown 1940: 195). The monograph by Marshall (1976) on the !Kung, discussed in Section 2.1 on kinship terms, also contains interesting information on joking relationships in this speech community, which is spread over three countries, Botswana, Namibia, and Angola. Joking relationships among the !Kung follow strict lines of kin affinal and kin relationships, thereby reconfirming the relevance of this generational notion.

> The !Kung were apparently not always assiduous in teaching their children the exact biological position of their kinsmen (whether a given man was Fa[ther's]Br[other] or Mo[ther's] Br[other], for instance), and a person would not always know why he applied a certain term to someone, but he would know that the term he used was proper, and he would know the proper joking status to observe; that would have been well taught him by his parents.
> (Marshall 1976: 204)

Marshall (1976: 205) observes that it is not proper to make blatantly insulting jokes to old people, for example by grandchildren with their grandparents. However, joking relationships between men allow them to accuse each other of having genital organs of excessive size or abnormal condition (castration or circumcision), or of being excessively preoccupied with sexual intercourse, unable to leave their wives long enough to go hunting. As one !Kung consultant explained to the author, such joking is not only amusing, it is also useful in that it teaches people, "young men especially, not to lose their tempers, but to have poise, instead, in their social relations" (Marshall 1976: 206).

10.3 "First wave" and more recent approaches

Work on politeness strategies has burgeoned since the quintessential contribution of Brown and Levison (1987), as becomes clear from the over fifty pages of references published by Dufon et al. (1994). Brown and Levinson's model is still frequently mentioned in professional journals like the *Journal of Politeness Research, Intercultural Communication Studies, Language in Society, Multilingua,* or *the Journal of Pragmatics.* However, as is common with scientific models, which involve certain abstractions in order to cover as many variables as possible, various features of this model have also been criticized, as is discussed next. This discussion is followed by an elaboration upon the question of the extent to which it is useful and meaningful to talk about "waves" in theoretical approaches to anthropological linguistics and the closely related discipline of interactional sociolinguistics.

Criticism on the most influential model from the "first wave", Brown and Levinson (1987), concerns not only their assessment of what is or is not considered polite from an intercultural perspective, as shown below, but also theoretical premises such as Grice's "Cooperative Principle", consisting of maxims which are assumed to enhance effective communication in social interactions. Hakulinen and Karlson (1977), quoted in Lehtonen (1985), present a witty discussion of "the silent Finn" as a popular image in Finland, thereby parodying Gricean conversational maxims by proposing additional principles in order to remain uncommunicative, like "do not speak", or, if there is no choice, "drink as much alcohol as possible".

On a more serious level, Grice's maxims were already being criticized before they became an integral part of Brown and Levinson's model. Based on her observations about social interactions in Madagascar, in particular among Malagasy peasants, Ochs Keenan (1976) claims that fulfilling informational needs is not necessarily a basic norm in a speech community. From her American perspective,

Malagasy speakers are less informative in their information exchanges than Americans. Ochs Keenan (1976: 70) explains this behaviour as being motivated by the fact that new information in villages where everybody knows everybody is rare, and therefore a commodity: "As long as it is known that one has that information and others do not, one has some prestige over them". A second reason, according to the same author, is the fear of committing oneself explicitly to some particular claim, and thereby being made responsible for the information communicated (Ochs Keenan 1976: 70). Ochs Keenan further observes that this may apply to past as well as future events. Moreover, misinformation may lead to *tsiny* 'guilt' for the speaker and *henatra* 'shame' for the speaker's family.

Ochs Keenan (1976: 77) points out that women in Malagasy society are more likely to satisfy the informational needs of hearers than men. As further observed by the same author (p. 78), in Western societies, being informative also varies with the social roles of interlocutors. Being discreet rather than informative is important for lawyers, priests, or press agents. Among speakers of Malagasy, this behaviour is also reflected in the tendency to mask the exact identity of individuals in utterances, e.g., by avoiding the use of personal names. Hence, terms of personal reference that specify individuals as distinct from other members of the community are avoided in favour of terms that do not make this distinction.

The case studies discussed above all refer to specific contexts where one withholds information; they do not appear to question the fundamental relevance of Grice's maxim of quality as a general conversational principle. Keenan and Ochs (1979: 156), for example, observe that "[i]t would be incorrect to infer from our descriptions of Malagasy social behavior that the Malagasy are always uninformative (...)". What is required is a specification of the domains in which the maxim is expected to hold.

Scholars from Asia and Africa have also criticized the egocentric and individualistic conceptualization of face (or public self-image), instead calling for a more community-oriented framework. Matsumoto (1989) points towards the importance of a sociocentric, context-bound (as against an egocentric, individualistic) conception of personhood in Japanese culture, thereby emphasizing the importance of group membership and social hierarchies. "Acknowledgment and maintenance of the relative position of others, rather than preservation of an individual's proper territory, governs all social interaction", as stated by Matsumoto (1989: 405) with respect to the Japanese speech community. Showing deference, according to this view, is not a negative politeness strategy showing minimal imposition, but rather a positive politeness strategy showing a positive relationship and interdependence between two interlocutors, as in the following example (Matsumoto 1989: 409; no glossing provided):

(127) doozo   yorosiku   onegaisimasu
'I ask you to please treat me well'

The importance of communal interdependence has also been emphasized by speakers of Chinese. Mao (1994: 459) argues that "Chinese face emphasizes not the accommodation of individual 'wants' and 'desires' but the harmony of individual conduct with the views and judgements of the community". Hence, these terms should be translated as 'public image'.

Authors familiar with specific communities of practice in Africa have also argued that the Brown-and-Levinson model focuses too strongly on individuals. Nwoye (1989, 1992) points out that individualistic notions of face pose problems for African notions of identity, which involve "group face", i.e., it is the self-image of the community which is at stake. As a speaker of Igbo (southern Nigeria), the author also emphasizes the dual manifestation of face: "group" and "individual" face.

A similar point of critique is found in Gough (1996) for Xhosa, and de Kadt (1992, 1995) for Zulu. Other authors from different parts of the continent have repeated the same criticism. For example, Ige (2010) reports on investigations carried out in South Africa among young male speakers of Zulu (referring to themselves as *Zulu-bradas* 'Zulu brothers'). Here too, respondents to the study show that "their collective identity tends to supersede their individual identity and may result in suppression of the individual self" (p. 3050).

Authors sometimes differ in their interpretation of the emic perspectives of speakers. According to Yahya-Othman (1994: 159), group face or collective needs, which she refers to as the "third party", are important in social interactions among Swahili speakers. Podobińska (2001: 212, passim) on the other hand denies the presence of a notion of "group face" ("face collective") in her extensive study of politeness strategies in Swahili. It would be interesting to compare these and other contributions on politeness strategies in Swahili, such as Habwe (2010) or Kraska-Szlenk (2018), in order to identify domains where interpretations differ. Of course, these may be caused by different factors, regional, generational, and urban versus rural, while how the data were collected is probably crucial.

Pointing towards the importance of "group face" (as a third party) in specific speech communities or communities of practice is no doubt important for a proper understanding of emic perspectives. But such criticism can be incorporated and accounted for by assuming that "face" as a metaphorical concept for an analytical category is itself an etic concept, whose emic interpretation as an individual attribute or as a group attribute is to some extent culture-specific. Face thus serves as a *pars pro toto*, involving metonymic extension, thereby expressing "group image" as an alternative to "self-image", and entailing the recognition of a participant's place in social hierarchies. The handling of the notion of "face" in this respect would be similar to other key factors, such as P(ower), which is also less about actual power, in the sense of ability to control someone else either legally or based on tradition, and more about the subjective interpretation of power relations between community members.

Shweder and Bourne (1984) relate the slightly different conceptualizations of personhood to the stereotypical Western conception of the person as egocentric and individualistic, and a sociocentric conception of personhood for other parts of the world, particularly in pre-industrial societies. Whether this somewhat evolutionistic perspective on personhood can be upheld is an "empirical matter", so to speak, as future developments as a result of globalization should show.

One more fundamental point of critique concerns the assumption by Brown and Levinson (1987) that "more indirect" always means "more polite". It should be pointed out that "being direct" is in fact mentioned by Brown and Levinson (1987: 130) as the first strategy in their list of negative-face strategies, the motivation for this strategy being efficiency (Appendix III).

However, a number of authors have shown that the issues are more fundamental, thereby preparing the ground for approaches which do not treat speech acts as inherently fixed positive-face, negative-face, or off-record strategies, i.e., as objectivized entities, but instead as dynamic phenomena which can be manipulated as discursive strategies.

Watts et al. (1992) and Ide (1993) are among the first authors to try to link their own emic perspective on the discursive meaning of speech acts to the taxonomy proposed by Brown and Levinson (1987). They distinguish between the speaker's perspective and the scientific perspective (compare Table 22), the first referred to by Watts et al. (1992) as first-order politeness and the latter as second-order politeness (this terminological dichotomy has also been employed by other authors since).

Table 22: (Im)politeness models and terminological variation.

Hymes (1962)	Watts et al. (1992), Ide (1993)	Present study
emic perspective	first-order perspective	contextualized
etic perspective	second-order perspective	decontextualized

The important observations of Watts et al. (1992) and Ide (1993) show that contexts matter in the proper interpretation of politeness strategies. Before discussing this rather fundamental issue, one other point of criticism is taken up as a prelude, namely that speech communities may select certain strategies for culture-specific reasons, thereby – at least on the first account – contradicting Brown and Levinson's (1987) taxonomy of politeness strategies.

In her contribution on cross-cultural pragmatics, Wierzbicka (2003) raises another point: "From an English speaker's point of view, Polish ways of speaking may appear to reflect dogmatism, lack of consideration for other people, inflexibility, a tendency to be bossy, a tendency to interfere, and so on. On the other hand, from a Polish speaker's point of view, English ways of speaking may be seen as reflecting a lack of warmth, a lack of spontaneity, a lack of sincerity" (Wierzbicka 2003: 50).

Blum-Kulka (1987) also argues that for Hebrew speakers in Israel indirectness does not necessarily indicate politeness. A similar point is made by Lwanga-Lumu (1999) for speakers of Luganda in Uganda. In her research among university students, involving questionnaires distributed to 100 Luganda speakers and 100 Luganda speakers acquiring English as a second language, nine request types were investigated: Want Statements, Query Preparatory, Obligation Statements, Mild Hints, Suggestory Formula, Mood Derivable, Hedged Performative, Strong Hints, and Performatives. Lwanga-Lumu (1999: 88) states that "[i]n Luganda, the highest level of politeness is constituted by a "Want Statement" such as the following (no glossing provided):

(128) Njagala kunjazikako ku bifunze bwewandiise mu sommo lya jjo.
'I want you to lend me a little bit your notes from yesterday's lecture.'

This statement may be preceded by an address term, such as *madam* or *teacher* (Lwanga-Lumu 1999: 91). One could argue therefore that the use of honorifics provides a negative-face frame within which directness is allowed (if a specific speech community or community of practice opts to do so).

For Luganda speakers taking part in the research by Joy-Christine Lwanga-Lumu, "Explicit Performatives" such as the following are perceived as the least direct (Lwanga-Lumu 1999: 89; no glossing provided):

(129) Nsaba kunyongerayoko kubudde nsobole okmaliriza emboozi yange mu ssabiiti ejja
'I am requesting you to grant me a little more time, so that I can finish my essay in the coming week.'

While in native English hinting is considered a polite strategy of requesting, in Luganda hinting is not perceived as very polite and is therefore ranked low on the scale. Moreover, people who hint a lot are considered sneaky and less honest (Lwangu-Lumu 1999: 90).

The questionnaire used by Lwangu-Lumu was developed by Blum-Kulka and Olshtain (1984). This method has been criticized by Sommer and Vierke (2011: 23) as an "imposition of standardized contexts (particularly in the discourse completion tasks), as well as for applying criteria of description that have been decided upon in advance and that might not be relevant in all cultural contexts". The crucial modifying words here are "standardized" and "all cultural". The following examples from the language of wider communication in eastern and central Africa, Swahili, serve as a further illustration of the problems of arriving at an objectivized (etic) taxonomy of politeness strategies.

Rüsch (2012) describes regional differences in style between Swahili speakers in Kenya and Tanzania, based on interviews with speakers, who were also consulted in order to unveil their emic perspectives.

Tanzanian Swahili:
(130) tafadhali na-omb-a u-ni-let-e-e chai
please 1SG:SU.PRS-beg 2SGSU-1SG:OB-bring-APP-SUB chai
'Please, I beg/request that you bring me tea!'

Kenyan Swahili:
(131) (tafadhali) let-a chai
please bring.IMP-IND tea
'(please), bring tea!'

Such differences result from the different interpretations of linguistic politeness strategies between Tanzanian and Kenyan speakers of Swahili. The Kenyans interviewed by Rüsch interpreted the Tanzanian style (130) as over-polite, while Tanzanians consider Kenyans to be rude in their utterance of requests (131). Such examples show that, depending on the region, different assessments may be found within one and the same speech community of what is or is not polite. Such statements also need to be seen in the context of the alternative strategies which speakers have at their disposal; the imposition of strategies cannot simply be assessed out of context.

Byon (2006) and Song (2014) describe a strategy which allows speakers to be direct as part of negative politeness strategies in Korean, a language with different registers in verb conjugations, as well as pronominal address forms used as honorifics (as part of negative politeness strategies). These are summarized in Table 23.

Table 23: Pronouns in Korean (Byon 2006).

Person	Neutral	Polite
1SG	na	jeo
1PL	uri	jeohui
3SG	isaram	ibun
3PL	isaramdeul	ibundeul
2	neo, dangsin, jane, seonsaengnim, or the more archaic forms eoreusin and daeg	

Song (2014) identifies a preference for direct speech acts in situations where the honorific system as a negative-face strategy plays a role. One way of interpreting this constellation is that it is not the verbal act as a whole that should be characterized as "direct", but rather only particular aspects. In this respect such strategies may be interpreted as elaborations of a negative-face strategy called "be direct", and motived by minimizing "the imposition by coming rapidly to the point, avoiding the further imposition of prolixity and obscurity" in the sense of Brown and Levinson (1987: 130). The case study of Luganda by Lwanga-Lumu (1999) discussed above mentions the use of honorific address forms such as *madam* or *teacher* (referring to a knowledgeable person), providing a negative face frame for a direct statement.

There appear to be culture-specific motivations for such embedding of different face-threatening strategies. Based on his own deep knowledge of social interaction among speakers of Hamar, Strecker (1988: 154–170) also proposes to modify and extend the Brown-and-Levinson model. One analytical issue the author struggles with is the combinations of strategies which speakers may use, for example negative and positive politeness in one and the same situation. Strecker (1988: 156) describes the case of a female guest visiting the homestead of relatives and asking for some sorghum (the staple food of the Hamar people). She starts with a negative-face strategy:

(132)   'I don't imagine there'd be any chance of anyone giving me some sorghum. People are just too mean these days'

After that, she switches to a positive-face strategy by claiming common ground, namely knowledge about proper behaviour in the society of which speaker and hearer(s) are part, with the following utterance: 'One never refuses in Hamar a handful of sorghum to one's in-laws' (Strecker 1988: 156).

At least two lessons may be learned from Strecker's in-depth analysis of speech acts in Hamar. First, a proper interpretation of these (im)politeness strategies is only possible for hearers or addressees by situating the speech acts within the specific frames in which they are uttered, not just on the basis of their inherent (decontextualized meaning). Second, speakers may shift frames in one and the same interaction, and consequently they may also shift between different (im)politeness strategies. The preferred kinds of shifts would appear to be specific to the speech community or community of practice in which they are used, and such preferred scenarios of act sequences need to be learned or acquired by speakers. One may invoke the customs and traditions of the community to which one belongs, as Strecker (1988: 156) assumes to be the explanation in the case from Hamar above. In other communities, a sarcastic or ironical remark followed by a positive-face speech act may constitute a preferred and thus conventionalized strategy.

In the same way in which directness may be part of negative-face strategies under specific conditions selected by a community, being indirect or using an off-record strategy may show social proximity, and thus be among the positive face strategies used between intimates under specific social conditions. Kasper (1990: 200), for example, argues that indirectness in Japanese may also express empathy between participants, symbolizing a high degree of shared presuppositions rather than indicating social distance between speaker and hearer. It may thus be useful from an analytical point of view to differentiate between interactional discourse, whose primary goal it is to establish and maintain social relationships (such as between relatives), and transactional discourse, which involves a closer observance of Grice's Cooperative Principle, Kasper argues.

Proverbs as idiomatic expressions are inherently part of off-record strategies (flouting Grice's maxim of quality), because they can only be understood by somebody who is familiar with the actual meaning of what is said. At the same time, a number of authors have observed their popularity as a strategy for expressing positive concern for the addressee where the social distance is low. Obeng (1996: 522) notes that in Akan discourse (Ghana) proverbs are used as a mitigating strategy minimizing or softening the force of a potential offense without the essence of a message vanishing. Using proverbs in such a context is of course only effective if many presuppositions are shared, otherwise it is not possible for the speaker to be understood. Not being explicit as a sign of intimacy also allows the speaker to take into account potential sensitivities of the addressee.

In another contribution on (im)politeness strategies in Akan, Agyekum (2004b) lists the use of "invectives" as the most offensive but also the most frequently used strategy for impoliteness, with non-verbal forms of communication forming the least offensive strategy. As argued by Kofi Agyekum, the degree of offence is usually influenced by the audience present, the context, and the time of its use. Again, this is an indication that such utterances need to be situated. It is only within their proper discursive contexts that their intended meaning can be (or is most likely to be) deduced.

In what is sometimes referred to as a "second wave" in politeness research, Watts (2003: 260) initiates an alternative analytical approach towards politeness strategies by focusing on situated (discursive) contexts. In fact, Brown and Levinson (1987) point towards such an approach in their discussion of off-record strategies in languages, for example on p. 225, where it is observed that an utterance like *John's a pretty sharp/smooth cookie* could be either a compliment or an insult, depending on which of the connotations of *sharp* or *smooth* are latched onto. Watts (2003), however, argues that the proper assessment of all speech acts (i.e., both positive-face and negative-face and face-threatening acts) requires a context. Watts (2003: 254, passim) consequently argues that the claims made by Brown and Levinson (1987) and related studies of a (universally valid) objectification of the notion of politeness are impossible and therefore misguided.

However, by making such a claim Richard Watts contradicts his own argumentation to some extent (a point also made by Hasegawa (2009) in her review of Watts (2003)). If all strategies were context-sensitive and, more importantly, language-specific or culture-specific, it should be impossible to make generalizations about politeness (and impoliteness) strategies across these boundaries. This is obviously wrong from an empirical point of view. Contrary to Watts (2003), therefore, it is assumed here that the taxonomy of speech acts as presented in Brown and Levinson (1987) is essentially correct, as the examples given above from languages such Turkana and Hamar help to show, as well as various other phenomena, such as the distinction in the domain of social deixis between honorific and non-honorific pronouns, to mention but one widespread phenomenon.

In the absence of an alternative model, equally detailed and elaborate in terms of size and depth, as well as able to account for a wide range of speech acts and their cultural interpretation, it makes sense to try and understand where and how culture-specific manipulation by speakers occurs and for what social reasons. The purpose is therefore not to save a particular model "at all costs", but rather to construct a model capable of explaining a range of conversational strategies which do not seem to fit into the first account because of their ambiguous structure, as illustrated in the next examples.

Let us get back to "being direct without being impolite", claimed to be a preferred strategy of speakers of Hebrew and Polish, amongst others. A frequently encountered, popular stereotype, also found in YouTube clips on what is assumed to be "typically Dutch", is the use of bald-on statements combined with positive face strategies by primary language speakers of this language. Various visitors with Anglo-American backgrounds staying in the Netherlands told the present author that it took them some time to get used to such communication strategies.

"You Dutchmen don't beat around the bush in order to get to the point or say what you really think, do you?", was the comment of one acquaintance who had been working for a Dutch company for several years. He admitted that during his first years in the Netherlands he had felt insulted at times, wondering why people in that part of the world seemed not to consider the personal feelings of others.

Of course, the emic perspective of community members growing up with Dutch as a first language is a different one. It should be added that within the Netherlands, "being direct" as a stereotype used to be associated with speakers from the so-called "Randstad", the triangle between Amsterdam, Rotterdam, and The Hague. Due to modern media and people's increased mobility, regional differences are vanishing, not only in that dialect differences are disappearing but also differences in speech styles. By being direct one shows that one does not have a hidden agenda and that one is sincere, i.e., one adheres to Grice's maxims of quality and quantity.

Corresponding to this and presumably as part of the same language ideology, there is a strong dislike of so-called "white lies", as Brown and Levinson (1987: 115–116) call this (positive) face strategy, used when one is confronted with the necessity of stating an opinion. From the Dutch cultural perspective, "white lies", told in order to avoid hurting somebody's feelings, are interpreted as a strategy for keeping important and relevant information from others. Being direct as part of a language ideology thus becomes an index for integrity (or lack thereof, if one comes up with "white lies"). It should also be pointed out that in social interaction in Dutch, discourse particles play a crucial role as a perlocutionary dimension of speech acts. For example, in the following utterance the attitude marker *hoor* (from the verb *horen* 'hear) serves as an important hedging strategy for a direct statement, even in situations where social distance and/or power relations may be considered high from an intercultural perspective:

(133) Ik   vind dat   niet, hoor
       1SG   find that not   ATT
       'I don't really agree with that'

There is a popular stereotype among members of the same speech community (again, also manifest in YouTube clips where speakers reflect upon their habitus) that social distance and power relations are relatively small in the Netherlands, i.e., that social structures are flat, just like most of the country. Whether this is correct from a socio-economic point is irrelevant, as we are talking about dominant emic perspectives. Sharifian (2011: 177) uses the metaphor of "language as a 'memory bank' for the cultural conceptualisations that have evolved throughout the history of a particular speech community". How and why these habitus features developed in this small country cannot be explained by anthropological-linguistic principles. They may be a reflex of resistance against domination and occupation by powerful neighbours over the past five centuries, such as Spain, France, and Germany, such that freedom of opinion is treasured. But of course this emic perspective is the result of language-ideological principles as formulated by Irvine and Gal (2000).

Human interaction becomes rather more intricate from an intercultural perspective, if speakers say exactly the opposite of what they actually mean, something apparently made possible when interactants share a lot of common ground. In such situations, interpretations of speech acts as instances of certain politeness strategies become rather intricate, as the following example of mock impoliteness or banter derived from the personal experience of the present author while based in Cologne, Germany, should illustrate. One day, a group of Afro-Germans in the Cologne subway were exchanging experiences they had apparently had with weird characters while enjoying the nightlife in the metropole over the years. Interestingly, they addressed each other as "nigger", thereby showing that "face threats" are minimal when age mates are close. Such insults in fact appeared to reconfirm the intimacy of their personal relations. In other words, a speech act cannot be interpreted as insulting until the hearer has chosen to interpret it as such *within a given context*, an important point raised by Eelen (2001) in his critical account of politeness theories.

Again, comparable examples can be found in descriptions of greeting strategies in an African context, for example in Wolof joking greetings and mocking insults where social bonds are close and social hierarchies do not play a role (Irvine 1974: 180–183). Another example is given by Nassenstein (2016a: 251–252) in his analysis of the Swahili-based youth language Yabacrâne (Democratic Republic of the Congo), where terms like *pantshi* 'idiot' or *imbecile* 'dumb person' may be used as a part of joking relationships and male bonding, i.e., as (contextualized) positive-face politeness strategies rather than impoliteness strategies.

A further example potentially causing confusion from an intercultural perspective again derives from a German-speaking environment, and relates to two distinct conversational implicatures of the German greeting *Schönen Tag noch!* 'have a nice day'. In terms of instrumentality, a change in amplitude (for example a strong rather than a minimal high-low accent drop between the second and third word) shows which emotive reading or conversational implicature is intended, potentially a wish that the other person will not have a nice day. (The role played by prosody in impoliteness strategies is also discussed in Culpeper 2005: 52–62.) This strategy is not commonly used in the neighbouring speech community speaking a closely related language, Dutch.

The hermeneutics of the "said" and its conversational implicatures can already be complex from an intercultural perspective. But the hermeneutics of the "unsaid" assumes knowledge about shared background knowledge and inferences about the unspoken intentions of its speakers. In his intellectually demanding monograph *The Said and the Unsaid*, the linguistic anthropologist Tyler (1978: 435) argues that the interpretation of meaning is derived through a dynamic process, and that speech events change and emerge in the course of interaction. The present author does not share Tyler's view that meaning cannot be investigated as an objective entity studied apart from its users, as progress made in formal semantics as an autonomous linguistic-semantic theory shows. This applies, for example, to the logical implications of the use of negation markers or quantifiers such as *nobody* as opposed to *everybody* in English: *Nobody knows English* vs. *Everybody knows English*. But if a speaker of Hamar calls out to others 'kill him', when a young boy from the neighbouring Nyangatom (Bume) community, driven by hunger, visits a Hamar hamlet (an example discussed in Section 10.1 on off-record strategies), he can do so without implying that the boy should indeed be killed. This is so because competent Hamar speakers have learned about elders' flouting of Grice's maxim of quality through sarcasm as part of their language socialization. Hence, exactly as Strecker (1988: 136) states in his analysis of such contradictory statements as used by Hamar speakers, through such strategies and shared knowledge they are claiming common ground and conveying that they are co-operators.

It is important therefore to view "truth" and "felicity" as two independent dimensions. The latter concept relates utterances to situations in which they are appropriate or felicitous. Children acquiring Hamar through socialization have to learn that a community member with authority may deliberately invert the truth value of a statement or command. And this is where a "theory of mind" (knowing what the other person actually intends to say) comes in.

The claim that meaning should be interpreted as enaction, rather than reflecting internal mental representations, may sound somewhat abstract at first encounter. But as a matter of fact, this is what the above examples show. It is the frame within which they are uttered and the corresponding contextualization cues which enact the intended interpretation of these utterances and thereby their actual meaning, which is the opposite of what Grice's maxims might suggest. In his monograph *Cultural Linguistics*, Palmer (1996) adds a further useful dimension to the interpretation of meaning in this respect by distinguishing between situated meaning, based on conventionalized interpretations (which help us in making sense of what we have already experienced and know), and emergent meaning, whereby we place new experiences into new frames and thus rise to new meanings. The "invisible hand" of speakers, and more specifically the use of specific words in new bridging contexts, may cause situated meanings to change.

Grice (1975) was certainly aware of some of the inherent problems of his proposed maxims, for example the maxim of relation (or relevance): "Though the maxim itself is terse, its formulation contains a number of problems that exercize me a good deal: questions about what different kinds and focuses of relevance there may be, how these shift in the course of a talk exchange, how to allow for the fact that subjects of conversations are legitimately changed, and so on. I find the treatment of such questions exceedingly difficult, and I hope to revert to them in later work" (Grice 1975: 58). Such reservations are of course important from a methodological point of view, but they can possibly be accommodated without questioning the fundamental importance of the Gricean maxims, namely by taking recourse to contextualization cues as well as frames and scenarios.

A major challenge from an analytical point of view is to bring the insights from anthropological linguistics, cognitive linguistics, and sociolinguistics together in a unified model of human communication from both an intracultural and intercultural perspective. The present author does not pretend to be able to achieve this intellectual challenge. However, Table 24 is a first attempt to list relevant parameters established within these fields of investigation. These should also reflect the domains about which individuals need to acquire explicit, implicit, and tacit knowledge in order to become competent speakers

Table 24: Methodologies contributing to an understanding of communicative competence.

Ethnography of communication
– Speech community
– Speech events
– Constituent factors of speech events
– Functions of speech
Cognitive linguistics and speech act theory
– Frames
– Scenarios (or schemas)
– Conversational maxims
(Im)politeness research
– Bald-on statements
– Positive-face (im)politeness strategies
– Negative-face (im)politeness strategies
– Off-record (im)politeness strategies

Table 24 (continued)

Conversation analysis
– Structure of turn-taking (pause, overlap, number of turns)
– Act sequences and concepts like schisming
Interactional sociolinguistics
– Community of practice
– Identity
– Language ideology
– Indexicality
– Performance
Non-verbal communication
– Facial expressions
– Gestures

Linking current (im)politeness models with a frame-and-scenario model (inspired by interactional sociolinguistics and cognitive linguistics) allows us to understand how speakers create situated discourse, where they may even mean the opposite of what they appear to be saying, following the Gricean maxims. This also implies that (im)politeness is ultimately in the eyes of the beholder (speaker and hearer). From a cognitive point of view, this requires the acquistion of frames and corresponding scenarios when growing up in a specific speech community or community of practice (depending on the situation). As part of this process, automatic routines are developed by our cognitive system based on experience, allowing for rapid on-line processing and situated interpretation (through framing), as with blind typing on a keyboard or driving a car. This mental process is presumably also comparable with what is known from other brain activities, such as smells; the brain ignores what is already familiar. Only when an unexpected situation occurs is a reframing of a conversational interaction with corresponding scenarios required.

Mastering the contextualization cues as signalling mechanisms used by speakers to indicate how they mean what they say is an important part of language socialization, as becomes particularly clear from the study of politeness and impoliteness strategies. And here we enter the third type of linguistic relativity (alongside the lexical and the grammatical domains discussed in Chapter 5), namely "speaking as a culturally constructed act", as Foley (1997: 249) calls this phenomenon.

Although some reservations have been expressed above about the model proposed by Watts (2003), his critical assessment of an essentially objectivizing discourse model in the "first wave" of (im)politeness research helps to introduce a dimension crucial for our understanding of cross-cultural differences in the assessment of specific speech acts. Moreover, Watts (2008: 213) formulates an elegant synopsis of the analysis of language use from an anthropological-linguistic point of view, very much along lines also propagated in the present monograph:

> Discursive behaviour entails using concepts stored in the form of frames, scripts and scenarios (and the complex networks linking these concepts) in momentary mental spaces which form inputs from which elements can be projected to mental spaces to construct conceptual blends. These blends provide the basis for new emergent meaning structures. They are completed by the projection of elements taken from related cognitive frames and some of the blends may be retained in reconstructing the very frames and scenarios from which they are projected. The input to conceptual blends, however, is not only linguistic. Visual, auditory, tactual and sometimes even olfactory stimuli help to complete the emergent meaning(s) in addition to and sometimes even in place of human language.
> (Watts 2008: 213)

While frames are prototypical representations of contexts, the concept of prototypicality is also used for other linguistic domains in this study. Examples of this, as well as various examples of frames, scripts, scenarios, mental space, and conceptual blending (a notion also used by Watts 2008 in order to explain conversational interaction) can be retrieved via the index to this book.

Some final observations on theories in the humanities and the social sciences would seem to be appropriate here. As shown in the discussion of interactional sociolinguistics in Section 8.4, sociolinguists like to distinguish between first-wave, second-wave, and third-wave approaches as chronologically ordered sequences of approaches towards language in society. The treatment of variables such as social class, gender, or age as more or less static units were central in the investigation of dialect variation and dialect change within languages (initiated through the brilliant contributions of William Labov). In more recent, "second-wave" approaches, networks as social aggregates are more central in sociolinguistic investigations. The "third wave", initiated in the 1990s by Penelope Eckert and other scholars through their work on communities of practice, focuses on "the engine of social practice, coordinating social and individual change", as Eckert (2019: 752) formulates it.

These various innovative sociolinguistic reflections have resulted in significant new insights. However, waves as metaphors presuppose a temporal sequencing. But as with real waves, they also tend to involve an intermixing as a result of them breaking and mixing on solid shores or rocks. And this is also what can be observed with sociolinguistic waves, which complement each other to a considerable extent, rather than excluding each other. Let us take the spreading of clicks as part of avoidance strategies in southern Bantu languages (as discussed in Chapter 5) as a phenomenon, in order to explain the relevance of each of these "waves". Variables such as gender (women against men) and age (*hlonipha* as a vanishing tradition) still play a role when trying to understand this historical development. Differing social networks between those living in urban versus rural areas are also relevant, if one wishes to understand the skewed distribution of *hlonipha*. They are ideological constructs and as such their boundaries are sometimes fuzzy, since their use depends on variable contexts; consequently, these may also be subject to manipulation and change, including the complete loss of clicks, for example when the language is spoken in an area where languages with clicks are rare.

The "third wave" in sociolinguistics again resulted in new insights about variation and the importance of communities of practice in explaining such variation. As Eckert (2019: 751) points out, "[t]he meaning potential of sociolinguistic variables in turn is based on their form and their social source, constituting a cline 'interiority' from variables that index public social facts about the speaker to more internal, personal affective states". Such empirical observations are indeed important, for example if one wants to understand the differing spread of *hlonipha* terms between individuals compared with terms which received general acceptance as standard in communities speaking Southern Sotho, Xhosa, or Zulu. Children growing up in a homestead acquaint themselves with *hlonipha* terms through the mother (although they themselves are not supposed to use them). As pointed out by Kunene (1958: 153), the Southern Sotho word for 'river', *noka*, used to be a *hlonipha* substitute for *molapo*, but is now used in everyday speech. Given the frequent similarity with family names, such vocabulary comes in useful for larger groups. By acquiring these latter terms, chances of making errors in the avoidance practice can be reduced. Moreover, their generalization across the speech community at large simplifies the communication between those who have to abide by these avoidance registers and those who are not obliged to do so. At the individual level or within smaller local networks, however, partly differing norms for performance may also need to be attended to. This integration of the social indexicality of variation, presumably, is what Eckert (2019: 751) refers to when she mentions "a cline of 'interiority" from variables that index public social facts about the speaker to more internal, personal affective states.

In line with developments in sociolinguistics, scholars in the field of linguistic anthropology or anthropological linguistics sometimes also like to distinguish between first-wave approaches (associated primarily with Brown and Levinson 1987 and related approaches), and newer, second-wave approaches from the second millennium onwards, also known as the "discursive approach", as found in Watts (2003) or Haugh (2007). The "third wave", associated with a focus on performative frameworks, also takes into account gender differences in politeness strategies; see Mills (2003) for a survey of earlier literature, or van der Bom and Grainger (2015) for more recent updates. But as with sociolinguistic waves, anthropological-linguistic waves again complement and supplement each other, rather than being mutually exclusive, according to the present author. There is a strong academic pressure, in particular in North American halls of science, to be innovative, or even better, to come up with "cutting edge" research in peer-reviewed scientific journals. As argued a couple of times in the present monograph, in actual fact this sometimes involves digging up older ideas without necessarily giving credit to those "oldies".

In spite of useful critical comments by the authors referred to above, Brown and Levinson's model remains a brilliant contribution whose empirical coverage is hard to supersede. Inspired by their work and that of others over the past decades, a number of excellent handbooks on face and intercultural pragmatics have appeared, among them Gudykunst and Mody (2002) and Spencer-Oatey (2000).

The present author shares the view expressed by Kádár and Haugh (2013: 104) concerning politeness research that "there are no purely 'first-order' or 'second-order' approaches to politeness". The nature of specific speech acts and their impact on the positive and negative face needs of speakers and hearers can only be understood if we assume there is a universal basis to their inherent character. Apart from this (decontextualized) "first-order" interpretation, one needs to account for the culture-specific selection of discourse strategies, i.e., for "second order", culture-specific (emic) interpretations; this dichotomy between "first order" and "second order" grading and classification also applies to impoliteness strategies.

In a recent handbook on intercultural communication edited by Rings and Rasinger (2020), the state of the art with respect to (im)politeness strategies is summarized, but the same handbook also contains interesting contributions on conversation analysis, the final theoretical model, introduced in Chapter 11.

11 Conversation analysis

While doing fieldwork on the Turkana language in northwestern Kenya between 1978 and 1980 in order to collect data for a doctoral dissertation, the present author also came to know fellow countrymen from the Netherlands. Whenever these expatriates from different parts of the Netherlands met, a frequently discussed issue involved intercultural miscommunication. "Getting to the point" rather than "beating around the bush" as a speech style is highly appreciated among speakers of Dutch, but less so in the different speech communities in Kenya, according to these Dutchmen. The expatriates were often surprised and sometimes irritated during meetings or social encounters by the extensive use of "pre-expansions" in conversations (as these would be called in modern conversation(al) analyses) with their Kenyan counterparts in regional development projects. Before the Kenyans would bring up their main reasons for a visit to a project leader, for example, they would begin with "small talk" in order to show social interest and to seek common ground. At times, the Kenyan colleagues would only "get to the point" (for example, in order to ask for a pay rise because of increased school fees for their children) on a subsequent visit, something which these Dutch speakers at times found annoying.

As this anecdote should help to illustrate, differences in the organization of conversations may also give rise to intercultural misunderstandings. Over the past decades, models of conversational interaction, as first developed for American English in the 1970s by the sociologists Gail Jefferson, Harvey Sacks, and Emanuel Schegloff (the latter being two students of the sociologist Erving Goffman), have turned out to be useful in explaining intercultural differences in conversational styles as well. This chapter first introduces analytical concepts from this model of talk in interaction, with examples from Acholi (based on Rüsch 2020a); in three subsequent sections these are further illustrated with examples from additional African speech communities.

11.1 Conversation analysis as a model

The analysis of dialogic pairs or, more generally, conversational interaction, has come to be known as "conversation analysis", after the pioneering work of the American sociologists mentioned above, as well as other more recent authors. With opening and closing routines one can observe the most basic type of sequences in conversational interactions, so-called *adjacency pairs*. These consist of two parts, whereby the second pair part (SPP or S) involves a reaction uttered by another person than the person uttering the first pair part (FPP or F), for example, when speaker A makes a statement or asks a question, thereby setting relevance constraints, and speaker B reacts or replies.

Greeting strategies, as illustrated in Chapter 7, are typical examples of act sequences manifesting such adjacency pairs. They also show that communities of practice may differ in their preferred organization, for example with respect to the number of turn-takings.

Turn-taking, as illustrated in Table 25, involving a sequence of two utterances following one another, produced by two different speakers, is based on the commonly observed rule that (most often) only one person speaks at a time. Sacks, Schegloff, and Jefferson (1974), in their systematics of turn-taking, establish fourteen rules related to this feature:

Table 25: Turn-taking rules (Sacks, Schegloff, and Jefferson 1974).

1	Speaker-change recurs, or at least occurs
2	Overwhelmingly, one party talks at a time
3	Occurrences of more than one speaker at a time are common, but brief
4	Transitions (from one turn to a next) with no gap and no overlap are common. Together with transitions characterized by slight gap or slight overlap, they make up the vast majority of transitions
5	Turn order is not fixed, but varies.
6	Turn size is not fixed, but varies.
7	Length of conversation is not specified in advance.
8	What parties say is not specified in advance.
9	Relative distribution of turns is not specified in advance.
10	Number of parties can vary.
11	Talk can be continuous or discontinuous.
12	Turn-allocation techniques are obviously used. A current speaker may select a next speaker (as when he addresses a question to another party); or parties may self-select in starting.
13	Various "turn-constructional units" are employed; e.g., turns can projectedly be "one word long", or they can be sentential in length.
14	Repair mechanisms exist for dealing with turn-taking errors and violoations; e.g., if two parties find themselves talking at the same time, one of them will stop prematurely, and thus repair the trouble

When comparing greeting strategies as ritualized speech cross-culturally, one can easily detect differences in the number of turns taken between interacting individuals. Greeting strategies in the eastern parts of the Netherlands (where traditionally Lower Saxon, a language halfway between Standard Dutch and

Standard German, is spoken) may involve just two turns: A says: "*moi!*" (phonetically [mɔy?]), and B replies: "*moi!*". In closely related varieties in northern Germany referred to as "Plattdüütsch", they are slightly more talkative and so a reduplicated form tends to be used, "*moinmoin*" (from a word also found in East Frisian, meaning 'nice, beautiful'). This greeting ritual contrasts rather dramatically with the greeting strategies described for African communities in Section 7.2.

Turn-taking, as the sequential organization of communication involving a succession of speakers, is clearly open to cultural diversification. Not only does the number of turns vary, especially with conventionalized phenomena such as greetings, but the pause length between turns is also subject to variation. Pauses may reflect a target of minimal overlap and minimal gap between turns or, alternatively, may involve longer silences between turns. As illustrated in Section 11.2, asking the right kind of questions in social interactions is something we also learn when socializing in a particular community. Meyer (2018) presents interesting new findings on overlap in multiparty conversations, an important but relatively poorly studied feature which is addressed in Section 11.3. Furthermore, we also have to learn how "(not) to get to the point" depending on where we grow up, as the examples discussed in Section 11.4 should illustrate.

Coordinating the end of one turn with the initiation of the next turn involves the establishment of *turn-constructional units* (TCUs). The transition to the next turn may consist of a one-word unit or a longer sentence as a marker of the *transition relevance place* (TRP). Speakers have different turn-allocation techniques at their disposal, for example other-selection by the current speaker, self-selection by others, or self-selection by the current speaker, as the following examples adapted from Rüsch (2020a: 69–70) illustrate. They may be accomplished by intonation (as with questions), or gaze as a turn-ascribing strategy ("who is to speak next?"), which may be used instead of or in addition to naming an addressee.

(134) Hellen: wà-bèdò   gàŋ p' Otema
            1PL:SU-be.PAST home POSS Otema
            'we were at Otema's place'
                     (0.97)

(135) Betty: ì   Acholi Inn
          LOC Acholi Inn
          'in Acholi Inn Hotel?'
              (0.4)

(136) Hellen: Acholi Inn   kò
               Acholi Inn   NEG
               'not Acholi Inn!'

(137) Hellen: Acholi Inn   wà-bèdò   làwór
               Acholi Inn   1PL:SU-be.PST   yesterday
               'we were in Acholi Inn yesterday'
                       (0.75)

(138) Hellen: nìnò   cà-ni   wà-bèdò   ì   Pà-, (0.49) jengo
               QNT-DEM   1PL:S-DEM   1PL:SU-be.PAST   LOC   Pajengo
               'the other day we were in Pajengo . . .'

(139) Betty: |--------G₁--------|

(140) Hellen: ↗farm!
               farm
               '. . .farm'

   G₁ Snaps her fingers three times while holding her arm up in the direction
   of the assumed place

The numbers at the ends of the turn-constructional units in these examples indicate the number of milliseconds between each unit and the next. Alternatively, overlap may occur between the two units. Overlap is not necessarily a matter of "people just not listening to each other", as pointed out by Jefferson (1984: 11). It may occur at a transition-relevant place, for example when a next speaker is not pre-selected and consequently the next two persons begin to speak simultaneously. The author refers to these as "transitional overlaps"; they may also occur when the next speaker starts a little bit before the current speaker has finished, since the latter has projected the turn end. A further type identified by Jefferson (1984) occurs where hearers take over the turn as soon as "topic recognition" occurs, thereby demonstrating that they have understood the point, hence the label "recognitial onsets". Another type, labeled "progressional points", may occur when hearers assist the speaker in his or her formulation because they have the impression that there is trouble in the progression of the talk (Jefferson 1984).

   To this one may want to add that the emic perspective, and thereby the intercultural perspective, also counts, and that overlaps count as such if actors themselves judge them to be overlaps. A succinct survey of the literature on overlap in different speech communities is given by Meyer (2018: 108–123).

Finally, changes in participation frameworks, referred to as *schisming* (after Egbert 1997), are relevant. The author distinguishes between three types of transformations, from a single conversation between four or more interactants to multiple conversations: 1. the schisming-inducer targets one particular participant and receives his/her recipiency; 2. the schisming-inducer targets one particular participant and receives recipiency from the targeted person as well as from one or more other participants; 3. the schisming-inducer targets several participants and gets recipiency from targeted as well as from non-targeted participants. This phenomenon is discussed in Section 11.4 on multi-party conversations in Wolof (Senegal).

Sequence organization, as another relevant feature of conversational structures, is about the way successive turns link up to form larger coherent series of interrelated communicative action (Schegloff 2007). In the anecdote presented above one already finds an example of cross-cultural differences in preferred strategies for sequence organization, involving adjacency pairs (with two turns as the minimal form), and expansions, or more specifically a so-called pre-expansion (before getting to the point in a conversation); alternatively, speakers may use insert-expansions or post-expansions. *Oh* or *okay* in English may be used as part of a post-expansion in order to claim information receipt (Schegloff 2007: 118). In this way a sequence closing may be introduced, for example, before moving to the next turn-constructional unit. These, and related structural properties, are discussed in more detail in Section 11.4 below.

Rüsch (2020a: 89) makes an interesting observation from an intercultural perspective, based on her extensive fieldwork in East Africa, concerning "the frequent omission of entire closing, and introductory, sequences at the end of telephone calls. Telephone calls often end without a farewell. Instead they are terminated abruptly or after only a minimal post-expansion like 'okay' or *àyà*", the latter interjection being characteristic for Acholi. This is not considered impolite but rather is seen "as an economically-guided behavior: The longer one speaks, the higher the cost for the call. Consequently, the good-bye sequence to close a call is dispensable" (Rüsch 2020a: 89).

Repair procedures address troubles in speaking, hearing, and understanding, and consequently may be initiated by the speaker through initiated repair (self-correction), or by the hearer, i.e., through other-initiated repair.

Dingemanse and Floyd (2014: 462) describe other-initiated repair in three languages which are geographically far apart from each other: Siwu (spoken in Ghana), Lao (in Laos), and Cha'palaa (Ecuador). They conclude that utterances in these three languages are characterized by the same three-turn structures; moreover, in all three languages some material from the first turn is repeated in the third turn, and the formal structure of the interjection is also similar.

(141) Siwu:
1   A   mámà   sɔ   ba
          mama   QT   come
          'Mama says "come"!'
2   B   aa?
          OIR.INTJ
3   A   mámà   sɔ   ba
          mama   QT   come

(142) Lao (whereby the digits indicate tone levels):
1   A   nòòj4   bòò1   mii2   sùak4   vaa3   nòòj4
          PSN   NEG   have   rope   QPLR.INFER   PSN
          'Noi, don't you have any rope. Noi?'
2   B   haa2?
          OIR.INTJ
          'Huh?'
3   A   bòò1   mii2   sùak4   vaa3
          NEG   have   rope   QPLR.INFER
          'Don't you have any rope?'

(143) Cha'palaa:
1   A   chundenashin
          sit-PL-POS-AFF
          '(youPL are) sitting'
2   B   aa?
          OIR.INTJ
          'Huh?'
3   A   ñuilla   kera'   chundenahshin
          2PL   see-SR   sit-PL-POS-AFF
          'YouPL (can be clearly) seen sitting'

The examples above are instances of other-initiated self-repair by the speaker. With other-initiated other-repair it is the hearer or addressee who clarifies an issue. Rüsch (2020a: 139–140) gives an example where these strategies are combined, i.e., where the conversational trouble is solved by both interactants.

(144) Susan   àwóbí   cà-nì   à-pé   gì   number
               boy   DEM-DEM   1SG:S-NEG   with   number
               'that boy whose number I don't have'

(145) Paul   mèné
             INTJ.which
             'which one?'

(146) Susan boda   àcέl-ì
             motorcycle.driver NUM.one-DEM
             'one of the boda drivers'

(147) Paul   okay Ocii kónò yâ
             okay Ocii or   MP
             'okay, that must have been Ocii (lit. how about Ocii?)'

(148) Susan Ocii kʊ̀
             Ocii NEG
             'not Ocii'

(149) Susan mà- mà   ŋwécɔ̀
             REL REL 3SG:SU.race.PRS
             'that, that one who drives'

(150) Susan kì   pìkìpìkì   pà   Monica nì
             COM motorcycle POSS monica DEM
             'with the motorcycle of Monica'

(151) Paul   aha Okema
             RT Okema
             'aha, Okema!'

(152) Susan Okema
             Okema
             'Okema'

In their cross-linguistic pragmatic typology of other-initiated repair (or collaborative repair), Dingemanse, Blythe, and Dirksmeyer (2014: 5) conclude "that different languages make available a wide but remarkably similar range of linguistic resources for this function". These include the use of interjections, question words, "apology-based" formulaic forms (like *sorry* in English), and repetition. The intersubjective forces behind these common strategies involve the management of trouble and responsibility (thereby affecting social relations and enhancing mutual understanding) as well as handling knowledge (Dingemanse, Blythe, and Dirksmeyer 2014: 33).

The initiators of conversation analysis (frequently abbreviated as CA) in the 1970s had to rely on recorded telephone calls and video recordings of domestic life for their analyses. But modern language documentation technology (as already discussed at different points in earlier chapters) allows for an elaboration that goes far beyond these original domains (see also Dimmendaal 2010 for a discussion). Rüsch (2020a: 26–38), in her detailed analysis of talk in interaction among speakers of Acholi (Uganda), presents a valuable discussion of ethical issues in this respect. Audio and video recording of course requires the consent of those recorded, or whose speech is used as (written) annotated data; in the case of children, consent from guardian adults is required. Rüsch (2020a: 37–38) also points out that recordings which included an audience were not made publicly accessible by the author. For the same ethical reasons, the settings for her investigations had to be staged or half-staged.

Recording without the consent of speakers in the present author's view is simply not done (Dimmendaal 2001: 68–69). Those of us claiming that no "natural data" can be assembled through staged settings are wrong; it can be done. As Dingemanse (2011: 11–12) points out in his study of ideophones in Siwu (a language spoken in Ghana), for which he used language documentation technology, "[t]he excitement about the camera usually wears off after some minutes, as people broach other topics in conversation and return to whatever activity is at hand (. . .)". The author himself usually stayed away from the scenes in which speakers were recorded.

Within the model of conversation analysis, transcription conventions were developed in order to mark specific phenomena. Some of these conventions are illustrated in the present chapter. Additional symbols are presented in studies such as Jefferson (2004), Mazeland (2006), and Meyer (2018). Most of these symbols from the notational system developed within conversation analysis are summarized in Appendix IV. Some of these are illustrated below, based on a pioneering study on conversation analysis by Gumperz (1992: 247–252). The first part of one of the texts in his study is included below, and involves a recorded and transcribed conversation between Don (D) and Lee (D).

(153)
1D: this is not a-
1L: ==of *course/ {[ac] it is not a secret//]
2D: =that it *is a secret*//=
2L: (1) =I haven't *said= it's a secret//]
      (2) {[ac] I didn't say it was a secret//}

(3) what I *said was/
(4) .. that it was *not a suitable course/ .. for you to *apply for//
(5) because it is ( )//
(6) .. {[lo] now if you *want to apply for it/}
(7) .. {[hi] of *course/) you can do what you *want//
(8) but/ {[hi] if you are *doing the twilight course at the *moment/}
(9) .. {[lo] it was *not something which- }
(10) .. Mrs N and Mr G *thought/ *originally/
(11) that it was *not something which/}
(12) but this is NOT the case//

The brief section above derives from a much longer text illustrating turn-taking between the two protagonists, Don and Lee. The italics indicate increased loudness in the heated argument between the two, whereas CAPS in the transcribed text indicate extra prominence. The transcribed conversation is also characterized by an overlap of utterances (indicated by =), and pauses of less than 0.5 seconds (indicated by ..). The final fall (//) and slight fall (/) indicate that "more is to come"; the brackets [ ] indicate that vocal and non-vocal non-lexical phenomena are involved, which interrupt the lexical stretch, such as laughter. For further details and analyses the reader is referred to Gumperz (1992: 236–247).

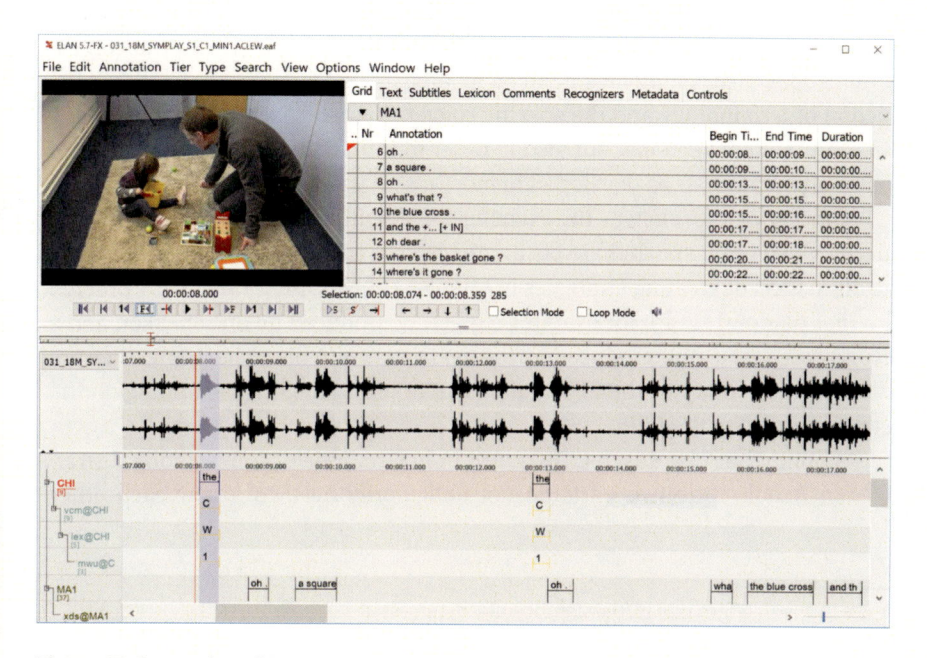

Picture 25: Screenshot of ELAN.

Modern technology and programmes such as ELAN (illustrated in Picture 25), an annotation tool for audio and video recordings, allow us to digitize transcribed texts, and also to annotate these in order to be able to search for specific issues, such as the frequency of overlap in conversations or pauses between turns, as well as accompanying non-verbal communication.[54]

A number of handbooks have appeared on conversation analysis, for example Atkinson and Heritage (1985), Drew and Heritage (2006a, 2006b), Liddicoat (2007), Sidnell (2009, 2010), Sidnell and Stivers (2012), and Clift (2016), showing how progress has been made in various domains of this relatively new but rapidly growing academic field.[55]

Over recent years, the original conversation analysis model has been further elaborated upon, as is shown in Rüsch (2020a) in her exemplary investigation of speech styles in Acholi, which serves as an illustration of the model here. With a range of studies having been published on Acholi, the grammatical structure of this language is reasonably well understood. A detailed account of language use however was still lacking, as is true for most African languages. Based on original fieldwork mainly in Gulu (Uganda), the author managed to diagnose a range of structural features of verbal and non-verbal communication of Acholi speakers, evolving from natural discourse in different contexts. She also made an effort to unravel the emic perspective of speakers on their speech behaviour through interviews with speakers, as well as by means of questionnaires on their conversational styles. Maren Rüsch's important monograph within the context of anthropological linguistics is taken as a basis below, not only for the introduction of terminology and the specific conversational features discussed in the three subsequent sections, but also in order to introduce additional concepts of conversation analysis as developed in more recent years.

A*djacency pairs*, such as the exchange of greetings, consist of two turns produced by two speakers, and are positioned next to each other, i.e., adjacently. As the discussion of greeting strategies in Chapter 7 shows, they are usually ordered as a first pair part (FPP), for example a greeting produced by one speaker, and a second pair part (SPP), produced by the next speaker in his or her reply; they are paired in the sense that the FPP requires an appropriate SPP, depending on the action initiated by the FPP.

As pointed out by Rüsch (2020a: 80) in her analysis of conversational strategies in Acholi, "the two parts do not obligatorily need to follow each other

---

54 See [https://archive.mpi.nl/tla/elan/download] (accessed 14 March 2021).
55 See also the online module with sound illustrations: [https://www.sscnet.ucla.edu/soc/faculty/schegloff/TranscriptionProject] (accessed 14 April 2021).

instantly: Adjacency pairs can be interrupted by inserted sequences and initiated by pre-sequences or followed by post-sequences". Pre-sequences, or pre-expansions, serve as a kind of check on a condition for the successful accomplishment of the first pair part and may have different functions. They may constitute pre-invitations, pre-offers, pre-announcements, pre-rejections, or pre-disagreements, for example, one motivation being "avoidance of problematic responses to a base FPP – most notably rejection (as with invitations, offers, requests, tellings-as-news, etc.), but also non-uptakes (as in troubled hearing or understanding)" (Schegloff 2007: 57).

In studies on speech styles and corresponding politeness strategies in African speech communities in contexts where social distance is low and interactants know each other well, authors frequently refer to the use of proverbs. Such a strategy is used in social interaction in Maninka, according to Bird and Shopen (1979: 94), in order to avoid a direct assertion of power, for example by a father over his son. When the latter wants to borrow the family car, the father may answer: 'Ah my son, the words of the elders are like the droppings of the hyena. Grey when fresh, they become clear with time.' The proverb reflects the traditional wisdom of the ancestors, and consequently "[t]he son no longer has only his father's opinion to contend with, but also the wisdom of many past generations" (Bird and Shopen 1979: 94).

Using such an off-record strategy embedded in an interaction otherwise characterized by positive-face strategies may thus be interpreted as a strategy of evasion and at the same time of persuasion. Strecker (1988: 155, passim) also makes reference to such "embedded intrusions" and, more generally, switches in face-saving strategies in his analysis of conversational interaction in Hamar (Ethiopia).

Obeng (1996: 540) also argues that proverbs in Akan society may perform this pre-sequencing role in the context of advice-giving, in order to prefigure potentially difficult upcoming issues. The actual message associated with the following proverb in Akan is the advice to abstain from alcohol (no interlinear glossing given by the author).

(154)   ɛnni adwen dɛ akyi nhwe Bremuu
        'do not let the tasty nature of mudfish force you to fish in the Birim River'

Proverbs may thus also be used as post-expansions, for example as a preclosing or closing strategy when giving somebody advice, sometimes combined with long stretches of talk as elaborate structures built around them, presumably because they depersonalize the advice.

The following three sections serve as illustrations and elaborations of different conversation strategies.

11.2 Asking the right questions

Duranti (1997a: 265) refers to the intellectual tension between conversation analysts and linguistic anthropologists due to fundamental disagreements in analytical procedures and data collection. The analysis of decontextualized speech in conversation analysis is potentially problematic for scholars interested in linguistic anthropology or interactional sociolinguistics, if situational, cultural, or historical contexts are ignored. The study by Rüsch (2020a) shows that such problems can be overcome, first of all by presenting the reader with exactly this information where needed. For virtually all examples in her monograph, the reader is informed about the spoken text from which the sentences are derived and where and how the text was collected. Apart from providing rich information about cultural features of the Acholi speech community, the reader also learns that the data were collected by using modern language documentation technology. As a result, difficulties in the methods used can be and in fact have already been overcome, as the following discussion should also help to show.

As a result of a concern for the documentation of endangered or nearly obsolete languages, several programmes were initiated from the late 1990s onwards to document these languages in different parts of the world using modern audio-visual means.[56] One of the projects emerging from these efforts was the documentation of ǂĀkhoe Haiǁom, a language in Namibia spoken by a community of around 200 individuals traditionally living as hunter-gatherers, whose endangered language was investigated in a multidisciplinary project by the anthropologist Thomas Widlok and two linguists, Gertie Hoymann and Christian Rapold.

In one publication emerging from the documentation project, Hoymann (2010) focuses on questions in ǂĀkhoe Haiǁom. The author thereby contributed to a project of the Max Planck Institute for Psycholinguistics (in Nijmegen, the Netherlands), the *Multimodal Interaction Group's Question and Response Project*. In this project, questions and their responses across ten languages (ǂĀkhoe Haiǁom, Danish, Dutch, English, Italian, Japanese, Korean, Lao, Tzeltal, and Yélî-Dnye) were collected and coded for a number of features. Initial results on the investigation of universals and cultural variation in turn-taking in conversation emerging from this research endeavour were published in Stivers et al. (2009) and in a special issue of the *Journal of Pragmatics* edited by Stivers, Enfield, and Levinson (2010).

---

[56] For further details, the reader is referred to the following links: http://dobes.mpi.nl/projects/ and [https://www.elararchive.org/] (accessed 15 April 2021).

In the special issue, Stivers and Enfield (2010) explain the coding scheme for question-response sequences in conversations. For all these languages, a minimum of 350 questions and their responses were collected from video recordings of natural conversations, and these were all coded. In order to make the datasets comparable, the question-response sequences used for the project came from seven conversations comprising 94 minutes of video-recorded conversation containing 408 questions. Three of these conversations (comprising 28 minutes of recordings and containing 133 questions) were task-based in that the participants, who knew each other, were given a picture book (*Frog, where are you?* Mayer 1994)) or shown video clips (the MPI "staged events" task clips; van Staden et al. 2001), and were asked to talk about them.

Questions may be divided into polar questions (also known as "yes-or-no" or "propositional" questions) and content (or "question-word") questions; in addition, there are so-called "alternative" questions, i.e., questions that give the addressee a choice of usually two possibilities for an answer. The following three examples from Hoymann (2010) illustrate these three types for ǂĀkhoe Haiǁom.

(155) uri   ra |gôa-e
jump PROG child-SN.A
'does the child jump?'

(156) tae-e   nē   e
what-3SN.A DEM 3SN.A
'what is this?'

In the data that was collected from ǂĀkhoe Haiǁom for the Questions Project there is no evidence to support a mode of communication that is radically unlike those of other cultural groups. Nevertheless, interesting differences in conversational features can be identified, for example that alternative questions are extremely rare in ǂĀkhoe Haiǁom (Hoymann 2010: 2728).

(157) ari-b   of   katsi-s-a   ra   !gû
dog-3SM or cat-3SF-A PROG walk
'does the dog or the cat walk?'

In her investigation of the way questions are posed in natural conversations in ǂĀkhoe Haiǁom, Hoymann (2010) studies the actions the questions are used for and the manner in which they are responded to. While the turn-taking device is confirmed by the data from this speech community, there are also some striking differences in the strategies observed, for example, in comparison with Japanese.

Picture 26: Hai∥om Bush camp in |Gomais (Mangetti-West, Namibia).⁵⁷

One significant property of this type of social interaction as emerging from the comparative project at the Max Planck Institute for Psycholinguistics in Nijmegen is that ǂĀkhoe Haiǁom silences between questions and answers are relatively long compared to those of the other languages. Such silences vary from the fast response time of Japanese speakers (7.29 ms) at one end of the scale, to the slow response time of ǂĀkhoe Haiǁom speakers (423.16 ms) and Danish speakers (468.88 ms) at the other.

Based on the audio-visual recordings, it could also be concluded that ǂĀkhoe Haiǁom speakers select a next speaker relatively less often than speakers of the other languages in the comparative study do. The actions or action types (as they are called in conversation analysis) listed in Table 26 and coded for in this project are:

Table 26: Action types in the conversational analysis of Hoymann (2010).

1.	information requests, which are what are often considered "real" questions, as their primary goal is to obtain information;
2.	repair initiators, which are questions that aim to clarify something that was misheard or misunderstanding, for example: "You're going where?";
3.	requests for confirmation, which are questions that seek confirmation for a previously held assumption, for example "So you're coming tonight?";
4.	assessments, which are information questions seeking agreement, for example: "Isn't it beautiful out today?";
5.	suggestions, offers and requests.

---

[57] Courtesy of the ǂAkhoe Haiǁom Dobes Project; see [https://dobes.mpi.nl/projects/akhoe/] (accessed 13 March 2021).

If ǂĀkhoe Haillom speakers perform certain actions more or less frequently than speakers of the other languages, this will of course affect the distribution of the question types. Thus, ǂĀkhoe Haillom has a markedly different distribution from the other languages in that it has a majority of content questions, whereas the other languages all have a majority of polar questions. For example, whereas ǂĀkhoe Haillom has 58.5% content questions and 41.5% polar questions in the corpus, more than 80% of the questions in Japanese are polar questions. The major action types for polar and content questions in ǂĀkhoe Haillom are information requests and repair initiators. One conclusion to be drawn from the database is that ǂĀkhoe speakers virtually never request confirmation, while in the other languages requests for confirmation make up between 20% and 50% of all questions. Since requests for confirmation are always made using polar questions, not making any requests for confirmation (as a highly coercive strategy), as is usual among ǂĀkhoe Haillom, dramatically reduces the overall number of polar questions.

There are also seven questions in the ǂĀkhoe Haillom database seemingly said to oneself, so-called "out-louds", also known as "broadcast talk". These questions do not seem to be specifically designed to pressure anyone for an answer, i.e., no next speaker is selected, and indeed, these questions often do not receive a response. Only two of the seven cases in this collection are answered and four receive no response at all (Hoymann 2010: 2735). ǂĀkhoe speakers also ask more repair-initiating questions than speakers of most of the other languages, except Korean. Most of the repair initiation is done using content questions.

The frequent reliance on open questions, i.e., content questions ('where', 'what' etc.), provides the answerer with greater "freedom" in choosing a type of answer than a polar question would, as the latter constrains the recipient to 'yes' or 'no' answers. The culture of ǂĀkhoe speakers leads them to pose questions in a way that is less coercive and less restrictive on the answerer than is the case with speakers of other languages. Hoymann (2010) relates these differences from the other speech communities investigated in the question-answer project to the social constellation of ǂĀkhoe Haillom speakers, which may be characterized as a society of intimates.

Presumably related to this latter property of this speech community, the ǂĀkhoe Haillom data show a high number of questions that get no response or uptake, around 23% (Hoymann 2010: 2734). This puts ǂĀkhoe at the highest end of the "no response" scale for the ten languages compared in the project, together with Lao (in Laos). This frequent lack of responses in turn-taking in ǂĀkhoe can be explained, according to Hoymann (2010), by a cultural difference that causes speakers not to select a next speaker, as this would pressure the person for an answer. The author accords this behaviour to speakers' concerns for individual independence. The reluctance to pose direct questions, or questions that strongly pressure recipients to answer by selecting a speaker, leads to a higher proportion of content questions or open questions and almost no requests for confirmation using yes-or-no questions.

Sugawara (1996, 1998a: 238), in his study of the IIGana people in Botswana, argues that their form of speaking is "deeply rooted in the form of life specific to hunting-gathering societies". The author also claims that a defining feature of interaction in this San community is the speakers' seeming indifference or lack of concern with the attention of their conversation partners. This interpretation presumably reflects a cultural perspective geared primarily by the investigator's own cultural background as a speaker of Japanese. An alternative interpretation, in line with the results of investigations in Hoymann (2010) on ǂĀkhoe Haillom (discussed above), would be that this habitus reflects a mutual concern for individual independence or privacy.

In a society where different communities of practice co-exist, which also occasionally interact with each other, such differences in communicative strategies may easily lead to intercultural misunderstandings. In Canada and the United States, where First Nation communities were confronted with new cultures imposed upon them, including alternative fashions of speaking, such confrontations at times took on dramatic forms, lingering on in modern times to some extent. Saville-Troike (1985: 13) observes, with respect to Navajo speakers in the United States, that the "Navajo temporal pattern of silence in turn-taking between questions and answers (. . .) occupies a significantly longer time-space than that generally used by monolingual English speakers".

Foley (1997: 252–253) discusses cultural misunderstandings emerging from different cultural practices between Australian Aboriginals and middle-class white Australians, for example in courtrooms. In keeping with his conventions, an Aboriginal witness "may launch into a long monolog, undirected to any particular participant, including the questioning lawyer, in keeping with his conventions. This runs counter to the intention of the questioning lawyer, who, true to his own conventions for speaking, wants to break up the answer into a set of short paired question and response utterances, determined by his preplanned array of questions" (Foley 1997: 253). In a globalizing world, it is useful at least to be aware of such alternative conventions, as the last example in the next section should also help to illustrate.

11.3 Overlap in conversations

Conversation theory as a model was developed primarily in order to deal with dyadic participation frameworks, with schisming allowing for more complex interactions than just one speaker/hearer pair. However, social encounters and corresponding speech behaviour can be way more complex, as Meyer's (2018) case study on Wolof helps to show. The author presents a detailed analysis of conversational interactions in two Wolof-speaking villages in northwestern Senegal. Meyer (2018: 14) characterizes his micro-ethnographic approach as radically empiricist, and as an attempt "to base its analysis on concrete hard data provided in particular by video recordings and complemented by observations, interviews and document research". A major purpose of his detailed study is the investigation of overlap in conversations, as this is a feature of what to outsiders sometimes appears to constitute a chaotic participation framework.

> Perhaps the most striking feature of Wolof multiparty conversations is that they initially appear "chaotic", as Reisman (1974 (. . .)) had expressed it in regard to Antiguan conversations. The first impression is that permanently several speakers talk at once and constantly interrupt each other without thereby creating a deep problem for the course of the conversation. A second, more thorough, look, however, reveals that this impression is wrong and due to several tacit assumptions derived from our experience as competent actors in our own society. These assumptions suspended, Wolof multiparty conversations reveal, to the contrary, to be well ordered, but not in all their aspects in accordance with the turn-taking principles established by conversation analysis. (Meyer 2018: 4)

The setting investigated by Christian Meyer, in collaboration with his Senegalese colleagues Anna Marie Diagne and Malick Faye, is a public space, namely the 'village square', known as *pénc* in Wolof. The latter is in paradigmatic contrast with *kër* 'compound', which represents the (more) private space of the extended family.

Pénc conversations usually involve about a dozen men seated on mats under the shady trees of this village square. Their conversations are frequently held in smaller groups of two, three, or four active participants at once, and involve a constant reshaping of participation roles. For example, a speaker may turn into a hearer and vice versa, and an over-hearer may turn into an addressee. Figure 16 gives a schematized "representation of one such village square interaction between individuals, whereby the numbers express topics such as 1. working morale of the villagers, 2. rain, 3a. laziness 1, 3b. laziness 2, 4. Njaga's story. The connecting lines visualize the positions of individuals participating in the development of a thread after a topic has been introduced.

Apparently, individuals may participate in several threads and probably listen to more than one speaker at once (Meyer 2018: 178). Participants involved in discussions shift between threads more than the thread itself changes its topic. As this schematic representation helps to visualize, threads constantly split up or re-converge, thereby also affecting the number of individuals involved in discussing a specific topic.

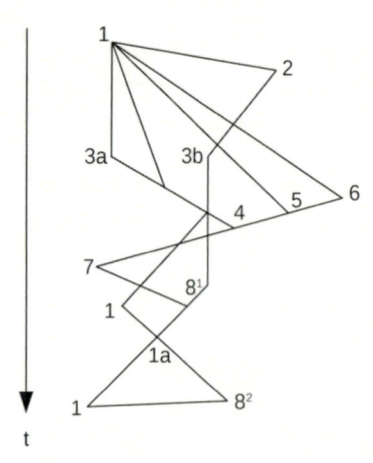

Figure 16: Pénc conversation threads in a Wolof village (reproduced with kind permission from Christian Meyer).

Characteristically, the individual focuses of the participants sitting together on the village square are constantly shifting, although there is still speaker selection and turn allocation. In line with this behaviour, there is also schisming and converging and joining in conversations. Picture 27 shows such a Wolof conversation taking place in a village square.

Picture 27: Wolof village square meeting (reproduced with kind permission from the Habilitation of Christian Meyer).

In his analysis of such village square meetings, Meyer (2018: 192) differentiates "between a process of conversational fission that is well prepared and unambiguously introduced by bodily signs (posture, gaze) and vocal signals (that Egbert [1997] calls schisming), and another one that occurs in an unanticipated manner through a first start overlap at a transition relevance place which is not managed by withdrawal by either of the parties talking in overlap, but by the subsequent establishment of two 'subgroups'." Here, Meyer (2018: 192) refers to an early fieldwork report by Sigman (1981) on fission involving conversations between more than two persons where two or more participants may self-select to speak simultaneously. This situation is either repaired by one or more speakers becoming silent, or two or more simultaneous conversations being started. This initial simultaneous talk may be an invitation to fission and may also involve a search by the simultaneous speakers for an available subgroup of listeners.

The interactional "footing" is organized differently in Wolof; in particular, the boundaries of dyads, triads, or interaction systems in general are often undefined, so that systemic effects are generated which lead to more frequent and unproblematic overlaps than presumed by canonical conversation analysis (Meyer 2018: 262) Hence, the canonical turn-taking system is more adequate for joint and collaborative focused interactions than the semi-focused interactions with multi-party conversations running simultaneously, as shown by Christian Meyer in his monograph. Elsewhere in the world, such simultaneous conversations or overlaps may also be observed, of course, at parties or similar social gatherings, as well as during the exchange of greetings.

Gaze in this type of conversational interaction does not necessarily signal addressivity in terms of turn-taking, or at least it does so less than in languages like English (Meyer 2018: 195, passim). Only when the joint focus is left vague in some of its aspects may overlap occur in an unproblematic way, as suggested by such Wolof polyadic conversations. Also, in communicative behaviour in which gaze plays a lesser role in the signaling of recipiency and attention, the longer and grammatically more elaborate status of assessments and repetitions might be exploited as signaling recipiency or turn claiming. In such situations, it is not always easy to establish a conversational dyad and to be listened to; there appears, at least occasionally, to exist a preference for not easily passing on the turn once gained (Meyer 2018: 188). In his study on gestures in Wolof, Meyer (2014: 1169) further observes that "[c]onversational functions that are fulfilled in Western conversations by gaze (selection of addressee, signaling of listenership) are adopted by touch and contact gestures among the Wolof. Moreover, gestures are often combined with touch or even performed in tactile ways so that the body of the interlocutor is used as a resource".

The issue of repetition and its intersubjective meaning in conversation is discussed in detail by Rüsch (2018: 157–173). Repetition by the same person, in order to reinforce or intensify something a person has just said, can be observed in the documentary *Lorang's Way*, when the main protagonist makes reference to somebody from the neighbouring ethnic group, the Dodoth, in northeastern Uganda (who speak Karimojong), called Lowual (probably Lobwal; GJD), who is very rich.

Lorang first refers to him as *Lobwal ɲɛkabaran(ɪ)* 'Lobwal the rich man', and then repeats his name several times, also praising the latter as being "number one" when it comes to material wealth (Picture 28).

Picture 28: Lorang emphasizing the name of a rich Dodoth (Karimojong) person.

Self-repetition (or autophonic repetition) constrasts with diaphonic repetition (allorepetition or other-repetition). In Acholi, "diaphonic repetition can be used to simply confirm another speaker's assumption, or to answer a question (. . .), it can be part of 'participatory listenership' (. . .), or it can show agreement and empathy (. . .)".

In addition to that, repetition is used as a device of "repair resolution" (Rüsch 2020a: 159–160). The latter feature is illustrated by the following examples from Acholi (Rüsch 2020a: 163–164).

(158) Hellen: ɛ́h   én   àyé   wòn
                RT   3SG:S   CFM   father
       'yes, he is indeed the father'

(159) Susan: ɛ́ntɔ́   lùtínɔ̀   pà   nyèk   mègò   nɔŋɔ
                but   NMZ.PL:child   POSS   co-wife   motherhood   3SG:S:find.PRS
       'but they are children of stepmothers it seems?'

(160) Hellen: lùtínɔ̀   pà   nyèk   mègò
                NMZ.PL:child   POSS   co-wife   motherhood
       'they are children of stepmothers'

The structural counterpart of overlap, namely lapses, has also been discussed within conversational analysis as a model. Hoey (2017) discusses cross-linguistic strategies for managing such so-called lapses during conversational interactions, for example sequence re-completion, a strategy whereby participants bring to completion a sequence of talk that was already treated as complete. For further details see Hoey (2017) as well as Rüsch (2020a), who discusses lapses and pauses in Acholi conversation.

Apart from the pioneering studies by Rüsch (2020a, 2020b), sources on conversational strategies in African languages are relatively scarce, although a number of scholars from Japan have worked on this topic. Unfortunately for the scientific community at large, several of their publications are in Japanese, such as Sugawara (1998b). In a study published in English, Kimura (2001) discusses speech styles in the Baka speech community in the border area of Cameroon, the Democratic Republic of the Congo, and the Central African Republic, whose members have a hunter-gatherer lifestyle, these days combined with agriculture and fishing. The author argues that in Baka conversations both utterance overlap and long silences are more frequent than in Bakwele, a (non-related) language spoken by neighbouring farmers. According to him the observed overlaps in Baka conversations are also cooperative rather than confrontational (aiming at strategic interruption). Kimura (2003: 33) claims that this synchronization, or parallel distributed interaction, is also observable in the polyphonic singing and dancing of Baka people.

In a similar approach, again using conversation analysis, Sugawara (2009, 2012) reports on turn-taking strategies among |Gui speakers in Botswana, whose sequential dynamics are also characterized by prolonged stretches of talk when multi-party interactions occur. According to Kazuyoshi Sugawara, opposing motives underlie conversational overlaps in this community, both antagonistic and cooperative (showing mutual entrainment of speaking activities).

11.4 Pre-expansions and pre-closing strategies

The "etic grid" developed by Hymes (1968) for the description of "fashions of speaking" is still useful and enlightening more than fifty years down the road, as shown by Kießling, Neumann, and Schröter (2011) in their analysis of specific speech events in Isu, a language spoken in Cameroon. The setting the authors report upon is a public hearing on the occasion of the inauguration ceremony of the chief of the Isu. A chief is usually referred to as *Fon* in the Grassfields area of Cameroon, where this language is spoken. During the inauguration ceremony, there is also space for the public to offer feedback on local problems. The message form analyzed by the authors is a piece of discourse accompanying the inauguration of the new chief. Participants include an individual whose role it is to protect the chief from inappropriate questions from the audience.

Triadic communication as a channel between speech participants also plays a role in this community, as it does in other parts of the Cameroonian Grassfields, according to Kießling, Neumann, and Schröter (2011: 95–96, footnote 7).[58] They point out that complaints in the Grassfields cultures are for the most part addressed, not directly to the causer of the complaint but to a third-party mediator, for example to a village representative, referred to as "quarterhead" in their study. This strategy also constitutes a means of showing reverence to status-superiors, thereby cementing or at least supporting social relationships rather than threatening them. The complaints do not seem to be regarded as impositions, but rather as honourable responsibilities which upgrade the social importance and authority of the addressee, as argued by Kießling, Neumann, and Schröter (2011: 96).

One interesting feature of speech act sequences with this type of discourse in Isu is the use of complaints to prepare to request advice in the community, "to the extent that a complaint without requestive intention is barely to be found" (Kießling, Neumann, and Schröter 2011: 106). "[A] complaint could rather be classified as a directive in the Grassfields' cultures, i.e., a speech act that is to cause the hearer to take a particular action", as argued by Kießling, Neumann, and Schröter (2011: 89).

Before embarking upon a discussion of act sequences as part of such speech events in Isu, Kießling, Neumann, and Schröter (2011) first apply the more traditional ethnography of communication as a descriptive and analytical tool, as Isu has a rather rich vocabulary or set of constructions at hand in the domain of complaints, requests, and apologies, "which form a functional complex in that these acts are actually pragmatically interrelated, which is also reflected in the local terminology" (Kießling, Neumann, and Schröter 2011: 84). These facts are of course relevant for an investigation of the emic perspective of community members. Thus, in Isu, the concept of apology is derived from a requestive type of concept (Kießling, Neumann, and Schröter 2011: 85).

(161) bwɔ́ʔ kə́wɔ́   'beg for something on which the requester can lay no rightful claim'
       bwɔ́ʔ kə́wɔ́ nə̀ 'beg addressee to forget'

In Mɛn, a related language spoken in the same area and also discussed to some extent in the same article, the verb *fóʌʔtə̀* in fact covers three semantic domains

---

[58] Blench (2010) is another source discussing lexical registers in different Grassfields chiefdoms and reflecting social hierarchies between the Fon (king and nobility), village heads and leaders, and commoners.

and may be translated as 1. 'confess (as a speech act verb belonging to the domain of representative verbs)'; 2. 'complain (as a speech act verb belonging to the domain of expressive verbs)'; and 3. 'apologize (as a speech act belonging to the domain of performative verbs)'. Since Isu is treated in considerably more detail by Kießling, Neumann, and Schröter (2011), Isu rather than Mɛn is focused upon here. Isu has several verbal constructions in the complaint domain (Kießling, Neumann and Schröter 2011: 87–88), including the following, also reflecting social hierarchies (of superiors and inferiors) and showing the mediation of complaints (i.e., the non-identity of addressee and causer of the complaint):

(162)   dzài   'say, complain directly to the causer of the
        say   complaint'
        dìy-dzài   'cry for change, complain to a superior (not
        cry-say   identical with the causer of the complaint)'
        dìy utswɔ̂d   'lament misfortune or calamity'
        cry sorrow/trouble/torment
        kwà   'shout, express dissatisfaction to an inferior,
                                          admonish'

In the second part of Kießling, Neumann, and Schröter (2011), the analysis of performance plays a central role. The speech event analyzed by the authors, *dìy-dzài*, a complaint (legal case) issued by a local community during an inauguration ceremony for a new chief in a local village, where the community members are also allowed to ask for feedback on local problems, is framed by an elder through a question. The issue revolves around pastoral Fulani in the area, trespassing on Isu farmlands and thereby destroying crops. Table 27 is an attempt to summarize the main characteristics of the three stages described as part of the scenario by Kießling, Neumann, and Schröter (2011: 98–106) for this event. They also refer to the partly fragmentary style of speaking, characterized in Isu as *zém*, 'open up a little crack or wound something in order to have access to the inner part' (p. 102). The authors provide a full transcript of the elder's complaint and reactions by the mediator and chief (pp. 110–124) as well as annotations (pp. 126–136). The politeness strategies used by the protagonists may be characterized as bald-on statements, negative-face strategies, and off-record strategies in terms of Brown and Levinson (1987) (although these labels are not used by the authors).[59]

---

[59] The close link between 'complaining' and 'seeking judicial redress' may be more widespread, as suggested, for example, by the Dutch word for 'complain', *klagen*, which is used in the closely related language German for 'complain' as well as 'going to court'.

Table 27: Frame-and-scenario model of a complaint (Kießling, Neumann, and Schröter 2011).

Stages of the *dìy-dzài*	Microstructure
Stage I: *báb* 'ask' (elder)	
Stage II: *bə̀lì* 'answer' (chief)	Premature evasive reaction of the chief
Stage III: reiteration of the *dìy-dzài* (elder)	Upgrading and concretizing the complaint, resulting in advice, *tswò*, and offering help to the chief in public
Stage IV: *kìm* 'hush up' ("quarterhead")	Reply (*tswò*) in four steps: "First, he points to the speaker's violation of the clarity principle since the elder has cloaked his contribution in obscure imagery. Second, he points out the inappropriateness of the elder's contribution due to secrecy of its contents, since the sharing of knowledge about spiritual powers is confined to certain circles of initiates. Thirdly, he points out the inappropriateness due to breaching of communicative norms, as the elder's speech act of *tswò* should not have been performed in public. And fourthly he gives emphasis to his illocution by recurring to steps two and three, the secret content of the elder's proposal and the breach of communicative norms" (Kießling, Neumann, and Schröter 2011: 98–99).

With respect to each of the four steps or stages, the authors add different metalinguistic observations (pp. 99–105). With regard to stage I, it is noted that the elder starts by stating his intention explicitly and according to the norms. Next, he develops an argument clad in a series of rhetorical questions, allusions, and metaphors, as well as suggestions which become more concrete step by step.

At stage II, the new and still inexperienced chief answers in, what is called, a *tà-bə̀li* 'jump-answer' (premature) manner in Isu, because he apparently misunderstood the speaker's real intention (due to his inexperience).

At stage III, the complainant elaborates upon his initial complaint, also trying to invoke the chief's responsibility by suggesting to the latter that specific punishments for the aggressors (by using spiritual powers) need to be made, although he is not in a position to do so; moreover, such issues are not supposed to be dealt with in public, hence the "quarterhead" (a translation presumably of "maire de quartier") as mediator in the case intervenes, hushing the plaintiff up (at Stage IV). The purpose of this reaction is to make the complainant stop before his intentions become clear to the commoners in the audience, and also "to raise the chief's awareness that there is something more to understand here" (Kießling, Neumann, and Schröter 2011: 104). This act is followed by a request from the chief to the audience to show approval of the "quarterhead" by clapping.

Proper understanding of "veiled illocutions" (p. 106), as they are called by the authors, involves quite a bit more than understanding what is said, namely cultural knowledge, for example on what is proper verbal behaviour in public. Here again, reference may be made to the discussion in Section 8.4, in particular to Tyler's (1978) monograph *The Said and the Unsaid*.

Kießling, Neumann, and Schröter (2011) do not use conversation analysis for their analysis of Isu, but rather a model of speech act analysis proposed by Trosborg (1995) and Blum-Kulka and Olshtain (1984: 86–87). In line with these authors on language in social interaction, Kießling, Neumann, and Schröter use a very useful concept, that of "head (speech) act". In addition, notions like superordinate illocution and preparatory and supportive sub-acts are used, concepts that would seem to correspond to conversation analysis terms like pre-expansions and insert-expansions.

Kießling, Neumann, and Schröter (2011) also succeed in pinning down the point of transition from complaint to request (or advice) in the court case annotated and analyzed by them. Interestingly, they characterize the transition at stage III from dìy-dzài 'complain' into tswò 'advise' by the elder as a blending over point (p. 128). Blending as a concept, of course, has also been used as an important cognitive notion at different stages in the present monograph. But it has also been used with respect to conversation analysis, probably first by Watts (2008). In terms of the blending model proposed by Fauconnier and Turner (2002: 40), understanding what the speaker means involves "unpacking" the blend in order "to reconstruct the inputs, the cross-space mapping, the generic space, and the network of connections between all these spaces". When applying these analytical tools to the speech event described by Kießling, Neumann, and Schröter (2011), the following picture emerges.

The first step in the structure emerging from the conversational interaction between the complainant and the mediator involves "composition" (in terms of the model developed by Fauconnier and Turner 2002): The elements from input 1 (the complaint) and input 2 (the advice) make new relationships available that did not exist in either input. The next step in the interpretation involves "completion", in which knowledge from background frames is used by the mediator to create a larger meaning structure in the blend. As a result, he interprets the blend as a non-permissible illocution in the given context. Several background frames were apparently activated in the mind of the mediator (i.e., the village representative) after having heard the complaint and the advice (See Table 27). They all relate to the breaching of social norms of the Isu speech community (using obscure imagery, sharing knowledge about spiritual powers, giving advice in public). The third and final step in the speech events discussed here involves "elaboration" (Watts 2008: 296). Here, a larger meaning can be further developed in the subsequent construction of the verbal interaction. This is equivalent to what we, following Fauconnier (1997), shall call "running the blend" (Watts 2008: 296). In the speech event discussed here, it is the chief or *Fon* who takes on this role by asking for applause for the mediating "quarterhead" (Kießling, Neumann, and Schröter 2011: 105).

These examples show how specific illocutionary and perlocutionary acts are intimately linked in a manner that is probably characteristic of the area where the language is spoken (the Grassfields area in Cameroon), but not necessarily elsewhere. They show that speakers need to acquire specific frames and corresponding scenarios in order to understand such speech events. Moreover, those immediately involved need to be familiar with the appropriate politeness strategies for such events. Children socializing through the Isu language (in this case) have to learn about the various conversational implicatures while acquiring the language, either through instruction from peers or by deduction (through observation).

Duranti (1984, 1990) presents what appear to be similar interpretational challenges for outsiders in his analyses of traditional village council meetings in Samoa, known as *fono*. The function of the *fono* court and legislative body is conflict management as a cooperative endeavour, and re-establishing lost harmony. On the basis of his analyses of such meetings, Duranti (1984: 2) argues that "[r]ather than taking words as representations of privately owned meanings, Samoans practice interpretation as a way of publicly controlling social relationships rather than as a way of figuring out what a given person 'meant to say'". The speaker's original intentions and understanding of certain events at the time of the speech act seem at times irrelevant for those who interpret the words and assess his responsibility. Duranti (1988) hence argues that what an utterance means in a Samoan political debate is not what the speaker intends it to mean, but fundamentally what the powerful participants in the debate ultimately determine it to mean.

Like with the complaint cases in Isu, presumably, it is the conventionalized social processes of negotiation and interpretation that fix the ultimate meaning of such discursive acts. It is possible that the ultimate (emic) interpretation emerging from such a *fono* becomes less enigmatic to outsiders trying to understand what is going on, if one integrates the theory of conceptual blending into such conversational analyses (as with Isu above). But of course this can only be done properly by those who know about the conversational implicatures of the "said" as well as the "unsaid" in Samoan discourse.

Meaning is apparently not just something one communicates to others, but rather something one *creates* with others. That this creation is heavily conventionalized in linguistic and cultural practices is the fundamental insight of the Russian scholar Bakhtin, whose contributions on the philosophy of language and text analyses have also been translated into English (e.g., Bakhtin 1986). Nevertheless, a major challenge for future investigations on conversational strategies from a cross-cultural point of view is to understand how speakers of specific communities of practice or speech communities acquire such composition and completion processes.

As pointed out by Bhabha (2004), "hybrid (third) spaces" developed during colonial times through the creation of new varieties of former colonial languages such as the new Englishes, or new varieties of French or Portuguese in Brazil during colonial times. Examples of this can also be found in the present contribution, for example with greeting strategies in Chapter 8. One author contrasting such (new) speech styles in English as spoken in North America (presumably referring to the United States as well as Canada) and Portuguese as spoken in Brazil is Novinger (2003), in her study *Communicating with Brazilians: When "Yes" Means "No"*. The author argues that in Brazil one has to learn when "yes" means "no", a feature related to be being indirect. "North Americans like 'yes' and 'no' answers, and their thinking patterns tend to categorize concepts and events as either black or white. Brazilians tend to perceive matters along a spectrum of grays" (Novinger 2003: 197). The latter is usually communicated indirectly, for example, by "postponing an answer, saying that something might be difficult, or alluding to an imprecise future commitment, which by convention are used to indirectly communicate a 'no' answer" (Novinger 2003: 198).

Of course, there are more than 200 languages spoken in Brazil, and there are clearly distinct language ideologies among speakers of indigenous languages (as shown, for example, by Aikhenvald 2002), but also among descendants of people with African and European roots in different regions of the country. Allport (1954: 191) argues that "a stereotype is an exaggerated belief associated with a category. It justifies (rationalizes) our conduct in relation to that category. Categorisation is a cognitive process that involves the segmentation of the social world into social categories or groups. This is a cognitive process because typing entails filling in details about others according to 'pictures in our heads'". Nevertheless, the observations made by Novinger are interesting in that they reveal the emic perspective and interpretation of somebody with a North American background trying to use Brazilian Portuguese in a culturally appropriate way.

Novinger (2003: 163) further points out that interrupting is interpreted as a sign of interest and enthusiasm among speakers of Brazilian Portuguese (comparable to Tannen's 1985 description of involvement in social interaction among New Yorkers with a Jewish background). As further argued by Novinger (2003: 198–199), "Brazilians are more emotionally open and direct with their peers than are North Americans, and they do not feel they have really communicated with someone if they do not know what that person's feelings and personal opinions are (. . .) and Brazilians complain that North Americans are not direct in revealing what they 'really think', that is, their emotions, the mutual perception of indirectness is a two-way communication problem between Brazilians and North Americans".

Even if we are talking about stereotypes, it is still interesting to investigate to what extent there has been influence, particularly from West-African speech communities, on the habitus of Brazilian speakers when using the national language, Portuguese, not only in its grammar but also with respect to speech styles as part of a more general transfer of frames and scenarios by enslaved people mainly from West Africa to the Americas. In Brazil these issues are indeed a matter of vivid academic disputes these days (Alexander Cobbinah, personal communication).

The transfer of speech styles from one language onto another, as part of language shift, either by keeping the first language (i.e., through additive bilingualism), or by abandoning the original first language (i.e., through subtractive bilingualism), has been studied to some extent with respect to "new Englishes", for example by Polzenhagen (2007). Here, comparisons with communicative styles in the primary language of speakers help to understand where these originated from. Rüsch (2021: 198) gives a beautiful example from northern Uganda, where Acholi is the dominant regional language. In the latter language, so called (elliptic) repair initiation with a question word is a common strategy. The same strategy is used in the regional variety of English, as illustrated by the sign "Don't walk on the what? The grass" in Picture 29, taken at a café in the city of Gulu.

Similar processes of transfer of communicative styles must also have occurred in African languages as part of shifts in language solidarity outside European colonialism. Dimmendaal (2022c) discusses the emergence of such new languages and the creation of new speech styles in speech communities in central and eastern Africa.

Picture 29: Sign in a café in Gulu (reproduced here with kind permission from Maren Rüsch).

In the closing section of Chapter 5, reference was made to ethnocentric perspectives on the investigation of lexical-semantic fields in anthropological linguistics. Along similar lines, Ameka and Terkourafi (2019) have criticized current approaches to speech acts, conversational implicatures, (im)politeness, and conversation analysis, claiming that these theories and models are "based on observations of communicative practices in the West and tacitly treated as culturally neutral, while patterns of language use in non-Western communities have been used as testing grounds for Western usage rules and their assumed motivations". Much of their criticism, which in and by itself is well-founded, has been taken into account in the discussion of these four approaches towards pragmatic theory and practices above. But the reader is also encouraged to read their contribution in order to get a succinct summary of the ethnocentric pitfalls Ameka and Terkourafi (2019) identify.

12 Non-verbal communication

One strategy contributing to the expression of personal intentions, along with visual contact, is body language. The scientific investigation of body behavioural communication has come to be known as *kinesis* (or kinesics), after the Greek word for 'movement' κίνησις. Facial gestures, as instances of visible action, clearly perform such an interactive or interpersonal function. They may show the hearer which way an utterance is to be interpreted, by smiling while telling a funny story, or by putting on a solemn face in order to enhance the effect when telling a joke. Co-speech gestures perform a communicative function for the speaker as well as the hearer, with the information conveyed either supporting speech or providing additional information. Birdwhistell (1952) is among the pioneering studies on the way in which body motion is organized. But as the selective survey below should help to illustrate, a range of additional studies over the past decades have helped to enhance our understanding of this phenomenon, including from an intercultural perspective.

The fact that this dimension of human communication is introduced at a relative late point in the present monograph should not be interpreted as an indication of its peripheral role. On the contrary, body language, from facial expressions and arms and hands (also in combination) to body posture, plays a central role in most if not all speech communities. But it is probably better understood from an intercultural point of view once differences in verbal strategies have been discussed first. Kasanga (2011: 58) presents an example of intercultural miscommunication between a businessman from Uganda speaking Luganda and his British associate. While the British man expected a plain and direct explanation for a late report and suggestions for solutions, the former relied heavily on kinesis (nodding, grimacing, gesticulating) in line with his own cultural norms in order to explain the reasons for the delay. The result, apparently, was friction.

Non-verbal communication of course comes in different forms, not all of them necessarily involving body language. But for reasons of space these "surrogate languages" are only briefly discussed here before focusing on body language. Among them are the "abridging" signal systems involving whistling, which are attested in different parts of the world, such as the Canary Islands and Turkey, among the Akha and Hmong in southern Asia, and among the Kickapoo in Mexico.

Within an African context, whistled speech is probably best known from Kalenjin communities in Kenya, as first documented by the late Archibald Tucker (1904–1980) during his many research trips to eastern Africa, although his recordings and account of whistled speech among the Kalenjin were never published (Archibald Tucker, personal communication 1978). We can only be grateful for the documentation of this vanishing tradition in one variety of this dialect continuum in Kenya, Cherang'any, by Mietzner (2016: 248–249). "Whistling is a part of the secret language, learned and performed during the time of seclusion [during the initiation of boys and girls]", as noted by Mietzner (2016: 248), who also points out that she could not get any further information, due to its secret aspects. Whistling as a channel of communication is performed by Cherang'any people in various social settings, for example as an off-record strategy to show astonishment, unexpected pleasure, and contentment, in line with the preferred habitus of not "showing fear, joy, anger, love and other primary emotions" (Mietzner 2016: 248). In concrete terms, this communication channel involves the use of pitch (reflecting the tonal distinctions in the language) and duration (reflecting distinctive vowel length), as well as the spoken melody line (thereby also providing information on speakers' overt knowledge of the prosodic structure of their language), as illustrated in Figure 17.

Figure 17: Tonal melody of a whistled Cherang'any utterance (Mietzner 2016).

(163) á-mác-é   à-mwá   ʌ́-lé   káráárán   kíy-ìì
      1SG-want-IPVF   1SG-say   that   good   thing-DEM
      'I want to say that this thing is good'

In Oyda, a language spoken in Ethiopia, individuals have an additional personal name which is only whistled or sung, to hail or identify them for other purposes (Amha, Slotta, and Sarvasy 2021). These latter Oyda names are generally non-compositional and unique to individuals, i.e., produced without taking recourse to the actual language, for example, *léeteléetetóom* for someone whose proper name is *S'as'ima*. Interestingly, no *moyzé* 'name tune' may be shared by two or more living persons from the community, although a person may take on the name tune of a deceased person in addition to their own. A similar phenomenon is found in Yopno, a language spoken in Papua New Guinea, as described in the same article. As argued by the authors, mountainous environments may have played a role in the parallel development of these systems of name tunes, as these carry over a long distance, for example when trying to attract somebody's attention.

Tone plays a role in another phenomenon, that of tone riddles, which have been reported in different parts of Africa. Simmons (1955) describes such riddles for Efik (southeastern Nigeria), whereby the answer must contain the same number of syllables and the same sequence of tones as the question, as in the following reminder to mind one's own business:

(164) Q: àfák ɔ́kɔ̀k kéták utɔŋ
putting chewstick under ear
A: èsín ényìn kéŋkpɔ́ ówò
putting eyes in.thing of.person

Another more extensively investigated "surrogate language", also based on the imitation of prosodic structures of languages, or more specifically their tonal registers, is of course drum language. Akinbo (2019) presents a detailed modern, instrumental-phonetic investigation (using articulatory and acoustic data) of this phenomenon in Yoruba (Nigeria). There are various older sources, but Nketia (1971) on drum language in Africa is still an informative source in this respect.[60]

Texts printed on textiles known as *kanga* (a piece of cloth worn by women) and *leso* (a kind of scarf usually worn around the head) in Swahili constitute another indirect means of communication by women in eastern Africa, primarily in the form of proverbs (*mithali* in Swahili). As off-record strategies, these usually involve hints at proper social behaviour. Beck (2001) gives an analysis of a range of such Swahili proverbs (and idiomatic expressions), their stylistic properties, and social contexts where they play a role (interlinear glossing added by the present author).

(165) a-taka yote hu-kosa yote
3SG-want everything HAB-miss everything
'(s)he who wants everything misses out on everything' (Beck 2001: 99)

Off-record impoliteness (where the offence is conveyed indirectly by way of an implicature) thus also manifests itself on these kangas. Swahili culture is known for its appreciation of metaphor in general and of *mafumbo* 'enigmas'. These are found in some genres of poetry, but they also occur in various forms as means of indirect verbal communication (e.g., Yahya-Othman 1994). Together with sharp *vijembe* 'innuendos', they are particularly used by women, whether in the oral form

---

[60] Mobile phones are sometimes called the "new talking drums" of Africa, for example by de Bruijn, Nyamnjoh, and Brinkman (2009). The popularity of *emoticons* in electronic messages again show that language use is fundamentally multimodal and that intersubjectivity or mutual understanding and coordination around a common activity is a crucial component of social interaction.

as conversational strategies, or in the written form, printed on these pieces of cloth known as *kanga* and *leso*.

Similar colourfully printed cotton material without texts, called *kitenge* in the Swahili-speaking areas of East Africa, and *capulana* further south in Mocambique, are also, as clothing styles, indexical of a certain style; see Arnfred and Meneses (2018) for a discussion of their semantics.

With respect to non-verbal communication, there is still a lot to be discovered and documented, for example in terms of dress codes, which may convey information about age or status. Asangba Reginald Taluah (2018) discusses the way in which the traditional hat is worn by men in the Dagbani (Dagomba) speech community of northern Ghana, particularly at ceremonies. For example, a hat worn standing upright or directed to the sky is referred to as *dunia zerigu* 'one who carries the world', a posture reserved for rulers. When the hat is tilted towards the front, it is referred to as *kpe mani*, which literally translates as 'there is no one'. When the hat is tilted left, it is referred to as *mam beam* 'womb shell (lit. I do not hear anything)' by men who are spiritually strong. When the hat is tilted towards the right, it is referred to as *nlala* or *njavere* 'I do not want trouble'. A hat tilted backward is referred to as *mmali nyandolba*, which literally translates as 'I have followers'; most elderly persons will normally have their hats tipped backwards.[61]

Non-verbal communication involves other signs as well, such as tattoos or embroidery, as shown in the introduction to a volume edited by Agwuele (2015: 1–13), who also provides a succinct survey of literature on non-verbal communication with a special focus on Africa.

12.1 Facial expressions

Facial gestures in conversation serve referential as well as interactive functions. Use of the head to point may be universal (McCave 2007), but may be supplemented with facial expressions such as lip-pointing, i.e., pointing at somebody by protruding the lips in the direction of that person, rather than using the index finger or hand shapes as a referential strategy; this has been reported for all continents of the world (Enfield 2001; Wilkins 2003; Kita 2009). It is also commonly used across Africa as an alternative to using one's hands, which might be too obvious and thus disrespectful.

---

[61] Special thanks are to be expressed here to Asangba Reginald Taluah for his detailed information on dress codes in the Dagbani speech community.

Backchanneling in conversations may take on different forms, as illustrated in the preceding chapter. A related, non-verbal semiotic sign involves raising the eyebrows in order to acknowledge understanding of a statement. Confirming agreement or understanding for statements made by a speaker may also be rendered by nodding, with a sideways or up and down head motion.[62]

In the Volta Basin area of West Africa a backchannel signal is used as a response to "yes-or-no questions", when a hearer does not feel strongly about something. From an articulatory phonetic point of view, this sound is described as a "palatal nasal click" by Pillion et al. (2019). It is made with a post-alveolar release in the oral cavity, typically with a closed mouth (without any lip movement or movement of the facial muscles), and may be repeated several times to emphasize a speaker's disagreement. This click is often accompanied by a gentle shake of the head, thereby expressing a multi-modal form of negation.

Widlok (2016: 143) mentions facial expressions accompanying confirmation or denial in ǂAkhoe Haiǁom, a community in Namibia where speakers are reluctant to use yes-or-no questions in general (as discussed in Section 11.2). The affirmative *ĩhĩ* goes with a rising voice and with the eyebrows raised, although "half-way" values (flat prosody, one eyebrow slightly raised) are also possible. The negative *ĩ - ĩ* usually goes with a falling prosody, at least in its stand-alone version, and with narrowing of the eyebrows.

The important interactive function of facial expressions also becomes clear from the following examples, found across Africa and carried over into other parts of the world during colonial times by slaves originating from this continent, and known as "kiss-teeth" or "suck-teeth". This phenomenon is described as a "bilabial fricated click" by Lionnet (2020). Hollington (2017: 82) points out that this phenomenon, first discussed by Rickford and Rickford (1976), is performed by "drawing air through the teeth and into the mouth to produce a loud sucking sound. In the basic suck-teeth gesture, the back of the tongue is raised toward the soft palate and a vacuum is created behind a closure formed in the front part of the mouth". Hollington (2017: 82) explains that its function in non-verbal communication is to express contempt of another person. Ameka (2020: 213) points out that in Ewe the corresponding expression (*ɖu tsé* 'bite inside one's cheek') may also be used cathartically to express frustration about oneself. As a sound gesture, it features prominently across the African continent (probably reflecting an ancient Africanism), but also in the African Diaspora, especially in the Caribbean and the United States.

---

62 Additional gestures involving the head can be found under the following link: [https://www.youtube.com/watch?v=l2yv7kyZRqo] (accessed 20 February 2021).

There are various YouTube clips showing "teeth kissing", for example, in the interviews by the linguistic anthropologist Colman Donaldson in Bamako (Mali) with speakers of Bambara on the cultural background of *surunci*, as it is called in Bambara. It is also known as *tchip* (from the Wolof word for this phenomenon, *ciip*), for example in colloquial French. The upper line in the translation of the interviews in Bambara is written in the Tifinagh script (Picture 30).

Picture 30: Screenshot from YouTube on "teeth kissing" in Bamako (Mali).[63]

Another visual gesture of contempt or disapproval is the so-called "cut-eye" action (Rickford and Rickford 1976) by looking at the addressee for a while from the corners of one's eyes, blinking or rolling the eye and then turning one's face away and down quickly, in order to show disregard. Different languages in Ghana have terms for this act: *anikyie* (Akan), *ŋkutetre* (Ewe), *kpemɔ* (Gã) (Thompson and Agyekum 2016: 26).

In many parts of Africa, and presumably elsewhere too, it is traditionally taken as a sign of respect when younger people, particularly women, avoid eye contact in social interactions, as described for example by Treis (2005) in her detailed contribution on traditional language taboos among Kambaata women in Ethiopia, particularly with respect to their parents-in-law, whose eyes and names are to be avoided. Coly (2017) describes the notion of *kersa* in Wolof (Senegal), positively evaluated as 'shame', "out of respect for another person (generally for an older person) and out of an esteem that one does not want to lose (. . .) This person is never able to look another person in the face, an act that is interpreted as insolence, lack of respect" (Coly 2017: 118). In Wolof, this term is used in paradigmatic contrast with *wow bət* 'dry eye', expressing lack of respect for others.

---

63 See [http://www.youtube.com/watch?v=zt8nHLyqkOg] (accessed 5 April 2021).

This in turn may lead to what Wolof speakers refer to as *der bu yaqu* 'destroyed skin', a coercive metaphorical concept for "public dishonour" (Coly 2017: 117).

In his conversational analysis of Wolof, Meyer (2018: 263) mentions that gazing at an addressee in Wolof conversations usually signals confrontation or projective conflict with an adversary; a speaker may also gaze at a third party as witness (orally) while verbally addressing their adversary.

Avoiding eye contact as a sign of respect extends to many other parts of Africa (and elsewhere, presumably). Amberber (2001: 54) observes that "in Amharic being shy is typically regarded as a positive cultural attribute. It often incorporates evaluation in the visual domain – for example a shy person does not gaze or stare at people". The following compound nouns in Amharic also reflect this preferred habitus (as culture inscribed in mind and body).

(166)   aynaffar
         eye.dry
         'a shy person'

(167)   aynədərək'
         eye.dry
         'shameless, impudent, cheeky'

Gazing may also be interpreted as putting the evil eye on somebody, as observed by Coly (2017: 107) with respect to the Wolof speech community. Differences in the amount of gaze between speakers and hearers in social interactions, as well as the relative duration, are thus potentially significant from a cross-cultural perspective, as already observed in Kendon (1975a), one of the early sources on this phenomenon in conversational interaction.

One dimension of gaze in day-to-day interaction involves its function as a turn-taking device. Gaze direction may serve as a recipient selection strategy, as pointed out by Rüsch (2020a: 58) in her analysis of conversational strategies in Acholi (Uganda). But as shown in the discussion of conversation strategies among Hai‖om speakers (Chapter 11), mutual gaze or monitoring during turn-taking is not universal.

This position is confirmed in Meyer's (2018) monograph on Wolof speech communities where interactants know each other well. Speakers may gaze at an object or a "third party", i.e., another person than the addressee, who may react with a vocal signal. The addressee also does not necessarily gaze back, and instead may only react vocally like the "third party" (Meyer 2018: 229–230). Speakers explained that they like to look at third parties as witnesses or allies, usually choosing people who are known to share the opinion of the speaker. Speakers may also prod gently as a turn-allocation device, or nudge at the back of the third party, because there is not necessarily any face-to-face interaction.

The differential interactive function of facial expressions becomes clear, not only from the study of gaze in turn-taking devices, but also when interpreting speakers' intentions in social interactions. Tanaka et al. (2010) report on an investigation of cultural differences between 20 Japanese and 16 Dutch participants in the multisensory perception of emotion involving facial expressions (in particular the area around the mouth) and tone of voice. The results of this experiment, during which participants were asked to listen to audio recordings and watch video recordings, indicated that the Japanese speakers were more attuned than the Dutch speakers to vocal processing (voice) rather than facial expression in the multisensory perception of emotion (Tanaka et al. 2010: 1262). The Japanese participants' greater reliance on voice qualities than on facial expressions compared to the Dutch participants may be related to a cultural habit among speakers of Japanese of controlling the facial display of their own feelings more than speakers of Dutch tend to do, according to the authors. Showing a neutral facial expression, rather than showing anger, has also been claimed to be part of the habitus of other areas in Asia, as well as in Africa (see Chapter 9).

Culture-specific display rules may thus cover up emotional expressions to some extent. This also becomes obvious from pictures of facial expressions of two world leaders, the former president of the United States, Donald Trump, when lashing out at a reporter during a press conference (one of many similar pictures that can be found on the internet), and his Chinese counterpart Xi Jinping, of whom again a range of pictures may be found on internet, either with a neutral face, or smiling (Pictures 31 and 32).

Picture 31: Former president of the USA, Donald Trump, lashing out at journalists.

Picture 32: Xi Jinping, President of the People's Republic of China.

12.2 Gestures

There is no sharp division between verbal and non-verbal communication forms such as interjections, not least because the latter tend to be intimately linked with gestures in many languages (Ameka and Wilkins 2006). Grenoble, Martinović, and Baglini (2015: 110) in fact refer to a category of paralinguistic expressive features that they call "verbal gestures". The label itself, of course, is reminiscent of the term "vocal gestures", which is used as an alternative term for interjections by Ameka (1992a: 106). The latter term has the advantage of not being associated with "verbs", although Grenoble, Martinović, and Baglini (2015) of course use the term "verbal gestures" in paradigmatic contrast to gestures involving non-verbal communication.

Inspired by the pioneering contribution of Dialo (1985) on expressive elements in Wolof (to which the present author did not have access), Grenoble, Martinović, and Baglini (2015) define these as linguistic elements that are not lexical items per se (and so do not take derivational or inflectional morphology), neither do they occur in morphosyntactic frames, i.e., as part of words or sentences; they may include sounds or segments which stand outside a language's phonemic inventory but are still part of its communicative system. Semantically, they belong to the realm of emotive functions in language. The examples in Table 28 illustrate such verbal gestures for Wolof based on Grenoble, Martinović, and Baglini (2015: 115)

Table 28: Verbal gestures in Wolof (Grenoble, Martinović, and Baglini 2015).

GLOSS	DESCRIPTION	MANNER	MEANING
waaw	palatal/velar click (mouth closed) lateral click alveolar click	single instance repeated repeated	'yes'
déedéet	bilabial-dental click	repeated twice	'no'
ciipetu	bilabial-dental click	elongated suction through teeth	'I don't like this'
"hiss" ("the pis")	[s:]	elongated	attention-getting
waalis	whistle-1 whistle-2 whistle-3	flat intonation rising intonation rising-falling intonation	attention-getting calling expression admiration
"hmm"	nasal sound [m̥m?] mouth closed		'watch out, you are in trouble'

In coursebooks on southern Bantu languages like Xhosa or Zulu, such clicks tend to be described as follows: the bilabial click [ʘ] as the "kissing sound"; the dental click [|] as "what a pity click"; the palatal click [ǂ] as "the champagne cork popping click"; and the lateral click [ǁ] as the "cantering horse click".

The click sound referred to as *waaw* in Wolof and expressing 'yes (I get it)' is also used as a backchannel, whereas *ciipetu* corresponds to the well-known "suck-teeth" or "kiss-teeth" movement, found across Africa and the Caribbean. The elongated hissing sound is used in Wolof (and, in fact, in many parts of Africa) in order to get attention or to call out to someone; additional functions in Wolof are indicating admiration or expressing relief.

Lionnet (2020) describes the paralinguistic use of clicks in Laal in southern Chad and neighbouring zones. The use of the dental click (represented as [|] in the system of the International Phonetic Association) as a sound expressing negation or disagreement is presumably widespread across the world. The interjection /kây is reminiscent of the Hausa interjection with the same form and function, although this may be a coincidence.

(168) | kây!
NO EXCL
'really [what a horrible death it was]!'

The lateral click [ǁ] in Laal on the other hand expresses approval or endorsement ('yes'), and is also used as a backchanneling strategy in conversations ('yes, go on', 'I get it'). The (back-released velar) click [ʞ] (i.e., the inverted "k" symbol), indicating approval and agreement, has also been reported for languages such as Kanuri (Nigeria) and Mundang (Cameroon).

Other types of verbal gestures are found, for example as directed to domestic animals. Amha (2013) describes the use of such communication signs in Zargulla, a language of southwest Ethiopia. In this language, as well as in two languages belonging to the same (Omotic) language family, Maale and Wolaitta, interjectional directives are used (without any distinction between singular and plural forms) to summon the animal(s) to move closer to the speaker, or, alternatively, to disperse them. Interestingly, several of these cognates probably go back to a common proto-form in the shared ancestral language of Zargulla, Maale, and Wolaitta.

	Animal	Zargulla	Maale	Wolaitta	
(169)	chicken	lúk/ɓík'	lúkku	ɓík' ɓík'	(calling)
	chicken	čúk	čúkku	šúh/ šúk	(dispersal)

As is true more generally for interjections, Zargulla interjections also manifest a feature not found elsewhere in the language, namely the nasalization of vowels, as in the interjection used to disperse oxen, *wăă*. As illustrated in Section 6.3, cross-linguistically well-known clicks became incorporated into the regular sound system of southern Bantu languages belonging to the Nguni cluster, through borrowing from neighbouring Khoisan languages as a result of taboo strategies in the Nguni languages. There has been a lot of speculation about the origin of clicks, and the question of whether these sounds, found in Khoisan, the latter constituting an areal rather than a genetic grouping, represent archaisms of human language. The Khoisan area involves at least three independent language families, Northern Khoisan, Central Khoisan, and Southern Khoisan, with the Sandawe language in Tanzania (which also has clicks) probably being distantly related to Central Khoisan. Herbert (1990) gives an overview of different authors from the 19th and 20th century writing on the subject of the origin of these sounds in human language. For an updated survey of this phonetic phenomenon, readers are referred to Sands (2020). In line with Güldemann (2007), it is assumed in the present study that contact-induced transmission of clicks (as in the Tanzanian language Hadza, or in southern Bantu languages) as well as independent development (as in the initiate register Damin of the Lardil in Australia (Hale 1973), and possibly in Dahalo in Kenya (Güldemann 2007: 13)) are equally plausible explanations for the spreading of these sounds.

Gil (2013), like earlier authors on the subject, again takes them to be archaisms in human languages. But if they are indeed old, why did all languages across the world outside the African continent lose them as regular sounds of language systems (the Lardil register being a late innovation)? Clicks as paralinguistic – rather than linguistic – phenomena, on the other hand, are extremely common as human speech sounds (Güldemann 2007: 10). It is very likely, therefore, that these paralinguistic features left the African continent when modern humans started spreading as hunter-gatherers around the world some 70,000 years ago. As "noisy" sounds, they were rather "impractical" as regular sound units (phonemes) in the languages of human beings with such means of subsistence. As shown in the next section, the different San speech communities use sign language in addition to oral communication when they go hunting. Clicks are also rather marked, as children acquire these sounds at a relatively late stage. Whatever the reasons were for integrating such paralinguistic phenomena into the sound system of these languages, there must have been very strong cultural reasons for maintaining them. It is likely, therefore (though again speculative, as with any claims about their origin), that clicks only came to be used as linguistic units under specific social conditions, such as in ritual languages, from which they then spread within languages and across languages, as they did in the Bantu languages of southern Africa.

In their introduction to gestures in conversation, Seyfeddinipur and Gullburg (2014: 1) observe that people in different parts of the world exploit the oral modality as well as the manual modality, but that there are also differences between individuals in the extent to which gestures are used; moreover, as many of us know from personal experiences, there are also differences across cultures. Hand shaking is one such domain, usually accompanying greeting strategies, manifesting intercultural differences. Probably the most widely spread greeting gesture worldwide is the single-handed handshake, in which the right hand of one person grasps the right hand of the other. As a special sign of respect (e.g., because of age differences), the left hand may support one's right forearm in many parts of Africa.

One of the earliest contributions on gestures in an African context is found in Creider (1977) for East Africa. Sanders (2015) gives a detailed description with illustrations of handshakes accompanying greetings among speakers of Tonga in Malawi; several of the types described are also found in other parts of Africa (and beyond), and therefore repeated here. The author distinguishes between standing and seated greetings (the latter being typical of prearranged meetings (Sanders 2015: 116)), with formality playing a role in both domains. Standing greetings "typically involve interlocutors in passing and take place outside of the home. They may take place without any verbal exchange, or they may turn into longer conversations and recruit more members as other passersby stop and join the conversation" (Sanders 2015: 116).

Different elaborations of these are found across the African continent. Wolof speakers, for example, may grasp each other's left hands in addition to their right hands by crossing their arms. Among speakers of Turkana and other pastoral communities in East Africa one finds what may be called the "thumb handshake" (Sanders 2015: 117). It consists of a hand shake followed by a rotational pivoting at the web of the thumb and back into the normal handshake position, which may be repeated several times.

Announcing one's presence during a visit to a homestead by slowly clapping one's hands at the gate or entrance a few times, in order not to startle any of the persons one is visiting, also appears to be widespread in Africa. Also widespread across the continent is the habit of holding the wrist of the person with whom one would otherwise shake hands; the latter may avoid a handshake because his/her hands are dirty (from working on the land) or wet (because the person has washed his/her hands, for example after having been to the toilet).

Picture 33 is also found on the cover of *The Leopard's Spots* by the present author; it shows how the spokesman of the Tima community in Khartoum, Sudan, the late Nasradeen Abdallah, greets another elderly Tima person during a visit back to the Nuba Mountains. Rather than shaking hands with the elderly lady, he offers his wrist as a sign of respect, since he just washed his hands.

Picture 33: Holding the wrist instead of shaking hands.

Kissing the hand of a respected older male or female person and putting his or her hand on one's forehead is common in Islamic cultures, especially in northeastern Africa. Putting one's own hand, as an elderly person, on the forehead of children, as a kind of blessing, is found in a region ranging from Songhai or Tuareg speakers in Mali to speakers of Maa(sai) in Kenya or Tanzania. Alternatively, hand shaking and other types of immediate physical contact may be avoided. Instead, bowing the head, prostrating oneself, or genuflecting (and crouching) before a person of high social status, sometimes accompanied by clapping the hands, may be found.

Ameka (2006: 150) observes that in the West African Volta region, women in particular may show respect in greeting by lowering their bodies, as if about to genuflect, and give a slight bow. While women and men still sometimes practise bowing slightly, these days women seldom, if ever, lower their bodies in greetings. An elegant habit frequently observed in Ethiopia, especially among Amharic speakers, is that of lifting oneself for a second from a chair or bench, in order to pay respect to somebody passing by, usually combined with a slight bow in the direction of the person one greets.

For a detailed discussion of non-verbal contributions to conversation with numerous illustrations in one specific speech community, that of the Acholi in Uganda, the reader is referred to Rüsch (2020a: 255–312). The author also presents an interesting multimodal approach to action through gestures, gaze, and body in her survey.

One of the leading authorities on gestures, Adam Kendon, defined gestures accompanying verbal interaction, as a central feature of human interaction, as "any distinct bodily action that is regarded by participants as being directly involved in the process of deliberate utterance" (Kendon 1985: 215). The author distinguishes between the following types:

> gesticulation (for example waving the arms in vigourous talk) → language-like gestures (in order to state, persuade, seduce, urge, command, question, obey) → pantomimes → emblems → sign languages

Kendon's continuum, representing types of gestures and the question of whether speech is required, or less so, or not at all (as with sign languages), is taken as a basis for an initial discussion below. It is also compared with the study by McNeill (1992), who presents a slightly modified typology with some alternative names. McNeill (1992) also focuses on gestures involving the hands and arms, thereby distinguishing between the following types: iconics, metaphorics, beats, emblems, cohesives, and deictics. These are discussed with illustrations from Turkana (Kenya) and other communities, mainly from Africa. The focus on Turkana is related not only to the fact that the present author spent almost one and a half years in this speech community, but also because McNeill (1992: 153–154) makes reference to gestures in the community. David McNeill's inspiration for this focus on the Turkana apparently came from the ethnocinematographic trilogy *Turkana Conversations*, produced by the McDougalls (1977), which is also discussed in Chapter 7.

Picture 34: Socializing within the family (*Lorang's Way*).

Picture 34, which is a snapshot from *Lorang's Way* (McDougalls 1977), illustrates another phenomenon of relevance from an intercultural perspective, namely differences in the management of physical space between individuals, a domain the investigation of which has come to be known as proxemics (Hall 1963). The screenshot shows a situation characteristic of socializing among Turkana family members in their nomadic homesteads. Learning at which point one starts to invade other people's privacy constitutes a further dimension of non-verbal communication which is part of culturation and consequently relevant from an intercultural perspective. Readers from other parts of the world may take a situation as shown in this picture as an intrusion on personal space, particularly for adults.

However, when elderly Turkana people feel they have important things to say, they require more personal space, because gestures tend to be a significant part of getting a point across. Anybody from outside who has visited a Turkana pastoral homestead in northwestern Kenya, or who has seen the classic ethnocinematographic contributions of the McDougalls on these pastoralists living in northwestern Kenya (*Wife among Wives*, *Lorang's Way*, and *Wedding Camels*) has probably noticed this "personal body space" that speakers usually require for themselves when speaking. Picture 35 shows one of Lorang's wife's sisters, Naingiro, raising her hands, opening them up and spreading them out sideways in order to express emptiness in a (non-iconic) metaphorical sense. Picture 36 shows Lorang talking about the mysteries of life, again expressing in a non-iconic (i.e., culture-specific) metaphorical sense what it means to exist as a human being.

Picture 35: Naingiro talking about Lorang's life.   **Picture 36:** Lorang explaining about life.

While the gesture types discussed below are also known from other parts of the world, a number of these also appear to manifest some idiosyncratic features, as used, for example, by Turkana speakers, as discussed next.

The first concept in David McNeill's gesture model (McNeill 1992: 12–19, 147–164) is *iconics*. They imitate the movement or action to which they refer; in other words, the gesture exhibits the same act referred to in speech. Thus, bending a tree back to the ground may be expressed by manipulating the hand as if gripping something and pulling it from the upper front space and back down to near the shoulder. These gestures can be treated as part of what Kendon (1975a) calls pantomimes (the latter involving additional examples of miming or body motions of the type discussed above).

Metaphorics (as the second type) refers to gestures which are also pictorial (iconic), but they may also express an abstract idea or concept rather than a concrete object, in which case they are non-iconic, representing a so-called conduit metaphor. The idea of a genre of a narrative (as an abstract concept) may be presented as a bound (physical) container, for example, or a hand forming a cup as a bounded supportable subject may symbolize 'a question' in a sentence 'I have [a question]' (McNeill 1992: 149). Kendon (2004) also describes such conduit metaphors, for example the *grappolo* (purse-hand, whereby the fingers form an enclosed space or container, followed by the hand opening) in order to introduce a discourse topic, in his analysis of gestures in the city of Naples, Italy. Because of their often culture-specific meaning, such metaphorics may also function as emblems for a specific speech community or community of practice, and thereby become susceptible to ideological productions (Haviland 2004: 216).

In his discussion of gestures in Turkana, McNeill (1992: 154) points out that he is puzzled by one metaphorical gesture used by the protagonist Lorang in the documentary by the McDougalls, when the latter discusses the inquisitive nature of Europeans or white people (*ŋimusungui*). Based on his contacts with white people before he decided to return to his home area and raise a family there, Lorang has the impression that these foreigners want to extract every bit of information or knowledge from other people (like him), whenever they can (Picture 37).

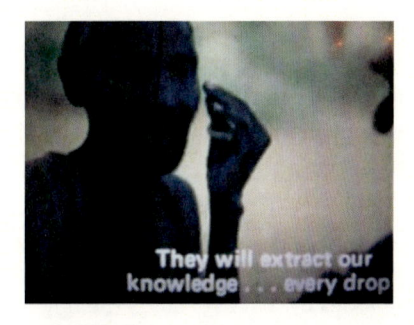

Picture 37: Lorang explaining about knowledge.

Although the abstract concept of knowledge is "entified" through a specific gesture made by Lorang, there is no boundary or container involved, according to McNeill (1992: 154). This would make such a gesture a "non-conduit metaphoric" gesture. There is, however an alternative interpretation, that of a conduit metaphor, whereby the head functions as the container from which these foreigners pick or pluck knowledge bit by bit.

Metaphors may also take on the form of culturally ratified versions of emblematic gestures, as shown in the pioneering contributions of Adam Kendon. Such emblematic gestures of course may also spread across language boundaries, especially in multilingual societies, for example as part of insults, and thereby of impoliteness strategies. Ameka (2020) discusses taboo expressions and shared maledicta containing "schatological and sex references as well as the mother theme" as areal invectives in the Lower Volta Basin in West Africa. The author also points out that these are multimodal, in that they may be combined with a thumb point gesture directed at the addressee (Ameka 2020:137). Another gesture which is also widespread across West Africa involves a particular movement of the arms in order to express rejection, by bending them at the elbows, making a fist with the hands, and moving the bent arms to hit the sides.

Beats (as a third category of gestures) may be found in statements where the beat coincides with the specific linguistic segment that does the summing up, for example in listing a specific procedure: 'first . . ., second, . . . third, . . . next,' As a phenomenon, they show similarities to the use of beats as measures (bars) in the time signature of music, hence the term. Beats are important for the pragmatic contents of an utterance, for example a simple flick of the hand with a summing up statement, thereby indexing the word or statement as significant.

Gestures belonging to the fourth category, *cohesives*, emphasize continuity (rather than discontinuities, in contrast to beats) because they serve to tie together thematically related but temporally separated parts of the discourse. By repeating this type of gesture, continuity may be suggested. In terms of their form, they can consist of gestures which are iconic, metaphoric, beats, or pointing gestures (deictics), which constitute the fifth and final category.

Deictics involve the cross-culturally familiar pointing which is also part of sign language. Across Africa it is common to use the whole hand (unless one wants to threaten somebody), as a pointing gesture which consists of "a communicative body movement that projects a vector from a body part. This vector indicates a certain direction, location, or object" (Kita 2003: 1). Picture 38, a screenshot from *Lorang's Way* (McDougalls 1977), shows this wide-hand pointing gesture.

However, when a young boy herding goats passes by, Lorang scolds the boy, named Eriyet, for trespassing on his territory (Picture 39). Pointing with his finger in this way is taken by speakers of Turkana as an ultimate warning not to let this happen again. Lorang's status as a rich and influential Turkana, who has also come of age, allows him to be very articulate and clear, using bald-on record statements without any face redress strategies in this case.

Wilkins (2003: 192), in his cross-cultural survey of the semiotics of pointing, states that there are cultures in which systematic pointing with the index finger

Picture 38: Lorang pointing at the homestead of one of his wives.

Picture 39: Lorang scolding a young boy.

is not attested, and consequently pointing is not a human universal in semiotic terms; moreover, where it occurs it may express different functions.

Another interesting deictic gesture which can be observed in *Lorang's Way* involves pointing in different directions with the fingers of both hands in order to express the presence of specific phenomena at different places (Picture 40); the protagonist also repeats his verbal message while continuing to show these gestures.

A further type of deictic hand gesture accompanying the oral modality may be observed in different parts of Africa when somebody wants to indicate the height of human beings as against animals (Picture 41). Rüsch (2020a: 261–263) describes and illustrates such differences in Acholi (Uganda).

The distinctive gestures used for the expression of the height of humans as against animals is widespread across the continent. Fehn (2011: 162), for example, shows that a similar distinction exists between humans and animals but also with objects in Ts'ixa (Botswana). The study on conversational strategies in Acholi by Rüsch (2020a) is also a rich source on non-verbal communication in this language, with extensive illustrations of the different types of facial and bodily movement discussed in the present study.

Picture 40: Lorang explaining about directions.

Picture 41: Expressing the height of humans as against animals in Acholi.

In urban centres across Africa, new varieties of contact languages have developed over the past decades, and along with them, gestures as part of these new speech styles. Due to the spreading of mobile phones and the internet, such registers are of course no longer typically associated with urban life these days, and may be found in rural areas as well. Moreover, they are not uniquely associated with younger people, as was often claimed in the earliest accounts of these languages; see Nassenstein and Hollington (2015) for a survey, and Nassenstein (2018) for a critical assessment of some earlier claims regarding the question of who the actual users of these languages are.

One such stylect is found in a number of varieties in South Africa. Brookes (2014: 63) points out that the "[s]killful use of the informal slang variety known as *Tsotsitaal* (whereby *tsotsi* refers to 'robber, criminal' in regional languages like Pedi, Sesotho and Setswana, and *taal* is the Afrikaans word for 'language') and of gestures, is a key part of their communicative performance". Brookes (2014: 71) identifies more than 150 quotable (conventionalized) gestures used by young males in Vosloorus, a township east of Johannesburg. These gestures are used in order to enhance visibility, to compel attention and for performance, as a kind of dramatic art form that can be appreciated by those within and outside the immediate interaction". For example, in order to show that one is streetwise and does not have a rural identity, the forefinger and last finger are directed towards the gesturer's eyes, "and the stroke is a diagonal movement across the face down from the right side and back up. More than one movement down and up means the person is very streetwise" (Brookes 2014: 65). Such gestures thus may be seen as indexes of urban identity, but they may also be used in order to be able to communicate in private in crowded conditions. For a more general discussion of the linguistic makeup of hybrid social identities in urban areas in post-apartheid South Africa, the reader is referred to Slabbert and Finlayson (2000).

Birdwhistell (1952, 1968) calls such conventionalized emblematic gestures *kinemes*, by analogy with linguistic units such as *phonemes* (sound units distinguishing meaning in a language) and *morphemes* (as the smallest meaningful grammatical units in a language). Similarly, *kines* (as the least perceptible units of body motion) parallel the linguistic use of the terms *phones* (or sounds) and *morphs* (as a string of sounds expressing a specific lexical or grammatical function). Birdwhistell also developed symbols for the transcription of bodily movements, for example "h∧" for the superior head nod.

Ray Birdwhistell's research among the Kutenai (Ktunaxa) First Nation of British Columbia had taught him that members of this community were capable of identifying non-members from a great distance by their posture and body movements. Birdwhistell (1968: 381) points out that "biculturalism" may extend into kinesics, as shown by his comparison of gestural and expressional patterning among Kutenai and (white Anglo-Saxon) American "body language". The recognition that a bilingual Kutenai moved in a consistently and regularly different manner when speaking Kutenai than when speaking English could not be understood until systematic analysis of the structure of American kinesics was undertaken. Saville-Troike (1978) suggests the term "dinomia" for the complementary use within the same society of two cultural systems (for example, at home and in school in the case of children).

A further fascinating aspect of body language involving deictics is its interaction with spatial orientation among Australian aboriginal communities, as documented by Levinson (1992) and Haviland (1993) among speakers of Guugu Yimithirr in the far north of Queensland. Instead of using body-relative locational descriptors such as 'in front of', or 'at the back of', speakers of Guugu Yimithirr use words corresponding roughly to the English words for 'north', 'south', 'east' and 'west'. In other words, these relational terms are not "body-centric" or "ego-centric", but "earth-centric" (as further discussed in Chapter 4 above).

Haviland (2004: 209–210) describes an additional phenomenon related to the absolute reference system of Guugu Yimithirr speakers for spatial orientation (as discussed in Section 4.1). A speaker reported twice on a boat he was on that capsized, after which he swam to shore. Immediately afterwards, a giant shark fin cut through the water where the protagonist and his companion had just been swimming. When telling this story, the storyteller preserved this absolute orientation in his gestures. In the first telling of this story of a capsized boat turning over to the west, recorded by John Haviland in 1980, the narrator gestures to his front, i.e., to the west, while being seated facing west. Two years later, when the same speaker was recorded telling this story of this boat capsizing towards the west, he was facing north. In order to indicate a westerly direction in the story's events, he made the gestures over his left shoulder on his side, as shown in Figure 18. In other words, for speakers of this language the coordinates remain constant, i.e., they do not rotate with them as they do for speakers using relative systems.

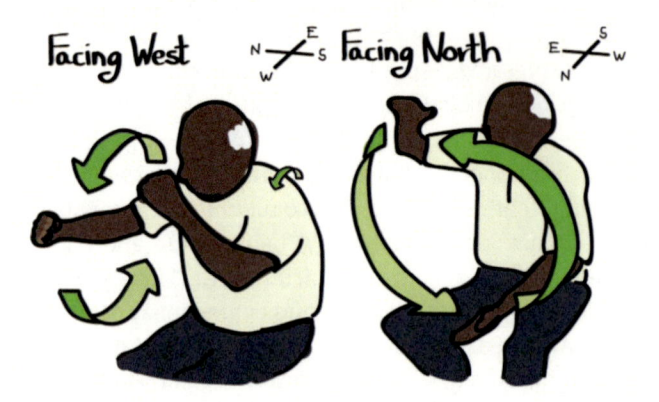

Figure 18: Gesturing in Guugu Yimithirr (kindly produced by Lennart Attenberger).[64]

In his discussion of these scenes, Haviland (2004: 204) makes reference to this combination of an emblematic and iconic gesture in Guugu Yimithirr (Guugu Yimidhirr), namely the open, empty palm of the hand expressing "nothing" in conjunction with "a sweeping, circular motion than can be seen as an iconic rendering of

---

[64] Based on screenshot from a documentary *Noord-Zuid-Oost-West* ('North South East West') for the Dutch television programme Noorderlicht, broadcast by VPRO in 1993, as part of an interview with the then director of the Max Planck Institute for Psycholinguistics in Nijmegen, the Netherlands, Stephen C. Levinson, who (2003a, 2018) also presents an extensive discussion of gestures in relation to spatial orientation. See [http://hdl.handle.net/11858/00-001M-0000-002E-36D6-1] (accessed 30 January 2021).

the rolling and tossing of the waves and the direction of the wind which carried the sunken boat's cargo away, suggesting that the loss of food and clothes was a consequence of the depicted movement of wind and waves". Such gestures consequently involve conceptual blending (in the present author's view), as they combine information on the position, direction, and orientation, as well as motion.

Unlike syntactic structures, gestures do not usually appear to combine smaller meaningful parts to create larger entities when combined with speech. However, when the verbal code is absent, they may in fact be combined, as further examples in the next section show. Modern audiovisual technology such as the ELAN programme provides unique opportunities to record and analyze such semiotic in detail, as illustrated by the screenshot Picture 42.

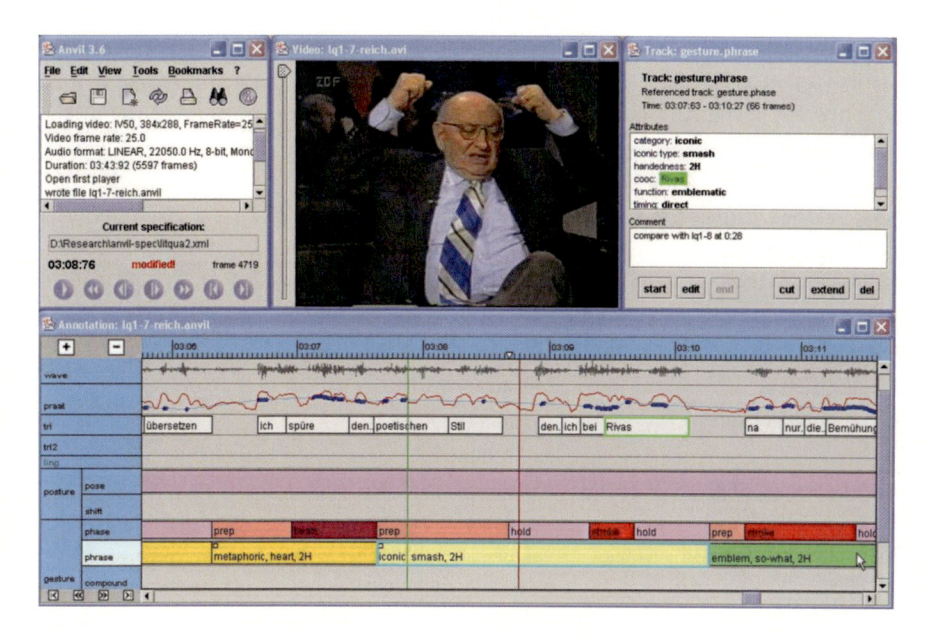

Picture 42: ELAN screenshot of a picture accompanying an utterance.

12.3 Sign language

In his typology of gestures, Kendon (1983) classifies sign language as a type of communication not involving any speech. Sign language as a language used in addition to oral communication and performed in a three-dimensional space, using hands, face, and the body, is probably best known within an African context from communities speaking Khoisan languages (as an areal grouping) in Southern Africa.[65]

These signs are used, for example, when hunting. Fehn (2011) presents an analysis of gestures in Ts'ixa, a language spoken by less than 200 persons residing mainly in Mababe village, Botswana. During hunting, iconic (symbolic) representations with the hand and arm represent images of an animal's shape or prominent body part, such as the trunk of an elephant or the long neck of a giraffe or ostrich. These may also be used outside the hunting context as illustrative gestures in storytelling and songs. As observed by Fehn (2011: 156), "[e]specially among male elders, they may also appear as co-speech gestures in natural communication".

Pointing gestures in the Ts'ixa community express deictic concepts but also temporal categories. While information conveyed by arm positions corresponds to local adverbs in Ts'ixa, information conveyed by hand shape and movement is not encoded verbally (Table 29). These examples show that gestures are not just a duplication of spoken language (Fehn 2011: 158–159).

Table 29: Arm positions in Ts'ixa pointing gestures (Fehn 2011:158–159).

Vertical arm position	Salient features of reference point	Corresponding local adverb
Below shoulder height	[+proximal] [+visible]	ŋxùà, ŋkùà
Shoulder height	[+distal] [+visible]	méxùà
Above shoulder height	[+distal] [-visible]	méŋkùà
	HANDSHAPES	
Index-finger pointing, with the palm facing downward	Pointing towards a specific object, location or direction	No corresponding deictic word
Open-hand pointing, with all digits extended	Vagueness with respect to object, location or direction; may be further emphasized by waving the hand slightly from side to side	No corresponding deictic word

With special purpose gestures denoting actions during hunting larger units can in fact be observed. Fehn (2011: 164) gives examples from Ts'ixa corresponding to a verbal representation 'There's a male kudu that side. Let's move around and kill it!', by using a sequence of gestures expressing 'male kudu', 'that direction', 'move around', and 'strike'.

---

[65] Hereditary deafness in local communities in Africa and elsewhere has also led to the development of sign languages outside the context of deaf education (Nyst 2020).

There is a widespread conviction amongst scholars that gestures are ancient features of human communication. Early authors like Hewes (1973), but also more recent authors like Corballis (2014), propagate a gesture-first scenario for the evolution of human language, and claim that language must have evolved from manual grasping and manipulation in primates to pantomime in our hominid forebears, gradually conventionalizing towards arbitrary linguistic symbols. Vocal production in nonhuman primates is inflexible, whereas manual action is flexible (as well as intentional and learnable). But of course vocal communication is also found in the animal kingdom (and, as modern research on orcas or dolphins amongst other species shows, quite complex too).

Rather than claiming that gestures were first and that switching to the oral modality to facilitate communication over long distances was a later development, Kendon (1975b) considers speech and gestures to have co-evolved. More recently, this hypothesis has been taken up and defended again by McNeill (2012). As a leading specialist in the field of gestures, McNeill claims that gestures and speech are unified and need to be considered jointly. McNeill (2012: 218–232) introduces the notion of "growth point", the whole of a gesture-language unit as the minimal psychological unit. Non-verbal communication goes hand in hand with speech. Criminal investigators use this knowledge when doing interviews with suspects and detecting incongruity, particularly between gestural and facial "leakage" of non-verbal messages and verbal messages, as these are partly out of voluntary control. As argued in McNeill (2012), the widely popular "gesture-first" theory, according to which language began as pure gesture without speech, fails this test twice, predicting what did not evolve, namely that speech supplanted gesture, and not predicting what did evolve, namely our own speech-gesture unity. An alternative, which McNeill (2012) calls "Mead's Loop" (after the philosopher George Herbert Mead), explains this unity. It too claims that gesture was essential to the origin of language, but not because it was "primitive" or more accessible. Rather, it says that speech could not have evolved without gesture, and nor could gesture have evolved without speech. Speech and gesture originated together, at the same time, in response to the same selection pressures.

There is still a lot to be discovered with respect to non-verbal communication from an intercultural perspective, a task which becomes more and more urgent in a globalizing world, because of diverging fashions of speaking leading to miscommunications on the one hand, and vanishing traditions worthy of being documented on the other. If the present monograph succeeds in encouraging scholars interested in the interaction between language, culture, and cognition to broaden and deepen our understanding of this as well as other anthropological-linguistic topics, and of course to take issue with the claims made here, a central goal of the present monograph will have been fulfilled.

Appendices

Appendix I: Kinship terminology in Tima (Schneider-Blum and Veit 2022)

For the description of kinship terminology in Tima, Murdock's (1968) typology based on sibling terminology is relevant. From his sample of 800 languages from different parts of the world, Murdock suggested seven types of terminological systems (Murdock 1968: 3–4):
Type A: The Kordofanian or Undifferentiated Sibling Type
Type B: The Yoruba or Relative Age Type
Type C: The Algonkian or Skewed Age Type
Type D: The Dravidian or Age-Sex Type
Type E: The European or Brother-Sister Type
Type F: The Melanesian or Relative Sex Type
Type G: The Siouan or Complexly Differentiated Type

The second subtype of Murdock's Type F (the Melanesian or Relative Sex Type) describes what one finds in Tima (Schneider-Blum and Veit 2022), namely three terms, glossed as 'sibling of the same sex', 'brother (woman speaking)', and 'sister (man speaking)'.

Appendix I: Kinship terminology in Tima (Schneider-Blum and Veit 2022)

Abbreviations: F – father; M – mother; Z – sister; B – brother; S – son; D – daughter

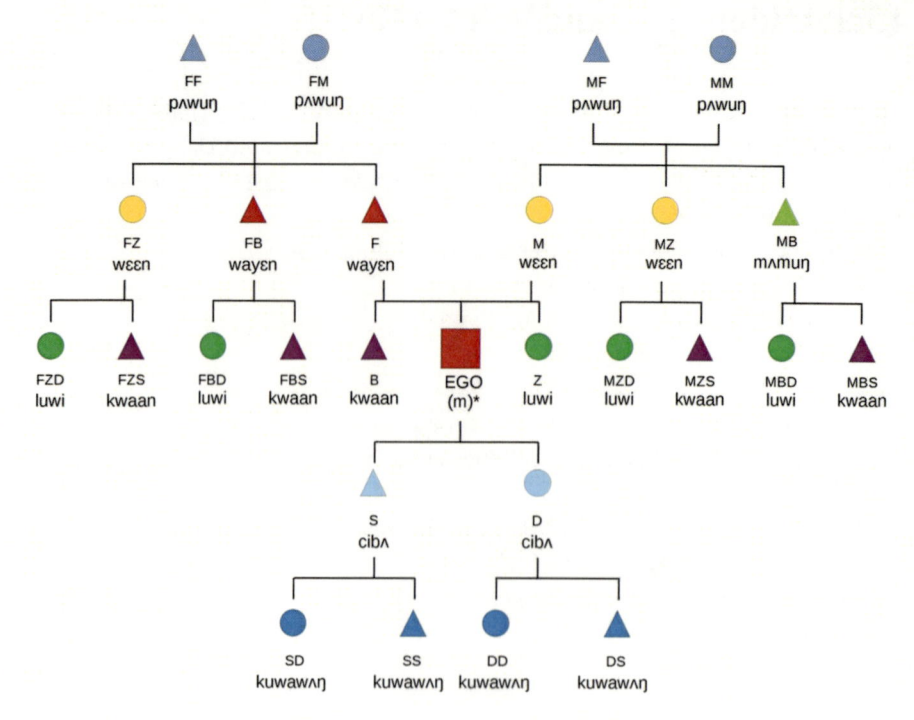

FF pʌwuŋ	FM pʌwuŋ				MF pʌwuŋ	MM pʌwuŋ

FZ wɛɛn	FB wayɛn	F wayɛn		M wɛɛn	MZ wɛɛn	MB mʌmuŋ

FZD luwi	FZS kwaan	FBD luwi	FBS kwaan	B kwaan	EGO (m)*	Z luwi	MZD luwi	MZS kwaan	MBD luwi	MBS kwaan

S cibʌ	D cibʌ

SD kuwawʌŋ	SS kuwawʌŋ	DD kuwawʌŋ	DS kuwawʌŋ

*When Ego is female the term for her 'brother' is *kinʌ* and the term for her 'sister' is *kwaan* ('sibling of the same gender').

Appendix II: Colour chart as used in Tornay (1978)

Appendix III: Politeness strategies (Brown and Levinson 1987)

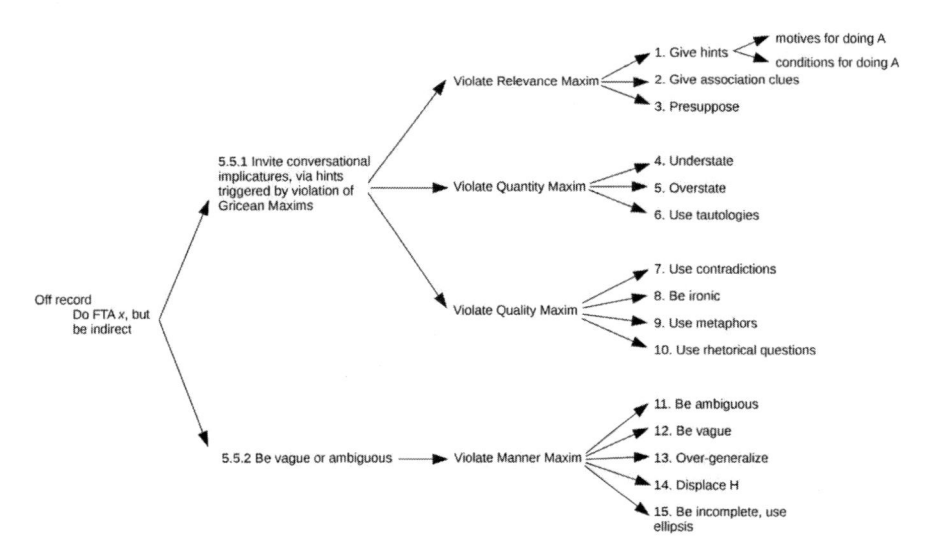

Off record — Do FTA *x*, but be indirect

- 5.5.1 Invite conversational implicatures, via hints triggered by violation of Gricean Maxims
  - Violate Relevance Maxim
    - 1. Give hints
      - motives for doing A
      - conditions for doing A
    - 2. Give association clues
    - 3. Presuppose
  - Violate Quantity Maxim
    - 4. Understate
    - 5. Overstate
    - 6. Use tautologies
  - Violate Quality Maxim
    - 7. Use contradictions
    - 8. Be ironic
    - 9. Use metaphors
    - 10. Use rhetorical questions
- 5.5.2 Be vague or ambiguous
  - Violate Manner Maxim
    - 11. Be ambiguous
    - 12. Be vague
    - 13. Over-generalize
    - 14. Displace H
    - 15. Be incomplete, use ellipsis

Appendix III a: Off record strategies (Brown and Levinson 1987: 214).

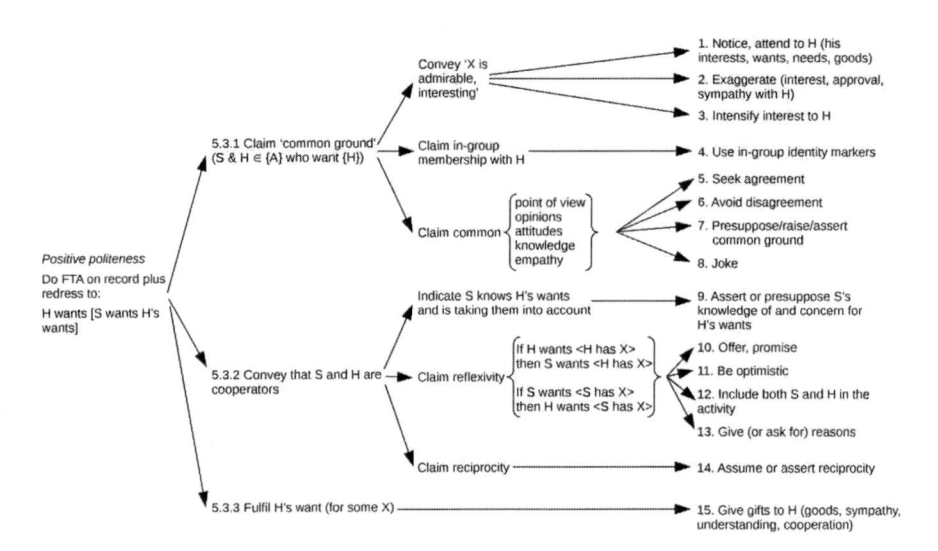

Positive politeness — Do FTA on record plus redress to: H wants [S wants H's wants]

- 5.3.1 Claim 'common ground' (S & H ∈ {A} who want {H})
  - Convey 'X is admirable, interesting'
    - 1. Notice, attend to H (his interests, wants, needs, goods)
    - 2. Exaggerate (interest, approval, sympathy with H)
    - 3. Intensify interest to H
  - Claim in-group membership with H
    - 4. Use in-group identity markers
  - Claim common {point of view, opinions, attitudes, knowledge, empathy}
    - 5. Seek agreement
    - 6. Avoid disagreement
    - 7. Presuppose/raise/assert common ground
    - 8. Joke
- 5.3.2 Convey that S and H are cooperators
  - Indicate S knows H's wants and is taking them into account
    - 9. Assert or presuppose S's knowledge of and concern for H's wants
  - Claim reflexivity
    - If H wants <H has X> then S wants <H has X>
      - 10. Offer, promise
      - 11. Be optimistic
    - If S wants <S has X> then H wants <S has X>
      - 12. Include both S and H in the activity
      - 13. Give (or ask for) reasons
  - Claim reciprocity
    - 14. Assume or assert reciprocity
- 5.3.3 Fulfil H's want (for some X)
  - 15. Give gifts to H (goods, sympathy, understanding, cooperation)

Appendix III b: Positive politeness strategies (Brown and Levinson 1987: 102).

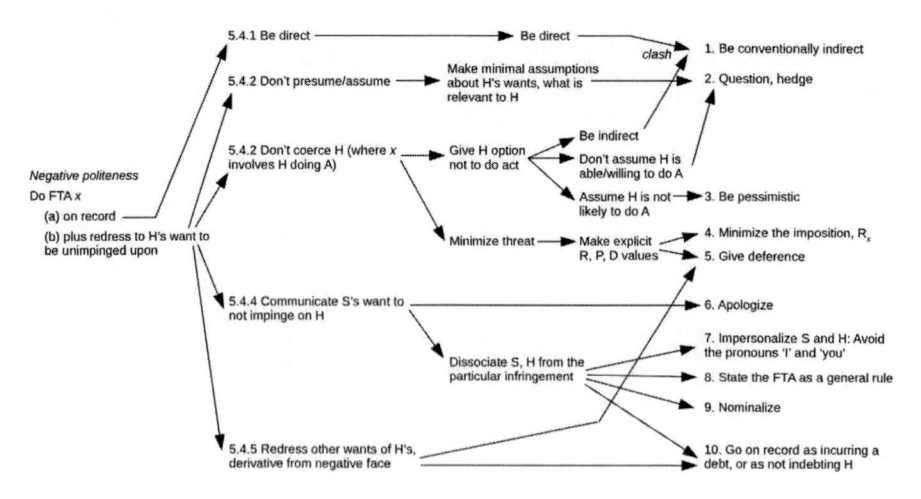

Appendix III: Politeness strategies (Brown and Levinson 1987)

Negative politeness
Do FTA *x*
(a) on record
(b) plus redress to H's want to be unimpinged upon

- 5.4.1 Be direct → Be direct → *clash* → 1. Be conventionally indirect
- 5.4.2 Don't presume/assume → Make minimal assumptions about H's wants, what is relevant to H → 2. Question, hedge
- 5.4.2 Don't coerce H (where *x* involves H doing A) → Give H option not to do act
  - Be indirect
  - Don't assume H is able/willing to do A
  - Assume H is not likely to do A → 3. Be pessimistic
  - Minimize threat → Make explicit R, P, D values
    - 4. Minimize the imposition, R_x
    - 5. Give deference
- 5.4.4 Communicate S's want to not impinge on H
  - 6. Apologize
  - Dissociate S, H from the particular infringement
    - 7. Impersonalize S and H: Avoid the pronouns 'I' and 'you'
    - 8. State the FTA as a general rule
    - 9. Nominalize
- 5.4.5 Redress other wants of H's, derivative from negative face → 10. Go on record as incurring a debt, or as not indebting H

Appendix III c: Negative politeness strategies (Brown and Levinson 1987: 131).

Appendix IV: Transcriptional symbols in conversation analysis

Additional symbols, including those related to gaze and gestures, can be found in Gumperz (1992), Jefferson (2004), Mazeland (2006), and Hoey and Kendrick (2017), who also provide a useful step-by-step procedure and analytical tools.

w[ord	left square bracket marks beginning of overlap
wor]d	right square bracket marks end of overlap
=	no break/gap
(.)	brief interval without talk, within or in between two utterances (untimed pause)
(0.0)	time elapsed in tenths of seconds (timed pause)
sto-	a hyphen indicates a cut-off
wor:d	prolonged sound stretch (the longer the sound, the more colons)
.	a period indicates a falling final pitch contour, a comma is a level or slightly rising pitch contour, a question mark indicates a high rising pitch contour, and an inverted question mark indicates a mid rising pitch contour
,	
?	
¿	
___	stress of a word/sound (the length indicates how light/strong the stress is)
↓↑	local pitch movement shifts into high (or rising) or low (falling) pitch
<slower>	the pace is slower than the talk surrounding it
>faster<	increase in speed of talk (higher pace than the talk surrounding it)
word=	latching, rush into next turn or segment
WORD	loud word compared to those surrounding
°word°	the degree signs signal a soft word compared to those surrounding
w(h)ord	laughter in word
£word	smile voice
(guess)	the transcriber is uncertain about the part of the utterance between parentheses (unclear hearing)
Hh	audible aspiration (exhalation)
.h	audible inbreath (inhalation)
((comment))	transcriber's comment

References

Aberra, Daniel. 2016. Grammaticalisation of the Amharic word *fit* "face" from a body part to grammatical meanings. *Journal of Languages and Culture* 7 (9). 86–92.
Adegbija, Efurosibina. 1989. A comparative study of politeness phenomena in Nigerian English, Yoruba and Ogori. *Multilingua* 8 (1). 57–80.
Agbedor, Paul & Assiba Johnson. 2005. Naming practices in Ewe. In Benjamin Lawrence (ed.), *A Handbook of Eweland*, 161–182. Accra: Woeli Publishers.
Agwuele, Augustine (ed.). 2015. *Body Talk and Cultural Identity in the African World*. Sheffield: Equinox.
Agyekum, Kofi 2002. The communicative role of silence in Akan. *International Pragmatics Association* 12(1). 31–51.
Agyekum, Kofi. 2004a. The sociocultural concept of Face in Akan communication. *Journal of Pragmatics and Cognition* 12 (1). 71–92.
Agyekum, Kofi 2004b. Invective language in contemporary Ghanaian politics. *Journal of Language and Politics* 3(2). 345–75.
Agyekum, Kofi. 2006. The sociolinguistic[s] of Akan personal names. *Nordic Journal of African Studies* 15 (2). 206–235.
Agyekum, Kofi. 2010. The sociolinguistics of thanking in Akan. *Nordic Journal of African Studies* 19 (2). 77–97.
Ag Youssouf, Ibrahim, Allen D. Grimshaw & Charles S. Bird. 1976. Greetings in the desert. *American Ethnologist* 3. 797–824.
Ahearn, Laura. 2012. *Living language: An Introduction to Linguistic Anthropology*. Chichester, UK & Malden, MA: Wiley-Blackwell.
Aikhenvald, Alexandra Y. 2002. *Language Contact in Amazonia*. Oxford: Oxford University Press.
Aikhenvald, Alexandra Y. (ed.). 2010. *Imperatives and Commands*. Oxford: Oxford University Press.
Aikhenvald, Alexandra. Y. 2016. *How Gender Shapes the World*. Oxford & New York: Oxford University Press.
Aikhenvald, Alexandra Y. & R. M. W. Dixon (eds.). 2014. *The Grammar of Knowledge: A Cross-Linguistic Typology*. Oxford: Oxford University Press.
Akinbo, Samuel. 2019. Representation of Yorùbá tones by a talking drum: An acoustic analysis. *Linguistique et Langues Africaines* 5. 11–23.
Akindele, Femi. 1990. A sociolinguistic analysis of Yoruba greetings. *African Languages and Cultures* 3 (1). 1–14.
Akkinaso, Niyi F. 1980. The sociolinguistic basis of Yoruba personal names. *Anthropological Linguistics* 22 (7). 275–304.
Alamin, Suzan, Gerrit J. Dimmendaal & Gertrud Schneider-Blum. 2012. Finding your way in Tima. In Angelika Mietzner & Ulrike Claudi (eds.), *Directionality in Grammar and Discourse: Case Studies from Africa*, 9–33. Cologne: Rüdiger Köppe.
Alba-Juez, Laura & J. Lachlan Mackenzie. 2019. Emotion processes in discourse. In J. Lachlan Mackenzie & Laura Alba-Juez (eds.), *Emotion in Discourse*, 3–26. Amsterdam: John Ben-jamins.
Albert, Ethel M. 1972. Culture patterning of speech behavior in Burundi. In John J. Gumperz & Dell H. Hymes, *Directions in Sociolinguistics. The Ethnography of Communication*, 72–105. New York: Holt, Rinehart & Winston.

Allan, Keith & Kate Burridge. 2006. *Forbidden Words: Taboo and the Censoring of Language.* Cambridge: Cambridge University Press.
Allport, Gordon W. 1954. *The Nature of Prejudice.* Reading, MA: Addison-Wesley.
Amberber, Mengistu. 2001. Testing emotional universals in Amharic. In Jean Harkins & Anna Wierzbicka (eds.), *Emotions in a Crosslinguistic Perspective,* 263–277. Amsterdam & Philadelphia: John Benjamins.
Ameka, Felix K. 1987. A comparative analysis of linguistic routines in two languages: Ewe and English. *Journal of Pragmatics* 11 (3). 299–326.
Ameka, Felix K. 1992a. Interjections: The universal yet neglected part of speech. *Journal of Pragmatics* 18 (2/3). 101–118.
Ameka, Felix K. 1992b. The meaning of phatic and conative interjections. *Journal of Pragmatics* 18 (2–3). 245–271.
Ameka, Felix K. 1994. Areal conversational routines and cross-cultural communication in a multilingual society. In Heiner Puerschel, Elmar Bartsch, Peter Franklin, Ulrich Schmitz & Sonja Vandermeeren (eds.), *Intercultural Communication, Proceedings of the 17th International L.A.U.D. Symposium Duisburg,* 23–27 March 1992, 441–469. Frankfurt a. M.: Peter Lang.
Ameka, Felix K. 1999. 'Partir, c'est mourir un peu': Universal and culture specific features of leave taking. In Jacob Mey & Andrzej Boguslawski (eds.), *'E Pluribus Una': The One in the Many,* 257–284. Odense: Odense University Press.
Ameka, Felix K. 2002. Cultural scripting for body parts for emotions: On 'jealousy' and related emotions in Ewe. *Pragmatics and Cognition* 10 (1). 1–25.
Ameka, Felix K. 2004. Grammar and cultural practices: The grammaticalization of triadic communication in West African languages. *Journal of West African Languages* 30 (2). 5–28.
Ameka, Felix K. 2006. 'When I die, don't cry': The ethnopragmatics of "gratitude" in West African languages. In Cliff Goddard (ed.), *Ethnopragmatics: Understanding Discourse in Cultural Context,* 231–266. Berlin: Mouton de Gruyter.
Ameka, Felix K. 2009. Access rituals in West African communities: An ethnopragmatic perspective. In Gunter Senft & Ellen B. Basso (eds.), *Ritual Communication,* 127–152. Oxford: Berg.
Ameka, Felix K. 2020. "I sh.t in your mouth: Areal invectives in the Lower Volta Basin (West Africa). In Nico Nassenstein & Anne Storch (eds.), *Swearing and Cursing: Contexts and Practices in a Critical Linguistic Perspective,* 121–144. Berlin & New York: Mouton de Gruyter.
Ameka, Felix K. & Anneke Breedveld. 2004. Areal cultural scripts for social interaction in West African communities. *Intercultural Pragmatics* 1(2). 167–188.
Ameka, Felix K. & James Essegbey. 2006. Elements of the grammar of space in Ewe. In Stephen C. Levinson & David Wilkins (eds.), *Grammars of Space: Explorations in Cognitive Diversity,* 359–399. Cambridge & New York: Cambridge University Press.
Ameka, Felix K & Stephen C. Levinson. 2007. Introduction: The typology and semantics of locative predicates: posturals, positionals, and other beasts. *Linguistics* 45(5–6): 847–871.
Ameka, Felix K. & Marina Terkourafi. 2019. What if …? Imagining non-Western perspectives on pragmatic theory and practice. *Journal of Pragmatics* 145. 75–85.
Ameka, Felix K & David P. Wilkins. 2006. Interjections. In Jan Ola Östman & Jef Verschueren (eds.), *Handbook of Pragmatics,* 1–19. Amsterdam and Philadelphia: John Benjamins.
Amha, Azeb. 2001. *The Maale Language.* Leiden: Research School CNWS, Leiden University.

Amha, Azeb. 2013. Directives to humans and to domestic animals: The imperative and some interjections in Zargulla. In Marie-Claude Simeone-Senelle & Martine Vanhove (eds.), *Proceedings of the 5th International conference on Cushitic and Omotic languages*, 211–229. Cologne: Rüdiger Köppe.
Amha, Azeb, James Slotta & Hannah S. Sarvasy. 2021. Singing the individual: Name tunes in Oyda and Yopno. *Frontiers in Psychology* 12: 667599. DOI:10.3389/fpsyg.2021.667599
Amoah, Quincy J. 2020. *Ejok! Experience, Language, and Aesthetico-Moral Expression in Karamoja*. Princeton, NJ: Princeton University PhD dissertation.
Andersen, Elaine S. 1978. Lexical universals of body-part terminology. In Joseph H. Greenberg (ed.), *Universals of Human Language, Vol. 3: Word Structure*, 335–368. Stanford: Stanford University Press.
Anderson, Stephen R. & Edward L. Keenan. 1985. Deixis. In Timothy Shopen (ed.), *Language Typology and Syntactic Description Vol. III: Grammatical categories and the Lexicon*, 259–308. Cambridge: Cambridge University Press.
Andree, Richard. 1878. Ueber den Farbensinn der Naturvölker. *Zeitschrift für Ethnologie* 10. 323–334.
Ankomah, Baffour. 2008. Secret Societies: Africa's Way Forward. *New African* 470.
Ansah, Gladys Nyarko. 2011. Emotion language in Akan: The case of anger. In Gian Claudio Batic (ed.), *Encoding Emotions in African Languages*, 119–137. Munich: LINCOM Europa.
Arnfred, Signe & Maria Paula Meneses. 2018. Mozambican capulanas. Tracing histories and memories. In Sheila Pereira Khan, Maria Paula Meneses & Bjørn Enge Bertelsen (eds.), *Mozambique on the Move: Challenges and Reflections*, 186–210. Leiden & Boston: Brill.
Asante, Molefi K. 1995. *The Book of African Names*. Trenton: Africa World Press.
Arensen, Jonathan E. 1988. Names in the life cycles of the Murle. *Journal of the Anthropological Society of Oxford* 19. 125–130.
Athanasiadou, Angeliki & Elżbieta Tabkowska (eds.). 1998. *Speaking of Emotions: Conceptualisation and Expression*. Berlin & New York: Mouton de Gruyter.
Atkin, Albert. 2010. Peirce's theory of signs. In Edward N. Zalta (ed.), *The Stanford Encyclopedia of Philosophy*, Metaphysics Research Lab, CSLI. [https://plato.stanford.edu/ entries/peirce-semiotics/] (accessed 15 February 2021).
Atkinson, J. Maxwell & John Heritage (eds.). 1985. *Structures of Social Action: Studies in Conversation Analysis*. Cambridge: Cambridge University Press.
Atran, Scott. 1998. Folk biology and the anthropology of science: Cognitive universals and cultural particulars. *Behavioral and Brain Sciences* 21. 547–609.
Atran, Scott, Douglas Medin & Norbert Ross. 2004. Evolution and devolution of knowledge: A tale of two biologies. *Journal of the Royal Anthropological Institute* 10. 395–420.
Augoustinos, M. & I. Walker. 1995. *Social Cognition: An Integrated Introduction*. London: Sage.
Austin, John L. 1962. *How to Do Things with Words*. Oxford: Oxford University Press.
Aziaku, Vincent E. 2014. Sociolinguistic perspectives of animal names among the Ewe of Ghana. In Rainer Vossen (ed.), *African Sociolinguistic and Sociocultural Studies,* 25–40. Cologne: Rüdiger Köppe.
Bakhtin, Mikhail M. 1986. *Speech Genres and Other Late Essays*. Austin: University of Texas Press.
Banti, Giorgio & Francesco Giannattasio. 2004. Poetry. In Alessandro Duranti (ed.), *A Companion to Linguistic Anthropology*, 290–320. Malden, MA & Oxford: Blackwell.
Barasa, David. 2017. *Ateso Grammar: A Descriptive Account of an Eastern Nilotic Language*. Munich: LINCOM.

Barasa, David & Gerrit J. Dimmendaal. To appear. When noun class overcomes gender: Contact-induced grammatical change in Ateso.
Bargery, Rev. G. P. 1951. *A Hausa-English Dictionary and English-Hausa Vocabulary*. London: Oxford University Press.
Bartlett, F. C. 1932. *Remembering*. Cambridge: Cambridge University Press.
Barsalou, Lawrence, W. 1992. Frames, concepts, and conceptual fields. In Adrienne Lehrer & Eva Feder Kittay (eds.), *Frames, Fields, and Contrasts: New Essays in Semantic and Lexical Organization*, 21–67. Hillsdale, NJ: Lawrence Erlbaum.
Bashir, Abeer. 2015. Address and Reference Terms in Midob. *Dotawo: A Journal of Nubian Studies* 2. 133–153.
Basso, Keith H. 1970. "To give up on words": Silence in western Apache culture. *Southwestern Journal of Anthropology* 26 (3). 213–230.
Bateson, G. 1972. *Steps to an Ecology of Mind*. New York: Ballantine.
Batic, Gian Claudio (ed.). 2011. *Encoding Emotions in African Languages*. Munich: LINCOM Europa.
Bauman, Richard. 1983. *Let Your Words Be Few: Symbolism of Speaking and Silence among Seventeenth-Century Quakers*. New York: Cambridge University Press.
Bauman, Richard & Joel Sherzer (eds.). 1974. *Explorations in the Ethnography of Speaking*. Cambridge: Cambridge University Press.
Baumgart, Ursula & Abdellah Bounfour (eds.). 2004. *Le proverbe en Afrique: Forme, fonction et sens*. Paris: L'Harmattan.
Beck, Rose Marie. 2001. *Texte auf Textil in in Ostafrika*. Cologne: Rüdiger Köppe.
Behrend, Heike. 2020. *Menschwerdung eines Affen: Eine Autobiographie der ethnographischen Forschung*. Berlin: Matthes und Seitz.
Behrens, Leila. 2007. Konservierung von Stereotypen mit Hilfe der Statistik. Geert Hofstede und sein kulturvergleichendes Modell. *Arbeitspapier* 51. Universität zu Köln: Allgemeine Sprachwissenschaft/Institut für Linguistik.
Beller, Sieghard & Andrea Bender. 2008. The limits of counting: Numerical cognition between evolution and culture. *Science* 319. 213–215.
Bender, M. Lionel. 1983. Color term encoding in a special lexical domain: Sudanese and Arabic skin colors. *Anthropological Linguistics* 25 (1). 19–27.
Benson, S. 2006. Injurious Names: Naming, disavowal, and recuperation in contexts of slavery and emancipation. In Barbara Bodenhorn & Gabriele vom Bruck (eds.), *The Anthropology of Names and Naming*, 177–199. Cambridge: Cambridge University Press.
Berlin, Brent. 1992. *Ethnobiological Classification: Principles of Categorization of Plants and Animals*. Princeton, NJ: Princeton University Press.
Berlin, Brent & Paul Kay. 1969. *Basic Color Terms: Their Universality and Evolution*. Berkeley: University of California Press.
Bhabha, Homi K. 2004. *The Location of Culture*. Abingdon: Routledge.
Bing, Janet. 1993. Names and honorific pronouns in Gborbo Krahn. In Salikoko S. Mufwene & Lioba Moshi (eds.), *Topics in African Linguistics, Papers from the XXI Annual Conference on African Linguistics, University of Georgia, April 1990*, 119–130. Amsterdam: John Benjamins.
Bird, Charles & Timothy Shopen. 1979. Maninka. In Timothy Shopen (ed.), *Languages and Their Speakers*, 59–111. Cambridge, MA: Winthrop Publishers.
Birdwhistell, Ray L. 1952. *Introduction to Kinesics*. Louisville, KY: University of Louisville Press.

Birdwhistell, Ray L. 1968. Kinesics. *International Encyclopedia of the Social Sciences* 8. 379–385.

Blažek, Václav. 1999. *Numerals: Comparative-etymological Analyses of Numeral Systems and their Implications*. Brno: Masarykova Univerzita.

Blench, Roger M. 2010. Imperial grammar and grassroots categories: Why we should take what people say more seriously. Paper presented at the Workshop on Loss and Gain in Grammar, University of Cologne, 24–26 October. [http://www.rogerblench.info/Language/Africa/ General/Imperial%20grammar.pdf] (accessed 20 January 2022).

Blench, Roger M. 2011. The interaction of phonaesthemes and templatic structures in Kolokuma Ịjọ ideophones. Unpublished paper, Cambridge, Kay Williamson Educational Foundation.

Blench, Roger M. & Selbut Longtau. 2016. Tarok young people's speech. *Sociolinguistic Studies* 10 (1/2). 219–234.

Blommaert, Jan. 2010. *The Sociolinguistics of Globalization*. Cambridge: Cambridge University Press.

Blommaert, Jan. 2015. Commentary: Superdiversity old and new. *Language and Communication* 44. 82–88.

Blommaert, Jan & Ben Rampton. 2011. Language and superdiversity. *Diversities* 13 (2). 1–21.

Bloomfield, Leonard. 1933. *Language*. New York: Henry Holt & Co.

Blount, Ben G. 1969. *Acquisition of Language by Luo Children. Working Paper 19*. Berkeley, CA: University of California, Language-Behavior Research Laboratory.

Blount, Ben G. 1970. The pre-linguistic system of Luo children. *Anthropological Linguistics* 12 (9). 326–342

Blount, Ben G. 1993. Luo personal names: Reference and meaning. In Salikoko S. Mufwene & Lioba Moshi (eds.), *Topics in African Linguistics, Papers from the XXI Annual Conference on African Linguistics*, University of Georgia, April 1990, 131–140. Amsterdam: John Benjamins.

Blount, Ben G. 2011. A history of cognitive anthropology. In David B. Kronenfeld, Giovanni Bennardo, Victor C. de Munck & Michael D. Fischer (eds.), *A Companion to Cognitive Anthropology*, 9–29. Malden, MA & Oxford: Wiley-Blackwell.

Blum-Kulka, Shoshana. 1987. Indirectness and politeness in requests: Same or different? *Journal of Pragmatics* 11. 131–146.

Blum-Kulka, Shoshana & Elite Olshtain. 1984. Requests and apologies: a cross-cultural study of speech act realization patterns (CCSARP). *Applied Linguistics* 5 (3). 196–213.

Blundy, Rachel. 2016. iPhone, Cola, and Kinky: What's in a Hongkongers name? *South China Morning Post*. https://www.scmp.com/news/hong-kong/article/1922277/iphone-cola-and-kinky-whats-hong-kongers-name (accessed 16 September 2020).

Boas, Franz. 1881. *Beiträge zur Erkenntniss der Farbe des Wassers*. Kiel: University of Kiel PhD dissertation.

Boas, Franz. 1891. Some general report on the Indians of British Columbia. *Report of the British Association for the Advancement of Science* 1890. 562–715.

Boas, Franz. 1911. Introduction to *The Handbook of North American Indians*, Vol. I, 1–83. Washington, D.C.: Bureau of American Ethnology Bulletin 40, Part 1, Smithsonian Institution.

Boisson, Claude. 1997. La dénomination des odeurs: variations et régularités linguistiques. *Intellectica* 24 (1). 29–49.

Bonvillain, Nancy. 1993. *Language, Culture and Communication: The Meaning of Messages*. Englewood: Prentice Hall.

Boroditsky, Lera. 2001. Does language shape thought?: Mandarin and English speakers' conceptions of time. *Cognitive Psychology* 43. 1–22.

Boroditsky, Lera, Lauren A. Schmidt & Webb Phillips. 2003. Sex, syntax, and semantics. In Dedre Gentner & Susan Goldin-Meadow (eds.), *Language in Mind: Advances in the Study of Language and Thought*, 61–79. Cambridge, MA: The MIT Press.

Bouquiaux, Luc. 2004. *Linguistique et ethnolinguistique. Anthologie d'articles parus entre 1961 et 2003*. Leuven-Paris-Dudley, MA: Peeters and SELAF.

Bouquiaux, Luc & Jacqueline M. C. Thomas. 1971. *Enquête et description des langues à tradition orale*. Paris: SELAF.

Bouquiaux, Luc & Jacqueline M. C. Thomas. 1992. *Studying and Describing Unwritten Languages*. Dallas: SIL International.

Bouquiaux, Luc & Jacqueline M. C. Thomas (eds). 2013. *L'ethnolinguistique – Haudricourt et nous, ses disciples*. Saint-Martin-au-Bosc: SELAF.

Bourdieu, Pierre. 1979. *Algeria 1960: The Disenchantment of the World, the Sense of Honour, The Kabyle House or the World Reversed*. Cambridge: Cambridge University Press.

Bourdieu, Pierre. 1991. *Language and Symbolic Power*. Cambridge, MA: Harvard University Press.

Bourdieu, Pierre. 1994. *Raisons pratiques: sur la théorie de l'action*. Paris: Editions du Seuil.

Bourgeot, Andre. 2009. Le code rural au Sahel au regard de la pauvreté des pasteurs: le cas des Touaregs du Niger. In Guillaume Duteurtre & Bernard Fayes (eds.), *L'élevage, richesse des pauvres: Stratégies d'éleveurs et organisations sociales face aux risques dans les pays du Sud*, 105–116. Versailles: Éditions Quae.

Bousfield, Derek & Miriam A. Locher (eds.). 2008. *Impoliteness in Language – Studies on its Interplay with Power in Theory and Practice*. Berlin: Mouton de Gruyter.

Boyd, Raymond. 2017. Zande insults. In Nicole Tersis & Pascal Boyeldieu (eds.), *Le langage de l'émotion: variations linguistiques et culturelles*, 55–79. Louvain & Paris: Peeters.

Brenzinger, Matthias. 1999. Personal names of the Kxoe: the example of Tcôò-names. In Mathias Schladt & Yvonne Treis (eds.), *Khoisan Forum* 10. 5–18.

Brookes, Heather. 2014. Gesture in the communicative ecology of a South African township. In Mandana Seyfeddinipur & Marianne Gullberg (eds.), *From Gesture in Conversation to Visible Action as Utterance*, 59–73. Amsterdam & Philadelphia: John Benjamins.

Brown, Cecil H. 1983. Where do cardinal direction terms come from? *Anthropological Linguistics* 25 (2). 121–161.

Brown, Cecil H. 1984. *Language and Living Things: Uniformities in Folk Classification and Naming*. New Brunswick, NJ: Rutgers University Press.

Brown, Cecil H. & Stanley R. Witkowski. 1981. Figurative language in a universalist perspective. *American Ethnologist* 83. 596–611.

Brown, Penelope. 2006. A sketch of the grammar of space in Tzeltal. In Stephen C. Levinson & David P. Wilkins (eds.), *Grammars of Space: Explorations in Cognitive Diversity*, 230–272. Cambridge & New York: Cambridge University Press.

Brown, Penelope & Suzanne Gaskins. 2014. Language acquisition and language socialization. In N. J. Enfield, Paul Kockelman & Jack Sidnell (eds.), *The Cambridge Handbook of Linguistic Anthropology*, 187–226. Cambridge: Cambridge University Press.

Brown, Penelope & Stephen C. Levinson. 1978. Universals in language usage: Politeness phenomena. In E. N. Goody (ed.), *Questions and Politeness: Strategies in Social Interaction*, 56–311. Cambridge: Cambridge University Press.

Brown, Penelope & Stephen C. Levinson. 1987. *Politeness. Some Universals in Language Usage*. Cambridge: Cambridge University Press.
Brown, Roger W. & Eric H. Lenneberg. 1954. A study in language and cognition. *The Journal of Abnormal and Social Psychology* 49. 454–462.
Bucholtz, Mary. 1999. "Why be normal?": Language and identity practices in a community of nerd girls. *Language in Society* 28 (2). 203–223.
Bucholtz, Mary & Kira Hall. 2004. Language and identity. In Alessandro Duranti (ed.), *A Companion to Linguistic Anthropology*, 369–394. Malden, MA & Oxford: Blackwell.
Bulmer, Ralph N. H. 1968. Karam Colour Categories. *Kivung* 1 (3). 120–133.
Bulmer, Ralph N. H. & Michael J. Tyler. 1968. Karam classification of frogs. *Journal of the Polynesian Society* 77. 333–385.
Burling, Robbins. 1964. Cognition and componential analysis: God's truth or hocus-pocus. In Stephen A. Tyler (ed.), *Cognitive Anthropology: Readings*, 419–432. New York: Holt, Rinehart & Winston.
Butler, Judith. 1990. *Gender Trouble: Feminism and the Subversion of Identity*. New York: Routledge.
Bühler, Karl. 1934. *Sprachtheorie: Die Darstellungsfunktion der Sprache*. Jena: Gustav Fischer.
Byon, Andrew Sangpil. 2006. The role of linguistic indirectness and honorifics in achieving linguistic politeness in Korean requests. *Journal of Politeness Research, Language, Behavior, Culture* 2 (2). 247–276.
Casson, Ronald W. (ed.). 1981. *Language, Culture and Cognition: Anthropological Perspectives*. New York: Macmillan.
Casson, Ronald W. 1983. Schemata in cognitive anthropology. *Annual Review of Anthropology* 12. 429–462.
Chala, Dejene Gemechu & Workineh Diribsa Gutama. 2019. The politics of personal name: Naming and self-renaming among the Oromo of Ethiopia. *Nordic Journal of African Studies* 28 (4). 1–21.
Chambers, Mary Ruth. 2009. *Which way is up?: motion verbs and paths of motion in Kubokota, an Austronesian language of the Solomon Islands*. SOAS, University of London: PhD dissertation. DOI:10.25501/SOAS.00026211
Chan, Eugene. *Numeral Systems of the World's Languages*. [https://mpi-lingweb.shh.mpg.de/numeral/] (accessed 20 April 2021).
Chen, M. Keith. 2013. The effect of language on economic behavior: evidence from saving rates, health behaviors, and retirement assets. *American Economic Review* 103 (2). 690–731.
Clamons, Cynthia Robb.1993. Gender assignment in Oromo. In Mushira Eid and Gregory Iverson (eds.), *Principles and Prediction: The Analysis of Natural Language*, 269–280. Amsterdam: John Benjamins.
Clark, Herbert H. 1996. *Using Language*. Cambridge: Cambridge University Press.
Clift, Rebecca. 2016. *Conversation Analysis*. Cambridge: Cambridge University Press.
Coly, Jules Jacques. 2017. Emotion, gazes and gestures in Wolof. In Anne Storch (ed.), *Consensus and Dissent: Negotiating Emotions in the Public Space*, 105–122. Amsterdam & Philadelphia: John Benjamins.
Comrie, Bernard. 2003. Left, right, and the cardinal directions. Some thought on consistency and usage. In Erin Shay & Uwe Seibert (eds.), *Motion, Direction and Location in Languages. In Honor of Zygmunt Frajzyngier*, 51–58. Amsterdam & Philadelphia: John Benjamins.

Comrie, Bernard, 2011. Numeral bases. In Matthew S. Dryer & Martin Haspelmath (eds.), *The World Atlas of Language Structures Online*. Leipzig: Max Planck Institute for Evolutionary Anthropology. [https://wals.info/chapter/131] (accessed 13 January 2021).

Conklin, Harold C. 1955. Hanunóo color categories. *Southwestern Journal of Anthropology* 11 (4). 339–344.

Conklin, Harold C. 1962. Lexicographical treatment of folk taxonomies. *International Journal of American Linguistics* 28. 119–141.

Conklin, Harold C. 1964. Hanunóo color categories. In Dell H. Hymes (ed.), *Language in Culture and Society: A Reader in Linguistics and Anthropology*, 189–192. New York: Harper and Row.

Conklin, Harold C. 1972. *Folk Classification: A Topically Arranged Bibliography of Contemporary and Background References Through 1971*. New Haven, CT: Department of Anthropology, Yale University.

Coote, Jeremy. 1992. Marvels of everyday vision: The anthropology of aesthetics and the cattle-keeping Nilotes. In Jeremy Coote & Anthony Shelton (eds.), *Anthropology, Art and Aesthetics*, 245–273. Oxford & New York: Oxford University Press.

Corballis, Michael C. 2014. The word according to Adam: The role of gesture in language evolution. In Mandana Seyfeddinipur & Marianne Gullberg (eds.), *From Gesture in Conversation to Visible Action as Utterance,* 177–197. Amsterdam & Philadelphia: John Benjamins.

Coupland, Nikolas. 2007. *Style: Language Variation and Identity*. Cambridge: Cambridge University Press.

Creider, Chet A. 1977. Towards a description of East African gestures. *Sign Language Studies* 14. 1–20.

Culpeper, Jonathan. 2005. Impoliteness and entertainment in the television quiz show: The weakest link. *Journal of Politeness Research* 1 (1). 35–72.

Culpeper, Jonathan. 2011. *Impoliteness. Using Language to Cause Offence*. Cambridge: Cambridge University Press.

Cysouw, Michael & Jeff Good. 2013. Languoid, doculect, and glossonym: Formalizing the notion 'language'. *Language Documentation & Conservation* 7. 331–359. [http://hdl.handle.net/10125/4606] (accessed 8 February 2021).

D'Andrade, Roy. 1995. *The Development of Cognitive Anthropology*. Cambridge: Cambridge University Press.

Danzinger, Eve. 2010. Deixis, gesture and cognition in spatial frame of reference typology. *Studies in Language* 34 (1). 167–185.

Darnell, Regna & Judith T. Irvine. 1997. A biographical memoir. In *Office of the Home Secretary, National Academy of Sciences: Biographical Memoirs*, Vol. 71. 279–299. Washington D.C.: National Academies Press.

Davies, Ian R. L. & Greville G. Corbett. 1997. Colour categories in African languages: A test of the Berlin & Kay theory of colour universals. In R. K. Herbert (ed.), *African Linguistics at the Crossroads: Papers from Kwaluseni*, 581–598. Cologne: Rüdiger Köppe.

Dawkins, Richard. 1976. *The Selfish Gene*. Oxford: Oxford University Press.

de Bruijn, Mirjam, Francis Nyamnjoh & Inge Brinkman (eds.). 2009. *Mobile Phones: The New Talking Drums of Everyday Africa*. Bamenda, CM & Leiden, NL: Langaa & African Studies Centre.

de Fina, Anna. 2007. Code-switching and the construction of ethnic identity in a community of practice. *Language in Society* 36 (3). 371–392.

de Kadt, Elizabeth. 1992. Requests as speech acts in Zulu. *South African Journal of African Languages* 12 (3). 101–106.

de Kadt, Elizabeth. 1995. The cross-cultural study of directives: Zulu as a non-typical language. *South African Journal of Linguistics/Suid-Afrikaanse Tydskrif vir Taalkunde,* Supplement 27. 45–72.

Demolin, Didier, Anthony Traill, Gilles Sicard & Jean-Marie Hombert. 2016. Odour terminology in !Xóõ. In Rainer Vossen & Wilfrid H. G. Haacke (eds), *Lone Tree. Scholarship in Service of the Koon, Essays in Memory of Anthony T. Traill,* 107–118. Cologne: Rüdiger Köppe.

Demaris, Ovid. 2019. *The Lucky Luciano Story, The Mafioso and the Violent 30s.* Mountain View, CA: Ishi Press.

Demuth, Katherine. 1987. Prompting routines in the language socialization of Basotho children. In Bambi Schieffelin & Elinor Ochs (eds.), *Language Socialization across Cultures,* 51–79. Cambridge & New York: Cambridge University Press.

Deng, Francis Madeng.1973. *The Dinka and Their Songs.* Oxford: Oxford University Press.

de Saussure, Ferdinand. 1916. *Cours de linguistique générale.* Paris: Payot.

Deutscher, Guy. 2010. *Through the Language Glass: Why the World Looks Different in Other Languages.* New York: Metropolitan Books and Henry Holt and Company.

de Valois, Russell L., Israel Abramov & Gerald H. Jacobs. 1966. Analysis of response patterns of LGN cells. *Journal of the Optical Society of America* 56. 966–977.

de Valois, Russell L. & Gerald H. Jacobs. 1968. Primate color vision. *Science* 162. 533–540.

de Voogt, Alex. 1997. *Mancala: The Board Game in Africa and Asia.* London: British Museum Press.

Dialo, Amadou. 1985. *Eléments expressifs du wolof contemporain: gestes, signaux oraux, unités significatives nasalisées, interjections, onomatopées, impressifs.* Dakar: Centre de linguistique appliquée de Dakar.

Diessel, Holger. 2012. Deixis and demonstratives. In Claudia Maienborn, Klaus von Heusinger & Paul Portner (eds.), *An International Handbook of Natural Language Meaning,* Vol. 3, 2407–2431. Berlin: Mouton de Gruyter.

Di Garbo, Francesca & Yvonne Agbetsoamedo. 2018. Non-canonical gender in African languages: A typological survey of interactions between gender and number, and between gender and evaluative morphology. In Sebastian Fedden, Jenny Audring & Greville G. Corbett (eds.), *Non-Canonical Gender Systems,* 176 –210. Oxford: Oxford University Press.

Dimmendaal, Gerrit J. 1983. *The Turkana Language.* Dordrecht: Foris Publications.

Dimmendaal, Gerrit J. 1991. Some observations on evolutionary concepts in current linguistics. In Walburga von Raffler-Engel, Jan Wind & Abraham Jonker (eds.), *Studies in Language Origins,* Vol. 2, 225–244. Amsterdam & Philadelphia: John Benjamins.

Dimmendaal, Gerrit J. 1995. Studying lexical-semantic fields in languages: nature versus nurture, or Where does culture come in these days? *Frankfurter Afrikanistische Papiere* 7. 1–29.

Dimmendaal, Gerrit J. 1996. Attitude markers and conversational implicatures in Turkana speech acts. *Studies in Language* 20. 259–284.

Dimmendaal, Gerrit J. 2000. Morphology. In Bernd Heine & Derek Nurse (eds.), *African Languages: An Introduction,* 161–193. Cambridge: Cambridge University Press.

Dimmendaal, Gerrit J. 2001. Places and people: Field sites and informants. In Paul Newman & Martha Ratliff (eds.), *Linguistic Fieldwork,* 55–75. Cambridge: Cambridge University Press.

Dimmendaal, Gerrit J. 2010. Language description and "the new paradigm": What linguists may learn from ethnocinematographers. *Language Documentation and Conservation* 4. 152–158.

Dimmendaal, Gerrit J. 2011. *Historical Linguistics and the Comparative Study of African Languages*. Amsterdam & Philadelphia: John Benjamins.

Dimmendaal, Gerrit J. 2014a. The grammar of knowledge in Tima. In Alexandra Y. Aikhenvald & R. M. W. Dixon (eds.), *The Grammar of Knowledge – A Cross-Linguistic Perspective*, 245–259. Leiden & Boston: Brill.

Dimmendaal, Gerrit J. 2014b. Attitude markers in Nilotic in a cross-linguistic perspective. *Studies in Nilotic Linguistics* 8. 1–14.

Dimmendaal, Gerrit J. 2015a. *The Leopard's Spots: Essays on Language, Cognition and Culture*. Leiden & Boston: Brill.

Dimmendaal, Gerrit J. 2015b. Semantic categorization and cognition. In Nancy Bonvillain (ed.), *The Routledge Handbook of Linguistic Anthropology*, 13–25. London: Taylor and Francis.

Dimmendaal, Gerrit J. 2018. Introduction. In Gertrud Schneider-Blum, Birgit Hellwig & Gerrit J. Dimmendaal (eds.), *Nuba Mountain Language Studies: New Insights*, 1–11. Cologne: Rüdiger Köppe.

Dimmendaal, Gerrit J. 2020. Linguistic isolates. In Rainer Vossen & Gerrit J. Dimmendaal (eds.), *The Oxford Handbook of African Languages*, 428–436. Oxford: Oxford University Press.

Dimmendaal, Gerrit J. 2022a. Nilo-Saharan – An overview. In Bedilu Wakjira, Ronny Meyer & Zelealem Leyew (eds.), *The Oxford Handbook of Ethiopian Languages*. London: Oxford University Press.

Dimmendaal, Gerrit J. 2022b. Comparative linguistics and language change in accretion zones: A view from the Nuba Mountains. In Na'ama Pat-El, Patience Epps & Danny Law (eds.), *Historical Linguistics and Endangered Languages: Exploring Diversity in Language Change*, 155–181. London: Routledge.

Dimmendaal, Gerrit J. 2022c. Emerging languages and the creation of new communicative styles. In Svenja Völkel & Nico Nassenstein (eds.), *Approaches to Language and Culture*, 77–100. Berlin: De Gruyter Mouton.

Dimmendaal, Gerrit J. & Franz Rottland. 1996. Projective space and spatial orientation in some Nilotic and Surmic languages. In Petr Zima (ed.), *Space and Direction in Languages*, 66–78. Prague: Institute of Advanced Studies at Charles University and Academy of Sciences of the Czech Republic.

Dimmendaal, Gerrit J., & Gertrud Schneider-Blum. To appear. Locative expressions and their semantic extensions in Tima. In James Essegbey & Enoch O. Aboh (eds.), *Locative Expressions*. Amsterdam and Philadelphia: John Benjamins.

Dimmendaal, Gerrit J., Gertrud Schneider-Blum & Nataliya Veit. To appear. Locative nouns, split ergativity and argument properties in Tima.

Dingemanse, Mark. 2011. *The Meaning and Use of Ideophones in Siwu*. Nijmegen: Radboud University PhD dissertation.

Dingemanse, Mark & Simeon Floyd. 2014. Conversation across cultures. In N. J. Enfield, Paul Kockelman & Jack Sidnell (eds.), *The Cambridge Handbook of Linguistic Anthropology*, 447–480. Cambridge: Cambridge University Press.

Dingemanse, Mark, Joe Blythe & Tiko Dirksmeyer. 2014. Formats for other-initiation of repair across languages: An exercise in pragmatic typology. *Studies in Language* 38 (1). 5–43.

Dioli, Maurizio. 2018. Nomad aesthetic: Cattle modifications among the northern Turkana of north west Kenya. *Pastoralism: Research, Policy, and Practice* 8 (1). 1–10.

Dixon, R. M. W. 1972. *The Dyirbal Language of North Queensland*. Cambridge: Cambridge University Press.
Dixon, R. M. W. 1982. *Where Have all the Adjectives Gone, and Other Essays in Semantics and Syntax*. Berlin: Mouton.
Dixon, R. M. W. 2010. *I am a Linguist*. Leiden & Boston: Brill.
Dixon, R. M. W. 2015. *Edible Gender, Mother-In-Law Style, & Other Grammatical Wonders: Studies in Dyirbal, Yidiñ, & Warrgamay*. Oxford: Oxford University Press,
Doke, Clement M. & Benedict W. Vilakazi. 1958. *Zulu-English Dictionary*, 2nd edition. Johannesburg: Witwatersrand University Press.
Douglas, Mary 1996. *Natural Symbols: Explorations in Cosmology*, 2nd edition. London: Routledge.
Dournes, Jacques. 1978. Les races de couleurs: Une optique jörai (Viet-Nam). In Serge Tornay (ed.), *Voir et nommer les couleurs*, 369–399. Nanterre: Service de Publication du Laboratoire de'Ethnologie et de Sociologie comparative de l'Université de Paris X.
Drew, Paul & John Heritage. 2006a. *Conversation Analysis. Volume III: Turn Design and Action Formation*. London: Sage.
Drew, Paul & John Heritage. 2006b. *Conversation Analysis. Volume IV: Institutional Interactions*. London: Sage.
Dufon, Margaret A., Gabriele Kasper, Satomi Takahashi & Naoko Yoshinaga. 1994. Bibliography on linguistic politeness. *Journal of Pragmatics* 21 (5). 527–578.
Duranti, Alessandro. 1984. Intentions, self and social theories of meaning: Words and social action in a Samoan context. *Center for Human Information Processing Report* No. 122. La Jolla, CA: Center for Human Information Processing.
Duranti, Alessandro. 1988. Intention, language, and social action in Samoa. *Journal of Pragmatics* 12. 13–33.
Duranti, Alessandro. 1990. Doing things with words: Conflict, understanding, and change in a Samoan *fono*. In Karen Ann Watson-Gegeo & Geoffrey M. White (eds.), *Disentangling Conflict Discourse in Pacific Societies*, 459–489. Stanford, CA: Stanford University Press.
Duranti, Alessandro. 1997a. *Linguistic Anthropology*. Cambridge: Cambridge University Press.
Duranti, Alessandro. 1997b. Universal and culture-specific properties of greetings. *Journal of Linguistic Anthropology* 7(1). 63–97.
Duranti, Alessandro. 2003. Language as culture in U.S. Anthropology: Three paradigms. *Current Anthropology* 44 (3). 323–347.
Duranti, Alessandro (ed.). 2004. *A Companion to Linguistic Anthropology*. Malden, MA & Oxford: Blackwell.
Duranti, Alessandro, Elinor Ochs & Bambi B. Schieffelin (eds.). 2011. *The Handbook of Language Socialization*. Malden, MA: Wiley Blackwell.
Dziebel, German Valentinovitch. 2007. *The Genius of Kinship: The Phenomenon of Human Kinship and the Global Diversity of Kinship Terminologies*. Amherst, NY: Cambria Press.
Eckert, Penelope. 2000. *Linguistic Variation as Social Practice: The Linguistic Construction of Identity in Belten High*. Cambridge, MA: Blackwell.
Eckert, Penelope. 2019. The limits of meaning: Social indexicality, variation, and the cline of interiority. *Language* 95 (4). 751–776.
Eckert, Penelope & Sally McConnell-Ginet. 1992. Communities of practice: Where language, gender, and power all live. In Kira Hall, Mary Bucholtz & Birch Moonwomon (eds.), *Locating Power, Proceedings of the 1992 Berkeley Women and Language Conference*, April 4–5, 89–99. Berkeley, CA: Berkeley Women and Language Group University of California.

Eelen, Gino. 2001. *A Critique of Politeness Theories*. London and New York: Routledge.
Egbert, Maria M. 1997. Schisming: The collaborative transformation from a single conversation to multiple conversations. *Research on Language and Social Interaction* 30 (1). 1–51.
Egblewogbe, E.Y. 1984. Personal names as a parameter for the study of culture: The case of Ghanaian Ewe. In François de Medeiros (ed.), *Peuples du Golfe du Bénin (Aja-Ewe)*, 209–220. Paris: Karthala.
Ekman, Paul, Wallace V. Friesen, Maureen O'Sullivan, Anthony Chan, Irene Diacoyanni-Tarlatzis, Karl Heider, Rainer Krause, William Ayhan LeCompte, Tom Pitcairn, Pio E. Ricci-Bitti, Klaus Scherer, Masatoshi Tomita & Athanase Tzavaras. 1987. Universal and cultural difference in the judgments of facial expressions of emotions. *Journal of Personality and Social Psychology* 53 (4). 712–717.
Elsworth, P. C. 1994. Sense, culture, and sensibility. In S. Kitayama & H. R. Markus (eds.), *Emotion and Culture: Empirical Studies of Mutual Influence*, pp. 23–50. American Psychological Association
Enfield, N. J. 2001. 'Lip-pointing': A discussion of form and function with reference to data from Laos. *Gesture* 1. 185–221.
Enfield, N. J. (ed). 2002. *Ethnosyntax: Explorations in Grammar and Culture*. Oxford: Oxford University Press.
Enfield, N. J., Paul Kockelman & Jack Sidnell (eds.). 2014. *The Cambridge Handbook of Linguistic Anthropology*. Cambridge: Cambridge University Press.
Enfield, N. J., Asifa Majid & Miriam van Staden (eds.). 2006. Parts of the body: cross-linguistic categorisation. [Special issue]. *Language Sciences* 28 (2–3). 137–360.
Enfield, N. J. & Anna Wierzbicka. 2002. Introduction: the body in description of emotion. [Special issue]. *Pragmatics and Cognition* 10 (1/2). 1–25.
Essien, Okon. 1997. What is in a name? A linguistic and cultural explication of Ibibio personal names. In H. Ekkehard Wolff & Orin D. Gensler (eds.), *Proceedings of the 2nd World Congress of African Linguistics*, Leipzig 1997, 103–130. Cologne: Rüdiger Köppe.
Evans, Nicholas. 2003. Context, culture, and structuration in the languages of Australia. *Annual Review of Anthropology* 32. 13–40.
Evans, Nicholas. 2009. Two *pus* one makes thirteen. *Linguistic Typology* 13 (2). 321–335.
Evans, Nicholas. 2010. *Dying Words: Endangered Languages and What They Have to Tell Us*. Oxford: Blackwell.
Evans, Nicholas & Stephen C. Levinson. 2009. The myth of language universals: Language diversity and its significance for cognitive science. *Behavioral and Brain Sciences* 32. 429–492.
Evans, Nicholas & David P. Wilkins. 2000. In the mind's ear: The semantic extension of perception verbs in Australian languages. *Language* 76 (3). 546–592.
Evans, Vyvyan. 2014. *The Language Myth: Why Language Is Not An Instinct*. Cambridge: Cambridge University Press.
Evans-Pritchard, Edward E. [1956] 1962. *Social Anthropology and Other Essays*. New York: Free Press.
Everett, Daniel L. 2012. *Language: The Cultural Tool*. New York: Pantheon Books.
Fabian, Johannes. 1983. *Time and the Other: How Anthropology Makes its Objects*. New York: Columbia University Press.
Farghal, Mohammed & Abdullah Shakir. 1994. Kin terms and titles of address as relational social honorifics in Jordanian Arabic. *Anthropological Linguistics* 6 (2). 240–253.

Fauconnier, Gilles. 1985. *Mental Spaces: Aspects of Meaning Construction in Natural Language*. Cambridge, MA: The MIT Press.
Fauconnier, Gilles. 1997. *Mappings in Thought and Language*. Cambridge: Cambridge University Press.
Fauconnier, Gilles & Mark Turner. 2002. *The Way We Think: Conceptual Thinking and the Mind's Hidden Complexities*. New York: Basic Books.
Faye, C. U. 1923–5. The influence of "Hlonipa" on the Zulu clicks. *Bulletin of the School of Oriental and African Studies* 3. 757–782.
Fehn, Anna-Maria. 2011. Some notes on traditional Ts'ixa gesture inventories. In Gabriele Sommer & Clarissa Vierke (eds.), *Speech Acts and Events in African Languages*, 145–168. Cologne: Rüdiger Köppe.
Ferry, Marie-Paule. 1977. Les noms des hommes et des masques chez les Basari du Sénégal oriental. In Geneviève Calame-Griaule (ed.), *Langage et cultures africaines: Essais d'ethnolinguistique*, 84–99. Paris: François Maspero.
Fillmore, Charles J. 1975a. An alternative to checklist theories of meaning. In Cathy Cogen (ed.), *Proceedings of the First Annual Meeting of the Berkeley Linguistics Society, February 15–17*, 123–131. Berkeley, CA: Berkeley Linguistics Society.
Fillmore, Charles J. 1975b. Topics in lexical semantics. In Roger W. Cole (ed.), *Current Issues in Linguistic Theory*, 76–138. Bloomington: Indiana University Press.
Fillmore, Charles J. 1976. Frame semantics and the nature of language. *Annals of the New York Academy of Sciences* 280. 20–32.
Fillmore, Charles J. & Collin Baker. 2009. A frames approach to semantic analysis. In Bernd Heine & Heiko Narrog (eds.), *The Oxford Handbook of Linguistic Analysis*, 313–340. Oxford: Oxford University Press.
Finlayson, Rosalyn. 1995. Women's language of respect: Isihlonipho Sabafazi. In Rajend Mesthrie (ed.), *Language and Social History. Studies in South African Sociolinguistics*, 140–153. Cape Town & Johannesburg: Philip.
Fleisch, Axel. 2020. Cognition and language. In Rainer Vossen & Gerrit J. Dimmendaal (eds.), *The Oxford Handbook of African Languages*, 780–794. Oxford: Oxford University Press.
Fleming, Harold, 2006. *Ongota: A Decisive Language in African Prehistory*. Wiesbaden: Harrassowitz.
Fleming, Luke, Alice Mitchell & Isabelle Ribot. 2019. In the name of the father-in-law: Patriarchy and the sociolinguistic prehistory of eastern and southern Africa. *Sociolinguistic Studies* 13(2–4). 171–192.
Foley, William A. 1997. *Anthropological Linguistics: An Introduction*. Oxford: Blackwell Publishers.
Foolen, Ad. 2019. The value of left and right. In J. Lachlan Mackenzie & Laura Alba-Juez (eds.), *Emotions in Discourse*, 139–158. Amsterdam and Philadelphia: John Benjamins.
Frake, Charles O. 1964. How to ask for a drink in Subanun. *American Anthropologist* 66 (6). 127–132.
Frake, Charles O. 1972. Struck by speech: The Yakan concept of litigation. In John J. Gumperz & Dell H. Hymes (eds.), *Directions in Sociolinguistics*, 127–132. New York: Holt, Rinehart & Winston.
Galton, F. 1853. *The Narrative of an Explorer in Tropical South Africa*. London: Murray. http://galton.org/books/south-west-africa/galton-1853-tropical-sa-1st.pdf (accessed 23 October 2020)

García, Ofelia & Li Wei. 2014. *Translanguaging: Language, Bilingualism, and Education.* New York: Palgrave MacMillan.

Gardner, Peter M. 1972. The Paliyans. In Marco G. Bicchieri (ed.), *Hunters and Gatherers Today,* 404–447. New York: Holt, Rinehart & Winston.

Gass, Susan M. & Joyce Neu (eds.). 2006. *Speech Acts across Cultures: Challenges to Communication in a Second Language.* Berlin & New York: Mouton de Gruyter.

Geeraerts, Dirk. 1988a. Where does prototypicality come from? In Brygida Rudzka-Ostyn (ed.), *Topics in Cognitive Linguistics,* 207–232. Amsterdam: John Benjamins.

Geeraerts, Dirk 1988b. Cognitive grammar and the history of lexical semantics. In Brygida Rudzka-Ostyn (ed.), *Topics in Cognitive Linguistics,* 647–677. Amsterdam: John Benjamins.

Geertz, Clifford. 1973. *The Interpretation of Cultures: Selected Essays.* New York: Basic Books.

Geiger, Lazarus. 1878. Über den Farbensinn der Urzeit und seine Entwickelung. Gesprochen auf der Versammlung deutscher Naturforscher in Frankfurt a. M., den 24.9.1867. In *Zur Entwickelungsgeschichte der Menschheit.* 2nd edn., 45–60. Stuttgart: Verlag der Cotta'schen Buchhandlung.

Gil, David. 2013. Para-linguistic usages of clicks. In Matthew S. Dryer & Martin Haspelmath (eds.), *The World Atlas of Language Structures Online.* Leipzig: Max Planck Institute for Evolutionary Anthropology. https://wals.info/chapter/142.

Gladstone, William Ewart. 1858. *Studies on Homer and the Homeric Age.* 3 Vols. Oxford: Oxford University Press.

Goddard, Cliff & Anna Wierzbicka (eds.). 2014. *Words and Meanings. Lexical Semantics Across Domains, Languages and Cultures.* Oxford: Oxford University Press.

Goffman, Erving. 1967. *Interaction Ritual: Essays on Face-to-Face Behavior.* Chicago: Aldine.

Goffman, Erving. 1971. *Relations in Public: Microstudies of the Public Order.* New York: Basic Books.

Goffman, Erving. 1981. *Forms of Talk.* Philadelphia, PA: University of Pennsylvania Press.

Goldschmidt, Walter. 1976. Absent eyes and idle hands: Socialization for low affect among the Sebei. In Theodore Schwartz (ed.), *Socialization as Cultural Communication,* 65–72. Berkeley, CA: University of California Press.

Goodenough, Ward H. 1956. Componential analysis and the study of meaning. *Language* 32 (1). 195–216.

Goodenough, Ward H. 1957. Cultural anthropology and linguistics. In Paul L. Garvin (ed.), *Report of the Seventh Annual Round Table Meeting on Linguistics and Language Study,* 167–173. Washington, D.C.: Georgetown University.

Goody, Esther. 1972. 'Greeting', 'begging', and the presentation of respect. In Jean S. la Fontaine (ed.), *The Interpretation of Ritual: Essays in Honour of A. I. Richards,* 39–72. London: Tavistock Publications.

Gough, David H. 1996. Thinking in Xhosa and speaking in English: The theory and practice of contrastive analysis. *South African Journal of Applied Language Studies* 4. 2–19.

Goyvaerts, Didier L. 1980. Counting in Logo. *Anthropological Linguistics* 22. 317–328.

Greenberg, Joseph H. 1946. *The Influence of Islam on a Sudanese Religion.* New York: J. J. Augustin.

Greenberg, Joseph H. 1963. *The Languages of Africa.* Bloomington & The Hague: Indiana University Press, Research Center in Anthropology, Folklore and Linguistics & Mouton.

Greenberg, Joseph H. 1978. Generalizations about numeral systems. In Joseph H. Greenberg, Charles A. Ferguson & Edith A. Moravcsik (eds.), *Universals of Human Language, Volume 3: Word Structure,* 249–295. Stanford, CA: Stanford University Press.

Greenberg, Joseph H., Charles A. Ferguson & Edith A. Moravcsik (ed.). 1978. *Universals of Human Language Volumes 1–4*. Stanford, CA: Stanford University Press.

Greenberg, Joseph H. 1980. Universals of kinship terminology: Their nature and the problem of their explanation. In Jacques Maquet (ed.), *On Linguistic Anthropology: Essays in Honor of Harry Hoijer*, 9–32. Malibu, CA: Undena Publications.

Greenberg, Joseph H. 1983. Some areal characteristics of African languages. In Ivan R. Dihoff (ed.), *Current Approaches to African Linguistics Vol. 1*, 3–31. Dordrecht: Foris.

Greenberg, Joseph H. 1986. On being a linguistic anthropologist. *Annual Review of Anthropology* 15. 1–24.

Gregersen, Edgar A. 1974. The signaling of social distance. In William W. Gage (ed.) *Language in its Social Setting*, 47–55. Washington, D.C.: Anthropological Society of Washington.

Grenoble, Lenore A., Martina Martinović, & Rebekah Baglini. 2015. Verbal gestures in Wolof. In Ruth Kramer, Elizabeth C. Zsiga & One Tlale Boyer (eds.), *Selected Proceedings of the 44th Annual Conference on African Linguistics*, 110–121. Somerville, MA: Cascadilla Proceedings Project.

Grice, H. Paul. 1975. Logic and conversation. In Peter Cole & Jerry L. Morgan (eds.), *Syntax and Semantics, Vol. 3: Speech Acts*, 41–58. New York: Academic Press.

Grimm, Nadine. 2012. Color categories in language contact: 'Pygmy' hunter-gatherers and Bantu farmers. *Proceedings of the Annual Meeting of the Berkeley Linguistics Society* 38: 31–45.

Grosfoguel, Ramón. 2007. The epistemic decolonial turn: Beyond political-economy paradigms. *Cultural Studies* 21 (2–3). 211–223.

Gudykunst, William B. & Bella Mody (eds.). 2002. *Handbook of International and Intercultural Communication*. Thousand Oaks, CA: Sage.

Guillaume, Antoine & Harold Koch (eds.). 2021. *Associated Motion*. Berlin: Mouton de Gruyter.

Güldemann, Tom. 2007. Clicks, genetics, and "proto-world" from a linguistic perspective. *University of Leipzig Papers on Africa*, 29.

Güldemann, Tom. 2018. Did Proto-Tuu have a paradigm of cardinal numerals? In Klaus Beyer, Gertrud Boden, Bernhard Köhler & Ulrike Zoch (eds.), *Linguistics across Africa*, 133–148. Cologne: Rüdiger Köppe.

Gulliver, Philip H. 1958. Counting with the fingers by two African tribes (Arusha and Turkana). *Tanganyika Notes* 51. 259–262.

Gumperz, John J. 1968. The speech community. In Pier Paolo Giglioli (ed.), *Language and Social Context*, 219–231. Harmondsworth: Penguin.

Gumperz, John J. 1975. Foreword. In Mary Sanches & Ben G. Blount (eds.), *Sociocultural Dimensions of Language Use*, xi–xxi. New York: Academic Press.

Gumperz, John J. 1982a. *Discourse Strategies*. Cambridge: Cambridge University Press.

Gumperz, John J. (ed.). 1982b. *Language and Social Identity*. Cambridge: Cambridge University Press.

Gumperz, John J. 1992. Contextualization and understanding. In Alessandro Duranti & Charles Goodwin (eds.), *Rethinking Context: Language as an Interactive Phenomenon*, 229–252. Cambridge: Cambridge University Press.

Gumperz, John J. & Jenny Cook-Gumperz. 1982. Introduction: Language and the communication of social identity. In John J. Gumperz (ed.), *Language and Social Identity*, 1–21. Cambridge: Cambridge University Press.

Gumperz, John J. & Dell Hymes.1964. The ethnography of communication. *American Anthropologist* 66(6). 137–153.

Gumperz. John J. & Dell H. Hymes (eds.). 1972. *Directions in Sociolinguistics. The Ethnography of Communication*. New York: Holt, Rinehart & Winston.

Gumperz, John J. & Stephen C. Levinson (eds.). 1996. *Rethinking Linguistic Relativity*. Cambridge: Cambridge University Press.

Habwe, John. 2010. Politeness phenomena: a case of Kiswahili honorifics. *Swahili Forum* 17. 126–142.

Hakulinen, Auli & Fred Karlsson. 1977. Den finländska tystnaden. Nagra teoretiska, deskriptiva och kontrastiva bidrag [The Finnish silence. Some theoretical, descriptive, and contrastive comments.] In Tove Skutnabb-Kangas & Olaug Rekdal (eds.), *Vardagsskrifter till Jan och Jens* [Working-day papers to Jan and Jens]. Uppsala: Institut för nordiska sprak.

Hale, Kenneth L. 1973. Deep-surface canonical disparities in relation to analysis and change: an Australian example. In Thomas Sebeok (ed.), *Current Trends in Linguistics*, Vol. 11, 401–458. The Hague: Mouton.

Hale, Kenneth L. 1975. Gaps in grammar and culture. In M. Dale Kindade, Kenneth L. Hale & Oswald Werner (eds.), *Linguistics and Anthropology. In Honor of C. F. Voegelin*, 295–315. Lisse: Peter de Ridder Press.

Hale, Kenneth L. 1986. Notes on world view and semantic categories: Some Warlpiri examples. In Pieter Muysken & Henk van Riemsdijk (eds.), *Features and Projections*, 233–254. Dordrecht: Foris.

Hale, Thomas A. 1998. *Griots and Griottes: Masters of Words and Music*. Bloomington, IN: Indiana University Press.

Hall, Edward T. 1959. *The Silent Language*. Garden City, NY: Doubleday.

Hall, Edward T. 1963. A system for the notation of proxemic behavior. *American Anthropologist* 65 (5). 1003–1026.

Harrison, K. David. 2007. *When Languages Die: The Extinction of the World's Languages and the Erosion of Human Knowledge*. Oxford & New York: Oxford University Press.

Hammarström, Harald. 2010. Rarities in numeral systems. In Jan Wohlgemuth & Michael Cysouw (eds.), *Rethinking Universals: How Rarities Affect Linguistic Theory*, 11–60. Berlin: Mouton de Gruyter.

Hanks, William F. 1996. *Language and Communicative Practices*. Oxford & Boulder, CO: Westview.

Hanks, William F. 2005. Explorations in the deictic field. *Current Anthropology* 46 (2). 191–220.

Hanks, William F. 2009. Fieldwork on deixis. *Journal of Pragmatics* 41 (1). 10–24.

Hardman, Martha J. 1981. Jaqaru color terms. *International Journal of American Linguistics* 41 (1). 66–68.

Harshberger, J. W. 1896. The purpose of ethnobotany. *Botanical Gazette* 21. 146–154.

Hasegawa, Yoko. 2009. Book Review: Politeness, Richard J. Watts (2003). *International Journal of the Sociology of Language* 199. 133–138.

Haugh, Michael. 2007. The discursive challenge to politeness research: an interactional alternative. *Journal of Politeness Research* 3 (2). 295–317.

Haviland, John B. 1992. Anchoring, iconicity, and orientation in Guugu Yimidhirr pointing gestures. *Cognitive Anthropology Research Group Working Paper 8*. Max Planck Institute for Psycholinguistics, Nijmegen, the Netherlands.

Haviland, John B. 1993. Anchoring, iconicity, and orientation in Guugu Yimidhirr pointing gestures. *Journal of Linguistic Anthropology* 3 (1). 3–45.

Haviland, John B. 1998. Guugu Yimithirr cardinal directions. *Ethos* 26 (1). 25–47.

Haviland, John B. 2004. Gesture. In Alessandro Duranti (ed.), *A Companion to Linguistic Anthropology*, 197–221. Malden, MA & Oxford: Blackwell.

Hayward, Richard. 1991. À propos patterns of lexicalization in the Ethiopian language area. In Daniela Mendel & Ulrike Claudi (eds.), *Ägypten im afro-orientalischen Kontext: Aufsätze zur Archäologie, Geschichte und Sprache eines unbegrenzten Raumes, Gedenkschrift Peter Behrens (Afrikanistische Arbeitspapiere Sondernummer)*, 139–156. Cologne: University of Cologne, Institute for African Studies.

Heider, Eleanor R. 1972. Universals of color naming and memory. *Journal of Experimental Psychology* 93. 10–20.

Heine, Bernd. 1997. *Cognitive Foundations of Grammar*. Oxford & New York: Oxford University Press.

Henrich, Joseph, Steven J. Heine & Ara Norenzayan. 2010. The weirdest people in the world? *Behavioral and Brain Sciences* 33 (2/3). 61–83.

Herbert, Robert K. 1990. The sociolinguistics of clicks in Southern Bantu. *Anthropological Linguistics* 32 (3/4). 295–315.

Herdt, Gilbert (ed.).1994. *Third Sex, Third Gender: Beyond Sexual Dimorphism in Culture and History*. New York: Zone Books.

Hewes, Gordon W. 1973. Primate communication and the gestural origins of language. *Current Anthropology* 14. 5–24.

Hickerson, Nancy. 1971. Review of Berlin and Kay (1969). *International Journal of American Linguistics* 37. 257–270.

Hickmann, Maya & Stéphane Robert (eds.).2006. *Space in Languages. Linguistic Systems and Cognitive Categories*. Amsterdam & Philadelphia: John Benjamins.

Hieda, Osamu. 1991. Koegu vocabulary with a reference to Kara. *African Study Monographs, Supplement* 14. 1–70.

Hill, Jane H. 1988. Language, culture and world view. In Frederick J. Newmeyer (ed.), *Linguistics: The Cambridge Survey*. Vol. 4: *Language: The Socio-Cultural Context*, 14–36. Cambridge: Cambridge University Press.

Hill, Jane H. 1999. Language, race, and white public space. *American Anthropologist* 100 (3). 680–689.

Hill, Jane H. & Judith T. Irvine. 1992. Introduction. In Jane H. Hill & Judith T. Irvine (eds.), *Responsibility and Evidence in Oral Discourse*, 1–23. Cambridge: Cambridge University Press.

Hill, Jane H. & Bruce Mannheim. 1992. Language and world view. *Annual Review of Anthro-pology* 21. 381–406.

Hoben, Susan J. 1976. The meaning of the second-person pronouns in Amharic. In M. Lionel Bender (ed.), *Language in Ethiopia*, 281–288. London: Oxford University Press.

Hock, Hans Henrich & Brian D. Joseph 1996. L*anguage History, Language Change and Language Relationship: An Introduction to Historical and Comparative Linguistics*. Berlin: Mouton de Gruyter.

Hoey, Elliott M. 2017. Sequence recompletion: A practice for managing lapses in conversation. *Journal of Pragmatics* 109. 47–63.

Hoey, Elliott M. & Kobin H. Kendrick 2017. Conversation analysis. In Annette M. B. de Groot & Peter Hagoort (eds.), *Research Methods in Psycholinguistics and the Neurobiology of Language: A Practical Guide*, 151–173. Hoboken (NJ): Wiley-Blackwell.

Hofstede, Geert. 1991. *Cultures and Organisations. Software of the Mind – Intercultural Cooperation and its Importance for Survival*. London/New York: McGraw-Hill.

Hogan, Sister Peter Marie. 1967. *An Ethnography of Communication among the Ashanti*. Austin, TX: Texas-Penn Working Papers in Sociolinguistics.

Hollington, Andrea. 2015. *Travelling Conceptualizations: A Cognitive and Anthropological Linguistic Study of Jamaican*. Amsterdam & Philadelphia: John Benjamins.

Hollington, Andrea. 2017. Emotions in Jamaican: African conceptualizations, emblematicity and multimodality in discourse and public spaces. In Anne Storch (ed.), *Consensus and Dissent: Negotiating Emotion in the Public Space*, 81–104. Amsterdam & Philadelphia: John Ben-jamins.

Hollington, Andrea. 2019. Muroora – reflections on women and taboo in Zimbabwe. *The Mouth* 4. 108–116.

Hollington, Andrea, Nico Nassenstein, Angelika Mietzner, Anne Storch & Sara Zavaree (eds.). 2020. The Other's Other. [Special Issue]. *Journal of Postcolontial Linguistics* 4.

Hombert, Jean-Marie. 1992. Terminologie des odeurs dans quelques langues du Gabon. *Pholia* 7. 61–65.

Homburger, Lilias. 1929. *Noms des parties du corps dans les langues Négro-Africaines*. Paris: Librairie Ancienne Honoré Champion.

Hoymann, Gertie. 2010. Questions and responses in ǂĀkhoe Haillom. *Journal of Pragmatics* 42. 2726–2740.

Huber, Hugo. 1969. 'Woman-marriage' in some East African societies. *Anthropos* 63/64. 745–752.

Hunn, Eugene. 1982. The utilitarian factor in folk biological classification. *American Anthropologist* 84. 830–847.

Hunn, Eugene. 2006. Ethnoscience. In Keith Brown (ed.), *Encyclopedia of Language and Linguistics*, 2nd edn., 258–260. Amsterdam: Elsevier.

Hunter, Linda. 1982. Silence is also language: Hausa attitudes about speech and language. *Anthropological Linguistics* 24 (4). 389–409.

Hurst, Ellen. 2008. *Style, Structure and Function in Cape Town Tsotsitaal*. Cape Town: Uni-versity of Cape Town PhD dissertation. [http://hdl.handle.net/11427/10934] (accessed 15 April 2021).

Hurst, Ellen & Rajend Mesthrie. 2013. "When you hang out with the guys they keep you in style": The case for considering style in descriptions of South African tsotsitaals. *Language Matters* 44(1). 3–20.

Hurst-Harosh, Ellen. 2020. *Tsotsitaal in South Africa: Style and Metaphor in Youth Language Practices*. Cologne: Rüdiger Köppe.

Huylebrouck, Dirk. 2019. *Africa and Mathematics: From Colonial Findings Back to the Ishango Rods*. Cham: Springer.

Hymes, Dell H. 1962. The ethnography of speaking, In Thomas Gladwin & William C. Sturtevant (eds.), *Anthropology and Human Behavior*, 13–53. Washington, D.C.: The Anthropology Society of Washington.

Hymes, Dell H. 1964. *Language in Culture and Society: A Reader in Linguistics and Anthropology*. New York: Harper & Row.

Hymes, Dell H. 1966. Two types of linguistic relativity (with examples from Amerindian ethnography). In William Bright (ed.), *Sociolinguistics: Proceedings of the UCLA sociolinguistics conference 1964*, 114–167. The Hague: Mouton.

Hymes, Dell H. 1968. The ethnography of speaking. In Joshua A. Fishman (ed.), *Readings in the Sociology of Language*, 99–138. The Hague: Mouton.

Hymes, Dell H. 1974. Ways of speaking. In Richard Bauman & Joel Sherzer (eds.), *Explorations in the Ethnography of Speaking*, 431–453. Cambridge: Cambridge University Press.
Ide, Sachiko. 1993. Preface: The search for integrated universals for linguistic politeness. *Multilingua* 12 (1). 7–11.
Ige, Busayo. 2010. Identity and language choice: 'We equals I'. *Journal of Pragmatics* 42. 3047–3054.
Ikoro, Suanu. 1994. Numeral classifiers in Kana. *Journal of African Languages and Linguistics* 15. 7–28.
Imai, Mutsumi & Dedre Gentner. 1993. Linguistic relativity vs. universal ontology: cross-linguistic studies of the object/substance distinction. In Katharine Beals, Gina Cooke, David Kathman, Sotaro Kita, Karl-Erik McCullough & David Testen (eds.), *What We Think, What We Mean and How We Say It: Papers from the Parasession on the Correspondence of Conceptual, Semantic and Grammatical Representations*, 171–186. Chicago: Chicago Linguistic Society.
Irvine, Judith T. 1974. Strategies of status manipulation in the Wolof greetings. In Richard Bauman & Joel Sherzer (eds.), *Explorations in the Ethnography of Speaking*, 167–191. New York: Cambridge University Press.
Irvine, Judith T. 1990. Registering affect: heteroglossia in the linguistic expression of emotion. In Catherine A. Lutz & Lila Abu-Lughod (eds.), *Language and the Politics of Emotion*, 126–161. Cambridge: Cambridge University Press.
Irvine, Judith T. 1992. Insult and responsibility: Verbal abuse in a Wolof village. In Jane H. Hill & Judith T. Irvine (eds.), *Responsibility and Evidence in Oral Discourse*, 105–134. Cambridge: Cambridge University Press.
Irvine, Judith T. 2009. Honorifics. In Gunter Senft, Jan-Ola Östman & Jef Verschueren (eds.), *Culture and Language Use*, 156–172. Amsterdam & Philadelphia: John Benjamins.
Irvine, Judith T. 2011. Société et communication chez les Wolof à travers le temps et l'espace. In Anna M. Diagne, Sascha Kesseler & Christian Meyer (eds.), *Communication wolof et société sénégalaise: Héritage et creation*, 37–70. Paris: L'Harmattan.
Irvine, Judith. 2017. Language and social hierarchy in West Africa. *Oxford Research Encyclopedia*. DOI:10.1093/acrefore/9780199384655.013.239
Irvine, Judith T. & Suzanne Gal. 2000. Language ideology and linguistic differentiation. In Paul V. Kroskrity (ed.), *Regimes of Language: Ideologies, Polities, and Identities*, 35–84. Santa Fe, NM: School of American Research Press.
Jakobi, Angelika. 1990. *A Fur Grammar – Phonology, Morphophonology, and Morphology*. Hamburg: Helmut Buske.
Jakobson, Roman. 1957. *Shifters, Verbal Categories, and the Russian Verb*. Cambridge, MA: Harvard University Aust Language Project.
Jakobson, Roman. 1959. On linguistic aspects of translation. In Reuben A. Brower (ed.), *On Translation*, 232–239. Cambridge, MA: Harvard University Press.
Jakobson, Roman. 1960. Closing statement: Linguistics and poetics. In Thomas A. Sebeok, (ed.), *Style in Language*, 350–377. Cambridge, MA: Technology Press & John Wiley & Sons.
James, William. 1890. *The Principles of Psychology*. New York: Henry Holt and Company.
Jaworski, Adam (ed). 1997. *Silence: Interdisciplinary Perspectives*. Berlin: Mouton de Gruyter.
Jefferson, Gail 1984. Notes on some orderlinesses of overlap onset. In V. d'Urso and P. Leonardi (eds.), *Discourse Analysis and Natural Rhetorics*, 11–38. Padova: CLEUP.
Jefferson, Gail 1986. Notes on latency in overlap onset. *Human Studies* 9. 153–183.

Jefferson, Gail 2004. Glossary of transcript symbols with an introduction. In Gene H. Lerner (ed.), *Conversation Analysis*, 13–31. Amsterdam & Philadelphia: John Benjamins.
Jernudd, Björn & Geoffrey M. White. 1983. The concept of basic colour terms: Variability in For and Arabic. *Anthropological Linguistics* 25 (1). 61–81.
Joswig, Andreas. 2019. *The Majang Language*. Amsterdam: Landelijke Onderzoekschool Taalwetenschap.
Kádár, Dániel Z. & Michael Haugh. 2013. *Understanding Politeness*. Cambridge: Cambridge University Press.
Kant, Emmanuel. 1781. *Kritik der reinen Vernunft*. Riga: Hartknoch.
Kasanga, Luanga A. 2011. Face, politeness, and speech acts: Reflecting on intercultural interaction in African languages and varieties of English. In Gabriele Sommer & Clarissa Vierke (eds.), *Speech Acts and Speech Events in African Languages*, 41–64. Cologne: Rüdiger Köppe.
Kasanga, Luanga A. & Joy-Christine Lwanga-Lumu. 2007. Cross-cultural linguistic realization of politeness: A study of apologies in English and Setswana. *Journal of Politeness Research: Language, Behaviour, Culture* 3 (1). 65–92.
Kasper, Gabriele. 1990. Linguistic politeness: Current research issues. *Journal of Pragmatics* 14 (2). 193–218.
Kay, Paul & Willett Kempton. 1984. What is the Sapir-Whorf hypothesis? *American Anthropologist* 86. 65–79.
Kay, Paul & Chad K. McDaniel. 1975. *Color Categories As Fuzzy Sets*. Language Behavior Research Laboratory, University of California at Berkeley, Working Paper 44.
Kay, Paul & Chad K. McDaniel. 1978. The linguistic significance of the meanings of basic color terms. *Language* 54. 610–646.
Kay, Paul, Brent Berlin & William Merrifield. 1991. Biocultural implications of color naming. *Journal of Linguistic Anthropology* 1. 12–25.
Katriel, Tamar. 1985. "Griping" as a verbal ritual in some Israeli discourse. In Marcelo Dascal (ed.), *Dialogue: An Interdisciplinary Approach*, 367–382. Amsterdam & Philadelphia: John Benjamins.
Keenan, Edward Louis & Elinor Ochs. 1979. Becoming a competent speaker of Malagasy. In Timothy Shopen (ed.), *Languages and Their Speakers*, 113–157. Philadelphia: University of Pennsylvania Press.
Keller, Rudi. 1994. *Sprachwandel: Von der unsichtbaren Hand in der Sprache*. 2nd edn. Tübingen: Francke.
Kendon, Adam. 1975a. Introduction. In Adam Kendon, Richard M. Harris & Mary R. Key (eds.), *Organization of Behavior in Face-to-Face Interaction*, 1–16. The Hague & Paris: Mouton.
Kendon, Adam. 1975b. Gesticulation, speech, and the gesture theory of language origins. *Sign Language Studies* 9. 349–373.
Kendon, Adam. 1983. Gesture and Speech: How they interact. In John M. Wiemann & Randall P. Harrison (eds.), *Nonverbal Interaction*, 13–46: Beverly Hills, CA: Sage Publications.
Kendon, Adam. 1985. Some uses of gesture. In Deborah Tannen & Muriel Saville-Troike (eds.), *Perspectives on Silence*, 215–234. Norwood: Alex.
Kendon, Adam. 2004. *Gesture: Visible Action as Utterance*. Cambridge: Cambridge University Press.
Khachaturyan, Maria. 2019. Inclusory pronouns in Mande: The emergence of a typological rarum. *Folia Linguistica* 53(1). 87–123.

Kießling, Roland & Maarten Mous. 2004. Urban youth languages in Africa. *Anthropological Linguistics* 46 (3). 303–341.
Kießling, Roland, Maarten Mous & Derek Nurse. 2008. The Tanzanian Rift Valley area. In Bernd Heine & Derek Nurse (eds.), *A Linguistic Geography of Africa*, 186–227. Cambridge: Cambridge University Press.
Kießling, Roland, Britta Neuman & Doreen Schröter. 2011. "O owner of the compound, those things you are saying – it is the talk of vagueness!": requesting, complaining and apologizing in two languages of the Cameroonian Grassfields. In Gabriele Sommer & Clarissa Vierke (eds.), *Speech Acts and Speech Events in African Languages*, 83–144. Cologne: Rüdiger Köppe.
Kilian-Hatz, Christa, and Mathias Schladt. 1997. From body to soul: On the structure of body part idioms. *Afrikanistische Arbeitspapiere* 49. 61–80.
Kimenyi, Alexandre. 1989. *Kinyarwanda and Kirundi Names: A Semiolinguistic Analysis of Bantu Onomastics*. Lewiston: Edwin Mellen Press.
Kimura, Daiji, 2001. Utterance overlap and long silence among the Baka Pygmies: Comparison with Bantu farmers and Japanese university students. *African Study Monographs* 26. 103–121.
Kimura, Daiji. 2003. Bakas' mode of co-presence. *African Study Monographs* 28. 25–35.
Kissine, Mikhail. 2020. Autism, constructionism and nativism. *Language* 96 (3). 1–35.
Kita, Sotaro (ed.). 2003. *Pointing: Where Language, Culture, and Cognition Meet*. Mahwah, N.J.: Lawrence Erlbaum Associates Publishers.
Kita, Sotaro. 2009. Cross-cultural variation of speech-accompanying gesture: A review. *Language and Cognitive Processes* 24 (2). 145–167.
Kita, Sotaro & James Essegbey. 2001. Pointing left in Ghana: How a taboo on the use of the left hand influences gestural practice. *Gesture* 1. 73–95.
Kirchhoff, Alfred. 1879. Über Farbensinn und Farbenbezeichnung der Nubier. *Zeitschrift für Ethnologie* 11. 397–402.
Koni Muluwa, J. 2010. La dénomination de plantes en mbuun, mpiin et nsong: Procédé de création lexicale et principes sémantiques. In Karsten Legère & Christina Thornell (eds.), *Bantu Languages: Analyses, Description and Theory*, 99–114. Cologne: Rüdiger Köppe.
Koops, Robert 2009. *A Grammar of Kuteb: A Jukunoid Language of Central Nigeria*. Cologne: Rüdiger Köppe.
Koptjevskaja-Tamm, Maria (ed.). 2015. *The Linguistics of Temperature*. Amsterdam and Philadelphia: John Benjamins.
Kövecses, Zoltán. 2000. *Metaphor and Emotion: Language, Culture, and Body in Human Feeling*. Cambridge & Paris: Cambridge University Press & Editions de la Maison des Sciences de l'Homme.
Kraska-Szlenk, Iwona. 2014. Semantic extensions of body parts: Common patterns and their interpretation. *Language Sciences* 44. 15–39.
Kraska-Szlenk, Iwona. 2018. Address inversion in Swahili: Usage patterns, cognitive motivation and cultural factors. *Cognitive Linguistics* 29 (3). 545–584.
Kremer, Arndt J. & Nadia Di Massi. 2008. *Küssen in Köln: Ein Kuss-Wegweiser durch die Domstadt*. Cologne: Emons.
Kroskrity, Paul V. 2004. Language ideologies. In Alessandro Duranti (ed.), *A Companion to Linguistic Anthropology*, 496–517. Malden, MA & Oxford: Blackwell.
Kunene, Daniel P. 1958. Notes on Hlonepha among the Southern Sotho. *African Studies* 17. 159–182.

Kutsch Lojenga, Constance L. 1994. *Ngiti: A Central-Sudanic Language of Zaire*. Cologne: Rüdiger Köppe.
Labov, William. 1972. *Sociolinguistic Patterns*. Philadelphia: University of Pennsylvania Press.
Lacan, Jacques. 1978. *Le moi dans la théorie de Freud et dans la technique de la psychanalyse*. Paris: Editions du Seuil.
Lakoff, George. 1987. *Women, Fire and Dangerous Things: What Categories Reveal About the Mind*. Chicago: Chicago University Press.
Lakoff, George & Mark Johnson. 1980. *Metaphors We Live By*. Chicago: University of Chicago Press.
Lakoff, Robin T. 1973. The logic of politeness: Or, minding your p's and q's. In Claudia W. Corum, Thomas C. Smith-Stark & Ann Weiser (eds.), *Papers from the Ninth Regional Meeting of the Chicago Linguistic Society*, 292–305. Chicago: Chicago Linguistic Society.
Langacker, R. W. 1991. *Foundations of Cognitive Grammar. Vol. 2: Descriptive Applications*. Stanford, CA: Stanford University Press.
Langley, Myrtle. 1979. *The Nandi of Kenya: Life Crisis Rituals in a Period of Change*. New York: St. Martin's Press.
Lavandera, Beatriz R. 2004. The social pragmatics of politeness forms. In Keith Brown (ed.), *Encyclopedia of Language and Linguistics, Vol. 2*, 1196–1205. 2nd edition. Elsevier.
Lave, Jean & Etienne Wenger. 1991. *Situated Learning: Legitimate Peripheral Participation*. Cambridge: Cambridge University Press.
Laver, John D. M. H. 1992. Linguistic routines and politeness in greeting and parting. In Florian Coulmas (ed.), *Conversational Routine: Explorations in Standardized Communication Situations and Prepatterned Speech*, 289–304. The Hague: Mouton.
Lee, Penny. 2009. Benjamin Lee Whorf. In Gunter Senft, Jan-Ola Östman & Jef Verschueren (eds.), *Culture and Language Use*, 256–272. Amsterdam & Philadelphia: John Benjamins.
Leech, Geoffrey N. 1980. *Explorations in Semantics and Pragmatics*. Amsterdam: John Benjamins.
Leech, Geoffrey N. 2014. *The Pragmatics of Politeness*. Oxford & New York: Oxford University Press.
Legère, Karsten. 2020. Language and ethnobotany. In Rainer Vossen & Gerrit J. Dimmendaal (eds.), *The Oxford Handbook of African Languages*, 732–749. Oxford: Oxford University Press.
Lehtonen, Jaakko & Kari Sajavaara. 1985. The silent Finn. In Deborah Tannen & Muriel Savil-le-Troike (eds.), *Perspectives on Silence*, 193–201. Norwood, NJ: Ablex.
Leikola, Kirsi. 2014. *Talking Manjo: Repertoires as Means of Negotiating Marginalization*. Helsinki: University of Helsinki PhD dissertation.
Lenneberg, Eric H. & J. Roberts. 1956. *The Language of Experience: A Study in Methodology*. Baltimore: Waverly Press.
Leonardi, Cherry. 2013. *Dealing with Government in South Sudan: Histories of Chiefship, Community & State*. London: James Currey.
Leslau, Wolf. 1959. Taboo expressions in Ethiopia. *American Anthropologist* 61 (1). 105–108.
Levinson, Stephen C. 1992. *Language and Cognition: Cognitive Consequences of Spatial Description in Guugu-Yimidhirr*. Working paper no.13. Nijmegen, the Netherlands: Cognitive Anthropology Research Group, Max Planck Institute for Psycholinguistics.
Levinson, Stephen C. 2003a. *Space in Language and Cognition: Explorations in Cognitive Diversity*. Cambridge: Cambridge University Press.

Levinson, Stephen C. 2003b. Contextualizing 'contextualization cues'. In Susan L. Eerdmans, Carlo L. Prevignano & Paul J. Thibault (eds.), *Language and Interaction, Discussions with John J. Gumperz*, 24–30. Amsterdam and Philadelphia: John Benjamins.

Levinson, Stephen C. 2018. Introduction: Demonstratives: Patterns in diversity. In Stephen C. Levinson (ed.), *Demonstratives in Cross-Linguistic Perspective*, 1–42. Cambridge: Cambridge University Press.

Levinson, Stephen C. & Penelope Brown.1994. Immanuel Kant among the Tenejapans: An-thropology as empirical philosophy. *Ethos* 22. 3–41.

Levinson, Stephen C., Penelope Brown, Eve Danzinger, Lourdes De Léon, John B. Haviland, Eric Pederson & Gunter Senft. 1992. Man and tree & space games. In Stephen C. Levinson (ed.), *Space Stimuli Kit 1.2*, 7–14. Nijmegen: Max Planck Institute for Psycholinguistics.

Levinson, Stephen C. & David P. Wilkins (eds). 2006. *Grammars of Space: Explorations in Cognitive Diversity*. Cambridge & New York: Cambridge University Press.

Lévi-Strauss, Claude. 1958. *Anthropologie structurale*. Paris: Librairie Plon.

Levitan, Carmel A., Jiana Ren, Andy T. Woods, Sanne Boesveldt, Jason S. Chan, Kirsten J. McKenzie, Michael Dodson, Jai A. Levin, Christine X. R. Leong & Jasper J. F. van den Bosch. 2014. Cross-cultural color-odor associations. *Plos One* [https://journals.plos.org/plosone/article?id=10.1371/journal.pone.01016] (accessed 20 May 2021).

Levy, Robert I. 1973. *Tahitians: Mind and Experience in the Society Islands*. Chicago: University of Chicago Press.

Leyew, Zelealem. 2004. The cardinal numerals of Nilo-Saharan languages. In Akinbi Akinlabi & Oluseye Adesola (eds.), *Proceedings of the 4th World Congress of African Linguistics, New Brunswick, 2003*, 237–258. Cologne: Rüdiger Köppe.

Leyew, Zelealem. 2011. *Wild Plant Nomenclature and Traditional Botanical Knowledge among Three Ethnolinguistic Groups in Northwestern Ethiopia*. Addis Ababa: OSSREA.

Lichtenberk, Frantisek. 2000. Inclusory pronominals. *Oceanic Linguistics* 39. 1–32.

Liddicoat, Anthony J. 2007. *An Introduction to Conversation Analysis*. London & New York: Continuum.

Lienhardt, Godfrey. 1961. *Divinity and Experience: The Religion of the Dinka*. Oxford: Oxford University Press.

Lienhardt, Godfrey. 1988. Social and cultural implications of some African personal names. *Journal of the Anthropological Society of Oxford* 19. 105–116.

Lionnet, Florian. 2020. Paralinguistic use of clicks in Chad. In Bonny Sands (ed.), *Handbook of Clicks*, 422–437. Leiden & Boston: Brill.

López Rúa, Paula. 2003. *Birds, Colours and Prepositions: The Theory of Categorization and its Applications in Linguistics*. Munich: LINCOM.

Lounsbury, Floyd G. 1956. A semantic analysis of the Pawnee kinship usage. *Language* 32. 158–194.

Lounsbury, Floyd G. 1964. A formal analysis of the Crow and Omaha-type kinship terminologies. In Ward H. Goodenough (ed.), *Explorations in Cultural Anthropology: Essays in Honor of George Peter Murdock*, 351–393. New York: McGraw Hill.

Loveday, Leo. 1981. Pitch, politeness and sexual role: An exploratory investigation into pitch correlates of English and Japanese politeness formulae. *Language and Speech* 24. 71–89.

Lucassen, Deborah. 1994. *Notes on Chai*. Leiden, NL: Leiden University MA thesis.

Lucy, John A. 1985. Whorf's view of the linguistic mediation of thought. In Elizabeth Mertz & Richard J. Parmentier (eds.), *Semiotic Mediation: Sociocultural and Psychological Perspectives*, 73–97. Orlando: Academic Press.

Lucy, John A. 1992a. *Language Diversity and Thought: A Reformulation of the Linguistic Relativity Hypothesis*. Cambridge: Cambridge University Press.

Lucy, John A. 1992b. *Grammatical Categories and Cognition: A Case Study of the Linguistic Relativity Hypothesis*. Cambridge: Cambridge University Press.

Lüpke, Friederike & Anne Storch. 2013. *Repertoires and Choices in African Languages*. Boston & Berlin: de Gruyter.

Lusekelo, Amani. 2018. Terms for cardinal directions in Eastern Bantu Languages. *Journal of the Humanities (Zomba)* 26. 49–71.

Lwanga-Lumu, Joy-Christine. 1999. Politeness and indirectness revisited. *South African Journal of African Languages* 19 (2). 83–92.

Lydall, Jean & Ivo Strecker. 1979. *The Hamar of Southern Ethiopia, Vol. 1: Work Journal*. Hohenschäftlarn: Renner.

Mackenzie, J. Lachlan & Laura Alba-Juez (eds.). 2019. *Emotions in Discourse*. Amsterdam: John Benjamins.

Mackie, Vera C. 1983. Japanese children and politeness. *Papers of the Japanese Study Centre* 6. Melbourne.

MacLaury, Robert E. 1992. From brightness to hue: An explanatory model of color-category evolution. *Current Anthropology* 33. 137–163.

MacLaury, Robert E. 2009. Taxonomy. In Gunter Senft, Jan-Ola Östman & Jef Verschueren (eds.), *Culture and Language Use*, 248–255. Amsterdam & Philadelphia: John Benjamins.

Madubuike, Ihechukwu. 1976. *A Handbook of African Names*. Washington, D.C.: Three Continents Press.

Majid, Asifa. 2012. Current emotion research in the language sciences. *Emotion Review* 4 (4). 432–443.

Majid, Asifa & Niclas Burenhult. 2014. Odors are expressible in language, as long as you speak the right language. *Cognition* 130 (2). 266–270.

Makoni, Sinfree & Alastair Pennycook (eds.). 2006. *Disinventing and Reconstituting Languages*. Multilingual Matters. DOI:10.21832/9781853599255.

Malinowski, Bronisław. 1923. The problem of meaning in primitive languages. In Charles K. Ogden & Ivor A. Richards (eds.), *The Meaning of Meaning: A Study of Influence of Language upon Thought and of the Science of Symbolism*, 296–336. London: Routledge & Kegan Paul.

Malinowski, Bronisław 1936. *The Foundations of Faith and Morals: An Anthropological Analysis of Primitve Beliefs and Conduct with Special Reference to the Fundamental Problems of Religion and Ethics*. London: Oxford University Press.

Malotki, Ekkehart. 1983. *Hopi Time: A Linguistic Analysis of the Temporal Concepts in the Hopi Language*. Berlin: Mouton Publishers

Manfredi, Stefano. To appear. An areal typology of kin terms in the Nuba Mountain Languages.

Mao, Lu Ming R. 1994. Beyond politeness theory: 'Face' revisited and renewed. *Journal of Pragmatics* 21. 451–486.

Marshall, Lorna.1976. *The !Kung of Nyae Nyae*. Cambridge, MA: Harvard University Press.

Mashiri, Pedzisai. 2005. The language of ethnic contempt: Malawian-Zimbabwean-Shona rivalry. *Zambezia: The Journal of Humanities of the University of Zimbabwe* 32(1). 1–29.

Mathiot, Madeleine. 1962. Noun classes and folk taxonomy in Papago. *American Anthropologist* 64 (2). 340–350.

Matisoff, James. 1979. *Blessings, Curses, Hopes and Fears: Psycho-ostensive Expressions in Yiddish*. Philadelphia: Institute for the Study of Human Issues.

Matisoff, James. 1986. Hearts and minds in South-East Asian languages and English: An essay in the comparative lexical semantics of psycho-collocations. *Cahiers de Linguistique Asie Orientale* 15 (1). 5–57.
Matsumoto, Yoshiko. 1989. Politeness and conversational universals – Observations from Japanese. *Multilingua* 8 (2/3). 207–221.
Maturana, Humberto R. & Francisco J. Varela. 1987. *The Tree of Knowledge: The Biological Roots of Human Understanding.* Boston: New Science Library.
Mauss, Marcel. 1968. *Sociologie et anthropologie.* Quatrième edition. Paris: Les Presses universitaires de France, 1968,
Mayer, Mercer. 1969. *Frog, Where Are you?* New York: Dial Books for Young Readers.
Mazeland, Harrie. 2006. Conversation analysis. In Keith Brown (ed.), *Encyclopedia of Language and Linguistics,* 2nd edn., 153–163. Amsterdam: Elsevier.
Mbaya, Maweja. 2002. Linguistic taboo in African marriage context: A study of the Oromo *Laguu. Nordic Journal of African Studies* 11 (2). 224–235.
Mbembe, Joseph A. 2016. Decolonizing the university: New directions. *Arts and Humanities in Higher Education* 15 (1). 29–45.
McClave, Evelyn. 2007. Potential cognitive universals. Evidence from head movements in Turkana. In Susan D. Duncan, Justine Cassell & Elena T. Levy (eds.), *Gesture and the Dynamic Dimension of Language: Essays in Honor of David McNeill,* 91–98. Amsterdam & Philadelphia: John Benjamins.
McDonough, Laraine, Soonja Choi & Jean M. Mandler. 2003. Understanding spatial relations: flexible infants, lexical adults. *Cognitive Psychology* 46 (3). 229–259.
McGruder, Juli H. 2004. Madness in Zanzibar: An exploration of lived experience. In Janis D. Jenkins & Robert J. Barrett (eds.), *Schizophrenia, Culture and Subjectivity,* 255–282. Cambridge: Cambridge University Press.
McIntyre, Joe A. 1980. The language of Hausa greetings: the social construction of hierarchy. *Afrika und Übersee* 63. 39–67.
McKnight, David. 1999. *People, Countries and the Rainbow Serpent: Systems of Classification among the Ladil of Mornington Island.* New York & Oxford: Oxford University Press.
Mc Laughlin, Fiona (ed.). 2009. *The Languages of Urban Africa.* London: Continuum
McNeill, David. 1992. *Hand and Mind: What Gestures Reveal about Thought.* Chicago & London: University of Chicago Press.
McNeill, David. 2012. *How Language Began: Gesture and Speech in Human Evolution.* Cambridge: Cambridge University Press.
McWhorter, John. 2014. *The Language Hoax: The World Looks the Same in Any Language.* Oxford: Oxford University Press.
Mead, Margaret. 1942. *Balinese Character: A Photographic Analysis.* New York Academy of Sciences.
Meerpohl, Meike. 2012. *The Tima of the Nuba Mountains (Sudan): A Social-Anthropological Study.* Cologne: Rüdiger Köppe.
Meeussen, A. E. 1975. Possible linguistic Africanisms (Fifth Hans Wolff Memorial Lecture). *Language Sciences* 35. Bloomington, IN: Indiana University.
Merleau-Ponty, Maurice. 1945. *Phénoménologie de la perception.* Paris: La Libraire Gallimard.
Mey, J. L. 2010. Reference and the pragmeme. *Journal of Pragmatics* 42 (11). 2882–2888.
Meyer, Christian. 2014. Gesture in West Africa: Wolof. In Cornelia Müller, Alan Cienki, Ellen Fricke, Silva Ladewig, David McNeill & Sedinha Tessendorf (eds.), *Body – Language – Communication* Vol. 2, 1169–1175. Berlin: Mouton de Gruyter

Meyer, Christian. 2018. *Culture, Practice, and the Body: Conversational Organization and Embodied Culture in Northwestern Senegal.* Stuttgart: J. B. Metzler.
Mickan, Anne, Maren Schiefke & Anatol Stefanowitsch. 2014. Key is a llave is a Schlüssel: A failure to replicate an experiment from Boroditsky et al. 2003. *Yearbook of the German Cognitive Linguistics Association (GCLA)* 2. 39–50.
Mietzner, Angelika. 2009. *Räumliche Orientierung in nilotischen Sprachen: Raumkonzepte – Direktionalität – Perspektiven.* Cologne: Rüdiger Köppe.
Mietzner, Angelika 2012. Spatial orientation in Nilotic languages and the forces of innovation. In Angelika Mietzner & Ulrike Claudi (eds.), *Directionality in Grammar and Discourse: Case Studies from Africa*, 165–175. Cologne: Rüdiger Köppe.
Mietzner, Angelika. 2016. *Cherang'any – A Kalenjin Language of Kenya.* Cologne: Rüdiger Köppe.
Mietzner, Angelika & Helma Pasch. 2007. Expressions of cardinal directions in Nilotic and in Ubangian languages. *SKASE Journal of Theoretical Linguistics* 4 (3). 17–31.
Mills, Sara. 2003. *Gender and Politeness.* Cambridge: Cambridge University Press.
Minsky, Marvin. 1975. A framework for representing knowledge. In Patrick Henry Winston (ed.), *The Psychology of Computer Vision*, 211–277. New York: McGraw Hill.
Minsky, Marvin. 1986. *The Society of Mind.* New York: Simon & Schuster.
Mitchell, Alice. 2015a. Extra-ordinary morphology in an avoidance register of Datooga. In Ruth Kremer, Elizabeth C. Zsiga & One Tlale Boyer (eds.), *Selected Proceedings of the 44th Annual Conference on African Linguistics*, 188–198. Somerville, MA: Cascadilla Proceedings Project.
Mitchell, Alice. 2015b. Words that smell like father-in-law: A linguistic description of the Datooga avoidance register. *Anthropological Linguistics* 57 (2). 195–217.
Mitchell, Alice. 2018. Allusive references and other-oriented stance in an affinal avoidance register. *Journal of Linguistic Anthropology* 28. 4–21.
Mitchell, Alice. 2020. "Oh, bald father": Kinship and swearing among Datooga of Tanzania. In Nico Nassenstein & Anne Storch (eds.), *Swearing and Cursing: Contexts and Practices in a Critical Linguistic Perspective*, 79–102. Berlin & Boston: Mouton de Gruyter.
Mitchell, Alice & Ayu'nwi N. Neba. 2019. Special-purpose registers of language in Africa. In H. Ekkehard Wolff (ed.), *The Cambridge Handbook of African Linguistics*, 513–534. Cambridge: Cambridge University Press.
Mncube, Francis Stephen Mabuta. 1949. *Hlonipa Language as Found among the Zulu-Xhosa Women.* Johannesburg: University of the Witwatersrand MA thesis.
Moodie, Jonathan & Rosey Billington. 2020. *A Grammar of Lopit – An Eastern Nilotic Language of South Sudan.* Leiden & Boston: Brill.
Moore, Henrietta L. 1986. *Space, Text and Gender: An Anthropological Study of the Marakwet of Kenya.* Cambridge: Cambridge University Press.
Morgan, Lewis H. 1871. *Systems of Consanguinity and Affinity of the Human Family.* Washington: Smithsonian Institute.
Morgan, Marcyliena. 2004. Speech community. In Alessandro Duranti (ed.), *A Companion to Linguistic Anthropology*, 3–22. Malden, MA & Oxford: Blackwell.
Morton, John. 1988. Sakanab: Greetings and information among the northern Beja. *Africa* 58 (4). 423–436.
Motte-Florac, Élisabeth & Gladys Guarisma (eds.). 2004. *Du terrain au cognitif – Linguistique, ethnolinguistique, ethnosciences – À Jacqueline M.C. Thomas.* Paris: SELAF.

Mufwene, Salikoko S. 1988. The pragmatics of kinship terms in Kituba. *Multilingua* 7 (4). 441–453.
Muñoz-Duston, Emma & Judith D. Kaplan. 1985. A sampling of sources of silence. In Deborah Tannen & Muriel Saville-Troike (eds.), *Perspectives on Silence*, 235–242. Norwood, NJ: Ablex.
Murdock, George P. 1949. *Social Structure*. New York: Macmillan.
Murdock, George P. 1968. Patterns of sibling terminology. *Ethnology* 7(1). 1–24.
Müller-Lyer, Franz C. 1889. Optische Urteilstäuschungen. *Archiv für Physiologie Supplement*. 263–270.
Mzamane, Godfred Isaac Malunga. 1962. *A Comparative Phonetic and Morphological Study of the Dialects of Southern Nguni Including the Lexical Influences of the Non-Bantu Languages*. Pretoria: University of South Africa PhD thesis.
Nachtigal, Gustav. 1972 [1879]. *Sahara and Sudan. Volume Four: Wadai and Darfur*. [Translated from the original German]. Berkeley & Los Angeles: University of California Press.
Naden, Anthony J. 1980. How to greet in Bisa. *Journal of Pragmatics* 4. 137–145.
Naden, Anthony J. 1986. Social context and Mampruli greetings. In George L. Huttar & Kenneth Gregerson (eds.), *Pragmatics in Non-Western Perspective*, 161–199. Dallas & Arlington: University of Texas & Summer Institute of Linguistics (SIL).
Nakamura, K. (2001). The acquisition of polite language by Japanese children. In K. E. Nelson, A. Aksu-Koç & C. E. Johnson (eds.), *Children's Language: Developing Narrative and Discourse Competence, Vol.10*, 93–112. Hillsdale, NJ: Lawrence Erlbaum Associates.
Nassenstein, Nico. 2016a. The new urban youth language Yabâcrane in Goma (DR Congo). *Sociolinguistic Studies* 10 (1–2). 235–259.
Nassenstein, Nico. 2016b. The metrolingual use of Swahili in urban Ugandan landscapes and everyday conversation. *Voices from Around the World* 2. https://kups.ub.uni-koeln.de/6502/
Nassenstein, Nico. 2018. "I swear they said this…": Kritische Gedanken zu afrikanischen Jugendsprachen und ihren Beschreibungspraktiken. *The Mouth: Critical Studies on Language, Culture and Society* 3. *[Critical Youth Language Studies: Rethinking Concepts]*. 29–63.
Nassenstein, Nico & Andrea Hollington (eds.). 2015. *Youth Language Practices in Africa and Beyond*. Berlin: Mouton de Gruyter.
Nassenstein, Nico & Anne Storch (eds). 2020. *Swearing and Cursing: Contexts and Practices in a Critical Linguistic Perspective*. Berlin & New York: Mouton de Gruyter.
Ndimele, Ozo-Mekuri & Eugene S. L. Chan (eds.). 2016. *The Numeral Systems of Nigerian Languages*. Port Harcourt: M & J Grand Orbit Communications Ltd.
Nebel, Arthur. 1979. *Dinka-English English-Dinka Dictionary*. Bologna: Editrice Missionaria Italiana.
Needham, Rodney.1971. Remarks on the analysis of kinship and marriage. In Rodney Needham (ed.), *Rethinking Kinship and Marriage*, 1–34. London: Tavistock.
Neethling, Bertie & S. J. Neethling. 2005. *Naming Among the Xhosa of South Africa*. New York: Edwin Mellen Press.
Newman, Paul. 1977. *Modern Hausa-English Dictionary / Sabon Kamus na Hausa zuwa Turanci*. Ibadan and Zaria: Oxford University Press.
Newman, Paul.1991. An interview with Joseph H. Greenberg. *Current Anthropology* 32. 453–467.
Newman, Paul. 2000. *The Hausa Language: An Encyclopedic Reference Grammar*. New Haven & London: Yale University Press.

Niedenthal, Paula M. 2003. Emotions. In Lynn Nadel (ed.), *Encyclopedia of Cognitive Science*, Vol. 1, 1115–1123. London, New York & Tokyo: Nature Publishing Group.

Nketia, J. H. Kwabena. 1971. Surrogate languages of Africa. In Thomas A. Sebeok (ed.), *Current Trends in Linguistics. Vol. 7: Linguistics in Sub-Saharan Africa*, 698–732. The Hague & Paris: Mouton.

Noonan, Michael P. 1992. *A Grammar of Lango*. Berlin and New York: Mouton de Gruyter.

Nortier, Jacomine & Margreet Dorleijn. 2013. Multi-ethnolects: Kebabnorsk, Perkerdansk, Verlan, Kanakensprache, Straattaal, etc. In Peter Bakker & Yaron Matras (eds.), *Contact Languages: A Comprehensive Guide*, 229–272. Boston & Berlin: Walter de Gruyter.

Novelli, Bruno. 1985. *A Grammar of the Karimojong Language*. Berlin: Dietrich Reimer.

Novinger, Tracy. 2003. *Communicating with Brazilians – When "Yes" Means "No"*. Austin, TX: University of Texas Press.

Ntahombaye, Philippe. 1983. *Des noms et des hommes: Aspects psychologiques et sociologiques du nom au Burundi*. Paris: Karthala.

Nureddeen, Fatima A. 2008. Cross-cultural pragmatics: Apology strategies in Sudanese Arabic. *Journal of Pragmatics* 40 (2). 279–306.

Nwoye, Gregory O. 1985. Eloquent silence among the Igbo of Nigeria. In Deborah Tannen & Muriel Saville-Troike (eds.), *Perspectives on Silence*, 285–291. Norwood, NJ: Ablex.

Nwoye, Onuigbo G. 1989. Linguistic politeness in Igbo. *Multilingua* 8 (2/3). 259–275.

Nwoye, Onuigbo G. 1992. Linguistic politeness and socio-cultural variations of the notion of face. *Journal of Pragmatics* 18. 309–328.

Nwoye, G. Onuigbo. 1993. An ethnographic analysis of Igbo greetings. *African Languages and Cultures* 6 (1). 37–48.

Nurse, Derek, and Gérard Philippson. 2003. Towards a historical classification of the Bantu languages. In Derek Nurse & Gérard Philippson, *The Bantu Languages*, 164–181. London: routledge.

Nyst, Victoria. 2020. Sign Languages. In Rainer Vossen & Gerrit J. Dimmendaal (eds.), *The Oxford Handbook of African Languages*, 899–904. Oxford: Oxford University Press.

Obeng, Samuel Gyasi. 1996. The proverb as a mitigating and politeness strategy in Akan dis-course. *Anthropological Linguistics* 38 (3). 521–547.

Obeng, Samuel Gyasi. 2001. *African Anthroponymy – An Ethnopragmatic and Morpho-phonological Study of Personal Names in Akan and Some African Societies*. Munich: LINCOM Europa.

Oboler Smith, Regine. 1980. Is the female husband a man? Woman/woman marriage among the Nandi of Kenya. *Ethnology* 19 (1). 69–88.

Ochs Keenan, Elinor. 1976. The universality of conversational postulates. *Language in Society* 6. 67–80.

Odoch Pido, John P. 2017. Indigenous knowledge in Acholi nicknames. *Regional Journal of Information and Knowledge Management* 2 (2). 1–13.

Oduyoye, Modupe. 1972. *Yoruba Names: Their Structure and Their Meanings*. Ibadan: Daystar Press.

O'Driscoll, Jim. 2009. Erving Goffman. In Sigurd D'hondt, Jan-Ola Östman & Jef Verschueren (eds.), *The Pragmatics of Interaction*, 79–95. Amsterdam & Philadelphia: John Benjamins.

Ohala, John J. 1984. An ethological perspective on common cross-language utilization of F_0 of voice. *Phonetica* 41. 1–16.

Ohta, Itaru. 1987. Livestock individual identification among the Turkana: The animal classification and naming in the pastoral livestock management. *African Study Monographs* 8(1). 1–69. The Center for African Area Studies, Kyoto University.

Onyango-Ouma, Washington & Jens Aagaard-Hansen. 2020. Dholuo kincepts in Western Kenya. *Studies in African Linguistics* 49 (2). 304–320.

Palmer, Gary B. 1996. *Toward a Theory of Cultural Linguistics*. Austin: University of Texas Press.

Pankhurst, Helen. 1992. *Gender, Development, and Identity: An Ethiopian Study*. London: Zed Books.

Parrott Hickerson, Nancy. 1980. *Linguistic Anthropology*. New York: Holt, Rinehart & Winston.

Pasch, Helma & François Mbolifouye. 2011. I am subordinate to Gbudwe, but your sovereign: Using a subject pronoun in object position in order to claim power. *Afrikanistik Online* 2011 (8). [https://www.afrikanistik-aegyptologie-online.de/archiv/2011/2907/] (accessed 12 January 2022).

Paulston, Christina Bratt. 1976. Pronouns of address in Swedish: Social class semantics and a changing system. *Language in Society* 5. 359–386.

Payne, Doris L. 1998. Maasai gender in typological perspective. *Studies in African Linguistics* 27. 159–175.

Payne, Doris L. 2003. Maa color terms and their use as human descriptors. *Anthropological Linguistics* 45. 169–200.

Payne, Doris L. 2020. Color term systems: Genetic vs. areal distribution in sub-Saharan Africa. In Rainer Vossen & Gerrit J. Dimmendaal (eds.), *The Oxford Handbook of African Languages*, 704–714. Oxford: Oxford University Press

Payne, Doris L. & Leonard Ole-Kotikash. 2005. *Maa Dictionary*. [https://pages.uoregon.edu/maasai/Maa%20Lexicon/lexicon/main.htm] (accessed 20 March 2021).

Pennycook, Alastair & Emi Otsuji. 2015. *Metrolingualism. Language in the City*. New York: Routledge.

Petrollino, Sara. 2016. *A Grammar of Hamar – A South Omotic Language of Ethiopia*. Cologne: Rüdiger Köppe.

Pillion, Betsy, Lenore A. Grenoble, Emmanuel Ngué Um & Sarah Kopper. 2019. Verbal gestures in Cameroon. In Emily Clem, Peter Jenks & Hannah Sande (eds.), *Theory and Description in African Linguistics, Selected papers from the 47th Annual Conference on African Linguistics*, 303–322. Berlin: Language Science Press. doi:10.5281/zenodo.3367152 (accessed 20 October 2020).

Pinker, Steven. 1994. *The Language Instinct: The New Science of Language and Mind*. London: Penguin Books.

Pinker, Steven. 2007. *The Stuff of Thought: Language as a Window into Human Nature*. London: Allen Lane.

Pike, Kenneth L. 1967. *Language in Relation to a Unified Theory of the Structure of Human Behavior*. The Hague: Mouton.

Planert, Wilhelm. 1905. Über die Sprache der Hottentotten und Buschmänner. *Mitteilungen des Seminars für Orientalische Sprachen zu Berlin 3. Abteilung Afrikanische Studien* 8. 104–176.

Podobińska, Zofia. 2001. *Politesse dans les actes pragmatiques (requête, suggestion, ordre) en swahili*. Warsaw: Dialog Academic Publishing House.

Polzenhagen, Frank 2007. *Cultural Conceptualisations in West African English – A Cognitive-Linguistic Approach*. Frankfurt a. M. & Berlin: Peter Lang.

Pritzker, Sonya E., Janina Fenigsen & James M. Wilce (eds.). 2020. *The Routledge Handbook of Language and Emotion*. London & New York: Routledge.
Pullum, Geoffrey K. 1989. The great Eskimo vocabulary hoax. *Natural Language and Linguistic Theory* 7. 275–281.
Pumphrey, M. E. C. 1937. Shilluk "royal" language conventions. *Sudan Notes and Records* 20. 319–321.
Quinn, Naomi & Dorothy Holland. 1987. Culture and Cognition. In Dorothy Holland & Naomi Quinn (eds.), *Cultural Models in Language and Thought*, 3–40. Cambridge: Cambridge University Press.
Quine, Willard van Ornam. 1960. *Word and Object*. Cambridge, MA: The MIT Press.
Quint, Nicolas & Stefano Manfredi, 2020. Le monts Nouba: une région riche de ses langues. *Faits de Langues* 51. 9–29.
Radcliffe-Brown, Alfred R. 1940. On joking relationships. *Africa* 13 (3). 195–210.
Radcliffe-Brown, Alfred R. 1952. On joking relationships. In Alfred R. Radcliffe-Brown (ed.), *Structure and Function in Primitive Society: Essays and Addresses*, 90–104. Glencoe, IL: The Free Press.
Raper, Peter E. 2009. Descriptive Zulu placenames of San origin. *Names: A Journal of Onomastics* 57 (1). 3–16.
Rapoo, Connie K. 2002. Naming practices and gender bias in the Setswana language. *Women and Language* 25 (1). 41–44.
Reda, Fikre Gebrekidan. 2015. *Tigrinya – English/Amharic Codeswitching*. Cologne: Rüdiger Köppe.
Reisman, Karl. 1974. Contrapuntal conversations in an Antiguan village. In Richard Bauman & Joel Sherzer (eds.), *Explorations in the Ethnography of Speaking*, 110–124. Cambridge: Cambridge University Press.
Remijsen, Bert & Otto Gwado Ayoker. 2020. A descriptive analysis of adjectives in Shilluk. *Language Documentation and Conservation* Special Publication 14: *A Descriptive Grammar of Shilluk*. http://hdl.handle.net/10125/24780
Rickford, John R. & Angela E. Rickford. 1976. 'Cut-eye' and suck teeth: African words and gestures in New World guise. *The Journal of American Folklore* 89. 294–309.
Rings, Guido & Sebastian Rasinger (eds.). 2020. *The Cambridge Handbook of Intercultural Communication*. Cambridge: Cambridge University Press.
Rivet, Alain. 2016. Des mots au génocide. *Le Patriote Résistant* 905. 6. [http://www.fndirp.asso.fr/wp-content/uploads/2016/02/6.pdf] (accessed 8 February 2021).
Robert, Stéphane. 2006. Deictic space in Wolof. In Maya Hickmann & Stéphane Robert (eds.), *Space in Languages. Linguistic Systems and Cognitive Categories*, 155–174. Amsterdam & Philadelphia: John Benjamins.
Rosch, Eleanor H. 1972a. Probabilities, sampling, and ethnographic method: The case of Dani colour names. *Man* 7 (3). 448–466.
Rosch, Eleanor H. 1972b. Universals in color naming and memory. *Journal of Experimental Psychology* 93 (1). 10–20.
Rosch, Eleanor H. 1977. Human Categorization. In Neil Warren (ed.), *Advances in Cross-Cultural Psychology* 1. 1–72. New York: Academic Press.
Rosch, Eleanor H. 1978. Principles of categorization. In Eleanor H. Rosch & Barbara L. Lloyd (eds.), *Cognition and Categorization*, 27–48. Hillsdale, NJ: Lawrence Erlbaum.

Roulon-Doko, Paulette. 1999. Les classifications en réseaux chez les Gbaya 'bodoe (Centrafrique). In Paul Valentin & Michèle Fruyt (eds.), *Lexique et cognition*, 181–190. Paris: Presses de l'Université de Paris-Sorbonne.

Roulon-Doko, Paulette. 2017. Une polarité d'exemplaire: Colère et Rire chez les Gbaya. In Nicole Tersis & Pascal Boyeldieu (eds.), *Le langage de l'émotion: variations linguistiques et culturelles*, 81–92. Louvain & Paris: Peeters.

Roulon-Doko, Paulette. 2019. Lexicalization patterns in color naming in Gbaya, a Ubanguian language of CAR. In Ida Raffaelli, Daniela Katunar & Barbara Kerovec (eds), *Lexicalization Patterns in Colour Naming: A Cross-linguistic Perspective*, 133–152. Amsterdam & Phila-delphia: John Benjamins.

Rudwick, Stephanie Inge. 2008. Shifting norms of linguistic and cultural respect: Hybrid sociolinguistic Zulu identities. *Nordic Journal of African Studies* 17 (2). 152–174.

Rüsch, Maren. 2012. *Höflichkeitsstrategien im Swahili: Eine Analyse anhand von Aufforderungen, Bitten und Vorschlägen*. Unpublished manuscript, University of Cologne.

Rüsch, Maren. 2018. Repetition in Acholi conversation. In Helga Schröder & Prisca Jerono (eds.), *Nilo-Saharan Issues and Perspectives*, 225–241. Cologne: Rüdiger Köppe.

Rüsch, Maren. 2020a. *A Conversational Analysis of Acholi. Structure and Socio-Pragmatics of a Nilotic Language of Uganda*. Leiden & Boston: Brill.

Rüsch, Maren. 2020b. Conversation analysis. In Rainer Vossen & Gerrit J. Dimmendaal (eds.), *The Oxford Handbook of African Languages*, 765–779. Oxford: Oxford University Press.

Sacks, Harvey, Emanuel A. Schegloff & Gail Jefferson. 1974. Simplest systematics for organization of turn-taking for conversation. *Language* 50 (4). 696–735.

Sagna, Serge & Emmanuel Bassène. 2016. Why are they named after death? Name giving, name changing, and death prevention names in Gújjolaay Eegimaa (Banjul). In Mandana Seyfeddinipur (ed.), *African Language Documentation: New Data, Methods, Approaches* (*Language Documentation & Conservation, Special Publication 10*), 40–70. Honolulu: University of Hawai'i Press.

Said, Edward W. 1978. *Orientalism*. London: Routledge and Kegan Paul.

Samarin, William J. 1965. Language of silence. *Practical Anthropology* 12 (3). 115–119.

Samarin, William J. 1969. The art of Gbeya insults. *International Journal of American Linguistics* 35 (4). 323–329.

Samatar, Said S. 1982. *Oral Poetry and Somali Nationalism. The Case of Sayyid Mahammad 'Abdille Hasan*. Cambridge: Cambridge University Press.

Sanders, Karen W. 2015. The convergence of language and culture in Malawian gestures: Handedness in everyday rituals. In Augustine Agwuele (ed.), *Body Talk and Cultural Identity in the African World*, 111–132. Sheffield: Equinox.

Sands, Bonny. 2020. *Click Consonants*. Leiden and Boston: Brill.

Santandrea, Stefano. 1944. The Luo of Bahr-el-Ghazal. Part 1: Tribal life and tribal organization. *Annali Lateranensi* 8. 91–145.

Sapir, Edward. 1916. *Time Perspective in Aboriginal American Culture: A Study in Method*. Canada Department of Mines, Geological Survey, Memoir 90.

Sapir, Edward. 1921. *Language. An Introduction to the Study of Speech*. New York: Harcourt Brace.

Saunders, Barbara A. C. 1992. *The Invention of Basic Color Terms*. Utrecht, NL: University of Utrecht PhD dissertation.

Sauter, Disa A., Olivier Le Guen & Daniel B. M. Haun. 2011. Categorical perception of emotional expressions does not require lexical categories. *Emotion* 11 (6). 1479–1483.

Savà, Graziano & Mauro Tosco. 2003. The classification of Ongota. In M. Lionel Bender, Gabor Takács & David Appleyard (eds.), *Selected Comparative-Historical Afrasian Linguistic Studies: In Memory of Igor M. Diakonoff*, 307–316. Munich: LINCOM.
Saville-Troike, Muriel. 1978. *A Guide to Culture in the Classroom*. Arlington, VA: National Clearinghouse for Bilingual Education.
Saville-Troike, Muriel. 1982. *The Ethnography of Communication*. Oxford: Basil Blackwell.
Saville-Troike, Muriel. 1985. The place of silence in an integrated theory of communication. In Deborah Tannen & Muriel Saville-Troike (eds.), *Perspectives on Silence*, 3–18. Norwood, NJ: Ablex.
Schaefer, Paul. 2015. Hot eyes, white stomach: Emotions and character qualities in Safaliba metaphor. In Elisabeth Piirainen & Ari Sherris (eds.), *Language Endangerment*, 91–110. Amsterdam & Philadelphia: John Benjamins.
Schaller, Susan. 1991. *A Man Without Words*. New York: Summit Books.
Schegloff, Emanuel A. 2007. *Sequence Organization in Interaction. Vol. 1: A Primer in Conversation Analysis*. Cambridge: Cambridge University Press.
Schegloff, Emanuel A., Gail Jefferson & Harvey Sacks. 1977. Preference for self-correction in organization of repair in conversation. *Language* 53. 361–382.
Schegloff, Emanuel A. & Harvey Sacks. 1984. Opening up closings. In John Baugh & Joel Sherzer (eds.), *Language in Use: Readings in Sociolinguistics*, 69–99. Englewood Cliffs, NJ: Prentice Hall.
Schieffelin, Bambi B. 1987.Teasing and shaming in Kaluli children's interaction. In Schieffelin and Ochs (eds.), *Language Socialization across Cultures*, 165–181. Cambridge & New York: Cambridge University Press.
Schieffelin, Bambi B. & Elinor Ochs (eds.). 1987. *Language Socialization across Cultures*. Cambridge & New York: Cambridge University Press.
Schieffelin, Bambi B., Kathryn A. Woolard & Paul V. Kroskity (eds.). 1998. *Language Ideologies: Practice and Theory*. New York & Oxford: Oxford University Press.
Schiffrin, Deborah. 1984. Jewish argument as sociability. *Language in Society* 13 (3). 311–335.
Schlee, Günther. 1989. *Identities on the Move: Clanship and Pastoralism in Northern Kenya*. Manchester: Manchester University Press.
Schneider, David M. 1984. *A Critique of the Study of Kinship*. Ann Arbor, MI: University of Michigan Press.
Schneider-Blum, Gertrud. 2012. Don't waste words – perspectives on the Tima lexicon. In Matthias Brenzinger and Anne-Maria Fehn (eds.), *Proceedings of the 6th World Congress of African Linguistics, Cologne, 17–21 August 2009*, 529–536. Cologne: Rüdiger Köppe.
Schneider-Blum, Gertrud (ed.). 2013a. *Nʌyʌyirʌk t̪amaa dumurik*. Cologne: Rüdiger Köppe.
Schneider-Blum, Gertrud. 2013b. *A Tima-English Dictionary. An Illustrated Lexicon of a Niger-Congo Language Spoken in the Nuba Mountains (Sudan)*. Cologne: Rüdiger Köppe. (Online version: [http://tima-dictionary.mine.nu/]; accessed 19 April 2021).
Searle, John R. 1969. *Speech Acts*. Cambridge: Cambridge University Press.
Searle, John R. 1976. A classification of illocutionary acts. *Language in Society* 5. 1–23.
Searle, John R. 1979. *Expression and Meaning: Studies in the Theory of Speech Acts*. Cambridge: Cambridge University Press.
Segall, Marshall H., Donald T. Campbell & Melville J. Herskovits. 1966. *The Influence of Culture on Visual Perception*. Indianapolis, IN: Bobbs-Merrill.

Sebba, Mark. 2012. On the notions of congruency and convergence in code-switching. In Barbara E. Bullock & Almeida Jacqueline Toribio (eds.), *The Cambridge Handbook of Linguistic Code-switching*, 44–57. Cambridge: Cambridge University Press.
Segerer, Guillaume & Martine Vanhove. 2019. Color naming in Africa. In Ida Raffaelli, Daniela Katunar & Barbara Kerovec (eds.), *Lexicalization patterns in colour naming: a cross-linguistic perspective*, 287–330. Amsterdam & Philadelphia: John Benjamins.
Senft, Gunter. 2009. Phatic communication. In Gunter Senft & Ellen B. Basso (eds.), *Ritual Communication*, 226–233. Oxford: Berg.
Senft, Gunter. 2012. Referring to colour and taste in Kilivila. Stability and change in two lexical domains of sensory perception. In Andrea C. Schalley (ed.), *Practical Theories and Empirical Practice: A Linguistic Perspective*, 71–98. Amsterdam & Philadelphia: John Benjamins.
Senft, Gunter & Ellen B. Basso (eds.). 2009. *Ritual Communication*. Oxford: Berg.
Senft, Gunter, Jan-Ola Östman & Jef Verschueren (eds). 2009. *Culture and Language Use*. Amsterdam & Philadelphia: John Benjamins.
Seyfeddinipur, Mandana & Marianne Gullberg (eds.). 2014. *From Gesture in Conversation to Visible Action as Utterance*. Amsterdam & Philadelphia: John Benjamins.
Sharifian, Farzad. 2011. *Cultural Conceptualisations and Language: Theoretical Framework and Applications*. Amsterdam & Philadelphia: John Benjamins.
Sharifian, Farzad (ed.). 2015 *The Routledge Handbook of Language and Culture*. London & New York: Routledge.
Sharifian, Farzad. 2017a. *Cultural Linguistics: Cultural Conceptualizations and Language*. Amsterdam & Philadelphia: John Benjamins.
Sharifian, Farzad (ed.). 2017b. *Advances in Cultural Linguistics*. Singapore: Springer.
Sherzer, Joel. 1974. *Namakke, sunmakke, kormakke*: Three types of Cuna speech event. In Richard Bauman & Joel Sherzer (eds.), *Explorations in the Ethnography of Speaking*, 263–282. Cambridge: Cambridge University Press.
Shweder, Richard A. & Edmund J. Bourne. 1984. Does the concept of the person vary cross-culturally? In Richard A. Shweder & Robert A. LeVine (eds.), *Culture Theory: Essays on Mind, Self and Emotion*, 158–199. Cambridge: Cambridge University Press.
Sidnell, Jack (ed.). 2009. *Conversation Analysis. Comparative Perspectives*. Cambridge: Cambridge University Press.
Sidnell, Jack. 2010. *Conversation Analysis. An Introduction*. Oxford: Wiley-Blackwell.
Sidnell, Jack & Tanya Stivers (eds.). 2012. *Handbook of Conversational Analysis*. Oxford: Wiley-Blackwell.
Sigman, Stuart J. 1981. Some notes on conversational fission. *Working Papers in Sociolinguistics* 91. Austin: Southwest Educational Development Laboratory.
Silverstein, Michael. 1972. Chinook Jargon: Language contact and the problem of multi-level generative systems. *Language* 48(2). 378–406 [Part I] and 48 (3). 596–625 [Part II].
Silverstein, Michael. 1976. Shifters, linguistic categories, and cultural description. In Keith H. Basso & Henry A. Selby (eds.), *Meaning in Anthropology*, 11–55. Albuquerque: University of New Mexico Press.
Silverstein, Michael. 1979. Language structure and linguistic ideology. In Paul R. Clyne, William F. Hanks & Carol L. Hofbauer (eds.), *The Elements: A Parasession on Linguistic Units and Levels*, 193–247. Chicago: Chicago Linguistic Society.
Silverstein, Michael. 2014. How language communities intersect: Is "superdiversity" an incremental or transformative condition? *Language and Communication* 44. 7–18.

Simeoni, Antonio. 1978. *Päri: A Luo Language of Southern Sudan. Small Grammar and Vocabulary*. Bologna: Editrice Missionaria Italiana.
Simmons, Donald C. 1955. Specimens of Efik folklore. *Folklore* 66. 417–124.
Slabbert, Sarah & Rosalie Finlayson. 2000. "I'm a cleva!": The linguistic makeup of identity in a South African urban environment. *International Journal for the Sociology of Language* 144. 119–135.
Slobin, Dan I. 1996. From "thought and language" to "thinking for speaking". In John J. Gumperz & Stephen C. Levinson (eds.), *Rethinking Linguistic Relativity*, 70–96. Cambridge: Cambridge University Press.
Smolders, Joshua A. G. 2016. *T'apo (Opuuo) number chart*. SIL International, Ethiopia. [https://www.academia.edu/30349186/T'apo_Opuuo_Number_Chart] (accessed 7 May 2021).
Soja, Nancy N., Susan Carey & Elizabeth S. Spelke. 1991. Ontological categories guide young children's inductions of word meaning: bject terms and substance terms. *Cognition* 38. 179–211.
Sommer, Gabriele & Abel Lupapula. 2012. Comparing address forms and systems: Some examples from Bantu. In Michael R. Marlo, Nikki B. Adams, Christopher R. Green, Michelle Morrison & Tristan M. Purvis (eds.), *Selected Proceedings of the 42nd Annual Conference on African Linguistics: African Languages in Contact*, 266–277. Somerville, MA: Cascadilla Proceedings Project.
Sommer, Gabriele & Clarissa Vierke (eds.). 2011. Speech acts and speech events in African languages. In Gabriele Sommer & Clarissa Vierke (eds.), *Speech Acts and Speech Events in African Languages*, 11–40. Cologne: Rüdiger Köppe.
Song, Sooho. 2014. Politeness in Korea and America: A comparative analysis of request strategy in English communication. *Korea Journal* 54 (1). 60–84.
Souag, Lameen. 2015. Non-Tuareg Berber and the genesis of nomadic Northern Songhay. *Journal of African Languages and Linguistics* 36 (1). 121–143.
Spagnolo, Lorenzo M. 1933. *Bari Grammar*. Verona: Missioni Africane.
Spagnolo, Lorenzo M. 1960. *Bari English Italian Dictionary*. Verona: Missioni Africane.
Spencer-Oatey, Helen (ed.). 2000. *Culturally Speaking: Managing Rapport through Talk across Cultures*. London: Continuum.
Stampe, David 1976. Cardinal numeral systems. *Chicago Linguistic Society* 12. 594–609.
Stivers, Tanya, N. J. Enfield, Penelope Brown, Christina Englert, Makoto Hayashi, Trine Heinemann, Gertie Hoymann, Federico Rossano, Jan Peter de Ruiter, Kyung-Eun Yoon & Stephen C. Levinson. 2009. Universals and cultural variation in turn-taking in conversation. *Proceedings of the National Academy of Sciences (PNAS)* 106 (26). 10587–10592.
Stivers, Tanya, N. J. Enfield & Stephen C. Levinson (eds.). 2010. question-response sequences in conversation across ten languages. *Journal of Pragmatics* 42 (10). 2615–2619.
Stivers, Tanya & N. J. Enfield. 2010. A coding scheme for question-response sequences in conversation. *Journal of Pragmatics* 42 (10). 2620–2626.
Stolz, Thomas, Ingo H. Warnke & Nataliya Levkovych. 2016. Colonial names in a comparative perspective. *Beiträge zur Namenforschung* 51 (3/4). 279–355.
Storch, Anne. 2011. *Secret Manipulations: Language and Context in Africa*. New York: Oxford University Press.
Storch, Anne. 2014. *A Grammar of Luwo: An Anthropological Approach*. Amsterdam & Philadelphia: John Benjamins.

Storch, Anne. 2017. Emotional edgelands. In Anne Storch (ed.), *Consensus and Dissent: Negotiating Emotion in the Public Space*, 193–212. Amsterdam & Philadelphia: John Benjamins.

Storch, Anne & Rainer Vossen. 2007. Odours and colours in Nilotic: Comparative case studies. In Doris L. Payne & Mechthild Reh (eds.), *Advances in Nilo-Saharan Linguistics*, 223–240. Cologne: Rüdiger Köppe.

Strecker, Ivo. 1976. Hamer speech situations. In M. Lionel Bender (ed.), *The Non-Semitic Languages of Ethiopia*, 583–596. East Lansing (MI): African Studies Centre.

Strecker, Ivo. 1988. *The Social Practice of Symbolization: An Anthropological Analysis*. London & Atlantic Highlands: The Athlone Press.

Strecker, Ivo. 1993. Cultural variations in the concept of 'face'. *Multilingua* 12 (2). 119–141.

Strecker, Ivo & Jean Lydall (eds). 2004. *The Perils of Face. Essays on Cultural Contact, Respect and Self-esteem in Southern Ethiopia*. Berlin: LIT.

Sugawara, Kazuyoshi. 1996. Some methodological issues for the analysis of everyday communication among the |Gui. *African Studies Monographs*, Supplementary Issue 22. 145–164.

Sugawara, Kazuyoshi. 1998a. The 'egalitarian' attitude in everyday conversation among the |Gui. In Andrew Banks, Hans Heese & Chris Loff (eds.), *The Proceedings of the Khoisan Cultures and Cultural Heritage Conference,* Cape Town 12–16 July 1997, 232–240. Cape Town: Infosource.

Sugawara, Kazuyoshi. 1998b. *Anthropology of Conversation (Living World of the Bushmen II)*. Kyoto: Kyoto University Press. (In Japanese)

Sugawara, Kazuyoshi. 2009. Speech acts, moves, and meta-communication in negotiation: Three cases of everyday conversation observed among the |Gui former-foragers. *Journal of Pragmatics* 41. 93–135.

Sugawara, Kazuyoshi. 2012. Interactive significance of simultaneous discourse or overlap in everyday conversations among |Gui former foragers. *Journal of Pragmatics* 44 (5). 577–618.

Suzman, Susan M. 1994. Names as pointers: Zulu personal naming practices. *Language in Society* 23. 253–272.

Takada, Akira. 2011. Preverbal infant-caregiver interaction. In Alessandro Duranti, Elinor Ochs & Bambi B. Schieffelin (eds.), *The Handbook of Language Socialization*, 56–80. Malden, MA: Wiley Blackwell.

Talmy, Leonard. 1988. Force dynamics in language and cognition. *Cognitive Science* 12 (1). 49–100.

Taluah, Asangba Reginald. 2018. Rethinking ritual: Decoding Dagbamba dress codes. Paper presented at the Forschungsseminar, Institute for African Studies and Egyptology, University of Cologne.

Taluah, Asangba Reginald. 2021. Grandmasters of the Drum: A Literary Linguistic Analysis of the Dagbamba Panegyrics. *The Mouth: Critical Studies on Language, Culture and Society* Special Issue 6.

Tanaka, Akihiro, Ai Koizumi, Hisato Imai, Saori Haramatsu, Eriko Hiramoto & Beatrice de Gelder. 2010. I feel your voice: Cultural differences in the multisensory perception of emotion. *Psychological Science* 21 (9). 1259–1262.

Tannen, Deborah. 1985. Silence: Anything but. In Deborah Tannen & Muriel Saville Troike (eds.), *Perspectives on Silence*, 93–111. Norwood, NJ: Ablex.

Tannen, Deborah & Muriel Saville-Troike (eds.). 1985. *Perspectives on Silence*. Norwood, NJ: Ablex.
Tannen, Deborah & Cynthia Wallat. 1987. Interactive frames and knowledge schemas in interaction. Examples from a medical examination/interview. *Social Psychology Quarterly* 50 (2). 205–216.
Tarr, Delbert H. Jr. 1979. *Indirection and Ambiguity as a Mode of Communication in West Africa: A Descriptive Survey*. Minneapolis, MN: University of Minnesota dissertation.
Tersis, Nicole & Pascal Boyeldieu (eds.). 2017. *Le langage de l'émotion: variations linguistiques et culturelles*. Louvain & Paris: Peeters.
Thomas, Jacqueline M. C., Serge Bahuchet, Alain Epelboin & Susanne Fürniss (eds). 2013. *Encyclopédie des Pygmées Aka II – Dictionnaire ethnographique Aka-Français (fasc. 11) – Voyelles*. Louvain: Peeters.
Thompson, John. 1991. Editor's introduction. In Pierre Bourdieu, *Language and Symbolic Power*, 1–31. Cambridge, MA: Harvard University Press.
Thompson, Rachel & Kofi Agyekum. 2015. Impoliteness: The Ghanaian standpoint. *International Journal of Society, Culture & Language* (Special Issue on African Cultures & Languages) 4 (1). 20–33.
Tierou, Alphonse. 1977. *Le nom africain: ou langages des traditions*. Paris: G.P. Maisonneuve et Larase.
Tomasello, Michael. 2003. *Constructing a Language: A Usage-Based Theory of Language Acquisition*. Cambridge, MA: Harvard University Press.
Tomasello, Michael. 2008. *Origins of Human Communication*. Cambridge, MA: The MIT Press.
Tornay, Serge. 1973. Langage et perception: La dénomination des couleurs chez les Nyangatom du sud-ouest éthiopien. *L'Homme* 13 (4). 66–94.
Tornay, Serge. 1978a. Introduction. In Serge Tornay (ed.), *Voir et nommer les couleurs*, IX–LI. Nanterre: Service de Publication du Laboratoire de'Ethnologie et de Sociologie comparative de l'Université de Paris X.
Tornay, Serge (ed.). 1978b. *Voir et nommer les couleurs*. Nanterre: Service de Publication du Laboratoire de'Ethnologie et de Sociologie comparative de l'Université de Paris X.
Traore, Dominique. 1965. *Comment le Noire se soigne-t-il? Ou médecine et magie africaines*. Paris: Presence Africaine.
Treis, Yvonne. 2005. Avoiding their names, avoiding their eyes: How Kambaata women respect their in-laws. *Anthropological Linguistics* 47 (3). 292–320.
Treis, Yvonne & Deginet Wotango Doyiso. 2019. "Issues and maize bread taste good when they're cool": Temperature terms and their metaphorical extensions in Kambaata (Cushitic). *Studies in African Linguistics* 48 (2). 225–266.
Trosborg, Anna. 1995. *Interlanguage Pragmatics: Requests, Complaints and Apologies*. Berlin & New York: Mouton de Gruyter.
Turner, Victor V. 1969. *The Ritual Process: Structure and Anti-Structure*. Ithaca: Cornell University Press.
Turner, Noleen S. 2000. Zulu names and indirect expression. *Names – A Journal of Onomastics* 48 (2). 127–137.
Turton, David. 1980. There is no such beast: Cattle and colour naming among the Mursi. *Man* 152. 320–338.
Tyler, Stephen A. 1978. *The Said and the Unsaid: Mind, Meaning, and Culture*. New York: Academic Press.
Ubahakwe, Ebo. 1981. *Igbo Names: Their Structure and their Meanings*. Ibadan: Daystar Press.

van der Bom, Isabelle & Karen Grainger. 2015. Journal of Politeness Research: Introduction. *Journal of Politeness Research* 11 (2). 165–178.
van Jaarsveld, G. J. 1988. Goeimôre, Good morning, Kgotso, Dumela, Sawubona: Opening routines and misunderstandings. *South African Journal of Linguistics* 6 (1). 93–108.
van Staden, Maren, Gunter Senft, N.J. Enfield & Jürgen Bohnemeyer. 2001. Staged events. In Stephen C. Levinson & N. J. Enfield (eds.), *Manual for the field season 2001*, 115–125. Nijmegen: Max Planck Institute for Psycholinguistics. doi:10.17617/2.874668
Veit, Nataliya & Gertrud Schneider-Blum. 2022. Kin-relational expressions of the Tima (Nuba Mountains, Sudan). In Alice Mitchell, Nico Nassenstein & Andrea Hollington (eds.), *Anthropological Linguistics: Perspectives from Africa*. Amsterdam/Philadelphia: John Benjamins.
Vermeulen, Jeroen. 2009. Edward Sapir. In Gunter Senft, Jan-Ola Östman & Jef Verschueren (eds.), *Culture and Language Use*, 234–247. Amsterdam & Philadelphia: John Benjamins.
Verschueren, Jef. 1984. Linguistics and crosscultural communication. *Language in Society* 13. 489–509.
Verschueren, Jef. 2012. *Ideology in Language Use: Pragmatic Guidelines for Empirical Research*. Cambridge: Cambridge University Press.
von Humboldt, Wilhelm. 1812. *Le prodige de l'origine des langues: Essai sur les langues du Nouveau Continent*. Paris: Éditions Manucius.
von Humboldt, Wilhelm. 1822. *Über das Entstehen der grammatischen Formen und ihren Einfluss auf die Ideeentwicklung*. Berlin: Akademie der Wissenschaften.
Vossen, Rainer. 2015. Faunal terminology and word formation in Nilotic languages: A typological approach. In Osamu Hieda (ed.), *Information Structure and Nilotic Languages*, 175–187. Tokyo: Research Institute for Languages and Cultures of Asia and Africa.
Vossen, Rainer & Gerrit J. Dimmendaal (eds.). 2020. *The Oxford Handbook of African Languages*. Oxford: Oxford University Press.
Völkel, Svenja. 2010. *Social Structure, Space, and Possession in Tongan Language and Culture – An Ethnolinguistic Study*. Amsterdam & Philadelphia: John Benjamins.
Völkel, Svenja. 2016. Tongan-English language contact and kinship terminology. *World Englishes* 35 (2). 242–258.
Völkel, Svenja & Franziska Kretzschmar. 2021. *Introducing Linguistic Research*. Cambridge: Cambridge University Press.
Vygotsky, Lev S. 1962. *Thought and Language*. Cambridge, MA: The MIT Press.
Wairungu, Michael. 2014. *"A Language of Many Hats". The Rise of Sheng and Other Linguistic Styles among Urban Youth in Kenya*. Charlottesville, VA: University of Virginia PhD dissertation.
Wassmann, Jürg. 1993. Finding the right path: The route knowledge of the Yupno of Papua New Guinea. *Cognitive Anthropology Research Group Working Paper 19*. Max Planck Institute for Psycholinguistics, Nijmegen, The Netherlands.
Watts, Richard J. 2003. *Politeness*. Cambridge: Cambridge University Press.
Watts, Richard J. 2008. Rudeness, conceptual blending theory and relational work. *Journal of Politeness Research: Language, Behaviour and Culture* 4 (2). 289–317.
Watts, Richard J., Sachiko Ide & Konrad Ehlich (eds.). 1992. *Politeness in Language: Studies in its History, Theory and Practice*. Berlin: Mouton de Gruyter.
Wescott, Roger W. 1970. Bini color terms. *Anthropological Linguistics* 12. 349–360.
Whorf, Benjamin Lee. 1956. *Language, Thought, and Reality. Selected Writings of Benjamin Lee Whorf*, edited and with an introduction by John B. Carroll. New York: Wiley.

Widlok, Thomas. 1997. Orientation in the wild: the shared cognition of Hai‖om bushpeople. *Journal of the Royal Anthropological Institute* 3 (2). 317–332.
Widlok, Thomas. 2008. Landscape unbounded: Space, place, and orientation in ǂAkhoe Hai‖om and beyond. *Language Sciences* 30. 362–380.
Widlok, Thomas. 2016. Small words – big issues: The anthropological relevance of Khoesan interjections. *African Study Monographs*, Supplement 52. 135–145.
Wierzbicka, Anna. 1999. *Emotions across Languages and Cultures: Diversity and Universals.* Cambridge: Cambridge University Press.
Wierzbicka, Anna. 2003. *Cross-cultural Pragmatics: The Semantics of Human Interaction.* Berlin: De Gruyter Mouton.
Wierzbicka, Anna. 2013. *Imprisoned in English. The Hazards of English as a Default Language.* Oxford & New York: Oxford University Press.
Wilkins, David P. 2003. Why pointing with the index finger is not a universal (in socio-cultural and semiotic terms). In Sotaro Kita (ed.), *Pointing: Where Language, Culture, and Cognition Meet*, 171–215. Mahwah, NJ: Lawrence Erlbaum.
Winawer, Jonathan, Nathan Witthoft, Michael C. Frank, Lisa Wu, Alex R. Wade & Lera Boroditsky. 2007. Russian blues reveal effects of language on color discrimination. *Proceedings of the National Academy of Sciences* 104 (19). 7780–7785.
Wnuk, Ewelina & Asifa Majid. 2014. Revisiting the limits of language: The odor lexicon of Maniq. *Cognition* 113.125–138.
Woolard, Kathryn A. & Bambi B. Schieffelin. 1994. Language ideology. *Annual Review of Anthropology* 23. 55–82.
Yahya-Othman, Saida. 1994. Covering one's social back: Politeness among the Swahili. *Text* 14 (1). 141–161.
Yahya-Othman, Saida. 1995. Aren't you going to greet me? Impoliteness in Swahili greetings. *Text* 15 (2). 209–227.
Yankah, Kwesi. 1995. *Speaking for the Chief: Okyeame and the Politics of Akan Oratory.* Bloomington: Indiana University Press.
Yigezu, Moges. 2018. Ngaalam: An endangered Nilo-Saharan language of southwest Ethiopia – a sociolinguistic survey on language vitality and endangerment. In Helga Schröder & Prisca Jerono (eds.), *Nilo-Saharan Issues and Perspectives*, 25–42. Cologne: Rüdiger Köppe.
Yimam, Baye. 1997. The pragmatics of greeting, felicitation and condolence expressions in four Ethiopian languages. *African Languages and Cultures* 10 (2). 103–128.
Yu, Ning. 1998. *The Contemporary Theory of Metaphor: A Perspective from Chinese.* Amsterdam: John Benjamins.
Zaslavsky, Claudia. 1999. *Africa Counts: Number and Pattern in African Languages.* 3rd edition. Chicago: Lawrence Hills Books.
Zucco, Gesualdo M., Rachel S. Herz & Benoist Schaal. 2012. *Olfactory Cognition – From Perception and Memory to Environmental Odours and Neuroscience.* Amsterdam & Philadelphia: John Benjamins.

Ethnographic documentaries

Chris Curling, Jean Lydall, Joanna Head, Veronika Hyks, & BBC. 1990. *Hamar Trilogy*. New York, NY: Filmakers Library.
Jean Lydall & Keira Strecker. 2001. *Duka's Dilemma*.
David & Judith MacDougall, *Turkana Conversations*, consisting of *Lorang's Way* (1977), *Wedding Camels* (1980), and *A Wife among Wives* (1981).

Subject index

act sequence(s) 159, 177–178, 259, 265, 270, 290
addressee(s) 86, 152, 154, 159, 182, 202, 234, 248, 250, 259, 271, 274, 281, 287, 290–291, 303–304, 314
addresser, addressor 154, 159
adjacency pairs 269–270, 273, 278–279
affinal 9, 13, 141, 251, 358
Africanism(s) 98, 221, 303, 357
allocentric 74, 81, 83, 87, 91
anthroponymy 125, 360
attitude marker(s) 175, 182–183, 185, 238, 341, 342
audience 159, 168, 193–194, 259, 261, 276, 289, 292
avoidance 4, 95, 125, 140–151, 205, 206–209, 212, 232, 235, 266–267, 279, 358

backchannel(ing) 183, 238, 302, 307
bald-on (see face-threatening act(s))
Basic Color Terms 37–42, 121, 336, 352, 364
beat(s) 311, 314
bilingual(s) 105, 108, 122, 202, 210, 317, 364
bionomenclature 3, 8, 14, 14–36, 57, 67, 109
blend(ing) 4, 45–46, 58, 60, 91, 93, 177, 190, 204, 214, 217, 266, 293–294, 319, 369
bongo-bongo-ist 55
broadcast talk 283

channel(s) 44, 105–106, 123, 154–155, 158–159, 176, 194, 228, 290, 299
chronotope 93
codeswitching 200, 209–210, 362
co-evolution VIII, 4, 23, 70, 98–103
cognitive anthropology 8–68, 178, 337, 339, 340, 348, 354, 369
cognitive grammar 5, 101, 346, 354
cognitive linguistics 6, 37–68, 100, 173, 215, 227, 264–265, 346, 353, 358
cohesives 311, 314
community of practice 5, 173, 191, 199, 214, 256, 259, 265, 313, 340
conative (function) 155, 183, 219, 334
consanguinity 8, 358

contextualization cue(s) 82, 116, 191, 225, 250–251, 263–265, 355
conventionalized (see also ritualized) 4–5, 66, 87, 103, 125, 192, 226, 237, 241, 243, 246, 259, 263, 271, 294, 316–317
conversation analysis 1, 6, 159–160, 227, 265, 268–297, 335, 339, 343, 349, 352, 355, 357, 363, 365
conversational implicature(s) 99, 176, 240, 242–243, 245–246, 250, 262–263, 294, 297, 341
conversational maxim(s) (see also maxim(s)) 234, 237, 252, 264
counting 18–22, 336, 346, 347
covert 136, 155, 196, 246, 249
cultural linguistics 6, 263, 361, 365

deference 11, 144, 166, 241, 246, 253
deictic 72, 74, 83, 95–97, 101–102, 134, 137, 200, 315, 320, 348, 362
deixis 4, 90–91, 93, 95, 98–103, 100, 129, 143, 238, 260, 335, 340, 341, 348
dinomia 317
directive(s) 155, 179–180, 290, 307, 335, 341
discourse marker(s) 169, 175, 181–183, 185
discursive 169, 182, 191, 237–238, 243, 249, 255, 260, 266, 268, 294, 348
dyadic 5, 159, 164, 187, 192–194, 284
dysphemism 206

earth-centric 75
echoing (see repetition)
egocentric perspective VIII, 4, 72, 74, 78, 87, 98, 100, 102, 161
emblems 311, 313
embodied 60, 103, 172, 184, 215, 218, 358
embodiment 2, 218
emic 4, 225, 228, 235, 254–255, 257, 261–262, 268, 272, 278, 290, 294–295
emoticons 300
emotion(s)
emotive 155, 174–175,183, 185, 262, 306
ends 158–159, 162, 272
erasure 195–196, 200

esoterogeny 203
ethnobotany 24, 348, 354
ethnography of speaking 4, 6, 151, 152–154, 336, 350, 351, 362, 365
ethnosyntax 98, 344
etic 4, 152–161, 173, 224, 234, 255, 257, 289
etic grid 156, 161, 173, 224, 289
evaluative morphology 117, 175
evidentiality 101, 103
expansion(s) 131, 140, 144, 201, 222, 273
- insert-expansion 273
- post-expansion 273, 279
- pre-expansion(s) 269, 273, 279, 289–297
expressive (function) 68, 155, 169, 180, 291, 306
eye contact 144, 152, 167, 188, 303–304

face-threatening act(s) (FTA) 235–236, 241, 245–246, 260, 264
- bald on/bald-on 236, 242, 245–246, 260, 264, 291
- negative face/negative-face 234–237, 240–241, 243, 246–247, 255–260, 264, 268, 329
- off record/off-record 235–236, 242–246, 249–251, 255, 259–260, 263–264, 279, 291, 299–300, 329
- positive face/positive-face 234–238, 242, 243–247, 255, 259–262, 264, 279, 329
face-to-face model 81–87
facial expression(s) 6, 213–215, 228, 265, 298, 301–305, 344
female husband(s) 12, 360
folk taxonomy/taxonomies 24, 26, 29, 32, 34, 340, 356
footing 179, 287
fractal recursivity 195–196, 200
frame 75, 166, 177–178, 185, 189–192, 223, 256, 258, 263, 345
frame of reference 61, 73–75, 82–83, 340
- absolute 72, 74–79, 82, 87, 214, 234, 318
- intrinsic 73–75, 78, 81, 85–86, 241
- relative 60, 67, 72–75, 79, 86–87, 90, 116, 156, 163, 166, 188, 189, 234, 244, 253, 270, 304, 318
frame-and-scenario model 5, 161, 173, 177–178, 191, 215, 265, 292

fundamental neural responses 46, 67
fuzzy set(s) 34, 44–45, 352

gaze 271, 286–287, 304–305, 311, 339
genre 158–159, 162, 176, 300, 313, 336
genotype(s) 4, 135
gesture(s) 6, 20, 21, 94, 95, 160, 170, 178, 204, 209, 232, 265, 287, 298, 301–303, 306–321, 338, 339, 340, 344, 345, 347, 348, 349, 352, 353, 357, 361, 362, 363, 365
globalization 23, 66,-67, 255, 337
great Eskimo vocabulary hoax 66, 107, 362
growth point 321

habitus 6, 142, 168, 191, 205, 212, 222–223, 226, 228–230, 261, 284, 296, 299, 304–305
heteroglossia 201, 351
hlonip(h)a 146–149, 267, 345, 358
honorific(s) 95–97, 117, 194, 200, 205, 241, 258, 260, 336
hybrid space 201
hypocoristic(s) 130–132

iconic(s) 103, 128, 196, 218, 311–314, 318, 320
iconization 195–196
icons 103, 200
identity 13, 97, 133, 135, 144, 174, 177, 186, 195–196, 199, 202, 206, 238, 249, 253–254, 265, 291, 317, 333, 339, 340, 343, 347, 351, 361, 363, 366
ideology 12, 97, 133, 149, 164, 186, 196, 203, 204, 210, 226, 261, 265, 351, 365, 369, 370
illocution(ary) 180–182, 244, 292–294, 364
inclusory (reference) 98–100, 352, 355
index(es) 103, 143, 160, 169, 173, 174, 175, 186, 196, 198, 227, 261, 266, 267, 301, 314, 317, 320, 370
indexicality 125, 186, 196, 265, 267, 343
instrument(ality) 73, 133, 158, 160, 162, 194, 262, 300
intercultural communication 160, 181, 252, 268, 334, 347, 362
interjection(s) 175, 181, 183–185, 214, 219–220, 248, 273, 275, 306–308, 334, 335, 341, 370

intersubjective VIII, 4, 158, 181, 191, 275, 287

joking relationship(s) 238–239, 251–252, 262, 362

key 1, 8, 37, 78, 100, 104, 115, 124, 138, 158–162, 166, 171, 182, 186, 194, 199, 228, 233, 238, 255, 316, 358
kincepts 10, 361
kinemes 317
kinesics 298, 317, 336, 337
kinesis 298
kinship 3, 8–16, 24, 32, 34, 37, 56–57, 60, 100, 131, 142, 146, 150, 247, 250, 325–326, 343, 347, 355, 358, 359, 364, 369
kiss-teeth (see also suck-teeth, teeth kissing) 302, 307

language documentation 171, 227, 276, 280, 340, 342, 362, 363
language ideology (see also ideology) 133, 149, 196, 203, 210, 226, 261, 265, 351, 370
language practice(s) 150, 195, 202, 205, 208, 350, 395
language socialization 5, 180–181, 187–192, 263, 265, 338, 341, 334, 364, 367
languaging 5, 202
languoid 5, 202, 340
lapses 288–289, 349
left 20, 70, 74–77, 80, 85, 91, 301, 309, 318, 339, 345, 353
lip-pointing 301, 344
locution(ary) 180

matronymicon 124
maxim(s) (see also conversational maxim(s)) 233–234, 236–237, 242, 246, 252–253, 259, 261, 263–265
meme 122
mental space(s) (see also space) 93, 266, 345
message content 159
message form 154–155, 159, 191, 289
metalanguage 10, 26, 28, 29, 40–41, 44, 50, 54, 55, 184, 213, 219–220
metalinguistic 155–156, 204, 292

metaphor(s) 218–219, 233, 261, 300, 313, 350, 353, 364, 370, 106, 209, 216
metaphorical 4, 11, 17, 19, 35, 58–60, 91, 94, 106, 118, 189, 215, 217–218, 223, 224, 233, 254, 304, 312–313, 368
metaphoric(s) 311, 313
metonymic (extension) 11, 17, 59, 60, 91, 217, 220, 254
metonymy 58, 147
metrolingualism 5, 202
multilingual 20, 35, 108, 122, 189, 191, 197, 201–203, 207, 209–210, 314, 334, 356
multimodal(ity) 6, 204, 209, 280, 300, 310, 314, 350
Munsell colour chart 39, 40–45, 55, 120–121

name strategy 108–109, 214
Natural Core Model 32, 34
Natural Semantic Metalanguage 184, 220
negative face (see face-threatening act(s))
network(s) 45, 67, 117, 124, 135, 147, 156, 161, 178, 207, 227, 266–267, 293
nickname(s) 51, 125–126, 131–132, 134, 137, 139, 360
norm(s) 5, 128, 146, 154, 157–159, 162, 173, 174, 185, 198, 200, 210, 232, 233, 247, 252, 267, 292–293, 298, 363

off-record (see face-threatening act(s))
olfactory 3, 61–68, 266, 370
onomastic(s) 124–151, 132, 209, 353, 362, 368
othering 128, 197–198
otherness 197
overlap(s) 214, 265, 270–272, 277–278, 284–289
overt 116, 136, 155, 196, 246, 248, 299
ox songs 176–177

participant(s) 8, 39, 40, 76, 80, 95, 98–100, 155–156, 158–159, 161–163, 167, 171–172, 174, 177–178, 188, 191–192, 227, 235, 240, 244, 259, 273, 281, 284–287, 289–290, 293, 305, 311
participant observation 8, 80, 161, 244
patronymicon 124

phatic (communion, communication) 155–156, 159, 167, 183, 219, 334, 365
perlocution(ary) 180–181, 185, 261, 294
performance(s) 5, 39, 105, 147, 160, 176, 180, 186–187, 195, 204–210, 230, 239, 247, 265, 267, 291, 316–317
phatic 155–156, 159, 167, 183, 220, 334, 365
phenotype(s) 4, 135
poetic (function) 155, 175–176, 247
positive face (see face-threatening act(s)
post-expansion(s) (see expansion(s))
post-sequence(s) (see sequence(s))
power 1, 38, 60, 97, 128, 133, 140, 165, 176, 190, 195, 234–236, 239, 241, 245, 248, 255, 261, 279, 338, 343, 361, 368
practice(s) (see language practice(s))
pragmemes 178
pre-closing 289–297
pre-expansion (see expansion(s)
pre-sequences (see sequence(s))
prototype(s) (theory) 3, 9, 12, 14–15, 34, 44, 50, 67, 178, 187, 214
proxemics 311–312, 348
psycho-collocation(s) 217, 357

questionnaire(s) 161, 198, 244, 256–257, 261, 278

radical translation 28–29
receiver 86, 154–155, 159, 193, 240
referential (function) 67, 95, 102, 155, 163, 167, 183–184, 250, 301
referential indexicals 102
register(s) 1, 95, 97, 142–144, 149, 179, 182, 194, 197, 199–200, 203, 205–206, 208–209, 232, 237, 246, 257, 267, 290, 300, 308, 316, 358
relative space (see space)
repair 270, 273–275, 282–283, 288, 296, 342, 364
– other-repair 274–275
– self-repair 273–274
repetition(s) 200, 238, 275, 287–288, 363
right 20, 64, 70, 74–77, 80, 85, 91, 228, 280, 301, 309, 317, 339, 335, 356, 369

ritualized (see also conventionalized) 66, 152, 159, 165, 168–171, 176–177, 187, 226, 246–248, 270

Sapir-Whorf hypothesis 107–108
scenario 161, 177, 239, 264, 291
scene(s) 45, 75, 102, 104, 111, 143, 154, 159, 168, 171, 173, 176, 173, 178, 186, 189–191, 193, 201, 203, 215, 227, 230, 276, 318
schema(s) 54, 161, 166–167, 178, 227, 264, 368
– cultural schema 8, 128
– event schema 161, 167, 178, 227
– ideological schema 200
– image schema 218
– knowledge schema 179, 224
– participation schema 166,
– perspective schema 161
– proposition schema 227
– role schema 166, 227
– sequencing schema 161
schisming 265, 273, 284, 286, 344
script(s) 169, 178, 194, 220, 266, 303, 334
sender 154–155, 159
sequence(s) 41, 43–44, 132, 142, 152, 159, 169, 177–178, 207, 244, 259, 265, 266, 269–270, 273, 279, 281, 289–290, 300, 320, 349, 364, 366
– post-sequence(s) 279
– pre-sequence(s) 279
sequence organization 273, 364
setting(s) 80, 154–155, 159, 161, 162, 164, 173–174, 192, 228, 244, 270, 285, 289, 347
Sheko 199
shifters 102, 351, 365
shunning 227
sign language(s) 119, 160, 308, 311, 314, 320, 319–321, 360
single-file model 81–82, 86–87
situation 5, 83, 102, 154, 158–159, 165, 174, 177–178, 182, 214, 225, 234, 237–238, 258, 265, 287, 312
social practice(s) 195, 266, 343, 367
space(s) 45, 60, 93, 197, 208, 233, 249, 266, 284, 285, 289, 293, 295, 312, 313, 319, 334, 338, 339, 342, 345, 349, 350, 354, 355, 358, 362, 367, 369, 370

- physical 71–90
- relative 72
- social 91–98

space grammar, see cognitive linguistics

space kit 80

speech act(s) 4, 119, 159–161, 169, 177, 179–181, 185, 192, 235–237, 241, 243–244, 246–247, 255, 258–262, 266, 268, 290–294, 297, 337, 341, 345, 346, 347, 352, 353, 365, 367

speech act theory 161, 173, 179, 185, 284

speech community VII, IX, 5, 8, 11, 13, 50, 55, 76, 91, 93, 98, 103, 109, 121, 128, 130, 149, 153, 154, 160, 168–169, 172–173, 193, 200, 214, 226, 228, 234, 239, 242, 249, 251, 252, 253, 256, 257, 259, 261, 262, 264, 265, 267, 280, 281, 283, 289, 293, 301, 304, 310, 311, 313, 347, 358

style(s) VII, 132, 166, 175, 179, 186–187, 197, 199–200, 204, 229, 257, 269, 291, 301, 340, 343, 350, 351

stylect 5, 142, 209, 316

suck-teeth (see also kiss-teeth, teeth kissing) 302, 307

surrogate (language(s)) 193, 298, 300, 360

symbol(s) 49, 103, 148, 149, 157, 241, 276, 307, 317, 321, 343, 352

taboo(s) 20, 61, 94, 142–144, 147, 150, 206–207, 242–243, 308, 314, 334, 350, 353, 354, 357

Taxonomic Hierarchy Model 32, 36

teeth kissing (see also kiss-teeth, suck-teeth) 303

teknonymy 131, 141, 147

theory of mind VIII, 100, 119, 263

third space 46, 201

toponomasticon 139

toponymy 125, 138–140

totalization 98

translanguaging (see also languaging) 202, 204, 210, 346

triadic 5, 159, 187, 192, 334

turn-taking 193–194, 290, 334

verbal gestures (see also gesture(s)) 306–307, 334, 347, 361

WEIRD people 55, 119–123, 161, 349

whistle(d speech) 298–299

Language index

|Gui 289
!Kung 13, 42, 251–252, 356
!Xóõ 62–64, 341
ǂĀkhoe Haillom 78, 182–184, 280, 282–283, 284, 302, 304, 350, 370
Gǁana 188
ʿĀmmiyya (Arabic) 244

Acholi (Achooli) 29, 131, 182–183, 269, 271–273, 276, 278, 280, 288–289, 296, 304, 310, 315–316, 360, 363
Adnyamathanha 100
Afrikaans 138, 148, 167, 209, 316
Aguaruna 36
Akan 128–129, 133, 135, 193–194, 216–217, 233, 250, 259, 279, 303, 333, 335, 360, 370
Akha 298
Amharic 96–97, 133, 142, 172, 184, 210, 213–216, 222, 304, 310, 333, 334, 349, 362
Anywa 21
Apache 227, 336
Arabic 21, 28, 54, 127, 130–132, 162–163, 165, 191, 194, 208, 222–223, 233, 244, 336, 352
– Jordanian 141, 344
– Juba Arabic 210
– Sudanese 26, 45, 55, 109, 203, 210, 233, 244
Arunta 28–29
Arusha 20, 347
Ashanti 225, 350
Ateso (Teso) 83–84, 88, 90, 335
Avestian 38
Awngi 36
Aymara 94

Baale 59, 69, 137
Baka 289, 353
Bakwele 289
Bambara 128, 188, 303
Bari 43, 88, 127, 366
Bassari 125

Beja 162, 172, 358
Bemba (Chibemba) 117, 175
Bini (Edo) 46, 369
Bodho 210
Bongo 210
Botatwe 216
Bulu 56
Burunge 46

Camus 220
Carapana 26
Chai 69
Chaʻpalaa 273–274
Cherangʻany 60, 81–83, 128, 139, 299, 358
Chichewa 67
Chinese 60, 65, 118, 133, 233, 254, 305, 370
Chinook (jargon) 200–200, 365
Cornish 87
Cuna 226, 365

Daga 25, 29
Dagbani 176, 194, 301
Daju 55
Dakota 60
Damara 22
Dani 120–121, 214, 362
Danish 244, 280, 282
Datooga 143–144, 206–208, 250, 358
Dinka 43, 51, 53, 94, 125, 137, 167, 176, 194, 210, 341, 355, 359
Djaru 75
Dogon 216
Dutch 65, 76–77, 97, 104, 125, 140, 189–191, 214, 223, 229, 260–262, 269, 270, 280, 291, 305, 318
Dyirbal 72, 116, 343

Edo (Bini) 46
Eegimaa 127–128, 363
Efik 299–300, 366
English 6, 8, 10, 12, 14, 22, 26, 27, 28, 29, 31, 32, 34, 35, 36, 39, 40, 41, 44, 45, 46, 47, 48, 49, 50, 53, 54, 55, 56, 57, 58, 61, 62, 65, 66, 67, 74, 75, 82, 85,

86, 91, 94, 95, 103, 104, 105, 106, 107,
108, 109, 110, 111, 112, 113, 114, 115,
118, 122, 125, 127, 129, 132, 133–134,
137, 138, 148, 154–162, 167, 174, 175,
176, 179–180, 183–184, 185, 196, 199,
201, 208, 209, 210, 213, 216, 217, 218,
219, 220, 221, 222, 224, 229, 231, 233,
234, 236, 240, 243, 244, 250, 256, 263,
269, 273, 275, 280, 284, 287, 289, 295,
296, 317, 333, 334, 336, 338, 343, 347,
352, 355, 357, 359, 361, 362, 364, 366,
369, 370
Eskimo (see also Inuit) 9, 39, 66, 362
Ewe 89, 125, 127, 165, 169, 170–171, 193,
219, 302–303, 333, 334, 335, 344

Fijian 87
Finnish 252, 348
Fon 193
French 3, 23, 35, 41, 56, 124, 132, 170,
201–202, 207–209, 244, 295, 303
Fulani (Fulbe) 141, 291
Fur (For) 45, 137, 351, 252 Fulani (Fulbe)
Fuṣḥa (Arabic) 244

Gā 193, 303
Gbaya 36, 47, 184, 226, 363
Gbeya 248–249, 363
German 2, 38, 38, 39, 65, 86, 114–115, 124,
197, 215, 223, 227, 244, 262, 271, 291,
358, 359
Greek 6, 38, 93, 124, 167, 171, 298
Gumuz 21, 36 , 38
Gurage 150
Gusii 13
Guugu Yimithirr (Yimidhirr) 28, 74–78,
317–319, 348, 354
Gyeli 56

Hamar (Hamer) 94, 115, 168, 226, 236–243,
258–260, 263, 279, 356, 361, 371
Hanunóo 24, 31, 54, 340
Hausa 16, 18, 43, 57, 73, 98, 103, 128,
131–132, 138, 150, 162, 188–191, 216,
220–221, 226, 307, 336, 350, 357, 359
Haya 144
Hebrew 106, 122, 124, 154, 244, 256, 260

Hmong 298
Hopi 107, 356

Ibibio 42, 125, 344
Iceland(ic) 124
Igbo 59, 126, 162, 216, 225, 227, 254, 360, 368
Inuit (see also Eskimo) 39, 66, 227
Ipai 174–175
Isu 289–294
Italian 137, 174, 229, 280, 366
Iwaidja 25

Jahai 61
Jaqaru 47, 348
Jaminjung 75
Japanese 3, 60, 114, 160, 180–181, 228, 233,
241, 253, 259, 280–284, 289, 305, 353,
355, 356, 357, 359, 367
Javanese 212
Jörai 47, 343
Jur-Lwoo 62

Kafa 199–200
Kalenjin 60, 139, 298, 358
Kaluli 188, 364
Kambaata 142–143, 147, 223, 303, 368
Kana 113–114, 117, 351
Kanuri 307
Karanga 54
Karimojong 130–131, 137, 168, 194, 206,
238, 248, 287–288, 360
Katla 203–204
Kayardild 75
Kerewe 144
Kgalagadi 78
K(h)rahn (Gborbo, Wobé, Guéré)
134, 336
Kickapoo 298
Kinyarwanda 206, 208, 353
Kirundi (Rundi) 126, 353
Kituba 12, 15, 359
Kobon 20
Koegu 88, 349
Kolokuma Ịjọ (Izọn) 175, 337
Komo 21
Korean 104–105, 156–157, 257–258, 280,
283, 339

Kpelle 21
Kunama 173
Kuteb 61–62, 353
Kwakiutl (Kwa'kwala) 29, 46, 121
Kxoe (Khwe) 33, 138–139, 149, 338

Laal 307
Langila 208
Lango 216, 360
Lao 273–274, 280, 283
Lardil (Damin) 308
Latin VIII, 26, 32, 124, 135
Lingala 208
Logo 17–18, 346
Lopit 99–100, 103, 358
Lower Saxon 104
Luba 128
Luganda 256–258, 298
Luo 11, 126–127, 188, 337, 363, 366
Luwo 11, 64, 210, 366

Maale 72, 307, 334
Maa(sai) 136, 175, 205, 220, 310, 361
Maba 54–55
Majang(ir) 17
Malagasy 252–253, 352
Malay 65
Malinke 19
Mampruli 162, 359
Mangbetu 137
Maniq 61, 370
Mano 98–99
Mbukushu 138
Mbuún 353
Mɛn 291
Mende 59
Midob 130, 336
Mimi 55
Mohawk 87
Mossi 193
Mpiin 31, 353
Munda 23
Mundang 307
Mursi 53–55, 368

Nandi 12, 205–206, 354, 360
Nara 173

Ndebele 146
Ngaalam 199, 370
Ngiti 18–19, 354
Ngombe 42
Nouchi (French) 207
Nsong 353
Nuer 21, 172
Nyakyusa 144
Nyangatom 18, 50–51, 54, 243, 263, 368

Ogori 162, 333
Old Irish 89
Opuuo (Opo) 21, 23
Oromo 21, 35–36, 115, 133, 143, 172, 339, 357
Oropom 198
Oyda 299, 335

Paliyan 226, 346
Päkoot 138–139, 168, 237
Päri 60, 366
Pedi 316
Polish 256, 260
Portuguese 140, 295–296

Randuk (Arabic) 207
Russian 42, 109, 110, 123, 201, 244, 294, 351, 370

Quechua 60

Safaliba 217, 364
Samburu 220
Sami 39
Samoan 167, 294, 343
Sebei 212, 346
Seneca 87
Sesotho 188, 317
Setswana 146, 132–133, 316, 352, 362
Shabo (Mikeyir) 199
Sheko 199
Sheng (Swahili) 207–209, 369
Shilluk 194, 210, 219, 362
Shinasha 36
Shona 42, 144, 250, 356
Shoshoni 26
Siwu 273–274, 276, 342

Somali 175–176, 363
Songhay 229, 310, 366
Southern Paiute 25
Southern Sotho (see also Sesotho) 147, 267, 353
South Fore 214
Spanish 114–115, 196, 201
Swahili 19, 31, 58, 86, 94, 103, 122, 149, 162, 207–209, 221–223, 237, 254, 257, 262, 300–301, 348, 353, 359, 361, 363, 370
Swazi 146
Swedish 97, 361

Tadaksahak 229
Tagdal 229
Tahitian 212
Tamil 234, 236, 243–244
T'apo 23, 366
Tarahumara 108–109
Tarok 61, 337
Thai 135–136
Tigrinya 150, 210, 362
Tima VIII–IX, 9, 26–28, 32, 45–50, 54, 58–59, 65, 73, 85, 88–89, 101–103, 109, 129–130, 135, 161, 203–204, 218–219, 309, 325–326, 333, 342, 357, 364, 369
Tirma 69
Tonga(n) 30, 46, 56, 77, 309, 369
Ts'ixa 315, 320, 345
Tuareg (Touareg, Tamashaq) 162–164
Tugen 129
Tupuri 216
Turkana 9, 19–20, 51–52, 54, 88, 90, 91, 94, 138–139, 150, 160, 168–169, 171–172, 176–177, 180, 182, 186, 198, 211, 223, 236, 237–242, 260, 269, 309, 311–315, 341, 342, 347, 357, 361, 371
Tzeltal 33, 36, 41, 74, 77–80, 82–83, 88, 109, 234, 236, 241, 244, 280, 338

Vedic 38

Warlbiri (Warlpiri) 75, 348
Wolaitta (Wolayita) 172, 307
Wolof 90, 160, 164–166, 193, 216, 247, 262, 273, 285–287, 303–304, 306–307, 309, 339, 341, 347, 351, 357, 362

Xhosa 67, 125, 146, 148–150, 254, 267, 306, 346, 358, 359

Yabacrâne (Swahili) 208–209, 262, 359
Yanké (Lingala) 208–209
Yapese 14
Yélî-Dnye 280
Yiddish 171, 356
Yoruba 125, 162, 300, 325, 333, 360
Yucatec (Maya) 110–113, 117, 215
Yupno (Yopno) 84, 299, 335, 369

Zande 97, 249, 338
Zargulla 183, 307–308, 335
Zulu 126, 139, 146–150
Zuni 40, 107